KNOWLEDGE MANAGEMENT, BUSINESS INTELLIGENCE, AND CONTENT MANAGEMENT

The IT Practitioner's Guide

OTHER AUERBACH PUBLICATIONS

KNOWLEDGE MANAGEMENT, BUSINESS INTELLIGENCE, AND CONTENT MANAGEMENT

The IT Practitioner's Guide

Jessica Keyes

CRC Press
Taylor & Francis Group
Boca Raton London New York

CRC Press is an imprint of the
Taylor & Francis Group, an **informa** business
AN AUERBACH BOOK

CRC Press
Taylor & Francis Group
6000 Broken Sound Parkway NW, Suite 300
Boca Raton, FL 33487-2742

First issued in paperback 2019

ISBN-13: 978-0-8493-9385-3 (hbk)
ISBN-13: 978-0-367-39084-6 (pbk)

Library of Congress Card Number 2005057127

Library of Congress Cataloging-in-Publication Data

Keyes, Jessica, 1950-
    Knowledge management, business intelligence, and content management : the IT practitioner's guide / by Jessica Keyes.
        p. cm.
    ISBN 0-8493-9385-X
    1. Information technology. 2. Information resources management. 3. Knowledge management. I. Title.

T58.5.K478 2006
658.4'038--dc22   2005057127

Visit the Taylor & Francis Web site at
http://www.taylorandfrancis.com

and the CRC Press Web site at
http://www.crcpress.com

This book is dedicated to my family and friends.

PREFACE

Business in the 21st century has become increasingly competitive as it has become global. A plethora of new technologies and business processes such as business intelligence, content management, supply chain management, customer relationship management, and enterprise resource management has resulted in the rise of new information types and inter-relationships that require knowledge of diverse areas such as raw materials, customer requirements, and manufacturing. Taken individually, this information provides value only to the process in which it exists. However, as a component of a knowledge management system, this raw data is transformed into the knowledge that will provide competitive advantage.

Knowledge management (KM) has been defined as the identification and analysis of available and required knowledge, and the subsequent planning and control of actions, to develop these into "knowledge assets" that will enable a business to generate profits and increase its competitive position. The major focus of knowledge management is to identify and gather content from documents, reports, and other sources and to be able to search that content for meaningful relationships. A variety of business intelligence, artificial intelligence, and content management methodologies and tools are the framework upon which knowledge management operates.

Studies have shown that knowledge management, content management, and business intelligence are important because:

1. The rate of innovation in the marketplace is rising, so knowledge must evolve and be assimilated at an ever faster rate.
2. Workforce reductions are impacting the level of expertise in a typical organization.

3. Globalization increases complexity and a need to manage this increasing complexity.
4. A change in strategic direction may result in the loss of knowledge in a specific area.

Information intelligence will provide a complete discussion of knowledge management for the IT practitioner. This book will discuss creation, protection, development, sharing and management of information, and intellectual assets using business intelligence, among other knowledge sharing and analytical techniques.

Additional material is available from the CRC Web site: www.crcpress. com/e_products_downloads/download.asp?cat_no=AU9385.

ABOUT THE AUTHOR

Jessica Keyes is president of New Art Technologies, Inc., a high-technology and management consultancy and development firm started in New York in 1989. She is also a founding partner of New York City-based Manhattan Technology Group.

Keyes has given seminars for such prestigious universities as Carnegie Mellon, Boston University, University of Illinois, James Madison University, and San Francisco State University. She is a frequent keynote speaker on the topics of competitive strategy and productivity and quality. She is former advisor for DataPro, McGraw-Hill's computer research arm, as well as a member of the Sprint Business Council. Keyes is also a founding board of directors and member of the New York Software Industry Association. She has recently completed a two-year term on the Mayor of New York City's Small Business Advisory Council. She is currently a professor of computer science at Fairleigh Dickinson University's Graduate Center as well as the University of Phoenix, where she is an area chairperson, and at Virginia Tech. She has been the editor for WGL's *Handbook of eBusiness* and CRC Press' *Systems Development Management* and *Information Management*.

Prior to founding New Art, Keyes was managing director of R&D for the New York Stock Exchange and has been an officer with Swiss Bank Co. and Banker's Trust, both in New York City. She holds a master of business administration from New York University where she did her research in the area of artificial intelligence. She is currently pursuing her doctorate.

A noted columnist and correspondent with over 200 articles published, Keyes is the author of 19 books, including *Auerbach's Software Engineering Handbook*, *Software Configuration Management*, and *Implementing the IT Balanced Scorecard*.

CONTENTS

Appendices

INFORMATION INTELLIGENCE

Knowledge management (KM) has been defined as the identification and analysis of available and required knowledge, and the subsequent planning and control of actions, to develop "knowledge assets" that will enable a business to generate profits and increase its competitive position. This book will provide the framework for the strategic use of the "information intelligence" processes — business intelligence, content management, and knowledge management.

1

THE NEW INTELLIGENCE: THE BIRTH OF THE KNOWLEDGE MANAGEMENT INDUSTRY

The introduction of computers led to an unmanageable pro-liferation of data, which stimulated the birth of knowledge management (KM). To understand KM and all of its compo-nents (i.e., business intelligence, content management, etc.), it is necessary to first discuss the precursors to KM.

1.1 BURIED IN INFORMATION

Magicians, who are masters of optical illusions, convince breathless audiences that their tricks work by magic. But the tricks really result from precision sleight of hand, split-second timing, and careful planning. And Merlin's code prevents the brotherhood of magicians from ever whispering its secrets. Knowledge is all that separates the knowing from the unknowing, the magician from the audience. Knowledge is elusive (especially in large organizations), inconsistent, unripe, and buried in information.

Pick up a copy of *The New York Times*. There is more information contained between the front and back pages than we can possibly digest. Add to this the other 99 papers we will read this year, the 3000 notices or forms that we will read or complete, the 2463 hours of television we will watch, the 730 hours of radio we will listen to, and you have something called an *information explosion*.

According to Linda Costigan Lederman (1986), who devised these statistics for her piece "Communication in the Workplace," this does not even take into account the number of hours spent exchanging information in conversations. And should we not include information that is signaled by nonverbal means, such as the wink of an eye, a firm handshake, or a nod of the head.

Soothsayers predict that the amount of information that we are expected to absorb will double every four to five years. Even now, more information has been generated for mass distribution in the last three decades than in the previous five thousand years.

Maybe it is more than an information explosion; perhaps it is more like a glut. And with this glut comes the breakdown of our ability to mess with or even retrieve the information we so labor to possess. Akio Morita, former chairman of Sony Corporation, believes that our capacity to retrieve this information is declining. In fact, he believes that out of all the information that we absorb, we can retrieve from our memories only a paltry 5 percent.

Alvin Toffler, in his much-acclaimed book *Future Shock* (1984), paints an even bleaker picture. He writes of an actual breakdown of human performance under these extraordinary information loads and demonstrates its relationship to psychopathology. Work is increasingly being done in one's head rather than at the desk, as we try to cope with managing this massive information overdose. The information that we must assimilate has become more abstract as technological innovators find new, clever ways to present it. And we do not just process one stream of data bits at a time. Some researchers refer to our need to deal with more than one information flow at a time as *polyphasic activity*. Visualize Sam riding his convertible to his next meeting. He grips the steering wheel in his left hand, a cellular phone in his right, and on his lap rests his miniature tape recorder. And in the passenger seat is his UltraLite computer.

This increasingly large information flow is forcing people to adapt to mastering and making judgments about it in shorter periods of time. You can compare this burgeoning quantity of information to an algae-infested pond that no longer has enough oxygen to support fish. We may actually be pushing to extreme limits the physical ability of people to process information. When that begins to happen, great amounts of information just pass by, which people cannot evaluate.

Born of this glut is a new phrase that all agree has distinct meaning. *Information anxiety*, a nice turn of phrase coined by Richard Saul Wurman (2000) in his book of the same name, is that chasm between what we think we should understand and what we really do understand. As those papers and magazines and books pile up unread on our nightstands, we grow increasingly uneasy at our inability to keep pace. And, exhausted, we fall asleep with yet another unfinished book by our side. Information anxiety, according to Wurman, "is the hole between data and knowledge.

It happens when information does not tell us what we want or need to know."

1.2 FROM BATCH TO DECISION SUPPORT

In the 21st century, we might achieve technological nirvana. For some, this might be the fusion of human and machine. A great debate has been raging on the technological, political, and even moral battlegrounds over the development of what we rather prosaically call an *artilect*.

An artilect would be a machine that exhibits intelligence (artificial) to the degree of surpassing its creators one day. These ultraintelligent machines inspire fear, loathing, and a great deal of fascination in the scientific community as well as in the general public. Could we bear living in a world "peopled by creations massively smarter than we are?" But we jump ahead of ourselves. There are no artilects to loathe or love; there is, however, the possibility of creating computer systems that are just about as bright as we are in narrower spheres of expertise.

The key is to create computer systems that present less but more significant or germane data. Several methods can be used to present, to the end user, the best mix of the detail with the composite data. All of these methods recognize a relationship between the type of decision maker and the detail presented.

1.2.1 Types of Decision Makers

There are three types of decision makers. At the bottom of the corporate hierarchy are the paper pushers. These are the people who do need to see all the data. They are the check processors, complaint takers, order takers, and customer service staff. These technical users need to input and review a wealth of data. Given the nature of the task, this is usually done in a rote fashion and not subject to complex decision making. At the other end of the spectrum are the organization's senior managers who use the information, gathered at the lower rungs, for strategic purposes. A whole range of vendor-sold EISs (executive information systems) are now in vogue. These sport flashy colors, touch screens, and sparse information displays. Data displayed here would most likely be sales projections, profitability numbers, and key competitive data. In the middle is (you guessed it) the middle manager or tactical user. In organizational terms, these are the professionals who are right in the firing line and need the most careful balance of data. These are the poor unfortunates who sit buried under that great avalanche of information.

Companies have always collected data and stored it in diverse corporate databases. Automobile manufacturers keep massive amounts of data on file, concerning their suppliers and dealership locations. For a long time, no one attached any strategic value to this mass of detail, that is, until Chrysler fell into the black pit of insolvency. Lee Iacocca tweaked this very set of databases to save Chrysler from a catastrophe much worse than rust. By moving to a different level of information analysis, Iacocca was able to convince members of Congress to support the loans that injected life into the veins of his company.

1.2.2 Filtering

There are a host of filtering methodologies for serving up this sort of strategic knowledge on a silver platter. For the most part, they are classified in three different ways. The monitoring method serves up data to the user on an exception basis. This can be variance reporting, in which the system produces only exceptions based on programmatic review of the data, for example, to review credit card payments and display only those accounts in which the payment was not received or the payment is below the minimum payment.

The advent of fourth-generation languages (4GLs), tools enabling the end user to access the corporate database with easy-to-use query syntax, has thrust the interrogative method of system tailoring to the popular forefront. This method takes into account the many occasions when the user cannot identify the set of information necessary to handle the day-to-day, *ad hoc* analyses required in complex decision-making environments. In these cases, all of the data elements need to be resident in an accessible database. And a tool needs to be in place to permit the user to easily and quickly develop queries and variations on these queries against this data.

When Banker's Trust, now part of Deutsche Bank, decided to get out of the retail business in the early 1980s, the data-processing effort to achieve this feat was enormous. One area that Banker's spun off rather quickly was the credit card subsidiary. The 4GL in use at that time was FOCUS (by Information Builders). The users and the accounting staff used this tool to great advantage to ensure a smooth transition of accounts to the many final resting places. Some accounts were spun off to a bank in Chicago, some to Albany, whereas the high-rollers stayed behind in newly minted, privileged accounts.

A model-oriented approach comes in many flavors. Human resource or facilities departments are good candidates for descriptive models, which can be organization charts or floor plans. On the other hand, a normative representation of data is a good fit for budgeting when the goal is to provide the best answer to a given problem. Economic projections are good targets for modeling methodologies that have the ability to handle uncertainty. The operations management students (among us) gleefully apply game theory to those problems in which there is a requirement to find the best solution in spite of a profound lack of information. An example of a problem that would use this type of strategy would be a competitive marketing system, in which data about the competition is scant or unknown.

1.2.3 Transforming Information into Knowledge

Perhaps the industry with the largest share of traditional systems is the banking industry. No one personifies banking more, or has done more for the banking industry, than Citicorp's former chairman emeritus, Walter Wriston. In his 17 years as CEO, he revolutionized the international banking environment, in which the interface between humans and machines permits easy access to complex information. Wriston predicted that artificial intelligence would become the norm and not the exception. He looks forward to a day when he can walk up to an expert system in a bank lobby that will be able to answer complex questions about his account. "Can I invest in a tax-free fund? Can I do brokerage transactions?"

Quaker Oats in Chicago was one of the first consumer-goods marketers to realize the potential of strategic information — i.e., knowledge. Several decades ago, it innovated a computer system to analyze some two billion facts about different products and competitors. The use of this system permitted Quaker Oats to understand the data and draw insights from it. This led them to the number one spot in product categories such as Rice-A-Roni and the ever-popular Aunt Jemima Pancakes.

Filtering is a mainstay in the marketing arena. For years, marketers have used smart software to filter relevancies out of the information glut. It all started with the first totally computerized census back in 1970. The Census Bureau recorded demographic data on computer tapes. This provided a plethora of information right down to the city block. By the time of the 1980 census, these stats had ballooned into 300,000 pages of statistics. And a whopping ten times that amount sat patiently on computer tapes. Today, this information is available on a desktop.

Many industries quickly followed suit. An investment service gathered data on some 5000 companies and offered this data along with smart filtering software. Individual.com started by sifting through full-text articles and pinpointing items of interest to its subscribers. Their take on their business is that they are operating an information refinery that takes a broad stream of raw data and turns it into actionable knowledge. Dean LeBaron agrees with this approach. He was very much in the *avant-garde* in the mid-1970s. That is when he preached the use of computers to improve the quality of investing. Batterymarch Financial Management is one of Boston's leading money management firms with a portfolio of over $11 billion. LeBaron runs Batterymarch as one large expert system. It is designed to operate the way an intelligent institutional investor would operate, if put on silicon substrate.

One of the most interesting expert-system success stories involved Campbell Soup. A senior technician was going to retire. Unfortunately, his expertise was going to retire as well. This fellow had decades worth of experience in determining where the problems were in the vast cookers that Campbell Soup used to make chicken soup. A few bubbles on the top meant one thing. A certain smell meant something else. Before he retired, Campbell Soup invested time and money in knowledge-engineering his expertise so that it could be stored in a knowledge base and used by his less-experienced successors.

1.3 A SHORT COURSE IN KNOWLEDGE REPRESENTATION

The science of artificial intelligence is the basis for most research on knowledge representation. The simplest method of capturing knowledge is through the use of rules, the medium of most expert systems. Because our lives are filled with decisions, it is quite natural to turn them into decision rules.

In general, a rule has two parts — a premise and a conclusion. For example, a premise might be "if it is cold and it is creamy," and the associated conclusion might be "then it is ice cream." Therefore, a *rule* is a conditional sentence starting with an IF segment and ending with a THEN segment. A rule, or *production rule* as it is sometimes called, stems from the need to make a decision. Look at the decision tree, another form of knowledge representation, in Figure 1.1.

Here, we are trying to determine whether a patient's bill for medical expenses should be reimbursed. Once the decision tree has been charted, it is not difficult to turn these into production rules. For example, the first

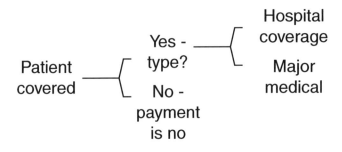

Figure 1.1 A decision tree.

rule would be: IF the patient is covered by insurance, THEN proceed to determine payment schedule.

Of course, rules in real knowledge-based systems are far more complex. For example, consider the following:

```
If ?X is in class REACTORS and
      The PRESSURE of the PRIMARY.COOLING.SYSTEM of?X
      Is DECREASING and
      The STATUS of
      The HIGH.PRESSURE.INJECTION.SYSTEM of ?X is ON
Then
      The INTEGRITY of
      The PRIMARY.COOLING.SYSTEM of ?X
            is CHALLENGED
Do ACTIVATE.ALARM
      GET.VALUE X 'PRIMARY.COOLING.SYSTEM'
```

You will notice a few things right away. First, this rule has three parts. The extra part is the DO, which permits the knowledge-based system to execute a procedure. You might also have noticed the ?X variable, which gives a knowledge-based system much of the same capabilities as a traditional system. However, that is where the similarity ends. Traditional computer systems execute instructions one statement at a time. Look at the sample BASIC programming language program that follows:

```
10 LET A = 10
20 LET B = 20
30 C = A + B
40 GOTO 60
50 PRINT C
60 GOTO 10
```

BASIC is a rigid sequential programming language (originally created to teach students how to program but then took on a life of its own under Microsoft's Bill Gates). Take a careful look at the code again. Does the value of C ever get printed? Line 40, the GOTO statement, prevents the program (as written) to ever execute line 50 — the PRINT statement.

The heart of a knowledge-based system is the inference engine, which is a program that has much functionality. It controls modules that access databases, the interface to the end user, as well as what we call a *knowledge base*. The typical expert-system-type knowledge base stores its knowledge in the form of rules. Rules do not execute in sequential order,

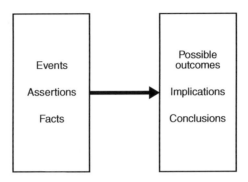

Figure 1.2 Forward chaining.

as do traditional programming languages. Instead, the rules are executed according to a grand design called a *control strategy*. The control strategy prescribes the method of searching through the knowledge base.

There are two major categories of searching. In forward chaining, as shown in Figure 1.2, we move from a set of assertions or facts to one or more possible outcomes. The way the rule application works is that the system searches for a value, where the conditions in the IF part of the rule are matched in memory (deemed to be true). If so, the THEN part is put into working memory. Applying a forward-chaining control strategy to a list of rules forces the execution of the rules from beginning to end. This is a sort of top-down reasoning approach. It reviews all known facts that either were entered at the very beginning or become known as other rules are triggered (that is, fired). In forward chaining, every bit of available evidence is examined, because the final goal is not predetermined.

A few examples might help explain a rather complicated topic. Suppose you have a personal computer. Now suppose the monitor goes on the fritz, and it just does not work. The screen is black. Well, there can be many solutions to this problem. Perhaps the monitor is not plugged in. Perhaps the power is out. We go from an event, a bad screen, to one of many possible outcomes. Our forward-chaining system would wind its way through rules that dealt with this topic trying to assist in figuring out what is wrong.

Let us look at another example. I call it "convict on the loose." Suppose I tell you that a killer or bank robber has broken out of jail. We know he hid some of the money he stole, but we do not know where. We also know that three of his former cronies turned state witnesses. While in prison, he boasted that when he got out of jail he would retrieve the loot and then seek revenge against his former cronies. We are a small police force. We need to know where to apply our meager resources. To solve this problem, we apply forward-chaining reasoning to come to a set of

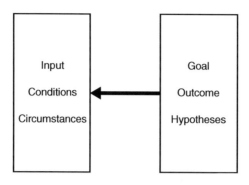

Figure 1.3   Backward chaining.

conclusions. In which direction was the killer or robber headed? Was he armed? Did he have a shovel? Where do the witnesses live? Which witness does he have the biggest grudge against?

The opposite of forward chaining is backward chaining. Shown in Figure 1.3, this strategy operates from the perspective that you already possess an outcome and are searching for the conditions or circumstances that would have led to that result. Here, the system tries to determine a value for the goal by identifying the roles that would conclude a value for the goal. Then the system backs up and tries to determine whether the IF clauses are true. Again, a couple of examples are presented to enlighten you. This time, we know that we have a bad graphics card, and we leaf through our rules to find out if a black screen is indeed symptomatic of this problem.

Or, if murder tickles your fancy, we have a story called "murder at midnight." Suppose we are called to the scene of a heinous murder. We have spent the last several months investigating the *modus operandi* of a notorious killer, Mr. X, who is still on the loose. The local constable asks, "Was this the work of Mr. X?" We can apply a backward-chaining control strategy to this problem. We already have a hypothesis about who did it. Remember that the constable asked the question about whether it was Mr. X. So, we backward chain through our rule base to determine if the inputs or conditions surrounding the murder really do lead us to the conclusion that it was Mr. X.

There are some very nice features that can be added to the inference engine's method of processing rules. One of the absolute must-haves is *truth maintenance.* This is the capability of stopping midway in a consultation, changing your mind, and having the system pick up and run with the ball, without having to start over. In a conventional system, if you change your mind, you are out of luck. You must stop the program, reenter the new inputs, and then restart the program. An inference engine with truth maintenance keeps track of the maneuverings through the knowledge base. If you change your mind, the inference engine backs up and resets the rules and the objects fired, giving you a clean slate. Now you can begin anew from practically any point that you desire.

Along with having the ability to change your mind during a consultation, there is always the chance that the session dredges up some rather uncertain decisions. Suppose that the police chief in the "convict on the loose" tale was not quite certain about how all of the evidence at the scene of the crime added up. He might reason as follows: "Well, if he had a shovel, then I am about 75 percent sure that he went looking for the loot. On the other hand, I am about 40 percent sure that a shovel means that he is out to look for one of his old cronies and beat him over the head with it." Is this not the way we reason when we are not quite sure about something? Some expert-system inference engines have this capability built right into the rule declaration function. These are called *confidence factors*, and they are used to assign a percentage of likelihood to the conclusion of a rule.

Most systems use both backward and forward chaining. We call this a *hybrid control strategy*. If you think about it, most complex systems would need this combined approach. For example, think of a knowledge-based system built to assist in the budgetary process. You would like the system to be able to answer questions about how to perform the budgetary process (forward chaining). You would also like the system to be able to produce a budget if you tell it to decrease expenditures by 5 percent (backward chaining).

In spite of all that you can do with rules, only a small subset of interesting problems can be handled using a purely rule-based approach. One reason is the possibility of combinatorial explosion, which occurs when the search space used by all of these rules becomes so large that it is impractical to run the system. For example, the average number of moves possible in a chess game is 35. If you look ahead only three moves, you need to examine 1.8 billion moves. The only computer that ever came close to having this capability was IBM's Deep Blue, which defeated Garry Kasparov in the late 1990s. Deep Blue thus became the first computer system to defeat a reigning world champion in a match under standard chess tournament time controls.

A large problem programmed in a purely rule-based format necessarily needs to support massive numbers of rules. Deep Blue derived its playing strength mainly out of brute force computing power. It is a massively parallel, 30-node, RS/6000, SP-based computer system enhanced with 480 special-purpose ASIC chess chips. Apart from those in the military, few computers as powerful as this one exist, making a rule-based knowledge system infeasible for very large, sophisticated problems.

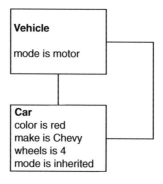

Figure 1.4 The object CAR.

Part of the problem is in the methodology that is used for searching through all of the chunks of knowledge in a forward-chaining strategy to find a match for a fact. One way in which developers cope with this problem is the implementation of what is called the *RETE algorithm*. The RETE algorithm is an efficient pattern-matching algorithm for implementing rule-based (expert) systems. The RETE algorithm was designed by Charles L. Forgy of Carnegie Mellon University in 1979, and refined by him in the 1980s. RETE has become the basis for many popular expert systems, including OPS5, CLIPS, JESS, and LISA. This algorithm can be thought of as an optimizer for rule-based systems. In a nutshell, RETE keeps track of which rules are true for a given knowledge-based state. In a very large system, however, even the RETE algorithm does not help.

A refinement to the typical rule-based expert system came with the advent of object-oriented programming (OOP). This methodology concentrates on data structures, as opposed to functions, for problem solving. Originating in the 1960s, the radical concept behind OOP is that a computer program is composed of a collection of individual units, or objects, as opposed to a traditional view in which a program is a list of instructions to the computer. Each object is capable of receiving messages, processing data, and sending messages to other objects.

Objects are a nice, neat way of defining knowledge. Look at the example of the object called CAR in Figure 1.4. The object CAR has several slots. Color is a slot, make is another slot, and number of wheels is a third slot. Each of these slots contains one or more values. The value of color is red, make is Chevy, and the wheels slot has a value of four. Notice that the value of the slot called *mode* is inherited from its parent. Objects are hierarchical in nature, similar to hierarchical databases. There is a parent–child relationship between an object and the one beneath it, in hierarchical order. Just as in a parent–child relationship, in which your child can inherit your hair color, an object can inherit some attribute from

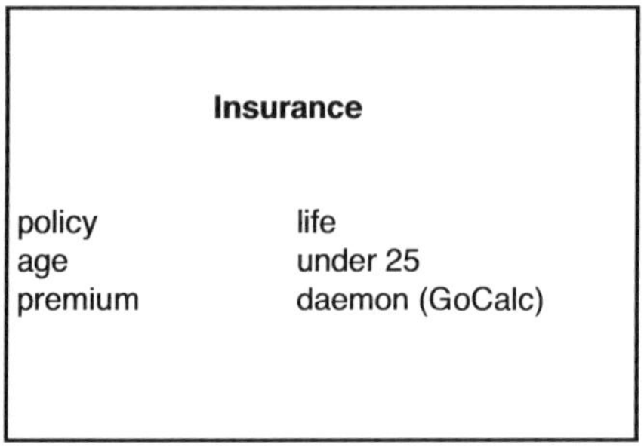

```
┌─────────────────────────────────────────────┐
│                                               │
│                  Insurance                    │
│                                               │
│   policy              life                    │
│   age                 under 25                │
│   premium             daemon (GoCalc)         │
│                                               │
│                                               │
└─────────────────────────────────────────────┘
```

Figure 1.5   Use of daemons.

its parent. For example, the object CAR inherits the value of mode from its parent. Let us also look at the slot called Insurance in Figure 1.5. This slot has something called a *daemon* attached to it. A daemon is a rule or procedure that will fire whenever this value is accessed. If the slot Insurance is accessed, then a procedure named GoCalc, which will recalculate the premium for this policyholder, will be automatically executed.

The attributes of object orientation make it perfect for developing knowledge-based systems. Aside from inheritance and the use of daemons, several other features are well worth noting. Each object can stand alone. We call this ability *encapsulation*. Looking at our example in Figure 1.5, you will note that this looks like a miniprogram. It has data and performs procedures. Because each object hides its data and procedures from other objects, one would expect a communication problem in the use of objects. On the contrary, OOP is well-known for its ability to pass messages as either inputs or outputs. When an object is passed a message, it checks to see whether it can handle the request. If it cannot, then it checks with its parent, which further checks with its parent, until the message is satisfied.

What you end up with is a loosely coupled network of virtual programs that mostly act independently. In a conventional programming language, there is specific code that indicates exactly how to carry out commands. In object-oriented languages, the message is simply passed; it is left to the object to figure out what is to be done next.

Jess (http://herzberg.ca.sandia.gov/jess/) is an example of this hybrid rules-based object-oriented knowledge-system development environment. Rather than a procedural paradigm, in which a single program has a loop that is activated only one time, the declarative paradigm used by Jess matches a rule with a single fact specified as its input and processes that fact as its output. When the program is run, the rules engine will activate one for each matching fact. Jess can be used to build Java applets as well as full applications that use knowledge in the form of declarative rules to draw conclusions and inferences. Because many rules may match many inputs, there are few effective general-purpose matching algorithms. The Jess rules engine uses the RETE algorithm.

1.4 DATA, INFORMATION, KNOWLEDGE, AND WISDOM — AND WHY WE NEED TO DO THIS

This chapter has discussed the birth of the KM industry. Once computer systems became a fact of life in the organization, the volume of data skyrocketed to unmanageable levels. Smarter systems, some using artificial intelligence techniques, began to gain mainstream acceptance. CEOs soon began to realize that that being a knowledge-driven organization was an important key to competitive advantage — and KM was born.

The goal of KM is to turn raw data into knowledge, if not wisdom, as shown in Figure 1.6.

That it is important to turn all of this raw data into knowledge is without question. Measuring the value of intellectual assets to ascertain the true value of an organization's future earning potential is almost turning into a field of its own.

Bruce P. Mehlman (2002), assistant secretary for technology policy for the U.S. Department of Commerce, gave a speech on intellectual property in the age of innovation at the Licensing Executives Society Spring Meeting in Washington, D.C.

Mehlman stressed that the wealth of nations is indeed changing. The impact of innovation and technology on our society is already profound and unmistakable. Just look at the outsized impacts of information industries. The information technology sector accounts for just 7 percent of all businesses in our economy. Yet, between 1996 and 2000, it drove 28 percent of the overall U.S. real economic growth and created jobs at twice the pace of other sectors, jobs that paid twice as much on average.

The growing importance of knowledge and innovation presents both good and bad news for the United States, relative to its global competitors. On the one hand, by almost any measure, America is the most innovative nation on earth.

- The United States generates the most patents per capita.
- The United States conducts more research and development than any other nation. The United States finances 44 percent of the total worldwide investment in R&D — equal to the combined total of Japan, the United Kingdom, Canada, France, Germany, and Italy.
- The U.S. workforce is more research intensive than other regions. Researchers represent only 5.3 percent of the overall workforce in Europe, as compared to 8.1 percent in the United States.

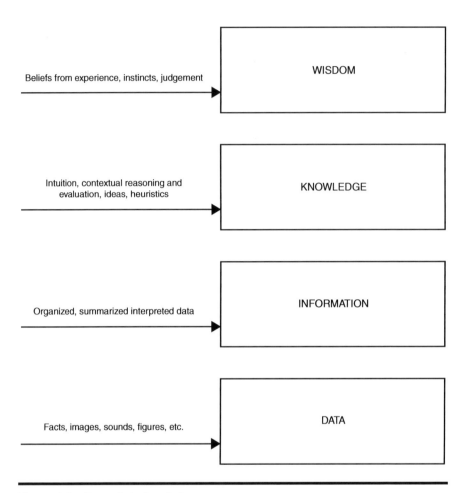

Figure 1.6   From data to wisdom.

- As measured by scientific publications, American scientific output exceeds those of the European Union and Japan (708 to 613 and 498, respectively) per million people.
- U.S. labs and universities remain a more attractive destination for the best and brightest young minds in the world. Of the PhDs who come here from China, 85 percent remain in the United States because it is a better place to do business. By contrast, many EU nations remain challenged when trying to attract top scientists and students.
- And perhaps most significantly, Americans have enjoyed the most rational, predictable, and consistent framework for intellectual property rights in the world, encouraging investment and rewarding innovation.

Notwithstanding the advantages and current leadership, the rest of the world is not blind to the importance of innovative capacity in the 21st century, and they are not standing still. America's global competitiveness faces pressure on multiple fronts including:

- *Education:* American students at the K-12 level continue to fall behind their international counterparts in math and science learning. U.S. eighth graders ranked 19th (out of 38 nations) in math and 18th in science in the 1999 Third International Math and Science Study.
- *Purchasing power parity:* When the CEO of an American multinational corporation was asked why they were moving so many R&D operations off shore, he replied that it cost 90 percent less to develop a PhD in Russia than in the United States. Just as manufacturing jobs have moved steadily abroad, innovation work may continue to globalize as highly skilled foreign labor proves cheaper.
- *Global R&D trends:* Although the United States accounts for 44 percent of worldwide R&D today, we accounted for 70 percent in 1970 (*Alliance for Science & Technology Research in America*). The European Union is racing to match our investments in nanotechnology, whereas Asian nations have collectively pulled ahead.

Our society, therefore, is facing threats from outside (global competition) as well as inside (failure of the educational system from middle school on up through college). Industry has no choice but to invest in systems that make us smarter.

1.5 EMBEDDING KNOWLEDGE MANAGEMENT IN THE ORGANIZATION

According to Pollard (2005) the expectations for KM are that it will be able to improve the following:

1. Growth and innovation
2. Productivity and efficiency reflected in cost savings
3. Customer relationships
4. Employee learning, satisfaction, and retention
5. Management decision making

KM can meet these goals if it is embedded within the organization using a bottom-up approach, rather than a top-down approach. Top-down approaches are usually forced upon employees and, hence, resisted or at least isolated. The bottom-up approach is somewhat akin to viral marketing, where you get one person enthusiastic about a product or service, who tells someone, who in turn tells someone else. By providing the tools, methodologies, training, and support on a unit or departmental level, you encourage employees to capture, share, and archive their knowledge for the good of the organization.

Of course, KM needs to have a focus. Pollard found that KM's safe haven seems to be the information technology department. This is quite a natural fit given KM's newly refocused definition, which includes topics such as organizational learning, technology transfer, competitive intelligence, data warehousing and business intelligence, document management (Davenport and Prusak, 2003), and its dependence on information technology resources.

Pollard suggests a number of techniques such as the following, to disseminate KM practices:

1. Do not force people to adapt. They must be self-motivated.
2. Change the job of knowledge professionals. In other words, get rid of those KM departments, and enable others to carry on these tasks (e.g., analysts, database administrators, and librarians can all go out and assist others to more effectively manage their information warehouses).
3. Stop collecting data centrally in a massive knowledge base. There is no reason why employees cannot store their domain of knowledge in their own private databases. Pollard makes a good point about respecting the privacy and confidentiality of personal information. This was quite a problem during the initial entry of artificial intelligence into the business world. People do not like to share what gives them their own personal competitive edge. For example, many financial investment houses never did get cooperation from their highly paid traders to build expert systems. After all, why should a trader give away what made him or her valuable to the firm? Of course, my own take on this is that a central KM repository needs to continue to exist, with the personal KM repositories used as inputs as well as outputs to the central store, where applicable.
4. Help people connect to experts inside and outside the organization.

The current craze over balanced scorecard (Kaplan and Norton, 1996) and performance management and measurement might also be used as a lever to further embed KM within an organization. Balanced scorecard has four perspectives, as shown in Figure 1.7. Each one of these perspectives defines a set of objectives, measures, targets, and initiatives to achieve the goals of that perspective. Although the "learning and growth" perspective is a natural fit for KM, the remaining perspectives should also

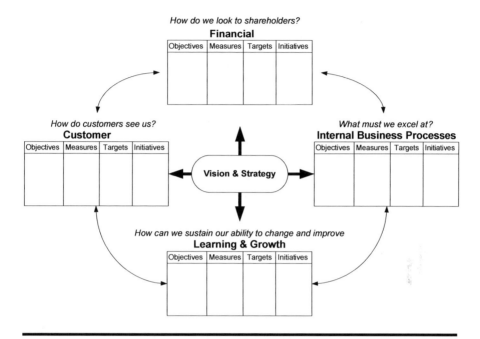

Figure 1.7   Balanced scorecard perspectives.

be considered. Balanced scorecard is best utilized when, similar to KM itself, it is cascaded through the organization. In other words, each unit or division should create its own scorecard, although it should tie in with the goals and objectives of the organizational scorecard. Adding goals, metrics, etc., for KM activities is a sure way to get these departments to at least consider usage within the department.

Finally, the role of the CEO should not be underestimated. Leaders challenge the process, inspire a shared vision, enable others to act, model the way, and encourage the heart (Lynch, 2003).

Sunassee and Sewry (2003) go a bit further and propose a framework for organizational KM. The proposed framework consists of three main interlinked components: knowledge management of the organization, knowledge management of the people, and knowledge management of the infrastructure and processes. They indicate that the organization needs to achieve a balance between these three subsystems to achieve a successful KM effort.

They stress that it is critical that the KM of the organization be carefully aligned to the overall business strategy of the organization. A close second in importance is an effort to make people feel as if they are part of the change process when implementing KM, including an emphasis on individual learning and innovative thinking.

The model also proposes a set of critical success factors such as the following that will serve to increase the chances of a successful implementation:

1. Align KM strategy with business strategy
2. Receive top management support
3. Create and manage knowledge culture
4. Use of pilot project
5. Create and manage organizational learning
6. Manage people
7. Choose the right technology
8. Include double-loop learning (Argyris [1976] proposes the double-loop learning theory, which pertains to learning to change underlying values and assumptions. The focus of the theory is on solving problems that are complex and ill-structured and which change as problem solving advances.)

1.6 WHERE DO WE GO NEXT?

Now that we understand how KM got its start and why it is important, our next chapter will delve into KM strategies.

References

Argyris, C., *Increasing Leadership Effectiveness*, New York: John Wiley & Sons, 1976.

Davenport, T.H. and Prusak, L., *What's the Big Idea?*, Boston, MA: Harvard Business School Press, 2003.

Kaplan, R.S. and Norton, D.P., *The Balanced Scorecard: Translating Strategy into Action*, Boston, MA: Harvard Business School Press, 1996.

Lederman, L.C. Communication in the workplace: the impact of the information age and high technology on interpersonal communication in organizations, in Gumpert, G. and Cathcart, R. (Eds.), *Intermedia,* New York: Oxford University Press, 1986, pp. 311–322.

Lynch, K., Leaders challenge the process, inspire a shared vision, enable others to act, model the way, encourage the heart, *The Kansas Banker, 93*(4), April 2003.

Mehlman, B.P., The Changing Wealth of Nations: Intellectual Property in the Age of Innovation, 2002. Retrieved August 9, 2005 from http://www.technology.gov/Speeches/p_BPM_020503_Wealth.htm.

Pollard, D., The future of knowledge management, *ExecutiveAction,* 130, January 2005. Retrieved March 24, 2005 from http://www.conference-board.org/publications/execaction_formac.cfm.

Sunassee, N. and Sewry, D.A., An investigation of knowledge management implementation strategies, *Proceedings of SAICSIT,* 2003, pp. 24–36.

Toffler, A., *Future Shock*, New York: Bantam, 1984.

Wurman, R.S., *Information Anxiety 2*, New York: Pearson, 2000.

2

KNOWLEDGE MANAGEMENT TRANSFER STRATEGIES

The U.S. Agency for International Development (2003) describes the "know who, know how, and know what" of knowledge management (KM) in three dimensions:

1. *Knowledge (experience)*
2. *Information (context)*
3. *Data (fact)*

Here, data is an explicit form of knowledge, and knowledge is a tacit form. They go on to describe how knowledge is converted between the tacit and explicit forms, as shown in Table 2.1.

If knowledge includes the experience and understanding of the people in the organization along with the information artifacts available within the organization and in the world outside, then KM must have a way to identify, collect, store, and transfer that knowledge within the organization, as shown in Figure 2.1.

In this chapter, we are going to talk about the framework under which KM operates and then delve into techniques for identifying, collecting, storing, and transferring knowledge within the organization.

Table 2.1 Examples of Converting between Tacit and Explicit Forms of Knowledge

Tacit to Tacit — **Socialization** Team members meeting and discussing	Tacit to Explicit — **Externalization** Dialoging within team, answering questions
Explicit to Tacit — **Internalization** Learning from a report	Explicit to Explicit — **Combination** E-Mailing a report

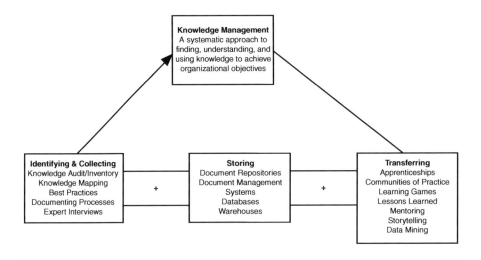

Figure 2.1 The process of knowledge management.

2.1 KM FRAMEWORKS

Corcoran and Robison (n.d.) provide a great checklist for successful management of corporate knowledge:

1. Identify or develop a strategy to support the knowledge base. It is a better idea to look for a business driver rather than just a technology platform. Ask how you can improve your business and measure the effectiveness.
2. Select the key business strategy that brings the most leverage to your business.
   a. Customer based — consolidation of information from employees, customers, etc., to create actionable intelligence
   b. Productivity based — creation of knowledge bases of employee expertise, including lessons learned

    c. Innovation based — integration of product development and R&D intelligence to bring products to market more quickly

3. Find a leader to drive the process; delegate.
4. Identify the knowledge products that will support the selected strategy. It is recommended that the organization start small, with a product or service from which you can get immediate payback. For example, to counter an emerging competitive threat, create a knowledge base of competitive intelligence from across the organization (e.g., sales, marketing, R&D, etc.).
5. Evaluate the sources of content within your organization.
   a. Identify sources of content (e.g., marketing and sales).
   b. Identify experts who gather, analyze, and organize information.
   c. Determine the gaps. Find out what people need to know that they cannot find.
   d. Determine how you can capture and document the informal information network within your organization.
6. Design a process for building and sharing knowledge. Develop a vision and mission. Determine incentives that will influence others to adopt your vision and mission. Incentives can be in the form of compensation, promotions, etc. Performance measurement is the key.
7. Create, integrate, and organize content.
   a. Determine project scope — for example, will individual or group creators put their knowledge in their own database? Will this be a corporatewide initiative, with designated builders and gate-keepers?
   b. Develop a methodology to capture best practices, research used, and lessons learned.
   c. Build a cross-functional project team to identify content; capture, organize, and communicate it; and make it accessible and usable. Three types of professionals are needed: content professionals, information technology professionals, and decision makers.
8. Identify the technology tools you need. What do you need to buy? What can you outsource?
9. Link content sources and users to create a flow of knowledge, creating a learning and sharing organization.
10. Measure the effectiveness of your efforts. Survey the users of and contributors to the knowledge base. Identify successes and increases in productivity. Develop appropriate metrics.

Siemens (n.d.) has developed a Knowledge Management Maturity Model (KMMM), loosely based on the Software Engineering Institute's widely used Capability Maturity Model (CMM). As shown in Table 2.2,

Table 2.2 **Software Engineering Institute's Capability Maturity Model**

Level	Focus	Key Process Area
5: Optimizing	Continuous process improvement	Defect prevention; technology innovation; process change control
4: Managed	Product and process quality	Process measurement and analysis; quality management
3: Defined	Engineering process	Organization process focus; organization process definition; peer reviews; training program; intergroup communication; software product engineering; integrated software management
2: Repeatable	Project management	Software project planning; software project tracking; software subcontract management; software configuration management; requirements management
1: Initial	Putting out fires	Ad hoc

Source: From http://www.sei.cmu.edu/.

the CMM, which is a framework closely followed by those who practice rigorous software engineering methodology, consists of five levels.

Seimen's KMMM utilizes the same five levels: initial, repeated, defined, managed, and optimizing, which constitutes its development model. The KMMM also has an analysis model, which is shown in Figure 2.2.

The analysis model creates transparency in all of the key areas of KM and, thus, provides a vehicle for improvement. The development model, on the other hand, provides the methodology for getting to the next level.

There are many ways for an organization to identify, store, and transfer knowledge. Some strategies will work better in one organization than another. Some may not be appropriate for specific types of content. The challenge is to identify and develop complementary ways to further KM and knowledge transfer in an organization.

2.2 KNOWLEDGE TRANSFER TECHNIQUES

In this section, we discuss a variety of knowledge transfer techniques that can be used to "cull" knowledge from people as well as processes. New York State utilizes many of these practices (2002).

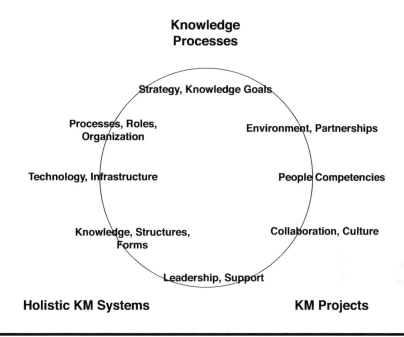

**Knowledge
Processes**

Strategy, Knowledge Goals

Processes, Roles,
Organization

Environment, Partnerships

Technology, Infrastructure

People Competencies

Knowledge, Structures,
Forms

Collaboration, Culture

Leadership, Support

Holistic KM Systems

KM Projects

Figure 2.2   Knowledge Management Maturity Model (KMMM) analysis.

2.2.1   Apprenticeships, Internships, and Traineeships

These are formal arrangements in which an experienced person passes along knowledge and skill to a novice.

2.2.2   Best Practices

The identification and use of processes or practices that result in excellent products or services. *Best practices* are ways of doing business, processes, methods, strategies, etc., that yield superior results. Best practices, sometimes called *preferred practices*, often generate ideas for improvements in other organizations or work units. They have been implemented and honed over time to a point where they are viewed as exemplary and should or could be adopted by others. A formal benchmarking process is often used to identify best practices. A full description of this technique is beyond the scope of this book; however, there are many books and other resources on the subject.

Identifying and sharing best practices is an important way to incorporate the knowledge of some into the work of many. Organizational structures tend to promote "silo" thinking, in which particular locations, divisions, or functions focus on maximizing their own accomplishments and rewards, keeping information to themselves and thereby suboptimizing the whole organization. The mechanisms are lacking in sharing of information and learning. Identifying and sharing best practices help build relationships and common perspectives among people who do not work side by side.

Best practices can also spark innovative ideas and generate suggestions for improving processes, even if a practice cannot be used in its entirety. The process of identifying them can also benefit employee morale. By highlighting or showcasing people's work, employees get organization-wide recognition for their work.

2.2.3 Communities of Practice

Communities are groups of individuals who share knowledge about a common work practice over a period of time, though they are not part of a formally constituted work team. Communities of practice generally cut across traditional organizational boundaries. They enable individuals to acquire new knowledge faster. They may also be called *communities of interest* if the people share an interest in something but do not necessarily perform the work on a daily basis.

A *community of practice* (COP) is a group of individuals sharing a common working practice over a period of time, though not a part of a formally constituted work team. They generally cut across traditional organizational boundaries and enable individuals to acquire new knowledge faster. For example, employees actively involved in multiparty, multi-issue settlement negotiations formed a monthly discussion group at which they explored process issues, reviewed lessons learned, and shared tools and techniques. COPs can be either more or less structured depending on the needs of the membership.

COPs provide a mechanism for sharing knowledge throughout one organization or across several organizations. They lead to an improved network of organizational contacts, supply opportunities for peer-group recognition, and support continuous learning, all of which reinforce knowledge transfer and contribute to better results. They are valuable for sharing tacit (implicit) knowledge.

To be successful, COPs require support from the organizations. However, if management closely controls their agenda and methods of operation, they are seldom successful. This is more of an issue for communities of practice within organizations.

Communities of practice can be used virtually anywhere in an organization: within one organizational unit or across organizational boundaries, with a small or large group of people, in one geographic location or multiple locations, etc. They can also be used to bring together people from multiple agencies, organized around a profession, shared roles, or common issues.

They create value when there is tacit information that, if shared, leads to better results for individuals and the organization. They are also valuable in situations in which knowledge is being constantly gained, and sharing this knowledge is beneficial to the accomplishment of the organization's goals.

There are different kinds of COPs. Some develop best practices, some create guidelines, and others meet to share common concerns, problems, and solutions. They can connect in different ways: face-to-face, in small or large meetings, or electronically.

An organization or group of practitioners needs to decide which kind of community is best for it by determining what knowledge people need to share, how closely connected the community is, and how closely knowledge needs to be linked with people's everyday jobs. The supporting organization needs to be willing to make resources available to the community. These resources include enabling employees to participate at COP events as well as providing logistical and other support. Public and private entities that have created communities of practice say they work best when they set their own agenda and focus on developing members' capabilities. Management should not dictate. Smaller, more informal COPs will likely have fewer constrictions and less need for support.

The following are guidelines to be considered in forming a COP:

1. Determine the community's purpose. Link the community's purpose to the profession or organization's goals and objectives. Communities can be formed as helping communities that provide a forum for members to help each other solve everyday work problems; best practice communities to develop and disseminate best practices, guidelines, and procedures for members' use; knowledge-stewarding communities to organize, manage, and steward a body of knowledge from which community members can draw; and innovation communities for creating breakthrough ideas, knowledge, and practices.
2. Clarify roles and responsibilities. Roles can include the following, especially for larger, more formal COPs:
   a. *Functional sponsors:* Sponsors need to believe in the value of knowledge sharing. They encourage community growth and commitment of agency resources, act as champions for the community within the organization, and work with community leaders to resolve issues.
   b. *Core group:* A subset of the community, consisting of knowledgeable and experienced community members (subject matter

experts) to assist with start up of the group and to provide ongoing organizational support.

c. *Community leaders:* Active members of the community who help to focus the community, plan and schedule meetings and events, represent the community within the organization, manage day-to-day activities, etc.

d. *Members:* Membership should be voluntary. Members will continue to be actively engaged to the extent the community meets their needs, but the expectation must be set that members participate in community discussions, activities, and work.

e. *Facilitator to guide the community's process:* Facilitators provide process expertise, assist with the use of process tools, and help to create and maintain a collaborative environment.

f. *Logistics coordinator:* Coordinates calendars, schedules meetings and events, coordinates facilities, and arranges for equipment.

g. Other roles to consider include *functional support staff* and a *project historian.* Functional support staff help to arrange for databases to store and share community knowledge and establish mechanisms for online sharing of information through such tools as chat rooms or discussion lists. The project historian documents project decisions and events for reuse by the agency.

3. Identify community members. Membership is voluntary, but it is recommended that individuals who could learn from each other and have a stake in the community's success be identified and cultivated. Employees who are seen as experts or as trusted information sources add value to the community, and efforts should be made to recruit them.

4. Devise mechanisms for communication and collaboration. There can be a combination of face-to-face meetings and events, instant messaging or chat rooms, shared databases, videoconferencing, etc.

5. Hold an initial community workshop to engage member interest and stimulate continued involvement. At this meeting, the community's purpose should be clarified as follows:

a. Work should begin on building member relationships.

b. Ground rules should be decided and roles explained.

c. Methods for creating, capturing, and sharing knowledge should be discussed.

d. Consensus should be reached on the highest-priority knowledge needs.

6. Check community progress to identify and resolve any barriers that impede the community's success. This is often a function of the community leader and core group.

Appendix L provides an excellent guide for COP practitioners.

2.2.4 Documenting Processes

These processes comprise developing a written or electronic record of a specific work process that includes the business case for the process, steps in the process, key dates, relationship to other processes that come before and after, key players and contact information, any required references and legal citations, backup procedures, and copies of forms, software, datasets, and filenames associated with the process.

2.2.5 Document Repositories

These are collections of documents that can be viewed, retrieved, and interpreted by humans and automated software systems (e.g., statistical software packages). Document repositories add navigation and categorization services to stored information. Key word search capability is often provided to facilitate information retrieval.

Content management is discussed in more depth in Chapter 6. Appendix D and Appendix E provide some good information on content management.

2.2.6 Expert Interviews

In these sessions, one or more people who are considered experts in a particular subject, program, policy, process, etc., meet with others to share knowledge. Expert interviews can be used in many ways, including capturing knowledge of those scheduled to leave an organization, conducting lessons learned debriefings, and identifying job competencies. Expert interviews became popular more than two decades ago when they took corporate America by storm.

Expert interviews are a way of making tacit knowledge more explicit. A person can describe not only what was done but why, providing context and explaining the judgment behind the action. Interviews are often easier for the experts than having them write down all the details and nuances. Learners can ask questions and probe deeper to ensure understanding.

Making time with these sessions is probably the biggest challenge for both the experts and the learners. If the session is more formal with a large group of learners, some may be intimidated and need coaching.

Expert interviews can be used in many situations. The best place to begin is with people who have unique knowledge developed over a long period and are likely to leave the organization soon. The next step might be to identify mission-critical processes or programs in which only one or two staff have a high level of technical knowledge.

This process is probably most effective when someone facilitates the experience, setting the stage with participants, facilitating the exchange of any information prior to the interview, and handling scheduling or other logistics.

Identify the people you want to start with, both the experts and the learners, and the area of knowledge. Discuss with the experts the reasons for the interviews, who will be involved, and what you would like to focus on. If the learner needs to prepare for the session, the expert can identify how to do this and what resource materials would be helpful. It is also essential to ask the learners what they think they would like to know from the experts. If they have specific questions, provide these to the expert in advance so he or she can be prepared.

If the session is more formal, with larger numbers of experts and learners, a facilitator can help keep the session focused and on time. If the interview is a one-on-one meeting, a facilitator is probably not needed.

If audio- or videotaping, arrangements should be made in advance and equipment tested to ensure, for instance, that both experts and learners can be heard on tape.

2.2.7 Job Aids

Job aids are tools that help people perform tasks accurately. They include things such as checklists, flow diagrams, reference tables, decision tree diagrams, etc., that provide specific, concrete information to the user and serve as a quick reference guide to performing a task. Job aids are not the actual tools used to perform tasks, such as computers, measuring tools, or telephones.

A job aid can take many forms, but it is basically a document that has information or instruction on how to perform a task. It guides the user to do the task correctly and is used while performing the task, when the person needs to know the procedure.

A job aid can be as simple as a sticker on an answering machine that describes how to access messages. Types of job aids include:

1. Step-by-step narratives or worksheets sequencing a process
2. Checklists, which might show items to be considered when planning or evaluating
3. Flowcharts, leading the user through a process and assisting the user to make decisions and complete tasks based on a set of conditions
4. Reference resources, such as a parts catalog or telephone listing

Job aids are usually inexpensive to create and easy to revise. Using job aids can eliminate the need for employees to memorize tedious or complex processes and procedures. When a job aid is easy to access, it can help increase productivity and reduce error rates.

Job aids need to be written clearly and concisely, with nothing left to interpretation. They also need to be updated and kept current. Finding the time to create job aids can be a challenge; however, creation of good job aids produces benefits over the long term.

Consult with knowledgeable users to identify what job aids to develop. Create job aids that include only the steps or information required by the user. Keep the information and language simple, using short words and sentences. Do not include background information or other information extraneous to actual performance of the task; put that in another location. Use graphics or drawings, when appropriate, to more clearly demonstrate detail.

Use bold or italicized text to highlight important points. Use colors to code different procedures or parts of a process. Make sure the job aid can be easily accessed and is sturdy. A laminated wall chart hung near the place where a task is performed can be consulted more quickly than a piece of paper stored in a file.

Job aids are most appropriate for tasks that an employee does not perform frequently or for complex tasks. Tasks with many steps that are difficult to remember or tasks that can cost high if not performed correctly can benefit from having readily accessible job aids. Also, if a task changes frequently, a job aid would save time and reduce the chance for errors.

Job aids can be a good supplement to classroom training. Users can learn tasks in a classroom but will likely need something to rely on when on the job.

2.2.8 Knowledge Audits

Knowledge audits help an organization identify its knowledge assets, including what knowledge is needed and available. They provide information on how knowledge assets are produced and shared, and where there is a need for internal transfer of knowledge.

2.2.9 Knowledge Fairs

These events showcase information about an organization or a topic. They can be used internally to provide a forum for sharing information or externally to educate customers or other stakeholders about important information.

A *knowledge fair* is an event designed to showcase information about an organization or a topic. It can be organized in many ways using speakers, demonstrations or, more commonly, booths displaying information of interest to the attendees. One example is the Xerox Corporation's annual "team day" that showcases the work of various quality-improvement teams.

A large amount of information can be made available, and attendees can focus specifically on what they are interested in learning. Attendees can interact directly with the presenters, getting immediate answers to their specific questions. They can also establish contacts for further exploration of topics if needed.

Attendees often network with one another and with booth developers; this strengthens their teamwork. Knowledge fairs also provide opportunities to draw attention to best practices and recognize employee and team achievements.

Depending on the scope and size of the event, it can require a large amount of staff time for creating booths, putting information together to display, and for organization and logistics. The costs for space, materials, and resources can be high. The potential exists for participants to become overwhelmed with information.

Consider a knowledge fair in which there is a lot of information to share with a lot of people, and participants need a broader perspective, as well as an opportunity, to interact on a one-on-one basis on specific topics. A knowledge fair is an alternative to traditional presentations in which more interactive experiences are desirable.

2.2.10 Knowledge Maps and Inventories

These catalog information or knowledge available in an organization and where it is located. They point to information but do not contain it. An example is an experts or resource directory that lists people with expert knowledge who can be contacted by others in need of that knowledge.

Knowledge mapping is actually a process of surveying, assessing, and linking the information, knowledge, competencies, and proficiencies held by individuals and groups within an organization. Organizations use knowledge maps for many different uses. Some use it to compile company locators to find internal and external resources. Others use them to identify knowledge-sharing opportunities or knowledge barriers within cross-functional workgroups. Many organizations use knowledge mapping before developing formal communities of practice.

Knowledge mapping is a process that actually never ends, with a goal toward illustrating or road-mapping how knowledge flows throughout an organization. The process consists of the following steps:

1. Discover the location, ownership, value, and use of knowledge artifacts.
2. Learn the roles and expertise of people.
3. Identify constraints to the flow of knowledge.
4. Highlight opportunities to leverage existing knowledge.

A knowledge map describes what knowledge is used in a process and how it flows around the process. It is the basis for determining knowledge commonality, or areas in which knowledge is used across multiple processes.

The knowledge map describes who has the knowledge (tacit), where the knowledge resides (infrastructure), and how the knowledge is transferred or disseminated (social). Knowledge mapping is used to focus on both the strategic as well as tactical knowledge assets of an organization. On an enterprise level, it should be focused on strategic, technical, and market knowledge as well as the cross-functional linkages between divisions or business groups. On the tactical level, it should focus on the working group and the processes within that group.

At all levels, the knowledge map provides an assessment of existing or required knowledge and information as follows:

1. What knowledge is needed?
2. Who has this knowledge?
3. Where does this knowledge reside?
4. Is the knowledge tacit or explicit?
5. Is the knowledge routine or nonroutine?
6. What issues does it address?

The APQC's (American Productivity & Quality Center) Road Map to Knowledge Management (www.apqc.org) consists of five stages of implementation: stage 1: getting started; stage 2: develop strategy; stage 3: design and launch KM initiatives; stage 4: expand and support; and stage 5: institutionalize KM. Within this context, knowledge mapping is recommended in stage 2 or stage 3.

Process knowledge mapping analyzes a business process or method to identify the following:

1. Design milestones (where knowledge is needed)
2. Knowledge requirements (what knowledge is needed)
3. Routes for access and retrieval of knowledge (through people and technology)
4. Gaps between required skills and current skills

Questions that are asked during this process include these:

1. What do you need to know?
2. Where does the knowledge come from?
3. Who owns it?
4. What knowledge, tools, and templates exist today?
5. What knowledge, tools, and templates should be created?
6. What barriers or issues exist?

The method for mapping the process or focus area consists of the following steps:

1. Review critical processes.
2. Identify individual process steps within each process.
3. Determine routine and nonroutine tasks.
4. Identify key decision points and handoffs.
5. Locate owners of and stakeholders in high-value processes.
6. Follow the knowledge pathways through the organization using the interview methodology or brainstorming.
7. Inventory types of knowledge utilized and needed. Categorize the knowledge content (explicit, tacit, and embedded), the social capital (trust, interpersonal relationships, and cultural norms), and infrastructure (processes, tools, roles and responsibilities, and incentives).
8. Identify gaps, lack of connectivity, and information overload.
9. Develop a plan for collecting, reviewing, validating, storing, and sharing knowledge and information.
10. Create measurement criteria for each critical process step.

A sample knowledge process map might look like the one in Table 2.3.

Once the maps have been completed, they should be analyzed. For each process step, review the knowledge resources and determine these issues:

1. Do we leverage this today?
2. Is the knowledge available and accessible to everyone who needs it?
3. Are decisions made with all the right knowledge?
4. Where should we focus our improvement efforts?

Summarize the analysis for creating a list of key strengths and key opportunities.

Table 2.3 **A Sample Knowledge Map**

Process step	1. Conduct design session	2. Document product gap
Objective of step	Gather requirements for software	Clarify requirements not met by package
Infrastructure	Methods and tools database; deliverables database; project management guidelines	Vendor supplied methods; methods and tools database; deliverables database
Social capital	Discussion among consultants; connecting with subject matter experts	Discussion with vendor; discussion with technical consultants
Tacit knowledge	Knowledge of previous design sessions; estimating experience	Knowledge of developers' skills; knowledge of package capabilities

Note: Two columns are shown; additional columns may be added.

2.2.11   Learning Games

These structured learning activities are used to make learning fun and more effective, provide a review of material that has already been presented to strengthen learning, and evaluate how much learning has occurred.

Games can also be used to serve these ends:

1. To help people prepare for learning by testing current levels of knowledge
2. To apply a newly learned skill
3. To learn as they play the game
4. To practice what has been presented to reinforce the learning

Games improve knowledge transfer in several ways:

1. By increasing participation among all involved
2. By improving the learning process by creating an environment in which people's creativity and intelligence are engaged
3. By destressing learning by making it fun
4. By addressing the different ways in which different people best learn — through movement, hearing, and seeing
5. By adding variety to a training program; this helps to keep people actively involved

When games are used as an end in themselves and not as means toward an end, they waste time and can hamper learning. In addition, using too many games can destroy learning effectiveness. Games are usually used in conjunction with other learning methodologies, such as presentations and discussions. When you use them, or whether you use them at all, depends on the learning that you are trying to convey and whether games will help you meet your learning objectives.

Games used at the beginning of a program can measure existing knowledge and build immediate interest in the training material. Games used during a program can help people discover the learning themselves (which strengthens recall and commitment), practice using new knowledge or skills, or reinforce initial learning. Games used near the end of a program can test knowledge gained and people's ability to apply it in their work settings.

The prerequisites for games to be effective are as follows:

1. They must be related to the workplace by providing knowledge, reinforcing attitudes, and initiating actions that are important to job success.
2. They must teach people how to think, access information, react, understand, and create value for themselves and their organizations.
3. They must be enjoyable and engaging without being overly simplistic or silly.
4. They must allow for collaboration between learners.
5. They must be challenging but not unattainable.
6. They must permit time for reflection, feedback, dialog, and integration. In other words, games should be debriefed.

Examples of games include the following:

1. Quizzes
2. Scavenger hunts
3. Quiz show games, including those modeled on television game shows such as Jeopardy! or Family Feud
4. Board games, such as GOER's supervision central
5. "Name that" games
6. Sports-related games
7. Twenty questions

2.2.12 Lessons Learned Debriefings

These debriefings are a way to identify, analyze, and capture experiences, those that worked well and those that need improvement, so that others can learn from these experiences. For maximum impact, lessons learned debriefings should be done either immediately following an event or on a regular basis, and results shared quickly with those who would benefit from the knowledge gained. Hewlett-Packard refers to their lessons learned sessions held during and at the end of projects to share knowledge as *project snapshots*.

Sessions are conducted at the completion of a project or activity, or at strategic points during a project or work team's ongoing work, in which members of the team or group evaluate the process used and the results. They identify what was done right and what could be done better the next time.

These sessions identify and capture the things that went well and the things that could be improved, so that team or workgroup members are aware of and can use the broader team or group's learning in their future projects or work activities. Results can also be shared with future teams or other workgroups so they can learn from the experiences of others.

Making time to conduct lessons learned debriefing sessions and documenting the results are the biggest challenges. The sessions should be done as soon as possible after the completion of the project or activities, but not more than 30 days later. They could also be done at any strategic point during a project.

Lessons learned sessions work best when they are done as a formal review session in a functional meeting room, using facilitators and an assigned note taker. Develop ground rules for the session, e.g., listen to understand, respect others' contributions, no blaming, full participation, etc. Include appropriate people such as these:

1. Project sponsor
2. Project or work unit manager
3. Project team or work unit staff
4. Customers
5. Stakeholder representatives, including the manager with responsibility for the project oversight
6. Other appropriate executive management
7. Others, depending on the nature of the project or work, e.g., maintenance, information systems, technical services, and operations staff

The following rules should be observed:

1. Make sure lists of lessons learned are process oriented and are directed toward improving the work process, not individual performance.
2. Make sure feedback is constructive.
3. Describe specific behaviors and their effects.

4 Be nonjudgmental.
5 Identify actions and behaviors that would be more effective.
6 Recognize positive contributions.
7. See the Lessons Learned Form (Appendix A).

2.2.12.1 Debriefing Process Alternative A

Have groups of six to ten people answer the following questions, and consolidate responses for all the groups. Open-ended questions usually elicit the best responses. You may want to consider the commonality or strength of agreement on the responses. Select questions from the following, or develop your own questions:

1. What worked best on the project or activity?
2. What could have been better on the project or activity?
3. How can we improve the methodology to better assist in the successful completion of future projects or work activities?
4. What parts of the project or work resulted in meeting the specified requirements and goals? What helped ensure these results?
5. What parts did not meet specifications and goals? What could have been done to ensure that these were met?
6. How satisfied were the customers with the results? What was particularly good? What could have been done to improve customer satisfaction?
7. Were cost budgets met? Why or why not? What helped or hindered staying within budget?
8. What contributed to the schedule being met? What hindered it?
9. What appropriate risks were identified and mitigated? What additional risks should have been identified? What additional actions should have been taken to mitigate risks?
10. What communications were appropriate and helpful? What additional communications would have been helpful?
11. How did the project or activity management methodology work? What worked particularly well? What could have been done to improve it?
12. What procedures were particularly helpful in producing deliverables? What could have been improved? How could processes be improved or streamlined?

2.2.12.2 Debriefing Process Alternative B

Develop, post, and use a list of eight to ten items or objectives considered most important for success. The team leader or work-unit leader and facilitator could develop this list ahead of time or with participants at the beginning of the session. Possible items to help keep the discussions focused include these:

1. Customer expectations met.
2. All specifications achieved.
3. Work completed on time.
4. Work completed within budget.
5. Return on investment achieved.
6. Organizational goals met.
7. Positive experience for project or workgroup members.

Identify how well these items were accomplished (fell short, met, or exceeded expectations) Identify actions that contributed to or hindered the accomplishment of each of these objectives. See the following text for a possible template for meeting notes.

2.2.12.3   Debriefing Process Alternative C

Identify eight to ten major strategies, activities, or processes that helped the project or work unit as well as eight to ten major problems encountered during the project or activity and what could be done to address or prevent these problems in the future.

The responsibilities of the project or work unit manager are as follows:

1. Make all arrangements.
2. Ensure that right people are present.
3. Make sure necessary materials and documentation are available.
4. Communicate results to the right people throughout the organization.

The facilitator, of course, has typical facilitation responsibilities.

Surveys can also be used instead of (or to supplement) a meeting. Consider getting professional assistance in developing and administering a survey to a large group or to people outside the organization. The survey could be written questionnaires that could be mailed or administered during a meeting. Consider how it should be administered and to whom (sponsor, team, workgroup, customer representatives, consumers, or other stakeholders).

The following could be typical goals:

1. Review product delivered against baseline requirements and specifications.
2. Determine how well the needs of the customer have been met.

3. Determine whether the product or service was delivered effectively and efficiently.
4. Determine what could be improved.

2.2.13 Mentoring

In mentoring, an experienced, skilled person (mentor) is paired with a lesser skilled or experienced person (protege), with the goal of developing or strengthening competencies of the protege.

2.2.14 On-the-Job Training (OJT)

Most organizations use some form of OJT in which an experienced employee teaches a new person how to perform job tasks. If this happens at random or with no consistent written materials or processes, it is called *unstructured OJT.* A system of *structured OJT* differs in that specific training processes are written; training materials and guides exist and are used consistently by all those who train; training is scheduled; records are kept of training sessions; and trainers are given training on how to do OJT, how to give feedback, and several other factors.

OJT is any kind of instruction that takes place at the actual job site and involves learning tasks, skills, or procedures in a hands-on manner. It can be informal, such as when a person asks a co-worker to show how to perform a task, or part of a more formal structured OJT system. If part of a structured system, there are usually prescribed procedures for training that specify the tasks and skills to be learned and that sequence the activities to build on knowledge already acquired. There are also administrative processes requiring both trainer (sometimes called a coach) and trainee to certify that a particular task or skill has been mastered. Structured OJT is usually more effective than informal OJT; however, the informal type can also be valuable.

OJT can be very effective because someone skilled in performing the tasks does the training (the coach). With training done on the actual job site, it may not reduce productivity as much as taking a person off site to a classroom setting.

The cost is usually the coach's and employee's time. If a more structured approach is being taken, there are costs associated with training coaches and developing checklists and other materials. However, these costs can be amortized over time and over the number of trainees who use them.

Informal OJT can sometimes be a problem if the training objectives are not clearly stated and understood. If the training is presented in an off-the-cuff manner, it might not be taken seriously enough. Also, if the person doing the training is not adequately prepared, the training could be confusing and the time wasted.

Consider the following when deciding whether to use structured OJT:

1. When equipment or materials needed to perform the job are not replicable in a classroom environment.
2. When instruction needs to take place in small chunks so that taking the person away from the job site is not an efficient use of time.
3. When the number of people needing instruction is too small to efficiently organize a classroom session.
4. When showing someone how to do something, using real work is the most effective way of teaching.

One-on-one training should not be presented in a vacuum but as part of an overall training program that might include some classroom instruction, job aids (e.g., checklists — see Subsection 2.2.7), manuals, and demonstrations. The following text presents a step-by-step approach:

1. Prepare
   a. Analyze the job to figure out the best way to teach.
   b. Make a list of the tasks and associated knowledge and skills.
   c. Break the job tasks into steps, and note the key factors that relate to each step.
2. Present the process
   a. Put the employee at ease.
   b. Find out what the employee already knows about the job.
   c. Make the employee aware of the importance of the job or task and how it fits into the larger picture of what the employee does.
   d. Show the employee how to perform the task, and describe what you are doing.
   e. Stress the key points, and use appropriate job aids.
   f. Completely instruct one point at a time, at a rate slow enough for the employee to understand.
3. Test the performance
   a. Have the employee perform the job while you observe.
   b. Have the employee show you how he or she does each step of the job and describe what is being done.
   c. Ask questions and offer advice.
   d. Continue until you are satisfied that the employee knows the job or tasks.
4. Follow up
   a. Tell the employee who to go to for help.
   b. Check on the employee as often as you feel necessary.
   c. Encourage questions.
   d. Have employee perform independently with normal supervision.

2.2.15 Storytelling

This involves the construction of fictional examples or the telling of real organizational stories to illustrate a point and effectively transfer knowledge. An *organizational story* is a detailed narrative of management actions, employee interactions, or other intraorganizational events that are communicated informally within the organization. When used well, storytelling is a powerful transformational tool in organizations.

Storytelling uses anecdotal examples to illustrate a point and effectively transfer knowledge. There are two types:

1. *Organizational stories* (business anecdotes) are narratives of management or employee actions, employee interactions, or other intraorganizational events that are communicated within the organization, either formally or informally.
2. *Future scenarios* create a future vision for the enterprise that describes how life will be different once a particular initiative, change, etc., is fully implemented. They provide a qualitative way of describing the value of the initiative even before it starts.

Storytelling has many benefits:

1. Stories capture context, which gives them meaning and makes them powerful.
2. We are used to stories. They are natural, easy, entertaining, and energizing.
3. Stories help us make sense of things. They can help us understand complexity and help us in seeing our organizations and ourselves in a different light.
4. Stories are easy to remember. People will remember a story more easily than a recitation of facts.
5. Stories are nonadversarial and nonhierarchical.
6. Stories engage our feelings and minds and are, therefore, more powerful than using logic alone. They complement abstract analysis.
7. Stories help listeners see similarities with their own backgrounds, contexts, fields of experience, etc., and, therefore, help them to see the relevancy of their own situations.
8. Stories can be a powerful transformational tool. Stories of transformation were termed *springboard stories* by Stephen Denning.

Stories are only as good as the underlying idea being conveyed. Because stories are usually orally presented, the person telling the story must have good presentation skills. Stories are seldom used alone, but rather, they are combined with other approaches such as quantitative analyses, best practices, knowledge audits, etc. They impart meaning and context to ideas, facts, and other kinds of knowledge derived from other KM tools. Stories can be used to support decision making, aid communications, engage buy-in, or market an idea or approach. If being used to illustrate the value of a way of thinking, or explaining an idea, they are best used at the outset to engage the listener and generate buy-in.

In using storytelling, the message, plot, and characters must be considered. Determine what underlying message is to be conveyed (e.g., importance of organizational goals, impact of a change effort on an individual, end benefits associated with a change effort, how a process works, etc.). How does the story illustrate the underlying message (plot)? Who was involved in the story (characters)?

Think about the audience for the story. Whom is the story aimed at? What will each audience listening to the story do with the story's message? What message will be told to each audience? How do we tell each desired story?

Four different structures for using stories have been developed (Denning, 2001):

1. Open with the springboard story, and then draw out its implications.
2. Tell a succession of stories. The telling of multiple stories can help enhance the chances that the audience will cocreate the follow-up. Two examples are cited: You want to describe the benefits of a proposed change effort. Tell a story that only partly serves your purpose, and then extrapolate with an anecdote (e.g., a future scenario) that describes how the story will play out when the change effort is fully in place. Alternatively, tell a series of related stories that, taken together, illustrate various ways in which the change effort is leading to payoffs for colleagues.
3. Accentuate the problem. Start with describing the nature of a problem, tell the story, and draw out the implications.
4. Simply tell the story. This is useful when time is very limited and you want to plant a seed.

The story should:

1. Be relatively brief and have only enough detail for the audience to understand it. Too much detail and the listener gets caught up in the explicit story and not its message.
2. Be intelligible to a specific audience, so that it hooks them. It must be relevant to them.

3. Be inherently interesting; maybe because the problem presented is difficult, the old way of resolving it will not work. There is tension between the characters in the story, and there are unexpected events, or an element of strangeness exists.
4. Embody the idea you are trying to convey and provide an easy mental leap from the facts of the story to its underlying message.
5. Have a positive ending, to avoid people being caught up in a negative, skeptical frame of mind.
6. Have an implicit change message, especially if the audience is skeptical or resistant, because the audience can then discover the change message on their own and, therefore, make it their own idea.
7. Feature a protagonist with whom the audience can identify.
8. Deal with a specific individual or organization.
9. Have a protagonist who is typical of the organization and its main business.

True stories are generally more powerful than invented stories, and can serve as jumping-off points for future-scenario stories. Stories should be tested on individuals or small groups before being tried on large groups or in high-risk settings.

The stories must be simple, brief, and concise. They should represent the perspective of one or two people in a situation typical of the organization's business, so that the explicit story is familiar to the audience. Similarly, the story should be plausible; it must ring true to the listener. It needs to be alive and exciting, not vague and abstract. By containing a strange or incongruous aspect, the listener can be helped to visualize a new way of thinking or behaving. Stories, therefore, should be used to help listeners extrapolate from the narrative to their own situations.

Finally, storytellers must believe in the story (own it) and tell it with conviction. Otherwise, the audience will not accept it.

2.2.16 Training

Training encompasses a large variety of activities designed to facilitate learning (of knowledge, skills, and abilities or competencies) by those being trained. Methodologies can include classroom instruction, simulations, role plays, computer- or Web-based instructions, small and large group exercises, and more. It can be instructor-led or self-directed in nature.

2.3 WHERE DO WE GO NEXT?

In this chapter, we have focused on KM strategies. KM is a rubric that surrounds a wide variety of technologies. Some of these require that we extract or elicit the expertise from those experts within our companies. In Chapter 3, therefore, we will delve into knowledge-engineering techniques.

References

Corcoran, M.E. and Robison, C.A. (n.d.), Successful Management of the Corporate Knowledge Base: A Checklist for Top Management, Quantum2 (Thomson). Retrieved June 22, 2005 from http://quantum.dialog.com/q2_resources/management/q-chklst.pdf.

Denning, S., *The Springboard: How Storytelling Ignites Action in Knowledge-Era Organizations*, Woburn, MA: Butterworth-Heinemann, 2001.

New York State Department of Civil Service, Knowledge Management/Transfer, Report of the Knowledge Management Transfer Workgroup, November 2002. Retrieved June 22, 2005 from http://www.cs.state.ny.us/successionplanning/workgroups/knowledgemanagement /knowledgemanagetransfer.html.

Siemens (n.d.), Knowledge Management Maturity Model — KMMM. Retrieved August 9, 2005 from http://w4.siemens.de/ct/en/technologies/ic/beispiele/anlagen/kmmm_flyer_en.pdf.

United States Agency for International Development, Knowledge Mapping 101, September 22, 2003. Retrieved August 15, 2005 from knowledge.usaid.gov/KfD_Seminar_2.pdf.

3

KNOWLEDGE-ENGINEERING TECHNIQUES

Without proper information, it is difficult, if not impossible, to define or start a knowledge management project. Knowledge elicitation is fairly similar to the traditional elicitation of requirements, which is a staple of software engineering during the systems analysis phase. In this chapter, we will bring these two disciplines together — requirements elicitation and knowledge elicitation — to provide the reader with a foundation upon which their knowledge management systems can be productively and effectively built.

3.1 TWO LEVELS OF KNOWLEDGE ELICITATION

What do Mozart and Christian Heinecken have in common? Both were prodigies. Mozart, as we all know, composed minuets at the tender age of four. Heinecken memorized the Pentateuch before the age of one, mastered sacred history before the age of two, and was a whiz at geography and history at age three. He spoke French and Latin, as well as excelling in religious studies, while little Mozart was hammering away at his piano. Sadly, he died when he was but five. Their brilliance was extraordinary. Because their expertise was so intuitive and appeared at such an early age, it would have been devilishly tricky to try to conceptualize knowledge acquisition in the 18th century. Fortunately, the rest of us do not exactly qualify as prodigies. However, the task of knowledge acquisition is still a tough one. So how do we do it?

The hurdle to overcome is the difficulty in realizing what constitutes expertise. Expertise is not always connected to the smartest person around. In a rather fun study entitled "A Day at the Races," researchers Ceci and

Liker (1986) found that even racetrack handicappers with relatively low IQs could beat the experts. What this seems to be saying is that expertise may be less a function of intelligence and more the product of a skillful coding of experience.

This coding of experience is not done consciously by the expert but is the result of unconscious organization and structuring of new experiences. Experts are different from mere mortals. Most knowledge engineers do recognize this fact but also erroneously believe that the major difference is in the quantity of knowledge the expert has managed to accumulate. Certainly, quantity is one aspect, but there are qualitative differences as well.

The most obvious difference, according to Nobel Prize winner Niels Bohr, is that experts have experienced all the mistakes that can be made in a very narrow field. Experts have such depth of experience that when a new problem comes their way, they can see the whole picture. Novices, on the other hand, possess little experience and thus "do not see the forest for the trees." Perhaps the most interesting difference is that the expert's knowledge is organized more efficiently than that of the novice. Even with the same stimuli, the expert is able to recall more readily the pieces of the stimuli than can the novice. This was proved in a memory experiment done in the early 1970s, in which novice and expert chess players were shown boards of games in progress. The experts were able to recall more piece positions than the novices, because they were able to recall, from their experience, more patterns. A corollary experiment was done by showing both the experts' and novices' game boards with pieces strewn randomly about. Neither the expert nor the novice did better at this experiment, certainly proving the recall hypothesis.

What this seems to indicate is that the expert, by virtue of a good deal of experience, learns certain patterns that seem to be almost "burned" into his or her memory. A new problem exhibits traits that are similar in some ways and dissimilar in other ways to the set of experiences in memory. In fact, patterning is so ingrained that sometimes it leads to decision making by rote. This robotizing effect was demonstrated in a study using bridge players as guinea pigs. In this study, the rules of the game were changed dramatically. Here, each subsequent hand was to be led by the player who had played the lowest card on the last hand. This confused the expert bridge players and adversely affected their playing skills. It did not much bother the novices. Because their experience was not as yet ingrained, they had a much easier time adjusting to the new rules. What we have here is indelible knowledge. The ramifications are significant for the knowledge-engineering team.

This leads to a two-tier approach to knowledge engineering. Surface knowledge can be obtained through conventional software-engineering techniques. Often, this is done through direct articulation — typically, a series of loosely structured interviews. This process is labeled a *bottleneck* by Ed Feigenbaum, who is one the pioneers in this area. Here, the knowledge engineer asks rather spontaneous questions as the expert describes a particular case or actually goes through the steps of solving the problem. The loose structure of this method of knowledge acquisition serves only to capture procedural knowledge at the most superficial level. It does not capture the expert's greater abstract ability to apply this procedural knowledge at a more tactical or strategic level. Schon (1983), in his book *The Reflective Practitioner*, has labeled this deeper knowledge as *knowing-in-action*.

A second generation of methodology for knowledge acquisition comes from the research of psychology and computer science departments at universities. Research has shown a better way of grabbing the knowledge residing deep inside the expert.

3.1.1 Capturing Procedural or Surface Knowledge

A wide variety of software-engineering techniques can be used to elicit knowledge from experts. These methods include interviewing, questionnaires, observation, participation, documentation, research, business intelligence (BI), competitive intelligence (CI), reverse engineering, and benchmarking.

3.1.1.1 Interviewing

The most common method of gathering information is by interviewing people. Interviewing can serve two purposes at the same time. The first is a fact-finding mission to discover what each person's goals and objectives are with respect to the project, and the second is to begin a communications process that enables one to set realistic expectations for the project.

There are a wide variety of stakeholders who can and should be interviewed. *Stakeholders* are those who have an interest in seeing this project successfully completed, i.e., they have a stake in the project. Stakeholders include employees, management, clients, customers, partners, and even competitors.

Employees: It is amazing to me that some analysts develop systems without ever interviewing those whose jobs will be affected the most. This occurred most notably at the U.S. Post Office when the clerical procedures were automated in the 1980s. So little information was shared about what the new system was going to do that the clerks got the misimpression that they were to be replaced soon.

The number and type of employees that will need to be interviewed will depend on the type of system being developed. Systems generally fall into two categories: tactical and strategic. Tactical systems are usually transaction based, such as check processing, student registration, and medical billing, in which data volumes are high. These systems are usually accessed by clerical staff. Strategic systems are those that support the decision-making process and are utilized by middle and senior managers. It is possible for a system to be a hybrid of both these types. An example of this would be a transactional back end that collects data for analysis by managers at the front end.

Interviews can have some major obstacles to overcome. The interviewee may resist giving information out of fear, they may relate their perception of how things should be done rather than how they really do them, or they may have difficulty in expressing themselves. On the other hand, the analyst's own mindset may also act as a filter. The interviewers sometimes have to set aside their own technical orientation and make the best effort to put themselves in the position that the interviewee is in. This requires that the analyst develops a certain amount of empathy.

An interview outline should contain the following information:

1. Name of interviewee
2. Name of interviewer
3. Date and time
4. Objectives of interview (i.e., what areas are going to be explored, and what data is going to be collected)
5. General observations
6. Unresolved issues and topics not covered
7. Agenda (i.e., introduction, questions, summary of major points, and closing)

Recommended guidelines for handling the employee interview process include the following:

1. Determine the system type (tactical, strategic, or hybrid).
2. Make a list of departments affected.
3. For each department, either request or develop an organization chart that shows the departmental breakdown along with the name, extension, and list of responsibilities of each employee.
4. Meet with the department head to request recommendations and then formulate a plan that details the employees who are the best interview prospects. The best employees to interview are those (a) who are very experienced (i.e., senior) in performing their job function; (b) who may have come from a competing company

and, thus, have a unique perspective; and (c) who have had a variety of positions within the department or company.

5. Plan to meet with employees from all units of the department. In other words, if you are developing a knowledge-based system for the marketing function and you are interviewing the marketing department, you will want to meet with employees from the: marketing communications unit, marketing research unit, public relations group, etc. In some cases, you may find that interviewing several employees at a time is more effective than dealing with a single employee; interviewing a group of employees permits them to bounce ideas off each other.

6. If there are many employees within a departmental unit, it is not optimum to interview every one. It would be wrong to assume that the more people in a department, the higher the number of interviewees. Instead, sampling should be used. Sampling is used to (1) contain costs, (2) improve effectiveness, (3) speed up the data-gathering process, and (4) reduce bias. Systems analysts often use a random sample. However, calculating a sample size based on population size and your desired confidence interval is more accurate. Rather than provide a formula and instructions on how to calculate sample size, the reader is directed to the sample-size calculator located at http://www.surveysystem.com/sscalc.htm.

7. Carefully plan your interview sessions. Prepare your interview questions in advance. Be familiar with any technical vocabulary that your interview subjects might use.

8. No meeting should last longer than an hour. A half hour is optimum. There is a point of diminishing returns with the interview process. Your interviewees are busy and, usually, easily distracted. Keep in mind that some of your interviewees may be doing this against their will.

Customers: They have a unique perspective on the industry, which is worth capturing. Customers often have experiences with other vendors or suppliers and can offer insight into the processes that other companies use or those they have experienced.

Guidelines for interviewing customers include the following:

1. Work with the sales or marketing departments to select knowledgeable and cooperative customers.

2. Prepare an adequate sample size as discussed in the prior section.

3. Carefully plan your interview sessions. Prepare your interview questions in advance.

Companies and consultants: Other sources of potentially valuable information are other companies in the industry and consultants who specialize in the area of interest. Although consultants can be easily located and paid for their expert advice, it is wise to tread slowly when working with other companies who are current or potential competitors.

Guidelines for interviewing other companies include the following:

1. Work with senior management and marketing to create a list of potential companies to interview. This list should contain the names of trading partners, vendors (companies that your company buys from), and competitors.
2. Attend industry trade shows to meet and mingle with competitor employees, and listen to presentations made by competitor companies.
3. Attend trade association meetings; sit on policy and standards committees.

Suppliers: Product suppliers are also an important source of information. They know a great deal about how their products are being used and the general industry trends.

When interviewing anyone, it is important to be aware of how to ask questions properly. Open-ended questions are the best for gaining the most information, because they do not limit the individuals to predefined answers. Other benefits of using open-ended questions include putting the interviewee at ease, providing more detail, and inducing spontaneity; also, it is far more interesting for the interviewee. Open-ended questions require more than a "yes" or a "no" answer (Yates, 1993). An example of an open-ended question is "What types of problems do you see on a daily basis with the current process?" These questions allow individuals to elaborate on the topics and potentially uncover the hidden problems at hand that might not be discoverable with a question that requires a "yes" or a "no" answer.

One disadvantage of open-ended questions is that they create lengthier interviews. Another disadvantage is that it is easy for the interview to get off track, and it takes an interviewer with skill to conduct the interview in an efficient manner (Yates, 1993).

Closed-ended questions are by far the most common questions in interviewing. They are questions that have "yes" and "no" answers and are utilized to elicit definitive responses.

Past-performance questions can be useful to determine past experiences with similar problems. Interviewees are often reluctant to discuss problems; therefore, questions about past performance can allow the person to discuss an issue with similar problems. An example of how a past-performance question can be used is, "In your past job, how did you deal with these processes?"

Reflexive questions are appropriate for closing a conversation or if moving forward to a new topic. Reflexive questions are created with a statement of confirmation preceded by "Don't you," "Couldn't you," "Wouldn't you," etc.

Mirror questions are a subtle form of probing and prove useful in obtaining additional details on a subject. After the interviewee makes a statement, pause and repeat their statement back with an additional or leading question: "So, when this problem occurs, you simply move on to more pressing issues?"

Often, answers do not give the interviewer enough detail; so, one follows the question with additional questions to prod the interviewee to divulge more details on the subject. For example:

1. Can you give some more details on that?
2. What did you learn from that experience?

Merely sitting back and saying nothing is another more subtle prodding technique. The silence will feel uncomfortable, causing the interviewee to expand on his or her last statement.

3.1.1.2 Questionnaires or Surveys

If there are large numbers of people to interview, one might start with a questionnaire and then follow up with certain individuals who present unusual ideas or issues in the questionnaires. Survey development and implementation is composed of the following tasks:

1. Establishing the goals of the project — What do you want to learn?
2. Determining your sample — Whom will you interview?
3. Choosing interview methodology — How will you interview?
4. Creating your questionnaire — What will you ask?
5. Pretesting the questionnaire, if practical — Test the questions.
6. Conducting interviews and entering data — Ask the questions.
7. Analyzing the data — Produce the reports.

Just as in interviews, questionnaires may contain close-ended or open-ended questions or a combination of the two.

Survey creation is quite an art. Guidelines for creation of a survey include the following:

1. Provide an introduction to the survey. Explain why it is important that they respond to it. Thank them for their time and effort.
2. Put all important questions first. It is rare that all questions will be responded to. Those filling out the survey often become tired or bored with the process.
3. Use plenty of "white space." Use an appropriate font (e.g., Arial), font size (e.g., at least 12), and do skip lines.
4. Use nominal scales if you wish to classify things (e.g., "What brand is your computer? 1 = Dell, 2 = Gateway, 3 = IBM").
5. Use ordinal scales to imply rank (e.g., "How helpful was this class? 3 = not helpful at all, 2 = moderately helpful, 1 = very helpful").
6. Use interval scales when you want to perform some mathematical calculations on the results.

For example, "How helpful was this class?"

Not useful at all				Very useful
1	2	3	4	5

Tallying the responses will provide a score, which assists in making a decision that requires the use of quantifiable information. When using interval scales, keep in mind that not all questions carry the same weight. Hence, it is a good idea to use a weighted-average formula during calculation. To do this, assign a weight or level of importance to each question. For example, the earlier question can be assigned a weight of 5 on a scale of 1 to 5, meaning that it is a very important question. On the other hand, a question such as: "Was the training center comfortable?" can be assigned a weight of only 3. The weighted average is calculated by multiplying the weight by the score (w × s) to get the final score. Thus, the formula is:

$$S_{new} = w \times s$$

Several problems can contribute to a poorly constructed questionnaire. *Leniency* is caused by respondents who grade nonsubjectively — in other words, too easily. *Central tendency* occurs when respondents rate everything as average. The *halo effect* occurs when the respondent carries his good or bad impression from one question to the next.

There are several methods that can be used successfully to deploy a survey. The easiest and most accurate is to gather all respondents in a conference room and hand out the survey. For the most part, this is not realistic, so other approaches would be more appropriate. E-mail and traditional mail are two methodologies that work well, although you often

Table 3.1   Survey Attributes

Speed	E-mail and Web page surveys are the fastest methods, followed by telephone interviewing. Mail surveys are the slowest.
Cost	Personal interviews are the most expensive, followed by telephone and mail. E-mail and Web page surveys are the least expensive for large samples.
Internet usage	Web page and E-mail surveys offer significant advantages, but you may not be able to generalize their results to the population as a whole.
Literacy levels	Illiterate and less-educated people rarely respond to mail surveys.
Sensitive questions	People are more likely to answer sensitive questions when interviewed directly by a computer in one form or another.
Video, sound, graphics	A need to get reactions to video, music, or a picture limits your options. You can play a video on a Web page, in a computer-direct interview, or in person. You can play music when using these methods or over a telephone. You can show pictures in those first methods and in a mail survey.

have to supply an incentive (i.e., prize) to get respondents to fill out those surveys on a timely basis. Web-based surveys (Internet and intranet) are becoming increasingly popular as they enable the inclusion of demos, audio, and video. For example, a Web-based survey on what type of user interface is preferable could have hyperlinks to demos or screen shots of the choices.

The different approaches to surveys are summarized in Table 3.1.

3.1.1.3   Observation

Observation is an important tool that can provide a wealth of information. There are several forms of observation: silent and directed. In silent observation, the analyst merely sits on the sidelines, pen and pad in hand, and observes what is happening. If it is suitable, a tape recorder or video recorder can record what is being observed. However, this is not recommended if the net result will be several hours of random footage.

Silent observation is best used to capture the spontaneous nature of a particular process or procedure. For example, observation is used in the following situations:

1. When customers interact with staff
2. During group meetings
3. On the manufacturing floor
4. In the field

Directed observation provides the knowledge engineer with a chance to microcontrol a process or procedure so that it is broken down into its observable parts. At one accounting firm, a tax system was being developed. The knowledge engineers requested that several senior tax accountants be coupled with a junior staff member. The group was given a problem, as well as all the manuals and materials they needed. The junior accountant sat at one end of the table with the pile of manuals and forms, and the senior tax accountants sat at the other end. A tough tax problem was posed. The senior tax accountants were directed to think through the process and then to direct the junior member to follow through on their directions to solve this problem. The catch was that the senior members could not walk over to the junior person nor touch any of the reference guides. This whole exercise had to be done verbally, using just their memories and expertise. The entire process was videotaped. The net result was that the knowledge engineer had a complete record of how to perform one of the critical functions of the new system.

3.1.1.4   Participation

The flip side of observation is participation. Actually becoming a member of the staff and thereby learning exactly what it is that the staff does so that it might be automated, is an invaluable experience.

3.1.1.5   Documentation

It is logical to assume that there will be a wide variety of documentation. This includes, but is not limited to, the following:

1. Documentation from existing systems (This includes requirements and design specifications, program documentation, user manuals, and help files. This also includes whatever "wish" lists have been developed for the existing system.)
2. Archival information
3. Policies and procedures manuals
4. Reports
5. Memos
6. Standards

7. E-mail
8. Minutes from meetings
9. Government and other regulatory guidelines and regulations
10. Industry or association manuals, guidelines, and standards (e.g., accountants are guided not only by in-house "rules and regulations" but also by industry and other rules and regulations)

3.1.1.6 Competitive Intelligence

Competitive intelligence (CI) is business intelligence that is limited to competitors and how that information affects strategy, tactics, and operations (Bock, 2000). It is often defined as a systematic and ethical program for gathering, analyzing, and managing external information that can affect your company's plans, decisions, and operations. The utilization of the Internet for the method of gathering information on individuals and companies has become widespread and automatic. CI enables management to make informed decisions about everything from marketing, R&D, and investing tactics to long-term business strategies.

CI data can be gathered from the following sources:

1. Internet discussion groups (listservs) and newsgroups (Usenet). Simple searches on the Internet can obtain expert discussions on issues that are on the Internet in listservs and Usenet. Often, a quick form of CI is to search these postings on the Internet for discussions of similar issues. The level of detail contained in these discussions is beneficial for not only things to do but also things that will not work (Graef, 2002). This is one of the quickest and most cost-effective methods of obtaining information.
2. Former employees of your competitors are often invaluable in providing information about your competitor's operations, products, and plans.
3. Your competitors' Web site usually contains marketing information about products and services offered, as well as press releases, white papers, and even product demos. Product demos enable the analyst and business manager to effectively "reverse engineer" the competitive product (i.e., see how it ticks).
4. If your competitor is a public company, then its investor relations Web page will contain a wealth of financial information such as annual reports. An alternative source of financial filings can be found at www.sec.gov. A company's 10-Q (quarterly) and 10-K (annual) reports contain information on products, services, products, budgets, etc.

3.1.1.7 Brainstorming

In a brainstorming session, you gather together a group of people, create a stimulating and focused atmosphere, and let people come up with ideas without risk of being ridiculed. Even seemingly stupid ideas may turn out to be "golden."

3.1.1.8 Focus Groups

Focus groups are derived from marketing. These are structured sessions in which a group of stakeholders are presented with a solution to a problem and then are closely questioned on their views about that solution.

Information gathering is a very intensive process. The more information one has, the more complete is the knowledge base. It has been said that turning information into knowledge is the creative skill of our age.

3.1.2 Capturing Tactical or Strategic Knowledge from Experts

There really is no best way to elicit knowledge from experts. The method used will be largely dependent on the circumstances surrounding the development of the knowledge base and the people involved in the project. Often, a combination of methodologies will do the trick when application of only one seems to miss the mark. There are many methods to choose from.

We already discussed the most popular form of knowledge acquisition. This is the free-flowing dialog between experts and knowledge engineers that can take place over several sessions or even one long brainstorming session. Although this is not the best methodology for retrieving deeply seated knowledge, it is an excellent method for acquiring procedural knowledge. This most certainly makes up a large part of an expert's knowledge. Many engineers video or audiotape the interview so that others can be involved in the interview process. Although this is a great idea, be forewarned that transcribing these tapes into notes is time consuming. One describer of this process noted that it took 100 hours of transcribing to capture 10 hours of interviews with an expert planner of airlift schedules.

3.1.2.1 Structured Interviews

A second form of interview is called a *structured interview*. This concept stems from the studies of social scientists and has been used largely in the area of psychotherapeutic interviews. The rule here is to plan the interview before you even get in the room with the expert. First, a meeting is called to discuss the problem domain. This general meeting will serve to provide enough information for the knowledge engineer to go back to the drawing board and carefully plan a second series of interviews, each of which will be structured around a specific topic. It is at these more structured meetings that a series of well-directed questions will be asked to elicit the knowledge that lies below the surface level.

3.1.2.2 Task Analysis

In 1987, two researchers conducted a study of people working on a problem-solving task. The researchers had people putting together a structure using an erector set. The methodology chosen by these experimental construction engineers was charted by the researchers. Hence, the logic was uncovered that was inherent in the problem solvers' reasoning.

This method can most certainly be applied to all classifications of problems. It can be done either silently, where the knowledge engineer merely observes the process, or by participation, where the knowledge engineer asks questions and the expert comments on the task.

3.1.2.3 Learning Rules from Examples

Instead of using various methodologies to directly elicit the reasoning behind the decision of the expert, a cadre of examples, when analyzed, should yield the same result. Here, a computer is fed cases or examples and their solutions. In the realm of artificial intelligence, the output would be rules or decision trees. Expert-system shells and case-based reasoning software provide these capabilities.

3.2 A KNOWLEDGE-ENGINEERING METHODOLOGY

About the only difference between knowledge-based systems development methodologies and traditional data processing methodologies is the all-important capture of knowledge, which is the essence of any knowledge-based system. Conventional systems contain minimal knowledge and loads of data, although knowledge-based systems process both data and knowledge.

At the beginning of this chapter, we have already discussed a series of techniques that can be used to uncover knowledge. Appendix I contains a plethora of additional knowledge-discovery techniques, courtesy of the government of the United Kingdom, as shown in Table 3.2.

Knowledge capture is, by itself, a really fuzzy process. There are many ways of doing it and no single best way. In all cases, great care must be

Table 3.2 Knowledge Discovery Techniques

Exit interviews
Speed dating
Mind mapping
After-action reviews
Project reviews
Baton passing
Virtual teams
Coaching and mentoring
Intellectual capital
Communities of practice
Social network analysis
Complex adaptive systems
Knowledge audits
Design of space
Knowledge harvesting
Domain knowledge mapping
Storytelling

taken to include not only expertise, but also common sense. For example, during the beta testing of a Ford Motor Company knowledge system to do credit analysis of car loans, the system goofed. It failed to notice that one 20-year-old applicant gave as "ten," the answer to the question of number of years of driving experience.

Another pitfall is to corral too many experts. This happened when DARPA, the research arm of the U.S. Department of Defense, tried to create an aircraft pilot knowledge system. A whole slew of pilots showed up as experts. Some were vastly experienced, and some were less so. It was impossible to achieve a consensus of opinion. And it was even more impossible to achieve a consistently high level of expertise.

3.2.1 Ten Steps for Creating a Knowledge System

3.2.1.1 Step 1: Creating a Knowledge Advisory Board

The charter of the knowledge advisory board (KAB) group, to be composed of "thought leaders" from all parts of the company, would be to address the needs of the organization in terms of possible knowledge-based system implementations. The KAB would be responsible for creating and prioritizing a list of possibilities.

3.2.1.2 Step 2: Creating a Team

Once a project from this list has been authorized, the next step is to find an able and willing knowledge expert. Just make certain that this person is really an expert and not just the first available individual around. The next step is to select a systems team. Just as in traditional systems development, it is a good idea to use a team approach. Knowledge system development projects need to be managed just as other projects. On top of that, there are really two components of the task. The one that people are most comfortable with is the traditional systems work that must be done. The second component is the elicitation of knowledge.

All knowledge systems will have components that require access to corporate data assets. For example, if you are building a knowledge system for budget analysis, you will need to gain access to the corporate expense file as well as the accounts payable and receivable files to be able to make predictions. Someone needs to perform the programming tasks required to get this functionality. These tasks are data-driven and require a certain skill set.

Another member of the team is the knowledge engineer. This person needs a very different skill set. The point here is that these two skill sets are quite different. Although it is possible to find a unique talent that can do it all, it is recommended that two people perform these two very different functions.

A good knowledge engineer will have certain hard-to-find qualities. They must have the ability to converse with the expert in the language of the expert. This person should also have the ability and the inclination to perform thorough research in the area chosen to be "knowledge-systematized." Finally, the knowledge engineer should have the literary capabilities necessary to document the results. What we have here is a rather unusual combination. Interestingly, a large number of systems have been developed by the experts themselves who (obviously) possess all these listed skills.

3.2.1.3 Step 3: Picking the Problem Domain

There are three simple rules of thumb to keep in mind when you select your problem. First, pick one you know well. It is not really a good idea to choose one that is so vague and not understandable to the team that successful development becomes a miracle of faith. Next, select a manageably sized problem. Do not attempt to create an organizationwide knowledge base on your first go-round. Instead, select one department and then one problem within that department. Last, pick a problem that matters.

The most suitable problems require application of knowledge rather than just data; in other words, choose a problem that requires decision making over number crunching. An example would be a system that advises a planner on how to put together a budget. This is a better choice than a system that just calculates the budget.

You want to make sure that you pick a problem for which knowledge is readily available. Do not just pick as a problem, "why were humans created?" It is an interesting problem. However, no one knows the answer even though there is a massive amount of philosophical and theological information on this subject, which might have been your intent from the start. Still, it is best to make sure that the expertise in solving a problem is available in your company before embarking on this effort.

If the problem is one that takes an expert a long period of time to solve (i.e., days and weeks rather than hours), then it might be wise to refine the problem into more manageable subproblems. The goal here is to develop knowledge systems for problems that exhibit depth in a narrow domain and then "glue" all of these knowledge bases together to attack broader strategic issues.

3.2.1.4 Step 4: Identifying the Problem

Once we select a problem, we must define it. This is actually more difficult than it sounds. There is often much noise associated with a particular problem. Hence, we must take care to define the actual problem and not just the symptoms of the problem. We also want to make sure that we do not define the problem either too broadly or too vaguely. To do so would run the risk of developing a bunch of incoherent rules, making the system virtually untestable.

Usually, the problem is formally defined at the first working meeting of the team. What we want to end up with is a written description of what this system is specifically supposed to do. Therefore, some ideas are tossed around over the course of the meeting to finally obtain a clear picture of the system. Consider the following example:

The goal of this project is to develop a smart budgetary system that will exhibit the following features:

1. Act as an advisor to the respective divisional budget administrators in leading them through the process of preparing the various forms required for the formal budget review.
2. Act as an advisor to the central administrative staff in tying all the divisional budgets together.
   a. Provide exception reporting and assistance in correcting these exceptions.

b. Act in an advisory capacity in determining how to apply budgetary constraints such that the least impact will be felt for the largest possible budget cut.

c. Perform budgetary calculation reporting, and provide an audit trail of changes made.

3.2.1.5 Step 5: Conceptualizing the Problem

We have spent a good deal of time lining up our pins. Now it is time to aim for a strike. In this phase of development, we need to concentrate on the specifics of the problem. A grassroots understanding of the problem and all of its vagaries is absolutely necessary.

To do this, the team should concentrate on the who, what, where, when, and how of investigative analysis. This is the beginning of the much-heralded knowledge-engineering process. The end goal is to develop a comprehensive view — what is often called *conceptual documentation.*

The first thing we want to know is who the end user will be. We want to know this because the consultation, which is the dialogue between the user and the system, should be tailored specifically for the level of worker using the system.

A budgetary system geared for low-level clerks will look different from one designed for accountants, which would look different from one designed for senior executives. In our budgetary expert system, the user is an accountant and, therefore, will design the system accordingly.

Now that we have the user figured out, let us take the time to understand the world that we live in. By this, I mean: where is the budget process located in relation to the rest of the department in which it operates? Let us look to the generalized domain flow diagram in Figure 3.1. This is a thumbnail sketch of what the finance department looks like. For the knowledge engineers on the team, the diagram serves the purpose of introducing them to the area in which the expert system will be used. For the expert, this serves as a reminder of the relationships between the process to be systematized and the rest of the operation. In this way, the team ensures that major inputs and outputs are not overlooked.

Now that we have the big picture, we need to fine-tune it a bit to see the specifics of our chosen task. Figure 3.2 shows the problem area's detailed flowchart. The key word here is "detailed." This diagram should show the specifics of the functionality of the job. At a minimum, it should show relationships to external sources such as outside databases, data manipulations to be performed, points of user interactions, and any areas of uncertainty. This exercise serves other purposes as well. For the knowledge engineer, this activity will serve to make the job functions

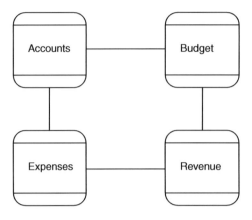

Figure 3.1 Generalized domain flowchart.

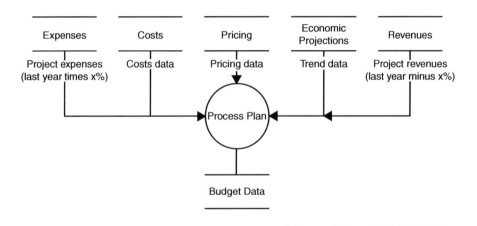

Figure 3.2 Problem area's detailed flowchart.

clear and specific. For the expert, it will serve as a sort of checklist to make sure that all bases are covered during the development process.

Many developers of expert systems do not perform these tasks. They run a risk. Unless they themselves are experts in the area in question, they run the risk of leaving out some all-important tidbit that can dramatically alter the way the system works.

The last activity in the conceptualization phase is to develop a series of use cases (see Appendix K). You need to develop several use cases that typify the process. This is the real meat behind knowledge engineering, and there are many ways to do it.

The wrong way is retrospective analysis. Asking an expert how a solution was arrived at is like asking a bird how it manages to fly. Nobody knows. Most people sequester themselves with the expert in a conference room and talk until all the knowledge has been siphoned out of the expert. A series of problems are discussed in this room, with the expert verbally solving the problems. Some even record or videotape these sessions. The point is that this is hard work, often very tedious and also cyclical. After you have uncovered a gem of knowledge, you should go back and review with the expert.

A careful set of notes should be maintained to complete the knowledge acquisition process. These notes should include what was learned from the use cases, problems encountered, and the conclusion or lack of conclusion.

3.2.1.6   Step 6: Formalizing the Problem

At this point, the team should all be experts. Hopefully, the problem should be so well defined that writing the specification should be a snap. Then, the process of knowledge engineering becomes very similar to the process of software engineering.

It is during the formalization stage that the knowledge-based system is specified and designed. Hardware, software, and the network will have to be designed, programmed, tested, and ultimately implemented. During this stage, a whole host of decisions has to be made, not the least of which is picking appropriate software tools with which to design the system.

The tools you select are dependent on the type of knowledge system that is being built. This book focuses on a combination of systems including data mining, data warehousing, content management, business intelligence, and all forms of knowledge-based systems. Different chapters in this book will cover all these different concepts. In particular, information available at www.crcpress.com/e_products_downloads/download. asp?cat_no-AU9385 provides a list of resources by category.

3.2.1.7   Step 7: Prototyping

In the formalization phase, a bunch of field notes are developed during all the interviews and videotaping sessions. These notes are then turned into something a bit more formal, i.e., the requirements specifications and design specifications.

Most expertise can be easily turned into pseudo code rules, the traditional purview of the design specifications in software engineering. One of the things I have learned over the years is that even if the project turns out not to be successful or is never pursued, the creation of rules is valuable for the users. The result is a procedures manual with that extra bit of expertise.

It is sound advice to build a prototype, although it largely runs the risk of making an enormous investment in time and money only to find that the problem is not suited to the type of system being built. Or you may find the knowledge base is faulty, the hardware is all wrong, or the software is all erroneous Pick any one or more of these. A prototype will find all these problems before you make a large commitment of resources. And the word *prototyping* is so comforting. Management expects little experimentation and few difficulties here — not so with real development. Knowledge-based systems are fundamentally more abstract than conventional systems; hence, the crutch of working with a prototype serves many purposes.

This prototype should certainly contain no more than 50 percent of the ultimate system; cut this number down if you can. So, if you developed 400 rules during the formalization phase, the prototype will have only 200 of these.

3.2.1.8 Step 8: Reformalizing or Reassessing the Problem

Once the prototype is complete, it is run to determine if the rules and objects are properly coded and if, in fact, all the rules and objects that need to be present are present. This phase is a reiteration of the initial formalization phase. The team must also make the determination whether or not the hardware and software chosen is indeed appropriate for the problem.

Although the prototype was checked out thoroughly while being built, it is important to run the use cases reconfigured as test cases against the prototype. Conclusions are then compared against those manually derived by the experts.

Because it is not possible to detail each and every tidbit of knowledge before undertaking this stage, running the prototype will uncover noticeable holes. These systems store their knowledge base discretely from the rest of the system, so it is a simple matter to enter the missing rules or objects. You may also notice that some of the rules are working incorrectly and must be changed. This process is not really much different from the traditional systems-testing methodology.

A stickier problem occurs when you find that the knowledge-based tool you selected does not quite measure up to your expectations. This could be because of several reasons, such as the following:

- The user interface is not adequate.
- The knowledge-based system is not able to process the final number of rules in the rule base.
- There is difficulty in getting to the external data needed.
- Hardware does not have enough memory.

- Hardware does not have enough disk capacity.
- Performance is degraded.
- There are conflicting rules.

Remember the budgetary system we discussed at the beginning of this chapter? The prototype passed with flying colors. We added a few new rules and objects when we realized that we had omitted a process clearly represented on our problem area, the detailed flowchart. We are glad that we had the diagram because it spurred us into remembering that we needed to factor in the process of economic projection. We also found some conflicting rules that we fixed. Our dry run to see if we could access our corporate databases was successful. All in all, the prototype was a success. Now it is time to see how good it really is. We are going to give it to the users.

3.2.1.9 Step 9: Testing

A knowledge-based system needs to be tested as thoroughly as a conventional system. It is hoped that through the use of a prototype and careful testing of this initial phase, the final testing period will be less than calamitous. In alpha (initial) testing, the system needs to pass muster with those people designated as experts in the user group. All during this process, you have worked with several experts, but there are other esteemed employees who should be given the opportunity to scrutinize the final system.

Once you have lived through that, the next phase of testing seems easy. In beta testing (or secondary testing), which is probably the most important type of testing you can do, you send out a system to the actual end users of the system.

These users need to be given adequate time to "test the waters" by themselves. At the same time, they should be given formal procedures for monitoring the session and noting any difficulties. Some of the techniques that auditors use to assess the correctness of the system can be applied here. These can be found in Chapter 9 of this book.

Use at least two to four end users for this process. Set up the system to run in tandem with the current system or manual procedures that this system will replace or assist. They should be made to feel free to comment on any difficulties, opinions, suggestions, or whatever else. After all, a side benefit of this phase is to make the "buy-in" to the system. And what better way than to have the users know that their opinions count?

This should be called a *pilot* and should last at least one month. You should also branch out from this base of four users and present this to nearly everyone within your reach.

3.2.1.10 Step 10: Maintaining the System

Have you ever heard of a system that does not need changing? Maintenance of knowledge-based systems is exactly the same as for traditional systems. The question now becomes — who should perform the maintenance function? Should it be the users? The development group? Or even a group set up to handle smart systems? The answer is, all of these, depending on the organization.

3.3 WHERE DO WE GO NEXT?

In this chapter, we focused on extracting or eliciting knowledge from experts within our domains. One of the tenets of knowledge management is innovation management. It is through innovation management techniques that our resident experts stimulate and expand upon their expertise. Chapter 4, therefore, will focus on enhancing innovation in the corporate environment.

References

Bock, W., Peter Drucker on Information and Information Systems, December 31, 2000. Retrieved July 27, 2005 from http://www.bockinfo.com/docs/drucker.htm.

Ceci, S.J. and Liker, J., Academic and nonacademic intelligence: an experimental separation, in *Practical Intelligence: Nature and Origins of Competence in the Everyday World*, Sternberg, R.J. and Wagner, R.K. (Eds.), Cambridge, MA: Cambridge University Press, 1986.

Curtis, G., Hoffer, J., George, J., and Valacich, J., *Introduction to Business Systems Analysis*, Boston, MA: Pearson Custom Publishing, 2000.

Graef, J., Using the Internet for Competitive Intelligence, CIO, 2002. Retrieved July 27, 2005 from http://www.cio.com/CIO/arch_0695_cicolumn.html.

Schon, D., *The Reflective Practitioner*, New York: Basic Books, 1983.

Yates, M., *Hiring the Best*, 4th ed., Holbrook, MA: Adams Media, 1993.

4

INNOVATION MANAGEMENT

KnowledgeBoard.com, the premier portal for the knowledge management community, refers to itself as "a self-moderating global community, thinking and collaborating on subjects around knowledge management and innovation in the worlds of business and academia." The WWW Virtual Library on Knowledge Management (http://www.kmnetwork.com/) defines knowledge management as catering to the critical issues of organizational adaptation, survival, and competence in the face of increasingly discontinuous environmental change. Essentially, it embodies organizational processes that seek synergistic combination of data- and information-processing capacities of information technology and the creative and innovative capacity of human beings. Thus, innovation has always been inexorably linked to knowledge management.

Simply put, the type of knowledge that allows an organization to be competitive is based on innovation. Therefore, it is important that the organization encourage and promote innovation within its ranks. In this chapter, we will discuss ideas and techniques to increase the "creative and innovative capacity of human beings."

4.1 SOURCES OF INNOVATION

Peter Drucker (2002), a well-known pundit in the field of business, wrote his book on innovation and entrepreneurship more than 20 years ago. In 2002, when his *Harvard Business Review* article was published, his ideas on the subject were just as relevant as they were when he first put pen to paper two decades ago.

Drucker identifies seven sources of innovation — four internal to the company and three external:

1. *Unexpected occurrences (internal).* Drucker considers unexpected successes and failures to be excellent sources of innovation because most businesses usually ignore them. An example would be IBM's first accounting machines, which were ignored by banks but later sold to libraries.
2. *Incongruities (internal).* The disconnect between expectations and results often provides opportunities for innovation. The growing market for the steel industry, coupled with falling profit margins, enabled the invention of the minimill.
3. *Process needs (internal).* Modern advertising permitted the newspaper industry to distribute newspapers at a very low cost, increasing readership (process need) dramatically.
4. *Industry and market changes (internal).* Deregulation of the telecommunications industry created havoc in the industry but provided ample opportunities for innovation.
5. *Demographic changes (external).* Japanese businesses surveyed changing demographics and determined that the number of people available for blue-collar work was decreasing. As a result, they have taken a leadership position in the area of robotics. However, they are not stopping at robotics for manufacturing. Sony's QRIO robot is an example of the future of robotics (http://www.sony.net/SonyInfo/QRIO/videoclip/).
6. *Changes in perception (external).* According to Drucker, although Americans are healthier than ever before, they worry more about their health. This change in perception has been exploited for innovative opportunities. An example is the proliferation of Web-based health sites, such as WebMD.com.
7. *New knowledge (external).* This is the traditional source of innovation. The first car. The first computer. The printing press. This source of information usually leads to innovation more radical than the other six sources mentioned by Drucker. There are two types of innovations based on new knowledge — *incremental* and *disruptive* (Harvard Business Essentials, 2003). An example of incremental innovation is the Pentium IV chip. There was the Pentium III chip that preceded it. Therefore, the Pentium IV represents just a slight increment of innovation over Pentium III. On the other hand, a radical innovation is something totally new, such as transistor technology. However, technological innovation does have one drawback — it takes much longer to implement. For example, although computing machines were available in the early 1900s, it was not

until the late 1960s that they were commonly used in business (http://www.computer.org/computer/timeline/timeline.pdf).

Drucker's framework for innovation is quite comprehensive. Most would agree with his assessment and would, however, use different categories for the sources. Palmberg (2004) asserts that innovation depends on the characteristics of the market and the broader environment in which the firm operates. Palmberg disagrees with Drucker's distinction between internal and external sources, saying that the distinction is artificial because collaboration and in-house activities are not mutually exclusive.

Palmberg proposes six categories: generic, science based, competitive, customer oriented, regulatory, and technology oriented. The first component ("generic") stems from the fact that sources of innovation are related to assimilation of generic technologies. The next component ("science based") is characterized by scientific breakthroughs and public research programs as the origin of innovation. Great importance is attached to collaboration with universities and research organizations. The "competitive" component is marked by collaboration with competitors. Alternatively, a firm might turn inward in their quest for sources of innovation in the face of competitive markets. The fourth component is referred to as "customer oriented" owing to the importance of market niche and customer demand, which spurs innovation. The fifth component is labeled "regulatory" because a variety of environmental, legal, and regulatory issues will suggest sources of innovation. The final component ("technology oriented") is characterized by sources of innovations related to scientific breakthroughs and new technologies.

4.2 GENERATING INNOVATION

According to the definition of innovation found on Wikipedia (http://en.wikipedia.org/wiki/Innovation), the question as to whether innovation is demand-led or supply-pushed is one of considerable debate. Wikipedia is a good example of innovation that is both. There was a demand in the marketplace for a free, Web-based encyclopedia. The technology of the Internet and the concept of the wiki, a Web application that lets users add and change content (http://en.wikipedia.org/wiki/Wiki), are excellent examples of supply-pushed innovation. The wiki was conceived and developed by Ward Cunningham in the middle 1990s.

Steve Lipscomb's World Poker Tour (Olmstead, 2005) is another example. Poker has taken America by storm, largely because of Lipscomb's innovative approach to the once-seedy concept of poker tournaments.

Both Lipscomb and Cunningham have what Drucker would refer to as "entrepreneurial personalities," but would be more commonly categorized as innovative or creative. Drucker's framework for sources of innovation is worthless without someone seeing these opportunities for what they are.

Drucker's article, therefore, falls short of actually describing how to generate the entrepreneurial or innovative personality. Couger et al. (1991), suggest a process for generating innovation via a series of bottom-up creativity techniques. A brief list of the best of these techniques is given in the following:

1. *Brainstorming* — This technique is perhaps the most common of all the techniques discussed here. It is used to generate a large quantity of ideas in a short period of time. My company often brings in consulting experts, partners, and others to brainstorm along with us.
2. *Blue slip* — Ideas are individually generated and recorded on a 3" × 5" sheet of blue paper. When done anonymously, people feel more at ease and readily share ideas. Because each idea is on a separate piece of blue paper, the sorting and grouping of similar ideas is possible.
3. *Extrapolation* — A technique or approach already used by the organization is stretched to apply to a new problem.
4. *Progressive abstraction technique* — By moving through progressively higher levels of abstraction, it is possible to generate alternative problem definitions from an original problem. When a problem is enlarged in a systematic way, it is possible to generate many new definitions that can then be evaluated for their usefulness and feasibility. Once an appropriate level of abstraction is reached, possible solutions are more easily identified.
5. *5Ws and H technique* — This is the traditional and journalistic approach of "who-what-where-when-why-how." Use of this technique serves to expand a person's view of the problem and assists in making sure that all related aspects of the problem have been addressed and considered.
6. *Force field analysis technique* — The name of this technique comes from its ability to identify forces contributing to or hindering the solution to a problem. This technique stimulates creative thinking in three ways — it (1) defines direction, (2) identifies strengths that can be maximized, and (3) identifies weaknesses that can be minimized.
7. *Problem reversal* — Reversing a problem statement often provides a different framework for analysis. For example, in attempting to come up with ways to improve productivity, try considering the opposite, how to decrease productivity.

8. *Associations/image technique* — Most of us have played the game, at one time or another, in which a player names a person, place, or thing and asks for the first thing that pops into the second player's mind. The linking or combining process is another way of expanding the solution space.

9. *Wishful thinking* — This technique enables people to loosen analytical parameters to consider a larger set of alternatives than they might ordinarily consider. By permitting a degree of fantasy into the process, the result just might be a new and unique approach.

The Harvard Business Essentials (2003) guide to managing creativity and innovation refers to idea generation as "opening the Genie's bottle." However, without management support and encouragement, idea generation is simply not possible. The key then is in how management interacts with and supports its employees.

Oren Harari (1993), a professor at the University of San Francisco and a management consultant, relates an interesting experience with one of his clients. While waiting for an appointment with this particular client, he overheard two of the manager's clerical assistants calling customers and asking them how they liked the company's product. Harari reflected that it was no wonder this manager had such a good reputation. When he finally met her, he offered his congratulations on her ability to delegate the customer service task to her staff. "What you talking about?" she asked, bewildered. "Why, your secretaries are calling up customers on their own," Harari replied. "Oh, really? Is that what they're doing?" she laughed. "You mean you didn't delegate that task to them?" "No," she said. "I didn't even know they were doing it. Listen, Oren, my job is to get everyone on my team to think creatively in pursuit of the same goal. So what I do is talk to people regularly about why we exist as a company and as a team. That means we talk straight about our common purpose and the high standards we want to achieve. I call these our *goal lines*. Then we talk regularly about some broad constraints we have to work with them, like budgets, ethics, policies, and legalities. Those are our *sidelines*."

"It's like a sport. Once we agree on the goal lines and sidelines, I leave it to my people to figure out how to best get from here to there. I'm available and attentive when they need feedback. Sometimes I praise; sometimes I criticize — but always constructively, I hope. We get together periodically and talk about who's been trying what, and we give constructive feedback to one another. I know that sounds overly simplistic, but I assure you that this is my basic management philosophy.

"And that's why I don't know what my assistants are doing, because it's obviously something they decided to try for the first time this week.

I happen to think it's a great idea, because it's within the playing field and helps keep high standards for being number one in our industry. I will tell you something else: I don't even know what they intend to do with the data they're collecting, but I know they'll do the right thing.

"Here's my secret: I don't know what my people are doing, but because I work face to face with them as a coach, I know that whenever it is they're doing is exactly what I'd want them to be doing if I knew what they were doing!"

The Harari story is one of my favorites because it encapsulates into one very brief story exactly what it is that a good manager is supposed to do to encourage innovative thinking in his or her employees.

Harvard Business Essentials (2003) refers to the need to create an "ambidextrous" organization — one that gets the work done today and also anticipates tomorrow's discontinuities. It goes on to provide a list of seven responsibilities for the organization's leaders. These run from the obvious (e.g., developing a culture that nurtures creativity and innovation, putting the right people in charge, etc.) to the less-than-obvious (e.g., improve the idea-to-commercialization process, think of ideas and projects in terms of a portfolio with distinct risk and return dimensions, etc.).

The obvious responsibilities are covered in depth by these authors, as well as many others. The most popular textbook on the subject of managing innovation is a book by Tidd et al. (2001), who developed a similar but more leadership-oriented model (http://www.wiley.co.uk/wileychi/innovate/website/pages/how/themodel.htm).

It is these less-than-obvious responsibilities that are the most intriguing, because, with these, the authors correlate creativity and innovation to financial goals, all important to me as the CEO.

4.3 COMPUTERIZED BRAINSTORMING

Human performance is what it all boils down to — enabling a person to perform at his or her full potential. In the beginning, we developed technology appliances to make the drudgery of clerical work less burdensome, and even to replace humans. Later, technology began to be used to help humans sort through massive information data stores. The age of the personal productivity appliance, the PC, began in the early 1980s and, during that decade and on into the new millennium, spurred an avalanche of productivity-enhancing tools that boggle the mind. But still, the emphasis was on productivity *enhancing*. What is really needed by companies searching for that elusive silver bullet of competitive leadership is some sort of tool that is productivity *producing*.

Marsh Fisher may just have found that silver bullet. You may have heard of Fisher — he was the original founder of the Century 21 real estate empire. Any business person would want to take advice from Fisher. After all, his business was worth billions. But Fisher wanted to offer more than advice; he wanted to offer ideas. Actually, he wanted to offer competitive advantage through creativity. Fischer calls this type of software *human performance technology.*

Fisher got the idea for creativity boosting back in the days when computers were large, monolithic mainframes, stuck away in the basements of office buildings, providing only a smattering of the functionality that has become available as a matter of course today. In 1964, Fisher was studying comedy writing. But he noticed that most of the other students in his class were much better at thinking on their feet than he was. They seemed to ad lib a lot better than he did. So, he started to look for some sort of a crutch with which he could at least become competitive.

He began to study the art of ad libbing, and comedy in general, and found that there is a unique association between the punch line and the set-up line. Related to both of these phrases is an assumed word or phrase. It is this word or phrase that associates the set-up line to the punch line.

When Fisher retired from Century 21, he began to study cognitive sciences, which is a combination of linguistics and computer science. One of the goals of cognitive science is to determine whether the mind can be mimicked in the mysterious task of problem solving.

Fisher describes problem solving as the three R's: recording, recalling, and reassociating. Recording of information is done spontaneously. Everything we say, hear, smell, or touch is stored in the grandest of all data banks — the human brain. Of course, once stored inside, it is sometimes very difficult to retrieve. This is the task of recalling or remembering. We have this massive warehouse of information in our subconscious, and trying to find something buried away can be quite difficult. Once an item of information is recalled, the R is deployed. We reassociate or recombine one or more items of information to produce an original creative idea.

Of course, if we had instant access to everything tucked away in our memories, the road to creativity would be much less arduous. Unfortunately, as we are reminded time and time again as we search in vain for the name of the person whom we just met in the hallway, this is usually not the case. Even if all humans were blessed with the gift of instant recall, there is still the third R to contend with: reassociation — the creative R, the R that gives us creative leverage.

In the 1960s, Fisher wanted to give humans a creativity shot in the arm by publishing a book of associations. By the time he was ready to do it, the PC had become so ubiquitous that he decided to write it in software. This is when IdeaFisher (http://www.ideacenter.com/how-if-works.html) was born.

The heart of IdeaFisher is the IdeaBank. This is where users look up related ideas and concepts. The IdeaBank is an organized storehouse of more than 65,000 ideas, words, phrases, and concepts. The software's cross-referencing capabilities create more than 775,000 associations. Ideas and concepts are organized by grouping related ideas. This method of organization is patterned after the way we naturally store information in the human brain. It explains the common experience of "one idea leading to another."

IdeaFisher claims that it can help us make something quite novel out of the fragmented and seemingly useless bits of information we deal with on a daily basis. Here is how it works:

In this example, we will join the product-planning group of a sock company. They are developing a plan to sell more socks in the summer months. In undertaking a challenge of this nature, it is important that the strategy team understand that this process actually consists of four sub-processes: (1) understanding the goal, (2) defining the strategy, (3) naming the product, and (4) finally, identifying the key attributes of the product for advertising and product positioning.

4.3.1 Understanding the Goal

Our first step is to fully understand the specific challenge. To do this, we normally get a group together to brainstorm to pick the goal, and the resultant ideas, apart and then piece them back together into a solution. Brainstorming relies on a series of questions and answers. But what if you cannot come up with the right questions? Fortunately, IdeaFisher comes with some add-ons in the form of various question banks. Questions are categorized along several lines, including developing a story script; developing a new product or service, developing a name; title, theme, or slogan; and developing a marketing strategy or promotional campaign. Because our goal is to develop a new line of socks, we will choose developing a new product service. Here, we look through a series of questions and pick the ones most appropriate to our goal. Questions such as: Does the customer fit into a particular category — a distinct type of thought and behavior (a stereotype)? What are the customer's relevant physical traits in addition to age and sex? List the person's relevant psychographics traits. What product or service characteristics are more important to this customer?

After each question is selected, the strategy team enters its responses and starts brainstorming. Our team brainstorms answers such as adult males and females of all ages; people at home and outside; likes to be outdoors, gardening, bird watching, etc.; socks should be fashionable; socks should be useful for outdoor activities; and socks should be made of a fabric that does not hold moisture or is hot. Once all of this is filtered into a series of key concepts, the team is ready to target the most relevant key concepts and move on to the next step.

After much debate, our team finally targets the key concepts of bird watching, color coordination, gardening, moisture, and useful outside activities. This, then, is the breakdown of the key elements in the marketing strategy. Defining a specific strategy is the next activity.

4.3.2 Defining the Strategy

To develop a feasible strategy to sell more socks in the summer, our team will use IdeaFisher's IdeaBank. Our team wants to begin with the socks key concept. Upon highlighting this word, the program will display all the topical categories that contain the word socks. IdeaFisher has multiple topics that deal was socks including black/gray, cleaning/dirty/clean, clothing/fashion/style, and push/pull/attract/repel. This last topic intrigues one of the members of the team, so it is highlighted to see the section titles on the next level. It turns out that there are close to 1000 idea words or phrases associated with push/pull/attract/repel categorized into groupings such as things/places, things that repel, things that attract, and abstractions/intangibles. The team decides to pursue things that repel. Highlighting this, they find some intriguing items such as anti-icer, body armor, car wax, and mosquito repellent. Clearly, these are the things that repel.

Marsh Fisher describes the act of creativity as one that involves coming up with new ideas whose revelation excites the creator so much that he or she exclaims, "A-ha!". Our fictitious team experiences this feeling when they realize the interesting possibilities of mosquito repellant on socks.

4.3.3 Naming the Product

Now that the team has decided upon their novel product, they need to come up with a good name for it — a good hook. Selecting a name for a product or service has many elements: It must be easily remembered; be descriptive; and tie in with the customer's perceived needs and values.

The team decides to compare two topical categories to create a new and unique name for the socks. The idea is to associate two disparate ideas and merge them together into a single word or phrase that creates a novel hook for the new product. Picking "socks" as the first key concept to compare, the team is prompted to pick one of many topical categories containing this word. The head of the team recommends that the team pursue limbs/appendages. "Outdoors" is the second word that the team wants to use in comparison. Again, a list of topical categories containing the word "outdoors" is displayed. This time the team picks camping/hiking/mountaineering. IdeaFisher takes over at this point and produces a listing of words and phrases found in both of these categories. This list serves as a jog to creativity. The team looks through the list bypassing blister, footing, footpath, and 55 other words and phrases. One word jumps out at them as the perfect name for the new line of socks: "surefooted."

So far, all in one sitting, the team has brainstormed the meaning of their challenge, defined their strategy, and named their product — in the space of hours rather than days. All that remains of their task is to identify key attributes for advertising and product positioning. To do this, the team decides to explore the key concepts in greater detail.

4.3.4 Identifying Key Attributes

The team decides that the key attributes they want to emphasize is the summer use of socks. So they select and highlight the word "summer." Ultimately, the team winds up with a host of summertime activities and hobbies that people in the target market might enjoy more with surefooted socks.

The final results of the IdeaFisher session, which began just a few scant hours earlier, are as follows:

1. Socks keep bugs away.
2. Color coordination with current athletic clothes and incorporation of reflective material in some models.
3. Lightweight material that does not hold heat or moisture inside.
4. An insect-repellent fabric that could be used for clothing, sleeping bags, and tents.

When Pabst Brewing Company customers began calling out "PBR" when ordering Pabst Blue Ribbon beer, Pabst knew it was onto something hot, but it needed more than just "PBR" to create a hot jingle — it needed some inspiration. That is when it turned to IdeaFisher to assist in writing a jingle that was based on abbreviations. This is what its fishing caught: "I'm gonna give my thirst some TLC, just PBR me ASAP." Pabst is not alone — IdeaFisher has been used to write copy for everything from beer to the Discover card.

4.4 SUSTAINABLE INNOVATION

In 2004, Procter & Gamble's chief technology officer G. Gil Cloyd was named *IndustryWeek*'s Technology Leader of the Year. According to Teresko (2004),

Cloyd has successfully shown how any company can contend with the classic innovator's dilemma — most innovations fail, but companies that do not innovate die. His solution, innovating innovation, resulted in P&G exceeding all of its financial goals in fiscal 2004. To do this, Cloyd leveraged a strategy designed to innovate innovation. The focus is on using technology and innovation to compete on multiple fronts simultaneously without spreading the corporate structure too thin. Among his changes were:

1. More collaboration
2. Strengthening external relationships
3. Expanding R&D's role to include not only knowledge generation, but also knowledge brokering
4. Utilizing computational modeling and simulation as the evolving solution for fast cycle learning

That P&G could achieve such startling financial results is a testament to the fact that changing the way businesses do business can lead to great creativity — and a tidy bottom line.

An interesting twist on reengineering was discussed in a recent *Time* magazine article (Taylor, 2005). The article discussed David Kelley, the founder of Ideo, who is on a mission to change the way businesses think. Ideo was originally a design firm but the dot.com bust forced Kelley to adapt this business model. Instead of "cool" products, Kelley began to focus on processes. For example, he streamlined the processes for admission into hospitals and new ways to stock supermarket shelves.

Ideo is now a business consultancy that specializes in reengineering companies to make them more efficient and innovative. The company uses transformational ideas directly from the design world and applies them to business processes. For example, Ideo once sent the CEO of P&G on a shopping trip to San Francisco's Mission District. In another example, top executives from Kraft were spirited away to a traffic control center to watch cars stop and start to determine whether this experience could influence their supply-chain management. Apparently it did, because Kraft cut in half the time it took to get products to retail.

Some are calling Ideo's ideas revolutionary. Kelley's goal is to merge business, design, and education together to both help the companies and train the next generation of business leaders to use a more innovative and emotional way of doing business. Maybe this is the "next big thing." Maybe it is not. Whatever it is or is not, it definitely gets those creative and innovative juices flowing within an organization, and that is all that matters.

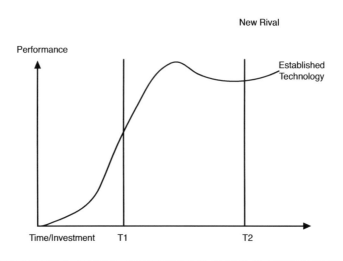

Figure 4.1   The S-curve for an established technology and a new rival.

4.5   THE S-CURVE AND INNOVATION MANAGEMENT

The S-curve, a quantitative trend extrapolation technique used in forecasting, has long been used in the technology industry. Many argue that this analysis is actually more useful to see where you have been than where you should go (Spencer, 2005). The S-curve is most often used to compare two competitive products in two dimensions, usually time and performance, as shown in Figure 4.1.

An excellent example of an S-curve can be found in Alexander (2001), in his discussion of the product innovation cycle. He discusses the S-curve of the ubiquitous automobile. The automobile was first introduced to the public in 1900 and became the plaything of the rich. Between 1900 and 1914, the automobile went through the lower curve of the cycle, or the innovation phase, at the end of which Henry Ford introduced the assembly line. Between 1914 and 1928, according to Alexander, the automobile went through its growth phase. It was during this phase that the automobile "caught on" and was adopted by the general public. By 1928, the automobile was in its maturity phase (the top part of the S-curve), and Ford was seeing leaner, meaner competition.

The S-curve can unleash unparalleled creativity when you realize that the time has come for your company to make its entry into the marketplace. For, it is at this point that you have got to get your product out there in a manner that effectively competes with established giants. This often translates to reverse engineering the competitive product and determining which features to adopt into your own product and then, essentially, one-upping them by adding new and novel features and/or services.

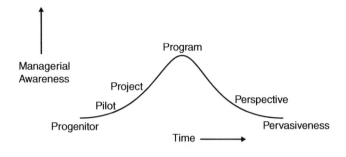

Figure 4.2   The P-cycle of a successful business idea.

For a company who is the "defender" of an established technology, the S-curve predicts at what point their leadership position might decline. Avoiding this should become their chief focus. Some companies practice what I like to call "continuous innovation" — Microsoft, for example. They practice all of the techniques in this chapter and then some, including operating skunk works, acquiring small companies that might become rivals (e.g., Hotmail.com), and leapfrogging the attacker's technology. This last technique is Microsoft's current tactic with the introduction of their new MSN search engine, which nicely rivals the Google.com powerhouse. Thus, Microsoft makes a good topic for a case history on knowledge and innovation management. But first, let us delve more into the link between creativity, innovation, and knowledge management.

4.6   HOW THE P-CYCLE IS IMPORTANT TO KNOWLEDGE MANAGEMENT

According to Davenport & Prusak (2003) the idealized life cycle of an idea within an organization is called the *P-cycle*, so named because each of its six stages starts with the letter "P" — i.e., progenitor, pilot, project, program, perspective, and pervasiveness, as shown in Figure 4.2.

The authors suggest that successful idea practitioners understand each idea's life cycle so that they might know where it might move next. There is an internal as well as external life cycle, and these might differ for many environmental reasons.

The P-cycle is somewhat similar to the traditional systems development life cycle (SDLC), in that both start with someone's bright idea (the progenitor). After a feasibility study has been performed, the next stage that the idea (or system) enters is the pilot. This is usually a scaled-down version of the grand idea such that stakeholders can determine if the idea is a fit for the company and whether it works. Once this has been proved to be true, we enter the project stage. At this point, a project plan is created; funding and other resources are allocated; and the work can begin. If successful, the idea (or system) can be implemented and is now referred to as an *ongoing program*. The program may spawn additional projects, all related to the original idea. The program is usually part of a strategic plan so that its goals can be cascaded down throughout the organization and, thus, used within many departments. Over time, the program is embedded within the corporate psyche and becomes firmly entrenched within the operating methods and controls of the company. At the beginning of this "rootedness," the idea can be said to be gaining perspective. By the time everyone in the company uses it on a daily basis, we reach the ideal end state for the P-cycle — pervasiveness.

The external P-cycle of an idea is similar to the internal P-cycle. There are usually five stages in the external life cycle of an idea: discovery, wild acceptance, digestion, decline, and hard-core. Understandably, the external life cycle of an idea often drives the internal life cycle — sometimes to the detriment of the idea.

Davenport and Wilson (2003) discuss the decline of the business process reengineering idea because the idea became too popular too soon in the external idea marketplace. Therefore, expectations within companies likely were raised too high, and the idea of reengineering never reached the pervasiveness state.

Davenport and Wilson also provide a framework that idea practitioners can follow to promote their ideas and see them through to implementation. The most salient ideas are summarized here:

1. *Idea identification:* The CEO should be an advocate of continual learning and growth. This means encouraging employees to read the latest, greatest business books, take courses, go to seminars, and network. The CEO should also be a supporter of KM because this provides a collaborative platform and methodology for knowledge and idea sharing. It is from these sources and using these tools that good ideas sprout.
2. *Advocating the idea:* An idea that is not heard is no idea at all. CEOs and other managers need to provide a pulpit for those advocating these great ideas. This may be through internal meetings, at retreats or even on the corporate intranet.
3. *Make it happen:* CEOs need to provide a slush fund so that these ideas at least progress to the pilot stage. This may be through a corporatewide R&D department or through individual departmental budgets. There also needs to be a way for these pilots to be seen and heard. Finally, if the pilot gets selected to move into the pilot stage, the CEO must provide the means to drive the idea through to the pervasiveness stage.

4.7 WHAT MAKES A BUSINESS GURU?

Business guru is a difficult term. Wikipedia, the free edit-your-own-content encyclopedia, which is itself a wonderful idea that has reached the pervasiveness stage, does not provide a formal definition of the term "business guru" but does define the term *guru* and its extension from a meaning of "Hindu religious teacher" to more general usage as "an expert of legendary proportions" (http://en.wikipedia.org/wiki/Guru). The term *guru* is nearly synonymous with "wizard" but implies that there is a history of being a knowledge resource for others.

Wikipedia also provided an interesting discussion on why people are attracted to gurus. Although it was written from the religious perspective, I would like to reprint it here with my annotations modifying the religious construct to the business construct:

> There are several reasons why people in Western cultures are attracted by gurus. The most common is that people look for the meaning of life (*business*) and are disillusioned in traditional religions (*business techniques and ideas*).

Wikipedia states that the gurus who are eloquent are the ones who are more likely to be unreliable and dangerous. Wikipedia quotes the scholar David C. Lane who wrote that a charlatan who cons people is not as dangerous as a guru who really believes in his delusions, and that the "bigger" the claims a guru makes, the bigger the chance that he is a charlatan or deluded. Of course, the context of this discussion is really a religious guru but I am gleeful to report that I see many parallels here. There is a fine line between a business guru and a huckster.

Gurus have some common attributes:

1. Creative
2. Tenacious
3. Zealots for their idea
4. Often quirky

According to Goldsmith (2003), innovative or creative personalities are often those who are inflexible and do not deal with others very well. He offers the examples of Ludwig von Beethoven, Thomas Edison, and Winston Churchill as those who have tremendous creativity but were not warm, friendly, accommodating, and cooperative. Creative people have a vision in mind; however, their difficulty is in expressing it to others. They frustrate themselves, as well as others, with their inability to effectively communicate.

The key then is to find these innovative personalities and integrate them into the company so that they can be productive, and not counterproductive as their personalities may force them to be. Pollard (2005) suggests that KM has become the organizational ghetto for the most creative minds in the business. So, this would be a wonderful place to nurture these innovative personalities.

Davenport and Wilson's (2003) idea framework, discussed earlier, provides a sound methodology that can be used by these innovators to take a company forward in idea generation and innovation.

4.8 KNOWLEDGE MANAGEMENT AT MICROSOFT

The software industry is hypercompetitive. Therefore, it is important for a software firm to hire only the best and the brightest — the gurus. However, Microsoft also realizes that knowledge should not be static, and so it embarked upon a project to create a competency-based skills profile, known as SPUD, to track and enhance employee competencies.

In the mid-1990s, the head of Microsoft's IT department hired Susan Conway to create the competency program. Conway, who had created similar competency-based programs at Computer Sciences and Texaco, soon created a pilot. SPUD (skills, planning, "und" development) focused on those skill sets and competencies required to stay at the bleeding edge of an extremely competitive industry.

The five major components of SPUD consisted of:

1. Developing a structure of competency types and levels
2. Defining the competencies or skills
3. Rating the performance or individuals based on the defined competencies
4. Implementing the knowledge competencies in an online system
5. Linking the competency model to training

Within each of the four competency types — entry level or foundation, local/unique, global, and universal — are two separate skill categories: explicit, which involves expertise in specific tools or methods, and implicit, which involves abstract thinking and reasoning skills. For example, knowledge of Microsoft Access is an explicit competency, whereas problem solving can be considered implicit. Going into the pilot, Microsoft identified 137 implicit competencies and 200 explicit competencies.

Within each competency, there were also four defined skill levels: level 1 (basic), level 2 (working), level 3 (leadership), and level 4 (expert). A sample competency description is shown in Table 4.1.

Table 4.1   Sample Competency Description

T430 Data Administration/Repository Management	
Definition: Development and maintenance of a flexible, efficient, and shared data environment, utilizing facilities such as data models, data definitions, common codes, reference databases, and data toolsets.	
Level 1: Basic knowledge of data administration and repository management	Basic knowledge of the principles and practices employed in the management of data and repositories Familiarity with information models and modeling Understanding of the rationale behind maintaining a centralized, reusable library of the business and enterprise models of a corporation
Level 2: Working knowledge of data administration and repository management	Working knowledge of the principles, practices, and tools associated with the access to and updating of local repositories
Level 3: Mastery of data administration and repository management	Knowledge and demonstrated expertise in data management Can assess the impact of functional/regional data changes on the enterprise model Able to integrate the business data and process models into the enterprise model Recognized as a data expert in a functional area
Level 4: Leadership and recognized expertise in data administration and repository management	Subject-matter expertise in the management of local, regional, and enterprisewide information/data models Recognized as a data expert in major functional areas Reviews information models for compliance, content quality, consistency, and impact on enterprise models

There are a variety of benefits to the competency model. These include:

1. Better fit of employee to specific job.
2. Ability of managers to find the right employee more quickly.
3. An organizational view of knowledge assets that is a valuable input into strategic planning.
4. Enables creation of detailed job descriptions so that item 1 of this list can be more easily achieved.

5. Enhanced ability to match employee to training offerings. Training can now be targeted at specific skill gaps.
6. General overall improvement in competencies of the entire firm. Theoretically, an improvement in the skill levels of individual employees should lead to an improvement of skill levels within the firm as a whole.
7. Improved employee morale as more offerings are targeted at specific employees.
8. Possibility that the model might become a vehicle for institutionalizing innovation. For example, Wi-Fi is a "hot" topic in 2005. Use of SPUD could force development of a competency in this area by requiring its presence in all job competency requirements.

It is obvious that the competency-based model has much potential if it is implemented properly and is generally accepted by all employees of the company.

The development of a competency-based model is necessarily time consuming, and a great deal of attention to detail is required for its success. This requirement alone might be sufficient to railroad its success. However, there are other weaknesses:

1. The person or persons creating the competency description might create an inaccurate description. They might not be privy to all the requirements of the job or may not be familiar enough with the job to provide an adequate level of detail.
2. Same job titles within different divisions might require different competency descriptions.
3. Job descriptions do change, leading to the possibility of an out-of-sync or out-of-date situation with the competency database. Maintaining a skills competency database is an expensive and time-consuming job.
4. It is sometimes difficult to assess and gauge implicit competencies within employees.
5. Online access to the competency database might enable managers to "raid" existing teams for members with desired competencies.
6. Individuals might feel that this information is a violation of their privacy and/or limit their potential within the company.

There has been some controversy amongst researchers about competency mapping as well. According to Lindgren et al. (2001), descriptions of competence are fragmentary and atomistic. Competence is usually categorized beforehand in an ad hoc manner, with weak connections to both empirical data and theory. This serves to confirm the model of competence itself rather than the workers' competence. Finally, regardless of the number of categories, competence profiles are static, indirect, and general descriptions concerning human competence. Competence profiles do not demonstrate whether workers actually use the competence in accomplishing work, i.e., the competency profiles may not be rooted in work practice.

4.9 SIX STEPS FOR INCREASING CREATIVITY AND PRODUCTIVITY

Harvard Business Essentials (2003) lists six steps for increasing creativity:
Make sure your company's goals are consistent with your value system. This is an interesting perspective in an era of few good jobs and trends toward outsourcing and offshoring.

In May of 2004, Elizabeth Lukin presented the results of a study about how Australians look at work (http://www.essentialmedia.com.au/news/1082351106_5696.html). She found the following, which is consistent with other studies on how Americans look at work:

1. Job insecurity is a big issue.
2. More and more permanent jobs are being replaced by temporary jobs.
3. Employees are experiencing unrealistic expectations, increased workloads, and lack of staff.

She concludes her discussion by saying that very few people can imagine their situation improving substantially. In fact, many believe things will only get worse. They see the gap between the rich and the poor growing, and they feel that they do not know where all this change will end up.

Managers need to realize that many, if not most, employees will harbor some or all of these feelings. Given the dire job market, they might opt to stay put rather than, as the Harvard text suggests, find a company whose goals match their values. Therefore, it is up to the manager to somehow ameliorate the level of anxiety that accompanies these feelings, such that creativity is not stifled.

Pursue some self-initiated activity by choosing projects in which your motivation is high. Few employees get to choose their own task assignments. However, savvy managers need to be aware that creativity is greatly enhanced when employees are motivated to do their jobs.

The better companies try to fit the employee to the task by creating a skills database. These permit managers to rapidly locate an employee who has the skills — and the motivation — to fulfill a particular work requirement.

However, there will always be times when the task the employee is expected to complete is simply not one that he or she is especially interested in. At this point, the good CEO will use a variety of motivating techniques.

Based on a study at Wichita State University, the top five motivating techniques are:

1. Manager personally congratulates an employee who does a good job.
2. Manager writes personal notes about good performance.
3. Organization uses performance as basis for promotion.
4. Manager publicly recognizes employee for good performance.
5. Manager holds morale-building meetings to celebrate successes.

One does not have to actually give an award for recognition to happen. Giving your attention is just as effective. The Hawthorne Effect says the act of measuring (paying attention) will itself change behavior.

Nelson and Blanchard (1994) suggest the following low-cost rewards recognition techniques:

1. Make a photo collage about a successful project that shows the people who worked on it, its stages of development, and its completion and presentation.
2. Create a "yearbook" to be displayed in the lobby that contains each employee's photograph, along with his or her best achievement of the year.
3. Establish a place to display memos, posters, photos, and so on, recognizing progress toward goals and thanking individual employees for their help.
4. Develop a "Behind-the-Scenes Award" specifically for those whose actions are not usually in the limelight.
5. Say thanks to your boss, your peers, and your employees when they have performed a task well or have done something to help you.
6. Make a thank-you card by hand.
7. Cover the person's desk with balloons.
8. Bake a batch of chocolate chip cookies for the person.
9. Make and deliver a fruit basket to the person.
10. Tape a candy bar for the typist in the middle of a long report with a note saying, "halfway there."
11. Give a person a candle with a note saying, "No one holds a candle to you."

12. Give a person a heart sticker with a note saying, "Thanks for caring."
13. Purchase a plaque, stuffed animal, or anything fun or meaningful and give it to an employee at a staff meeting with specific praise. That employee displays it for a while, and then gives it to another employee at a staff meeting in recognition of an accomplishment.
14. Call an employee into your office (or stop by his or her office) just to thank him or her; do not discuss any other issue.
15. Post a thank you note on the employee's office door.
16. Send an e-mail thank you card.
17. Praise people immediately. Encourage them to do more of the same.
18. Greet employees by name when you pass them in the hall.
19. Make sure you give credit to the employee or group that came up with an idea being used.
20. Acknowledge individual achievements by using employees' names when preparing status reports.

McCarthy and Allen (2000) suggest that you set up your employees for success. When you give someone a new assignment, tell the employee why you are trusting him or her with this new challenge. "I want you to handle this because I like the way you handled _____ last week." They also suggest that you never steal the stage. When an employee tells you about an accomplishment, do not steal her thunder by telling her about a similar accomplishment of yours. They also suggest that you never use sarcasm, even in a teasing way. Resist the temptation to say something like, "It is about time you gave me this report on time." Deal with the "late" problem by setting a specific time the report is due. If it is submitted on time, make a positive comment about timeliness.

Take advantage of unofficial activity. I know of few people who have the luxury of working on unofficial projects in larger companies. However, this is actually quite a good idea. Management should allow slack time to be used for creative purposes. Channels should be put in place such that any great idea nurtured during slack time has an equal opportunity to be presented for possible funding.

Be open to serendipity. The authors discuss how Scotchgard was invented by accident. My own company practices this technique. Several of our products were developed by accident by employees "playing around" with programming code. As a manager, it is very important that I be open to this sort of novel product development.

Diversify your stimuli. Employees should strive to rotate into every job they are capable of doing to induce intellectual cross pollination. This is not a new technique as it has been practiced for years within the high-tech industry. Rotating jobs is also a tenet of quality management systems, including ISO 9001 (http://standardsgroup.asq.org/news/psi/0207-PSIQA02.pdf).

Another recommendation is to get to know people who might spark your imagination. However, this is a personal preference, not shared by everyone. The challenge as a manager is, therefore, to somehow provide employees with a diversity of stimuli that might take them in new and different directions. This can be done by using some of the techniques in the last step, which follows.

Create opportunities for information communication — otherwise known as "meet and greet." Salespeople are natural networkers. These folks sign up for every event and learn a great deal by doing so. Other employees are somewhat less motivated to leave the office to attend industrywide gatherings, particularly as the employee gets older and has additional familial responsibilities.

Ideas to promote intellectual stimulation include:

1. Fund memberships to professional organizations
2. Fund subscriptions to trade and other magazines
3. Invite a variety of speakers to monthly staff meetings
4. Host industry events so that staff does not have to travel to get to them
5. Promote teaming within the company
6. Provide collaborative technologies such as a corporate intranet, video conferencing capabilities, instant chat, etc.
7. Fund continuous training
8. Fund higher-education opportunities

The Harvard six steps for increasing creativity are but a starting point for creating an innovative organization. All of this, however, still relies on the CEO being an advocate of innovation management.

4.10 REWARDING EMPLOYEES FOR INNOVATIVE IDEAS

There are two types of awards. *Intrinsic rewards* appeal to a person's desire for self-actualization, curiosity, joy, and interest in the work. *Extrinsic rewards* appeal to a person's desire for attainment: e.g., money, stock options, days off, tickets to ballgames, etc. Intrinsic rewards are intangible, whereas extrinsic rewards are quite tangible. As one of my employees says, "Show me the money."

Many of the motivation techniques discussed in this chapter could be considered intrinsic rewards. Extrinsic reward systems are more difficult to implement as there are usually budget considerations to deal with. In many companies, the methodology used to grant yearly raises can even be considered countermotivational. When I worked for the New York Stock Exchange, employees were rated on a scale of 1 to 5. The largest "rewards" (i.e., raises) were granted to the 5s. However, we were told to rate our employees using a bell-shaped curve. The result is that some 5s were cheated out of their fair share of the reward system.

This topic is so important that more than a few books have been written on it. Wilson (2002) talks about the use of spot bonuses, team celebrations, innovative employee benefits, and flex compensation. Pearce and Robinson (2005) discuss the subject of executive compensation in their textbook on strategic management, now in its ninth edition. Ideas that work for the senior managers should also work for the employee who greatly contributes to the profitability and/or competitive advantage of the firm:

1. Stock option grants
2. Restricted stock plan
3. Bonus income deferred, sometimes referred to as *golden handcuffs*
4. Cash based on accounting performance measures

Creating a workforce infused with innovation and creativity requires understanding how to work with people. You would be surprised (or maybe not) at how differently bosses look at things than do their staff, as shown in Table 4.2. The object, clearly, is to narrow the gap.

The first step is to understand your own motivations, your strengths as a manager, and your weaknesses. The best approach is probably to ask your peers and employees to make an anonymous appraisal of your performance as a manager. Have them rate such traits as listening and communications skills, openness, and attitude. Painful as this process may be, it will actually make you seem heroic in your employees' eyes. At the same time, it will give you some food for thought on ways to improve your own performance.

The second step — one that many managers pay only lip service to — can really make the difference between a motivated employee and one who feels that he or she is just another number. Take the time to learn about your employees and their families. What are their dreams? Then ask yourself how you, as a manager, can fulfill these dreams from a business perspective.

Perhaps the best way to learn about your employees is in a nonwork atmosphere — over lunch or during a company outing. As you learn more about your employees' motives, you can help each one develop a personalized strategic plan and vision. Ultimately, you could convert those horrible yearly performance reviews into goal-setting sessions and progress reports.

Table 4.2   What Do Employees Really Want?

What Employees Want	Items	What Employers Think Employees Want
1	Interesting work	5
2	Appreciation of work	8
3	Feeling "in on things"	10
4	Job security	2
5	Good wages	1
6	Promotion/growth	3
7	Good working conditions	4
8	Personal loyalty	6
9	Tactful discipline	7
10	Sympathetic help with problems	9

Source: From Kovach, K., Employee motivation, *Addressing a Crucial Factor in your Organization's Performance: Human Resource Development,* Ann Arbor, MI: University of Michigan Press, 1999.

Generating a positive attitude is the third step. Studies show that 87 percent of all management feedback is negative, and that traditional management theory has done little to correct the situation. Your goal should be to reverse the trend. Make 87 percent of all feedback good.

Respect for and sensitivity toward others remain essential in developing positive attitudes. Ask employees' opinions regarding problems on the job, and treat their suggestions and ideas as priceless treasures.

The partner of positive attitude in the motivational game is shared goals. A motivated workforce needs well-defined objectives that address both individual and organizational goals. This means that you should include all your employees in the strategic planning process. Getting the employees involved leads to increased motivation. It also acts as a quality check on whether or not you are doing the right thing. And you will close the communication gap at the same time.

Just setting a goal is insufficient. You have to monitor progress. The goal-setting process should include preparing a detailed road map that shows the specific path that each person is going to take to meet that goal. In my business, one of the things that IT professionals dislike the most is the feeling that they are left out of the business cycle. In essence, information technology is simply one brick of a grand strategic edifice.

IT staffers frequently complain that they rarely get to see the fruits of their labor. Distributing the IT function into the business unit mitigates this problem somewhat, but it is still up to the manager to put technologists into the thick of things — make them feel like part of the entire organization.

Finally, recognizing employees or team achievement is the most powerful motivating tool in the manager's toolbox. Appreciation for a job well done consistently appears on the top of employee "want lists." So, hire a band, have a party, send a card, or call in a clown — but thank that person or that team.

4.11 WHERE DO WE GO NEXT?

As knowledge becomes more important, organizations are restructuring themselves to better utilize this asset. Empowerment, flattening, and decentralization of the organization, and a focus on innovation and continuous improvement are all hallmarks of the modern enterprise.

In this new age, utilization of information and knowledge counts as much as its production. The ability to quickly utilize the knowledge and information of the entire workforce, and not just the "information elite," is critical. In Chapter 5, we will explore data management concepts, because data is the basis of all information and knowledge.

References

Alexander, M.A., The Innovation Wave and Secular Market Trends, 2001. Retrieved February 20, 2005 from http://www.safehaven.com/article-71.htm.

Couger, J.D., McIntyre, S.C., Higgins, L.F., and Snow, T.A., Using a bottom-up approach to creativity improvement in IS development, *Journal of Systems Management*, September 1991, pp. 23–36.

Davenport, T.H. and Prusak, L., *What's the Big Idea?*, Boston, MA: Harvard Business School Press, 2003.

Davenport, T.H. and Wilson, H.J., Turning mind into matter, CMP Optimize, 25, November 2003. Retrieved August 25, 2005 from http://www.optimizemag.com/issue/025/innovation.htm?articleId=17701007&pgno=1.

Drucker, P.F., The discipline of innovation, *Harvard Business Review 80*(8), 95–102, August 2002.

Goldsmith, B., Are you an Innovator or an Implementer, *Office Solutions, 20*(2), April–May 2003. Retrieved March 25, 2005 from Proquest.

Harari, O., Stop Empowering Your People, *Management Review,* 26–29, November 1993.

Harvard Business Essentials, *Managing Creativity and Innovation*, Boston, MA: Harvard Business School Press, 2003.

Kovach, K., Employee motivation, *Addressing a Crucial Factor in your Organization's Performance: Human Resource Development*, Ann Arbor, MI: University of Michigan Press, 1999.

Lindgren, R., Stenmark, D., Bergquist, M., and Ljungberg, J., Rethinking IT-support for managing competence, in *Proceedings of European Conference of Information Systems* 2001, Bled, Slovenia.

McCarthy, M. and Allen, J., *You Made My Day: Creating Co-Worker Recognition and Relationships*, New York: L-F Books, 2000.

Nelson, B. and Blanchard, K., *1001 Ways to Reward Employees*, New York: Workman Publishing, 1994.

Olmstead, L., How Steve Lipscomb reinvented poker and built the hottest business in America, *Inc. Magazine*, 80–92, May 2005.

Palmberg, C., The sources of innovations — looking beyond technological opportunities, *Economics of Innovation and New Technology, 13*(2), March 2004.

Pearce, J.A. and Robinson, R.B., *Strategic Management: Formulation, Implementation, and Control*, New York: McGraw-Hill, 2005.

Pollard, D., The future of knowledge management, ExecutiveAction, 130, January 2005. Retrieved March 24, 2005 from http://www.conference-board.org/publications/execaction_formac.cfm.

Spencer, A., The Technology S-Curve, January 2005. Retrieved February 20, 2005 from http://web.njit.edu/~aspencer/slides/s-curve.ppt.

Taylor, Chris, School of Bright Ideas, *Time,* March 6, 2005.

Teresko, J., P&G's Secret: Innovating Innovation, *IndustryWeek, 253*(12), December 2004. Retrieved March 25, 2005 from Proquest.

Tidd, J., Bessant, J., and Pavitt, K., *Managing Innovation: Integrating Technological, Market, and Organizational Change,* 2nd ed., Hoboken, NJ: John Wiley & Sons, 2001.

Wilson, T.B., *Innovative Reward Systems for the Changing Marketplace*, New York: McGraw-Hill, 2002.

5

DATA MANAGEMENT

The Data Management Association (www.dama.org) defines data management as the development and execution of architectures, policies, practices, and procedures that properly manage the full data life-cycle needs of an enterprise. Disciplines in data management include the following:

1. Data modeling
2. Database administration
3. Data warehousing
4. Data movement
5. Data mining
6. Data quality assurance
7. Data security
8. Metadata management (data repositories and their management)
9. Strategic data architecture

There is a difference between data and information. Data is stored in multiple applications systems on multiple platforms using multiple methods and is used to perform day-to-day operations. If this distributed data is grouped together in a meaningful format, it can provide valuable information to business organizations and their decision makers.

Data is captured using online transaction processing (OLTP) systems to perform mission-critical daily operations. Typically, many users simultaneously add, modify, delete, and view data using OLTP applications. OLTP systems are characteristically designed to process one transaction record at a time.

Information is derived from online analytical processing (OLAP) systems used for analysis, planning, and management reporting through access to a variety of sources. An OLAP system usually references information that is stored in a data warehouse. Use of this technology provides the facility to present a comprehensive view of the enterprise.

Data and information are extremely valuable assets. Data architecture defines an infrastructure for providing high-quality, consistent data to be used as the basis for decision support and executive information services as well as traditional transaction applications statewide.

In this chapter, we will focus on how data should best be organized so that it can provide the basis for knowledge management.

5.1 DATA MANAGEMENT

Data architecture defines all the components, interfaces, and processes for implementing and managing an integrated, cohesive data policy. These components are described in the following subsections.

5.1.1 Data

5.1.1.1 Text and Numeric Data

These are data fields comprising rows of information containing discrete values related to some business entity. Most operational databases are almost completely text and numeric data fields. Because there are discrete values, these can be individually retrieved, queried, and manipulated to support some activity, reporting need, or analysis.

5.1.1.2 Images

Scanned pictures of documents, photos, and other multidimensional forms can be stored in databases. The scanned image is a single data field and is retrieved and updated as a single fact. Software outside of the DBMS is used to manipulate the image.

5.1.1.3 Geographic Data

Geographic data is information about features on the surface and subsurface of the earth, including their location, shape, description, and condition. Geographic information includes spatial and descriptive tabular information in tabular and raster (image) formats. A *geographic informa-tion system* (GIS) is a hardware and software environment that captures, stores, analyzes, queries, and displays geographic information. Typically, geographic information is the basis for location-based decision making, land-use planning, emergency response, and mapping purposes.

5.1.1.4 Multimedia: Voice, Animation, and Video

Multimedia applications are increasingly used as we employ new modal-ities of communicating with users. Voice can be stored in a database to capture instructional, informative messages, which can then be played back rather than displayed as text. This helps in those situations in which keyboards and visual displays are difficult to utilize. Similarly, graphics, animation, and video offer an alternative way to inform users when simple text does not easily communicate the complexity or the relationships between informational components. An example might be a graphic display of vessels and equipment allowing drill down to more detailed information related to the part or component. Video may be useful in demonstrating some complex operation as part of a training program.

5.1.1.5 Objects

Objects are composites of other data types and other objects. Objects form a hierarchy of information unlike the relational model. Objects contain facts about themselves and exhibit certain behaviors implemented as procedural code. They also "inherit" the facts and behaviors of their parent objects up through the hierarchy. Relational databases store every-thing in rows and columns. Although they may support large binary object (LOB) fields that can hold anything, an object database can support any type of data combined with the processing to display it.

5.1.2 Databases

Databases organize data and information into physical structures, which are then accessed and updated through the services of a database man-agement system. A database is an organization method that links files together as required. In nonrelational systems (e.g., hierarchical, network, etc.), records in one file contain embedded pointers to the locations of records in another, such as customers to orders and vendors to purchases. These are fixed links set up ahead of time to speed up daily processing. A *relational database management system* (RDBMS) is software designed to manage a collection of data. Data is organized into related sets of tables, rows, and columns so that relationships between and among data

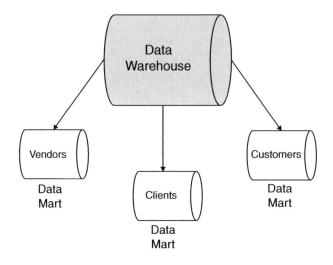

Figure 5.1   Data warehouse and its associated data marts.

can be established. For example, a vehicle database can contain two tables, one for customer information and one for vehicle information. An "owns" relationship is then established between the two tables.

A multidimensional database management system (MDDBMS) is specifically designed for efficient storage and retrieval of large volumes of data. Multidimensional databases are organized into fact tables and dimensions that intersect with the facts table to identify to what the fact pertains. Databases of this construction are used for OLAP.

5.1.3   Data Warehouse — Data Marts

A *data warehouse* is a database designed to support decision making in an organization or enterprise. It is refreshed, or batch-updated, and can contain massive amounts of data. When the database is organized for one department or function, it is often called a *data mart* rather than a data warehouse, as shown in Figure 5.1.

The data in a data warehouse is typically historical and static in nature. Data marts also contain numerous summary levels. It is structured to support a variety of elaborate analytical queries on large amounts of data that can require extensive searching.

A data warehouse is a record of an enterprise's past transactional and operational information, stored in a database designed for efficient data analysis and reporting (especially OLAP). Two basic ideas guide the creation of a data warehouse:

1. *Integration* of data from distributed and differently structured databases, which facilitates a global overview and comprehensive analysis in the data warehouse. Periodically, one imports data from enterprise resource planning (ERP) systems and other related business software systems into the data warehouse for further processing.
2. *Separation* of data used in daily operations from data used in the data warehouse for purposes of reporting, decision support, analysis, and controlling.

5.1.4 Operational Data Stores

The *operation data store* (ODS) is a database that consolidates data from multiple source systems and provides a near-real-time, integrated view of volatile, current data. An ODS differs from a warehouse in that its contents are updated in the course of business, whereas a data warehouse contains static data.

5.1.5 Data Access

Access to data falls into two major categories:

OLAP: Decision support software allows the user to quickly analyze information that has been summarized into multidimensional views. Traditional OLAP products, also known as *multidimensional OLAP,* or *MOLAP,* summarize transactions into multidimensional views ahead of time. User queries on these types of databases are extremely fast because the consolidation has already been done. OLAP places the data into a cube structure that can be rotated by the user, which is particularly suited for financial summaries, as shown in Figure 5.2.

OLTP: Online transaction processing means that master files are updated as soon as transactions are entered at terminals or received over communication lines. It also implies that confirmations are returned to the sender. They are considered real-time systems.

5.1.6 Replication

Replication is the process used to keep distributed databases up to date with a central source database. Replication uses a database that has been identified as a central source and reproduces the data to distributed target databases. As more and more data is being made available to the public over the Internet, replication of select data to locations outside the firewall is becoming more common.

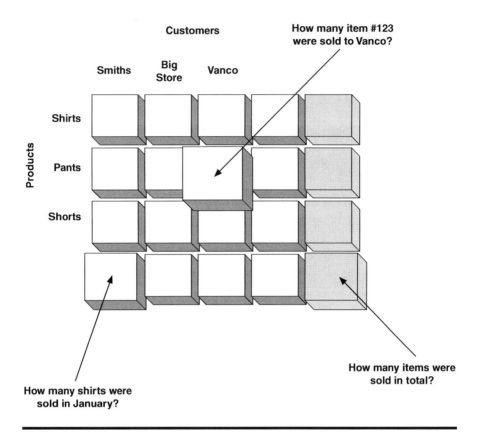

Figure 5.2   OLAP cube.

Replicated data should be accessed by applications in a read-only mode. If updates were allowed on replicated data, data would quickly become corrupted and out of sync. Updates should be directed to the database access tier in charge of updating the authoritative source, rather than to a replicated database.

Replication services are available from most relational database vendors for their particular products.

5.1.7   Resource Management

Resource management provides the operational facilities for managing and securing an enterprisewide, distributed data architecture. It provides a common view of the data, including definitions, stewardship, distribution, and currency, and allows those charged with ensuring operational integrity and availability the tools necessary to do so. Research needs to be done for all components in this category.

5.1.8 Security

Security becomes an increasingly important aspect as access to data and information expands and takes on new forms such as Web pages and dynamic content. The security policy needs to be examined to ensure that it provides for new types of databases and new data types, and that it can be enforced given the move to distributed data and Internet access.

5.2 DATA WAREHOUSE IS SOMETHING YOU DO

A data warehouse is something you do, not something you buy. A successful data warehouse does not have an end. Regardless of the methodology, warehousing environments must be built incrementally through projects that are managed under the umbrella of a data-warehousing program.

Most of the benefits of the data warehouse will not be realized in the first delivery. The first project will be the foundation for the next, which will in turn form the foundation for the next. Data warehousing at the enterprise level is a long-term strategy, not a short-term fix. Its cost and value should be evaluated across a time span sufficient to provide a realistic picture of its cost-to-value ratio.

The following seven components make up the enterprise data warehouse architecture. These components offer a high level of both flexibility and scalability for the enterprise wishing to implement a business intelligence solution.

5.2.1 Source Systems

A *data source system* is the operational or legacy system of record whose function is to capture the transactions of the business. Source systems should be thought of as outside the data warehouse, because we have no control over the content and format of the data. The data in these systems can be in many formats from flat files to hierarchical and relational RDBMSs such as Microsoft Access, Oracle, Sybase, UDB, and IMS to name a few. Other sources of data may already be cleansed and integrated, the data being available from operational data stores.

5.2.2 Data Staging Area

The *data staging area* is the portion of the data warehouse restricted to extracting, cleaning, matching, and loading data from multiple legacy systems. The data staging area is the back room and is explicitly off limits to the end users. The data staging area does not support query or presentation services. A data-cleansing tool may be used to process data in the staging area to resolve name and address misspellings, etc., as well as resolve other data cleansing issues by the use of fuzzy logic.

5.2.3 Data Warehouse Database

The warehouse is no special technology in itself. The *data warehouse database* is a relational data structure that is optimized for distribution. It collects and stores integrated sets of historical, nonvolatile data from multiple operational systems and feeds them to one or more data marts. It becomes the one source of truth for all shared data.

5.2.4 Data Marts

The easiest way to conceptually view a data mart is that a mart needs to be an extension of the data warehouse. Data is integrated as it enters the data warehouse from multiple legacy sources. Data marts then derive their data from the central data warehouse source. The theory is that no matter how many data marts are created, all the data is drawn from the one and only version of the truth, which is the data contained in the warehouse. Distribution of the data from the warehouse to the mart provides the opportunity to build new summaries to fit a particular department's need. The data marts contain subject-specific information supporting the requirements of the end users in individual business units. Data marts can provide rapid response to end-user requests if most queries are directed to precomputed, aggregated data stored in the data mart.

5.2.5 Data Extraction, Transformation, Load (ETL) Tools

These tools are used to extract data from data sources, cleanse the data, perform data transformations, and load the target data warehouse; it is used again to load the data marts. The ETL tools are also used to generate and maintain a central metadata repository and support data warehouse administration. The more robust ETL tools integrate with OLAP tools, data modeling tools, and data cleansing tools at the metadata level. Appendix J provides a good set of checklists for selecting and integrating a metadata repository.

5.2.6 Business Intelligence (BI)

Business intelligence provides the tools required by users to specify queries, to create arbitrary reports, and to analyze their own data using drill-down and OLAP functions. Putting this functionality in the hands of the power users allows them to ask their own questions and gives them quick and easy access to the information they need.

One tool, however, does not fit all. The BI tools arena still requires that we match the right tools to the right end users.

5.2.7 Metadata and the Metadata Repository

A *repository* is itself a database containing a complete glossary for all components, databases, fields, objects, owners, access, platforms, and users within the enterprise (see Appendix J for more information on selecting a repository). The repository offers a way to understand what information is available, where it comes from, where it is stored, the transformation performed on the data, its currency, and other important facts about the data.

The repository describes the data structures and the business rules at a level above a data dictionary. However, metadata has taken on a more visible role among day-to-day knowledge workers. Today, it serves as the main catalog, or map, to a data warehouse. The central metadata repository is an essential part of a data warehouse. Metadata can be generated and maintained by an ETL tool as part of the specification of the extraction, transformation, and load process. The repository can also capture the operational statistics on the operation of the ETL process.

5.3 DATA STORAGE STRUCTURES

There are a variety of techniques and tools that enable the organization to store and manage data:

Relational online analytical processing (ROLAP): These processing tools extract analytical data from traditional relational databases' structures. Using complex SQL statements against relational tables, ROLAP is able to create multidimensional views on the fly. ROLAP tends to be used on data that has a large number of attributes, when it cannot be easily placed into a cube structure.

Multidimensional online analytical processing (MOLAP): This is specially designed for the purpose of user understandability and high performance. A multidimensional database uses a dimensional model instead of a relational model. A *dimensional model* is a star schema characterized by a central "fact" table, as shown in Figure 5.3. One fact table is surrounded by a series of "dimension" tables. Data is joined from the dimension points to the center, providing a so-called star. The fact table contains all the pointers to its descriptive dimension tables plus a set of measurements of facts about this combination of dimensions.

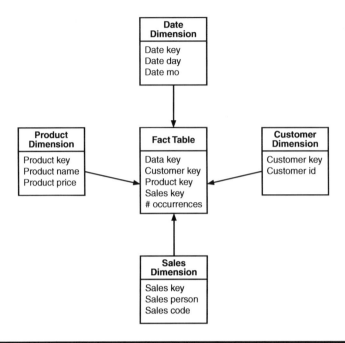

Figure 5.3 A dimensional model.

Hybrid online analytical processing (HOLAP): These tools use the best features of multidimensional and relational databases. Relational databases are best known for their flexibility. Until recently relational databases were weak in their ability to perform the same kind of multidimensional analysis that the multidimensional databases are specifically optimized for. The introduction of hybrid relational systems with enhanced abilities to manipulate star schemas has increased the OLAP capabilities of the relational world. Hybrid tools provide high performance for both general-purpose end users and power users.

Web-enabled online analytical processing (WOLAP)

CUBE: In a multidimensional database, a dimensional model is a cube. It holds data more as a 3-D spreadsheet rather than as a traditional relational database. A cube allows different views of the data to be quickly displayed. The ability to quickly switch between one slice of data and another allows users to analyze their information in smaller, meaningful chunks, at the speed of thought. Use of cubes allows the user to look at data in several dimensions; for example, attendance by department, attendance by attendance codes, attendance by date, etc.

5.3.1 Extraction, Transformation, and Load

Transforming data is generally performed as part of the preparation before data is loaded into the data warehouse and data marts. Understanding the business usage of this information and the specific business questions to be analyzed and answered are the keys to determining the transformations necessary to produce the target data mart.

ETL tools are used to extract data from operational and external source systems, transform the data, and load the transformed data in a data warehouse. The same tool is used to extract and transform the data from the warehouse and distribute it to the data marts. When a schedule is defined for refreshing the data, the data extraction and transformation schedule must be carefully implemented, so that it both meets the needs of the data warehouse and does not adversely impact the source systems that store the original data.

Extraction is a means of replicating data through a process of selection from one or more source databases. Extraction may or may not employ some form of transformation. Data extraction can be accomplished through custom-developed programs. But the preferred method uses vendor-supported data extraction and transformation tools that can be customized to address particular extraction and transformation needs as well as use an enterprise metadata repository, which will document the business rules used to determine what data was extracted from the source systems.

Data is transformed from transaction level data into information through several techniques: filtering, summarizing, merging, transposing, converting, and deriving new values through mathematical and logical formulas. All these operate on one or more discrete data fields to produce a target result having more meaning from a decision support perspective than the source data. This process requires understanding the business focus, the information needs, and the currently available sources. Issues of data standards, domains, and business terms arise when integrating across operational databases.

Cleansing data is based on the guideline of populating the data warehouse with quality data — that is, data that is consistent, is of a known and recognized value, and conforms to the business definition as expressed by the user. The cleansing operation is focused on determining those values that violate these rules and either reject or, through a transformation process, bring the data into conformance.

Data cleansing standardizes data according to specifically defined rules, eliminates redundancy to increase data query accuracy, reduces the cost associated with inaccurate, incomplete, and redundant data, and reduces the risk of invalid decisions made against incorrect data.

5.4 GOOD DATA MANAGEMENT PRACTICES

Performing and maintaining the functions of data management is an integral part of most large organizations. The rapid and expansive development of information management technologies has opened the door to a vast world of information that can be processed and analyzed with increasing speed and complexity. Ensuring that information (and the interpretations derived from it) is accurate is the key challenge for successful data management. Sound data management involves a series of actions that must be clearly defined, clearly understood, and diligently followed. The following discussion of data management roles and functionality was adapted from a white paper on data management prepared by the United States Forest Service (1998).

Achieving and maintaining data calls for the following roles to be assigned in the organization: data or project sponsors, data stewards, data and database administrators (DBAs), and system administrators. It will be these roles that facilitate the requirements of the data management functions.

5.4.1 Data Management Roles

Table 5.1 displays the relationship matrix between data management functions and corresponding roles of personnel. It is quite possible for roles to require both content knowledge and technical skills. As we move across the matrix from data sponsorship to system administration, the required skills phase from content oriented (program management level, data content level) to more highly technical in nature (systems, database management, GIS skills, etc.).

A description of each of these roles is given in the following subsections.

5.4.1.1 Data Sponsor

The *data sponsor* is an advocate for a particular information activity such as a spatial dataset or application. The person in the organization representing this role has a vested interest in the information activity and provides an appropriate level of support to ensure its success. The data sponsor normally has decision authority (at the management level) and approves resources available to the project.

Sponsor duties include the following:

1. To review project plans and assess relevancy to corporate information needs. The sponsor must inform management about the scope and effect of the project and its impact on the organization.

Table 5.1   Relationships of Data Management Functions and Roles People Play

Functions	Sponsor	Data Steward	Data Admin.	Database Admin.	System Admin./ISM
			Roles		
Development requirements	C	C	C/T	T	T
Identification enforcement standards		C	C/T	T	
Design implementation		C	C/T	T	T
Quality control data integrity		C	C/T	T	T
Backup and recovery			C/T		T
Data sharing		C	C/T	T	T
Change management/ change analysis		C	C/T		
Connectivity			C/T		T
Input and update		C	C/T		
Security			C	T	T
Metadata			C/T	T	
Training		C	C/T		

Note: C = Primary content knowledge required; T = primarily technical knowledge required; C/T = both content and technical knowledge required.

2. To serve as an advocate for the project. This advocacy role is not finished with the successful implementation of a dataset or application; it continues through evaluation and support of required future developments related to information need changes owing to technological advancements.
3. To collaborate in setting goals and priorities.
4. To ensure that staffing, funds, and other resources are available, in addition to making sure the appropriate data management roles are assigned and fulfilled.
5. To review the project's progress and use of resources.

Sponsor coordination responsibilities include the following:

1. Project sponsors must coordinate with counterparts at the leadership team level on budget and staffing issues. Implicit in this task is to ensure that adequate resources are available for the project.
2. Coordination is required at the planning level to ensure that priorities are clarified and that the project can proceed with the allotted resources.
3. The sponsor also coordinates with the roles of data steward, data administrator, and DBA at project initiation and periodically during the project life cycle.
4. Sponsors coordinate with higher-level counterparts in the program area the projects fall in.

Other sponsor requirements include these:

1. Every project must have clearly defined sponsorship.
2. Sponsorship is an ongoing responsibility that does not end with a project's implementation; this role extends through the project life cycle as well. Prior to beginning an information activity, a commitment to this responsibility must be comprehended and accepted.

5.4.1.2 Data Steward

Effective resource management requires data that is current, accurate, and readily available. To achieve this goal, responsibility for effective data management must be assigned to data stewards from top to bottom within the organization. Data automation and data sharing have increased the necessity of accurate and immediate data accessibility. It is the data steward's role that is essential to meeting these requirements.

The data steward's duties include the following:

1. To develop procedures and standards that ensure the data is both acceptable and accurate in the applicable program area. It is imperative that only data relevant to the organization's mission is collected and that the data is of sufficient quality. This also includes functioning as a liaison with the users of the data. The data steward must be assertive in asking for input when defining and managing corporate datasets.
2. To implement data standards. Stewards must define how the standards will be applied to the resources or programs.
3. To develop new standards when necessary. This includes maintaining state-of-the-art knowledge of existing data standards for the program.

4. To develop quality assurance and quality control plans. Examples include data gathering, updates, and sampling protocols for alpha-numeric databases and database edit rules.
5. To check data and databases to address the needs of others who use and share the data.
6. To initiate data sharing and exchange agreements when necessary.
7. To follow the life-cycle management or project planning and con-figuration management procedures in an application's develop-ment.
8. To determine user training needs and the resources necessary for user training (specific to the data and applications).
9. To determine data or application update needs and points of implementation. Included in this task is establishing periodic update cycles (either specific dates or frequency of updates) when relevant.
10. To establish and maintain data or application documentation; e.g., user manuals, data dictionaries, and metadata.
11. To serve as a point of contact for data or application.
12. To define access and security requirements for data or applications.
13. To comply with map accuracy standards when applicable.

Data steward coordination responsibilities include the following:

1. To coordinate with counterparts within the program area
2. To coordinate with the user community of the data or application
3. To coordinate with the data administrator, DBA, and data sponsor

5.4.1.3 Data Administration

The data administrator is responsible for the management of data-related activities. Two levels of data administration activities exist: system and project.

System-level functions deal with management issues. They include planning, developing data standards (in conjunction with data stewards), developing policies, establishing data integrity procedures, resolving data conflict issues, and managing data-resource-related DBMSs.

At the system level, data administration policies ensure careful man-agement of data, both at creation and during use. This management practice is necessary to maintain data integrity, maximize data use, and to minimize costs associated with data management and collection.

At the physical management level, we intentionally classify the DBA as a subcomponent of the data administrator role. The DBA differs from the data administration role in that it supports the development and use of a specific database system. The DBA role must fulfill the following tasks: defining user requirements, developing data models, training and consulting, establishing and monitoring data integrity, monitoring database usage, and controlling database changes.

Data administrator duties include the following:

1. Implement a program of data administration that meets the organization's vision with respect to consistency, shareability, and quality of data. This must reflect the business management requirements of the organization.
2. Develop strategies, policies, procedures, standards, guidance, and assistance needed for effective data administration.
3. Help to facilitate maximum data sharing capability and to eliminate data definition redundancies by promoting a common description and representation of data. Cooperation with data stewards is necessary to accomplish this task.
4. Promote data collection strategies to ensure that data is collected at the source and that key data collection surveys meet identified integration and business needs.
5. Establish and support strategies governing access, retention, and disposition of data.
6. Establish a communication program with customers and suppliers of information resources.
7. Maintain a repository of active sponsors and stewards for all information activities and components. Also, to ensure that stewardship responsibilities are properly established and maintained for the shared components.
8. Establish and support corporate strategies for data administration.
9. Promote a shared data environment that is both flexible and responsive to the changing business needs of the organization.
10. Establish an integrating framework (Enterprise Data Model) and work with development projects to ensure compatibility with the framework. The Enterprise Data Model will consist of a collection of models ranging from high-level strategic planning views through the implementation of shared databases.
11. Develop data and function modeling standards and procedures.
12. Develop and enforce standards for maintaining corporate data.
13. Participate in the review of all software releases to ensure compliance with data administration policy, procedures, and standards.
14. Facilitate the "change management" process for all corporate data.
15. Ensure that data administration standards comply with government and industry standards, in addition to providing for information exchange and operational compatibility.

16. Ensure compliance with metadata policy and facilitate the maintenance of official metadata records.
17. Facilitate customer access to metadata.
18. Promote data security. This task most notably includes identifying security requirements and assisting the identification of data security procedures and policies.

Data administration coordination responsibilities include the following:

1. The data administrator coordinates with the DBAs, data stewards, program area leads, project managers, and application developers by providing education, technical support, reviewing feedback, and developing good working relationships about the enterprise.
2. The data administrator serves as an internal consultant to help employees, managers, and developers locate and retrieve data pertaining to their information needs. This consultation helps provide leverage to the organization's data investment.
3. The data administrator serves as a coordination point between the various data stewards. By providing this type of coordination, data integration and standard consistency is maintained throughout the organization.

5.4.1.4 Database Administration

The focus of this subsection is the database administration subcomponent of data administration. It should be noted that the duties of the data administrator and DBA may overlap; these duties can be performed by one or more persons in the organization.

Both the DBA, who utilizes a technical perspective, and the data steward, who utilizes a content perspective, work together to build a framework that promotes and provides several data management functions. In simplest terms, the DBA is responsible for the database framework and all transactions (inputs and updates) associated with the dataset.

At the physical (project) level, the DBA must focus on the detailed needs of the individual users and applications. The database development aspect of data management shoulders the bulk of the responsibility for developing data models and database implementation. Data development involves the analysis (planning), design, building, maintenance, documentation, and monitoring aspect.

The duties of the DBA include the following:

1. Formulates a conceptual model of the database in conjunction with the system-level data administration requirements. As a result, the

DBA must be identified or assigned at a project's earliest stages to provide a background and establish the project's scope needed in the model.

2. Works closely with the system administrator to ensure that the physical environment is conducive to design and development, for example, by identifying appropriate physical space, networking, and establishing access criteria.

3. Coordinates with the data steward for the development and implementation of procedures that ensure data consistency, integrity, and quality.

4. Builds a data structure conducive to the enforcement of standards, developed at the system level of data administration as well as by data stewards. Although the ultimate responsibility for identification of standards related to the data and processes resides with the data steward, it is the responsibility of the DBA to build a data structure conducive to the enforcement of these standards.

5. Ensures that data structures are suitable for analysis and application development. Performs database tuning to ensure efficient input, update, and retrieval of data.

6. Monitors the dataset or application use and routinely reports back to the data steward regarding the use of a particular dataset or application.

7. Ensures that the dataset is readily available for sharing, both internally and externally.

8. Coordinates the identification, assessment of impacts, strategy, and implementation of change management procedures for a dataset.

9. Implements appropriate data security measures by aiding the control of access at several levels. Works closely with the system administrator to ensure this security exists at the appropriate levels (network, platform, data, and application).

10. Assesses current and new technology merit; e.g., the new technology or tool's performance, the change's cost ramifications at all levels, etc.

Database administration coordination responsibilities are the following:

1. DBAs must coordinate with project sponsors and data stewards to design and develop a data structure that meets their needs.

2. DBAs must coordinate with system administrators and other information support to ensure adequate physical environment and system security.

3. Coordinates the identification, impact assessment, strategy, and implementation of the change management procedures for the dataset.

5.4.1.5 System Administration and System Support

The system administrator's duties include the following:

1. Assesses existing computer resources and identifies additional needs.
2. Develops guidelines and offers consultation for optimum computer configurations.
3. Determines the online storage capacity, computer memory, and server, workstation, PC, and X-terminal configuration for the processing and management of data.
4. Monitors computer resources and makes recommendations for changes to the system.
5. Ensures that the systems are kept running and maintained with the latest technology.
6. Loads data onto the system and ensures its security. Provides security for corporate data via access control.
7. Provides access for maintenance of corporate data.
8. Performs scheduled data backups.
9. Archives historical data.

Coordination responsibilities include the following:

1. Coordinates with the data administrator and DBA to understand the nature and size of the datasets that will be worked with
2. Coordinates with the data administrator and DBA to ensure that backups and archives are performed when necessary
3. Works with the data administrator, DBA, and data stewards to ensure the needed security and data access
4. Coordinates with all individuals involved in the process to ensure that the systems meet project and organizational needs

5.4.2 Data Management Responsibilities

Data management functions, as shown in Table 5.2, are described in the following subsections.

5.4.2.1 Development and Management Requirements

Development and management requirements refer to management leadership's commitment toward the process of data development and data management. To be successful, management leadership must be totally involved in and prepared to commit people, time, and financial resources to the projects and associated tasks that they are sponsoring, not to mention using intelligent foresight during a project's resource analysis. It is important to make your resource specialists and managers available

Table 5.2 Data Management Functionality

	Data Management Functions
A	Development and management requirements
B	Identification and enforcement standards, design, and implementation
C	Data and mapping standards
D	Quality control, data integrity, and backup and recovery
E	Data sharing
F	Change management and impact analysis
G	Connectivity
H	Input and update
I	Security
J	Metadata
K	Training

when the important issues are defined and when working through analysis and data requirements. Although this may be a repetitive process taking place at the planning stages of identifying information needs and continuing throughout the life of the project, it is imperative to a project's proper development.

The actual event of defining "development and management requirements" is quite common; it occurs every time the details of a project are defined. For the purposes of this discussion, we are focusing specifically on defining the level of involvement of the spatial or associated-natural-resource data component of project planning.

5.4.2.2 *Identification and Enforcement Standards, Design, and Implementation*

Identification standards simply are guidelines to help maintain data collection or updates, definition, and validation protocol. *Enforcement standards* are guidelines to help ensure that the identification standards are followed. Both functions are based on the outcomes of the development and management requirement phase described in Subsection 5.4.2.1.

Successful implementation of data management depends on intelligent up-front data design; e.g., following up on the standard's agreements, constructing a data model, and setting up the actual system. The actual implementation should always follow the physical design process.

5.4.2.3 Data and Mapping Standards

To ensure that your databases, data entry forms, acceptable codes, applications, etc., are all shareable, consistent, and scientifically sound, data standards should be designed in advance. Given the large amount of data processing, it should be apparent that data collection standards are essential for data integrity.

5.4.2.4 Quality Control, Data Integrity, and Backup or Recovery

Before data can become corporate or shared, the appropriate mapping standards and data definition standards must be complied with via quality control.

Another important procedure that must be performed regularly, especially when a project or corporate dataset reaches a significant milestone, is data backup. Data backup protects the project's progress from any unanticipated system failures or user errors by saving it to the proper media and archiving it. To ensure real-time data integrity, recovery contingencies must also be in place.

5.4.2.5 Data Sharing

Sharing data is essential to most projects; multiple users must have access to the same data to make this type of data processing effective. Before data sharing can occur, the data, metadata, projection, and format must all be integrated. Data sharing has direct links with data security because certain users will have different types of access depending on their need or update responsibilities. Connectivity is also implicit in data sharing, which is discussed under Subsection 5.4.2.7.

5.4.2.6 Change Management and Impact Analysis

Impacts from data standard changes or technological changes (hardware or software upgrades) must be anticipated and planned for. Understanding the possible ramifications on certain end users, organizations, and applications must be accounted for during a project's planning.

5.4.2.7 Connectivity

Connectivity refers to how data is shared and distributed in a networked architecture. User requirements determine the scale of connectivity that is required; these requirements may or may not be apparent to the user community.

5.4.2.8 Input and Update

The actual collection, input, and update of data may take place in several different locations and several different steps. The technical side of data sharing has to do with the various data types; different types of data require different approaches to updating. Static data usually requires low maintenance, whereas dynamic data needs high maintenance (monitored by the specialist, the data steward, and the DBA). Update cycles are largely dependent on the dynamic or static nature of the data. Input and update protocols must be developed so that data stewards have standard methodologies to follow.

5.4.2.9 Security

A number of security levels exist in a multiple user interface: network, platform, and data. Security levels are based on user requirements, both internal and external to applications (e.g., databases). To help implement security access levels, a review process should be established.

Network security pertains to the different levels of security throughout the computer network and with firewall management. Platform security relates directly to access privileges according to the platforms you are operating on (e.g., IBM, DG, Prime, PCs, and associated operating systems). Here appears the issue of data access restrictions, normally set by the system administrator. Because data security is application specific, data stewards must determine the ownership requirements, and DBAs must then implement the requirements (e.g., RWE, RW, or R access).

5.4.2.10 Metadata

Metadata management requires proper documentation throughout the life cycle of any dataset. The term *metadata* is often loosely associated as being information about S/NR data. Technically, metadata is data about data. However, data dictionaries do not employ this definition, but a similar version.

5.4.2.11 Training

Appropriate training is imperative for those collecting and entering data, designing databases, and certainly, for those persons involved in the data management process. A certification process for some roles can be very valuable to ensure that consistent, sound, and accurate data is being collected and entered into the corporate database.

5.5 GUIDELINES

These guidelines, adapted from the State of Connecticut's manual *Data Management and Data Warehouse Domain Technical Architecture* (2002), are intended to provide a guide in the evaluation, selection, design, construction, and implementation of a data warehouse:

Guideline 1: Information is valued as an asset, which must be capable of being shared.

1. Need to develop policy pertaining to information stewardship. Requires determination of responsibility for accuracy, access authorization, historical trails, manipulation approval, definitions, and integrity relationships.
2. Information and its value must be identified by its current keepers. It must be authenticated and documented. Stewardship must be identified or assigned. The metadata must be capable of being universally available, so the data contained within can be leveraged by all authorized to use it.
3. A mechanism is required to maintain identified metadata information, which can be listed, categorized, show stewardship, level of privacy or security, and location of information. Need for unified metadata information management to make it accessible to all agencies.
4. Need to establish supporting policies for security, privacy, confidentiality, and information sharing. Requires data use agreements.
5. Data needs to be structured for easy access and management by adopting enterprise data standards.
6. Identified data should be used from existing sources but not recaptured by new developments.
7. Standards should be adopted to provide more global sharing capabilities.
8. Management tools will be required to maintain and manage a metadata repository.
9. Change control procedures need to be defined and adopted to ensure that the metadata repository is current.
10. Methodology is needed to publish and disseminate information on data available for sharing.
11. Requires creation of an enterprise data model.
12. Need to establish policy and procedures for maintaining timely and accurate enterprisewide geographic information.

13. Policies for service level agreements need to be defined to determine availability and level of service.
14. Need to provide enterprisewide systems that support the creation, storage, and retrieval of documents, images, and other information-rich objects that are used within processes or are exchanged with external organizations and constituents.

Guideline 2: The planning and management of the enterprisewide technical architecture must be unified and have a planned evolution that is governed across the enterprise.

1. A unified approach will require a change in cultural attributes.
2. Normal evolution will require prioritization and reprioritization across all IT initiatives.
3. Dependencies must be maintained.
4. The architecture must be continually reexamined and refreshed.
5. Short-term results versus long-term impact must be constantly considered.
6. Establishing enterprise architecture takes time and involves a lot of change.
7. Make sure that the chosen architecture has a broad range of capabilities to handle multiple needs and best-of-breed solutions in the marketplace (Internet, PDAs, and kiosks).
8. Planning for retirement of obsolete and nonstandard products.
9. Requires retraining of staff moving from obsolete technologies.
10. Need to develop in-house software engineers, data architects, DBA, and warehouse experts.

Guideline 3: Architecture support and review structures shall be used to ensure that the integrity of the architecture is maintained as systems and infrastructure are acquired, developed, and enhanced.

1. A structured project-level review process and authority will be needed to ensure that information systems comply with the IT architecture and related standards.
2. Processes incorporating the guidelines of this (technical) architecture must be developed for all application procurement, development, design, and management activities.
3. This compliance process must allow for the introduction of new technology and standards.
4. Conceptual architecture and technical domain guidelines should be used as evaluation criteria for purchasing as well as developing software.

5. Negotiate at the enterprise level to handle increase in compliant systems.
6. Need for open-mindedness when reviewing for compliance, possible need to broaden existing architecture, or considerations for possible exceptions.
7. Develop phaseout plans.
8. Inventory of who is using what architectures.

Guideline 4: Organizations should leverage a data warehouse and data marts to facilitate the sharing of existing information. This data warehouse will contain the one single version of "the truth."

1. Data warehousing must become a core competency of IT.
2. Data warehousing both requires and supplies configuration standards that need to be developed and maintained.
3. End-user tools must be provided to relieve the burden on programmers to provide this functionality.
4. End users become more knowledgeable about the information available to them. End users become more aware of and knowledgeable about the tools they need to access and analyze it.
5. The processes and procedures refreshing the data warehouse will require high levels of reliability and integrity.
6. Warehousing is not meant to replace shortcomings of transaction applications. Guidelines on maintaining data and data retention need to be developed.
7. Not all requests for data are simple in nature and appropriate for end-user tools. Not all data will be available to all users.
8. End users should be able to access the data without knowledge of where it resides or how it is stored.
9. Data warehouse architecture design requires an integrated design effort to provide usefulness. Full potential of a data warehouse will not be realized unless there is full participation throughout the enterprise.
10. User community must be made aware of the timeliness (as well as untimeliness) of information.

Guideline 5: IT systems should be implemented in adherence to all security, confidentiality, and privacy policies and applicable legal and regulatory requirements.

1. Need to identify, publish, and keep the applicable policies current.
2. Need to secure data elements.

3. Categorize access control; this may vary depending on the data and audience.
4. Need to monitor compliance with policies.
5. Must make the requirements for security, confidentiality, and privacy clear to everyone.
6. Education on issues of privacy and confidentiality must become a routine part of normal business processes.
7. Audit capabilities of data access.
8. Understanding that part of the stewardship role interprets security, confidentiality, and privacy.
9. All access requests for data that is not publicly available should be made to the data steward.
10. Requires a means to publish and implement changes to the status of data access requirements.

Guideline 6: The enterprise architecture must reduce integration complexity to the greatest extent possible.

1. Decreases the number of vendors, products, and configurations in the State's environment.
2. Must maintain configuration discipline.
3. Will sacrifice performance and functionality in some instances.
4. Will rely on components supplied by vendors, which will make the enterprise more vulnerable.
5. Need to factor cost of vendor dependency when figuring the total cost of ownership.
6. Determination of "the greatest extent possible" includes consideration of how reducing complexity can negatively impact providing critical client services.

Guideline 7: Consider reuse of existing tools and infrastructure before investing in new solutions.

1. Software license agreements and system development contracts should be written to allow for reuse across the enterprise.
2. Areas that provide clear advantages and business cost savings are likely to require quick adaptation.

Guideline 8: Systems must be designed, acquired, developed, or enhanced such that data and processes can be shared and integrated across the enterprise and with partners.

1. IT staff will need to consider the impacts on an enterprisewide scale when designing applications.
2. IT will need a method for identifying data and processes that need integration, when integration should take place, who should have access to the data, and cost justification for integration.
3. It will be necessary to coordinate, maintain, and arbitrate a common set of domain tables, data definitions, and processes across the organization.
4. Overintegration can lead to difficult data management and inefficient processes.
5. Use of metadata repository.
6. Enterprise integration teams composed of dedicated enterprise data architects and applications architects are required to assist in integration efforts.
7. Stewardship review of integration.
8. There is a need to evaluate the practicality of an integrated project before development.

Guideline 9: New information systems will be implemented after business processes have been analyzed, simplified, or otherwise redesigned as appropriate.

1. Need to have an agreed-upon business reengineering process.
2. Need to identify the business need for data.
3. Need to determine the legal requirement for retention of data.
4. New technology will be applied in conjunction with business process review.
5. Business processes must be optimized to align with business drivers.
6. Additional time and resources will have to be invested in analysis early in the systems life cycle.
7. Organizational change will be required to implement reengineered work processes.
8. May require regulatory or legislative change.

Guideline 10: Adopt a total cost of ownership model for applications and technologies that balances the costs of development, support, training, disaster recovery, and retirement against the costs of flexibility, scalability, ease of use, and reduction of integration complexity.

1. Will require looking closely at technical and user-training costs, especially when making platform or major software upgrades during the lifetime of the system.
2. Requires designers and developers to take a systemic view.
3. Need to selectively suboptimize individual IT components.
4. Need to develop a cost-of-ownership model.
5. Need to ensure coordinated retirements of systems.
6. Need to consider budget issues for staffing and training.
7. Need to develop a cost structure for providing access to shared information.
8. Need to provide funding for data costs that are not billable or recoverable.
9. Need to establish permanent, reliable funding mechanisms for developing enterprisewide geographic information such as aerial photography, satellite imagery, transportation, and hydrographic data layers.

Guideline 11: Infrastructure and data access will employ reusable components across the enterprise, using an n-tier model.

1. Component management must become a core competency.
2. Requires development of a culture of reuse.
3. Design reviews become crucial.
4. Data marts can be modularized without making components too small or too simple to do useful "work."

Guideline 12: The logical design of application systems and databases should be highly partitioned. These partitions must have logical boundaries established, and the logical boundaries must not be violated.

1. Applications need to be divided into coded entities (e.g., presentation, process, and data access).
2. For databases, there will be a need to develop competency in partitioning horizontally and vertically; this will result in more but simpler tables and views. Design reviews must ensure that logical boundaries are kept intact. Increases data management responsibilities of DBAs.
3. Requires increased analytical skills of project analyst to determine when partitioning takes place, based on expected data or access requirements.

Guideline 13: OLTP should be separated from data warehouse and other end-user computing and Internet access.

1. Data marts represent a type of configuration standard for physical partitioning.
2. Data warehousing and data marts must become core competencies of IT.
3. Business and IT must agree on the purpose and objective of the data warehouses.
4. Data redundancy will be necessary.
5. Data marts will not reflect the most current data.
6. It is not always necessary or even desirable to physically partition data as, for example, when there is a low scalability requirement.

Guideline 14: IT solutions will use industry-proven, mainstream technologies.

1. Need to establish criteria for vendor selection and performance measurement.
2. Need to establish criteria to identify the weak vendors and poor technology solutions.
3. Requires migration away from existing weak products in the technology portfolio.
4. Will reduce some solution choices.
5. Need to respond as changes in technology occur.

Guideline 15: Priority will be given to products adhering to industry standards and open architecture.

1. Need to establish criteria to identify standards and the products using them.
2. IT organizations will need to determine how they will make the transition to this mode.
3. Will reduce some solution choices.

Guideline 16: An assessment of business recovery requirements is mandatory when acquiring, developing, enhancing, or outsourcing systems. Based on that assessment, appropriate disaster recovery and business continuity planning, design and testing will take place.

1. Systems will need to be categorized according to business recovery needs (e.g., business critical, noncritical, or not required).
2. Alternate computing capabilities need to be in place.
3. Systems should be designed with fault tolerance and recovery in mind.
4. Plans for work-site recovery will need to be in place.

5. Costs may be higher.
6. Data must be capable of online backups to provide 24/7 availability.

Guideline 17: The underlying technology infrastructure and applications must be scalable in size, capacity, and functionality to meet changing business and technical requirements.

1. Scalability must be reviewed for both "upward" and "downward" capability.
2. May increase initial costs of development and deployment.
3. Will reduce some solution choices.

5.6 DICTIONARY OF DATA MANAGEMENT TERMS

Application: A set or logical grouping of data and automated procedures that support one or more business processes and information needs.

Attribute: Any detail that serves to qualify, identify, classify, quantify, or express the state of an entity. Any description of "a thing of significance."

Business function: What a business does or needs to do, irrespective of how it does it.

Business model: A collection of models representing a definition of a business. Components include models of objectives, functions, information, and technology.

Connectivity: How data is shared and distributed in a networked architecture.

Coordination: Sound working relationships between data stewards, the librarian or DBA function, system administration, and the data administration function need to be developed and supported. These relationships ensure that developed standards are adequately represented, maintained, and that access and database use is promoted.

Corporate data: Data that is needed across the organization and that must be shared or combined among offices. It is most valuable to the organization if corporate data is standardized, kept current, and managed in such a way that it addresses the needs of the project and the decision-making process.

Customer: A user or recipient of information management products and services.

Data: Symbols representing facts, ideas, or values that may be processed to produce information.

Data administration: The policies, procedures, and organizational responsibilities for managing the definition, security, access, and maintenance of data.

Database: A collection of interrelated data stored in a structured manner.

Data development life cycle: The data development life cycle begins at the data requirement's phase. The data development life cycle consists of analysis of need, design of structure, building the structure, documenting the approach, and monitoring results.

Data element: See *Attribute.*

Data management: The art of managing data and the processes for collecting, maintaining, and using it effectively to meet the organization's need to have solid information available. Data management consists of the daily and long-term development and upkeep of data on automated systems.

To effectively accomplish sound data management practices, an enterprise modeling approach needs to be implemented within each organization. This cannot be fully successful until information needs at different levels of the organization are represented. If grassroots standards are developed, there is a significant risk that the overall objectives of the organization may be missed and that developed applications will have a "stovepipe" narrow focus. If standards come down, it is quite possible they will not meet the field users' needs. Data stewards are responsible for developing standards within the context of these broader organizational business requirements. Clear responsibility for the data must be assigned to achieve good data management. Stewards must be identified at the levels of the organization (appropriate to the corporate data). Responsibility should be clarified through the establishment of performance expectations that specifically refer to the stewardship responsibility.

Data model: A structured representation of an organization's information. It includes entities, attributes, and entity relationships.

Data sharing: Usefulness to more than one user.

Data steward: Those personnel who ensure that the data complies with the respective program integrity standards. A data steward provides oversight and coordination.

Development and management requirements: Performing an analysis of the resources that will be required to support a project. Takes place every time the details of a project are defined.

Enforcement standards: Methods to ensure that all standards are being adhered to.

Function: What an organization does, will do, or should do; it defines what is done, not how or by whom. The types of activities that are required for us to perform sound data management practices.

Identification standards: Following protocol of how we collect or update, define, and validate data.

Information: Data that has been processed or interpreted. A majority of data evolves to information, which may in turn become data for a subsequent generation of information.

Information needs assessment: See *Needs assessment.*

Information structures: An end product of data modeling. Logical (versus taxonomic) representation of data components and their relationships.

Integrated application: An application designed to share data, screens, or behind-the-screens code with at least one other application.

Integrated database: (a) A set of tables designed to be shared among applications. (b) Where the official data tables for a given application reside.

Integrated information environment (IIE): The set of approaches, tools, and products that makes up an environment in which information is managed to achieve a high level of integration among systems and data.

Interpretation rules: Record of the rationale (logical and intuitive) and assumptions used to create interpreted data.

Lift-cycle management: A structured method for managing an application or automated system for its entire life cycle (initiation, design, development, implementation, operation, cancellation, or replacement).

Management: To treat with care, handle or direct with skill (Webster's dictionary).

Management direction: A statement of multiple-use and other goals and objectives, the management prescriptions, and the associated standards and guidelines for attaining them.

Management support: Management at all levels should be informed that data management and its component parts are an ongoing, never-ending process. Creating enterprise data models and developing data standards is a long process (multiyear), and the resulting products must be monitored and maintained over time.

Metadata: Data about data. Proper documentation of process and data content should take place throughout the life cycle of any dataset.

Monitoring: To watch, observe, or check, especially for a specific purpose; for example, to keep track of, regulate, or control (Webster's dictionary).

Needs assessment: The identification of the information need. This is generally a multidisciplinary effort and may be a formal information needs assessment (INA). The INA is developed with an enterprise modeling perspective relating the information need to the overall business requirement and is often tied directly to outstanding issues driving the need for analysis at a given scale. The end result is that a specific dataset is required to meet some information analysis requirement.

Network: An interconnected network of computers as referred to in distributed processing.

Normalization: A step-by-step process that produces either entity or table definitions that have (a) no repeating groups, (b) the same kind of values assigned to attributes or columns, (c) a distinct name, and (d) distinct and uniquely identifiable rows.

Operation: In other methodologies, the term *operation* has the same meaning as business function or elementary business function when used in a business context.

Physical database design: The database design that will support an organization's information requirement. It is derived from the analysis model and is driven by the technology used by the organization.

Physical model: Synonymous with physical database design.

Principal user: The person or group of people whom the database is designed to serve. These may be resource specialists, resource managers, decision makers, or policymakers.

Process: In other methodologies, the term *process* has the same meaning as business function or elementary business function when used in a business context.

Project management life cycle: From the perspective of the resource manager, projects are conceived, born, implemented, and monitored for compliance with standards that have roots in laws, executive orders, congressional mandates, and public input. Issues are then identified; a plan is developed, followed by an implementation and monitoring process. An information-needs assessment is one of the outflows of the project management life-cycle process.

Prototyping: A technique for demonstrating a concept rapidly to gain acceptance and check feasibility.

Relational database: (a) A database in which data is organized into one or more relations that may be manipulated using relational algebra. A *relation* is a named table (row by column) that identifies the set of occurrences of entities that have the same or common attributes. Relational algebra includes a set of relational operators, such as join and projection, to manipulate relations and the axioms of those operators. (b) A data storage, manipulation, and retrieval system that helps integrate information by emphasizing the flexible relationships among the data.

Relationship: What one thing has to do with another. Any significant way in which two things of the same or different type may be associated. Relationships are named to indicate their nature.

Repository: A database that acts as a storage place for knowledge about the business and information systems of an enterprise. The repository includes, but is not limited to, models, standards, requirements, definitions, and detailed designs.

Repository database administration: The policy, procedures, and organizational responsibility for managing the database implementation of the repository, which includes installing software, managing access to the database, performing backups, and tuning for performance.

Role: (a) A privilege assigned to allow specific users to perform specific functions. (b) A statement of the part a contact plays in relation to an interest.

Role-based access management (RBAM): Simplifies access management by granting access to menus, applications, report generators, and parts thereof to specified roles; people are then assigned to the roles.

Shared Data: Data shared between databases; not a single organization-wide database. Flexibility exists in the individual systems to keep information beyond that which is shared.

Sponsor: (a) An individual or organization officially assigned responsibility for the development and maintenance of one or more information systems. (b) An individual or organization responsible for ensuring that a particular information activity (such as a request to add a standard value or a request to develop an analysis program based on stored data) is carried out. The sponsor is not necessarily the exclusive provider of the resources for carrying out the activity. (c) The person or organization ensuring that a particular information activity such as a change request is carried out. This entails setting goals; making available time, funds, and other resources; participating in setting priorities; supporting employee participation; creating and maintaining support for integration; ensuring that sponsored changes are carried through to completion; and facilitating the acquisition of resources from other stakeholders. It should be noted that the sponsor is not the exclusive provider of resources. Other stakeholders may provide resources if they want to have an active role in the information activity. (d) The role of project sponsorship provides the overall direction and approval of the collection and acquisition of natural resource data. Project sponsors are responsible for evaluating the relevancy of the proposed project or activity within the corporate database. They also act as the liaison to higher leadership. (e) Sponsors and stewards would monitor development of interdisciplinary teams to proceed with project development. Sponsors plan and establish priorities for project development and reaffirm their support and involvement with the national efforts.

Staffing: Adequate staffing must be provided to the process that identifies the business requirements, data models, and standards. This goes beyond the naming of and assigning responsibility to data stewards. Individuals who are empowered to do the work are needed to manage the modeling tools and data dictionaries. Much of this work falls under the data administration function. Ongoing management of a diverse, integrated data resource cannot be accomplished with a staff of one person. The monitoring and maintenance of data models and data standards require a data administration staff of appropriate size to effectively manage the workload.

Stakeholder: (a) A stakeholder is responsible for providing input to decisions about information management objects (such as application modules or data tables) that impact the rest of his or her job. Anyone who has such an interest in the object is automatically a stakeholder, whether or not the person ever fulfills the responsibility of the role. Stakeholders include the users, customers, and managers of the data, processes, and systems. (b) Any person or position with an interest in an information system (IS) who would be affected by any change to that object. (c) A key member of an organization unit who defines and has a personal stake in achieving the goal of the unit. (d) Anyone who will be affected by the outcome of the decision.

Standards: Standards should be an outgrowth of data-modeling activities and not have a life all their own. Creating standards for a database, although beneficial in many ways, does not bring in the expected rewards if done without the benefit of knowing how they relate to the enterprise data model. Data sharing is maximized when standards are developed in the broader context.

Steward: (a) A steward is responsible for ensuring that the assigned object (such as a data model, an application module, a set of data, or a business process) has a structure that is logically consistent and accurately reflects business requirements, and that the data updates, availability, and performance are all adequately monitored for the requirements achievement. This includes ensuring that relevant policy is followed and that data integrity is maintained. (b) A position or organizational unit officially assigned responsibility for the development and maintenance of one or more information assets on behalf of the organization. (c) One whose job description makes him or her responsible for an information system object to ensure that the structure accurately reflects business requirements; the structure is logically consistent; and data updates, availability, and access speeds are adequate to meet business requirements. Stewardship can also be broken down into specific categories of information system objects to further describe the associated responsibilities. (d) A position or organizational unit officially assigned responsibility for the development and maintenance of one or more information assets.

Stewardship: The management of someone else's property.

System: (a) A total collection of interrelated programs, of equipment, of people, machines, and processes, or all of these; it is a very broad term. (b) A defined and interacting collection of real-world facts, procedures, and processes, along with the organized deployment of people, machines, and other resources that carry out those procedures and processes. In a good system, the real-world facts, procedures, and processes are used to achieve their defined business purposes within acceptable tolerances.

System administration: The policies, procedures, coordination, and organizational responsibilities for managing computer systems.

System integration: The blending of separate, inconsistent, and overlapping applications and their data into an information system.

Systems analysis: An approach to problem solving, in which the total system is considered before focusing on individual parts of the system. The term is used very broadly, for example, to describe the analysis of global ecosystems or political systems, but it may also apply to the analysis of a specific problem to be solved by a computer application.

Technology: The hardware and software used in conjunction with information management, regardless of the technology involved, whether computers, telecommunications, micrographics, or others.

Tools: Tools to aid in the management of data are a key ingredient in the success of a data management policy. Primary tools are data modeling and data repository (data dictionary) tools. The acquisition of these tools must be given a high priority.

Unique identifier: Any combination of attributes or relationships that serves, in all cases, to uniquely identify an occurrence of an entity, or one or more columns that will always supply a single row from a table.

5.7 WHERE DO WE GO NEXT?

Data is the basis of all information and, hence, knowledge. Online information is usually referred to as *content management*, which is the focus of Chapter 6.

References

GIS Center of Excellence of the U.S. Forest Service, Data Management: A Shared Perspective, 1998. Retrieved August 18, 2005 from http://ims.reo.gov/website/swop/html/swop_slide_show/swop_sdm_whitepaper/sdm.htm.

State of Connecticut, Data Management and Data Warehouse Domain Technical Architecture, June 6, 2002. Retrieved August 7, 2005 from http://www.ct.gov/doit/lib/doit/DATA_ARCHITECTURE_ver_20_6-6-2002.pdf.

6

CONTENT MANAGEMENT

In 2002, Nielsen Norman Group (http://www.nngroup.com) published a study on corporate intranet usability (Simplicity and enterprise search, 2003). The researchers looked at 14 separate intranets. The study emphasizes the importance of effective searching by noting what happens in its absence. They observed that poor search functionality was the single-greatest cause of reduced usability across the intranet studies. They found that search usability accounted for an estimated 43 percent of the difference in employee productivity between the best and worse intranets. The study also found that unsuccessful search users were using inefficient alternatives, or gave up altogether, bringing the return on investment (ROI) for the unused online assets down to zero.

The study measured users' performance for 16 common tasks. They found that a company with the least usable intranet would spend $3,042 per employee to cover time spent on the 16 tasks, although the cost of using the most usable intranet was only $1,563 per year. Extrapolating from these figures, the study concluded that the total annual cost of intranet use at various levels of usability for companies with 10,000 users to be the following:

- *Good usability: $15.6 million annually*
- *Average usability: $20.7 million annually*
- *Poor usability: $30.4 million annually*

Content can be delivered to the end user in a variety of ways — bots, search, push, browsing, and portal. This is referred to as knowledge flow. Bots, short for robots, are automated agents (i.e., software programs) that seek out information of interest and send it back to the end user on his or her request. Push technology, or server-push as it is sometimes known, is delivery of information that is initiated by the information server rather than by the end user. The information is "pushed" from a server to an end user as a result of a programmed request initiated originally by the end user. A portal is a Web site that serves as a single gateway to information and knowledge. Each of these methodologies requires that the content be managed in some way.

In this chapter, we will explore effective content-management techniques with an eye toward enhancing usability and functionality.

6.1 ENTERPRISE INFORMATION MANAGEMENT

Information is essential to running a successful business. There are four major elements to enterprise information management (EIM): correspondence management, workflow management, document management, and records management.

In a modern organization, these information assets might take the form of documents, multimedia objects, corporate public relations and advertising, technical documents, images, sounds, video, databases, knowledge bases, and any combination thereof.

For the most part, these systems are automated. EIM systems should be considered strategic investments, as they will affect the conduct of business in every part of the organization.

Most implementers of EIM systems recommend that there be a single, clear vision of the desired end result of implementing the EIM. This vision must be understood and supported by those at the very highest levels of leadership.

There are several varieties of EIM systems that can be implemented, as shown in Figure 6.1, which are as follows:

1. *Content management system (CMS):* Usually focus on intranet-based or Internet-based corporate content, including data and knowledge bases
2. *Document management system (DMS):* Focuses on the storage and retrieval of work documents (e.g., forms), in their original format
3. *Records management system (RMS):* The management of both physical and electronic documents

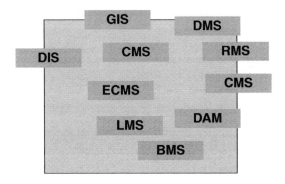

Figure 6.1 Enterprise information system components.

4. *Digital asset management (DAM):* Similar to RMS, but focused on multimedia resources such as images, audio, and video
5. *Brand management system (BMS):* Management of advertising and promotional materials
6. *Library management system (LMS):* The administration of a (corporate) library's technical functions and services
7. *Digital imaging system (DIS):* Automates the creation of electronic versions of paper documents (e.g., PDF files) that are input to RMSs
8. *Learning management system (LMS):* The administration of training and other learning resources; learning content management systems (LCMS) combine CMSs with LMSs
9. *Geographic information system (GIS):* Computer-based systems for the capture, storage, retrieval and analysis, and display of spatial (i.e., location-referenced) data

Enterprise content management systems (ECMSs) combine all of these within an organizational setting. We will delve into the most important of these in greater detail.

6.1.1 Content Management System

This digital content life cycle consists of six primary states: create, update, publish, translate, archive, and retire. For example, an instance of digital content is created by one or more authors. Over time, that content may be edited. One or more individuals may provide some editorial oversight, thereby approving the content for publication. Once published that content may be superseded by another form of content and thus retired or removed from use.

Content management is an inherently collaborative process. The process often consists of the following basic roles and responsibilities:

1. Content author — responsible for creating and editing content
2. Editor — responsible for tuning the content message and the style of delivery
3. Publisher — responsible for releasing the content for consumption
4. Administrator — responsible for managing the release of the content, ultimately placing it into a repository so that it can be found and consumed

A critical aspect of content management is the ability to manage versions of content as it evolves (i.e., version control). Authors and editors often need to restore older versions of edited products because of a process failure or an undesirable series of edits.

A CMS is a set of automated processes that may support the following features:

1. Identification of all key users and their roles
2. The ability to assign roles and responsibilities to different instances of content categories or types
3. Definition of workflow tasks often coupled with messaging so that content managers are alerted to changes in content
4. The ability to track and manage multiple versions of a single instance of content
5. The ability to publish the content to a repository to support the consumption of the content

CMSs take the following forms:

1. A Web CMS is software for Web-site management, which is often what is implicitly meant by this term
2. The work of a newspaper editorial staff organization
3. A workflow for article publication
4. A DMS
5. A single source CMS — in which content is stored in chunks, within a relational database
6. CMSs usually focus on intranet-based or Internet-based corporate content including data and knowledge bases

The Georgia.gov content management Web site sports the following features:

1. Predefined templates — utilize existing templates to support the structure of atypical agency Web site.
2. HTML editors — create Web content without knowing HTML by using the built-in HTML editor. It is as simple as cutting and pasting from Microsoft Word.
3. Predefined taxonomy — use a predefined structure to organize your content, enabling customers to find information easily and consistently.
4. Georgia.gov look and feel — use Georgia's trusted E-government brand designed as a result of extensive market and constituent research.
5. Training and implementation assistance — receive on-site training and implementation assistance to ensure successful completion of your initial Georgia.gov Web-site initiative.
6. Style guide — use the Georgia.gov style guide, a detailed document defining how to structure your Web content and applications.
7. Search engine — use the Georgia.gov search engine, a robust, state-of-the-art search engine to ensure that your customers find the information they need.
8. Predeployment quality assurance and testing — receive predeployment testing services that include a spell-check of your Web content, link checking, and a review for content completeness.

The Georgia.gov style guide, some 54 pages in length and located at http://www.georgia.gov/vgn/images/portal/cit_1210/3563842style_guide. pdf, provides guidelines on logo and tagline usage, icon design, color palette usage, typography, imagery, general design, as well as text and content.

CMSs allow end users to easily add new content in the form of articles. The articles are typically entered as plaintext, perhaps with markup to indicate where other resources (such as pictures, video or audio) should be placed. Hence, CMSs are multimedia enabled. The system then uses rules to style the article, separating the display from the content, which has a number of advantages when trying to get many articles to conform to a consistent "look and feel." The system then adds the articles to a larger collection for publishing.

A popular example of this is the wiki. A *wiki* is a Web application that allows users to add content, as on an Internet forum, but also allows anyone to edit the content. The free online encyclopedia called Wikipedia was created in this manner.

Figure 6.2 shows a typical formatted page on Wikipedia.

Note the "edit this page" tab at the top. Clicking on this tab gets you the display on Figure 6.3.

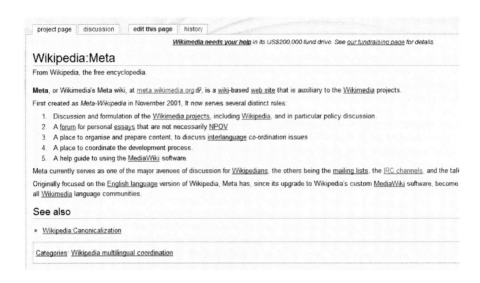

Figure 6.2 A typical formatted page on Wikipedia.

Figure 6.3 Editing the Wiki.

There are a variety of wiki engines, including UseMod, TWiki, Moin-Moin, PmWiki, and MediaWiki. A list of some of those available can be found at http://c2.com/cgi/wiki?WikiEngines.

Wikipedia, an example of a wiki, provides the following checklist to assist in selecting wiki software:

1. Who is developing it? A single person or a growing team?
2. Under what license is it distributed?
3. Who is using the wiki? A good wiki engine is likely to have a large group of existing users, and this is helpful if you need support running it.
4. Platform: should it run on a server or a local machine? Is online access needed? What OS does the machine run and is the wiki software ported to it?
5. Features for editors: easy-to-write (and powerful) formatting rules, WYSIWYG capabilities, sectional editing, easy to roll back to earlier versions, file upload, insert image, able to write complex formulae, etc.
6. Features for readers: table of contents, search, navigation bar, access statistics, article rating, and high-quality printable version.
7. User management: user personal page, personalized toolbar, and preferences.
8. Groupware features: forum, gallery, and message system.
9. Access controls: This is important for a company intranet with security considerations.
10. Be able to import external files (HTML, Microsoft Word document), export to external files (Microsoft Word document, PDF).
11. Customizable interface: Including main page, top bar, bottom bar, side bar, and skins.
12. Multilingual support.
13. Extensibility: What third-party plug-ins exist, and what mechanisms are there for creating them?
14. Portability: Are you locked into a particular package or wiki text format? Is it possible to export your text to other systems?
15. Scalability: Is it suitable for a large number of pages, or is it just lightweight wiki software? Most scalable wiki software needs a back-end database to store pages.
16. Ease of use: Is it easy to set up? Does it require PHP, SQL, and an additional Web server? Or are you looking for something simple, like a Wiki server?

The latest "hot ticket" in the content management arena is the Weblog or blog. A *blog* is a Web-based publication consisting primarily of periodic articles. Blogs range in scope from individual diaries to arms of political campaigns, media programs, and corporations. For example, Barack Obama, who is the senator from Illinois, maintains his blog at http://obama.senate.gov/blog/. They range in scale from the writings of one occasional author, to the collaboration of a large community of writers.

Many Weblogs enable visitors to leave public comments; others are non-interactive.

The format of Weblogs varies, from simple bullet lists of hyperlinks, to article summaries or complete articles with user-provided comments and ratings. Individual Weblog entries are almost always date- and time-stamped, with the newest post at the top of the page, and reader comments often appearing below it. Because incoming links to specific entries are important to many Weblogs, most have a way of archiving older entries and generating a static address for them; this static link is referred to as a *permalink*. The latest headlines, with hyperlinks and summaries, are frequently offered in Weblogs in the RSS or Atom XML format, to be read with a feed reader.

RSS is a family of XML file formats for Web syndication used by news Web sites and Weblogs. The abbreviation is used to refer to the following standards:

Rich Site Summary (RSS 0.91)
RDF Site Summary (RSS 0.9, 1.0, and 1.1)
Really Simple Syndication (RSS 2.0)

The technology behind RSS allows you to subscribe to Web sites that have provided RSS feeds; these are typically sites that change or add content regularly. To use this technology, you need to set up some type of aggregation service. You then have to subscribe to the sites that you want to get updates on. Unlike typical subscriptions to pulp-based newspapers and magazines, your RSS subscriptions are free, but they typically only give you a line or two of each article or post, along with a link to the full article or post.

The RSS formats provide Web content or summaries of Web content together with links to the full versions of the content and other metadata. This information is delivered as an XML file called *RSS feed*, *Webfeed*, *RSS stream*, or *RSS channel*. In addition to facilitating syndication, RSS allows a Web site's frequent readers to track updates on the site using a news aggregator.

RSS news readers are small programs that aggregate RSS feeds and display the story information. They allow you to scan headlines from hundreds of news sources in a central location.

A wide range of RSS readers can be easily downloaded from the Web. Some readers are Web-based although others require you to download a small software program onto your desktop. Most are free to use. (Several readers require Microsoft's .NET framework on your computer. They may be slightly more complicated to install if you do not have .NET.)

Google and Yahoo! both offer comprehensive lists of RSS readers. A few sample readers such as the following are also recommended for the purpose of evaluation:

Awasu — http://www.awasu.com/ (Windows)
Bloglines — http://bloglines.com/ (All OS, browser-based)
Amphetadesk — http://www.disobey.com/amphetadesk/ (Windows)
RSS Reader — http://www.rssreader.com/ (Windows .NET)
NetNewsWire — http://ranchero.com/netnewswire/ (Mac OS X)

The tools for editing, organizing, and publishing Weblogs are variously referred to as *content management systems*, *publishing platforms*, *Weblog software*, or simply *blogware*.

6.1.2 Document Management Systems/Electronic Document Management Systems

DMSs focus on the storage and retrieval of work documents (e.g., forms), in their original format. The key processes within the DMS are the following:

1. Feed — paper scanning or document importing.
2. Store — every organization has its own particular storage needs based on data volume, accessibility requirements, archival duration, etc. Choices include magnetic (such as typical desktop hard drives, RAID), optical (CD, DVD, WORM), magneto-optical storage technology, or a combination of these devices.
3. Indexing — tagging each document with some code for accessibility.
4. Control — one of the main advantages of an EDMS is that all documents of all types reside in the same computing environment. Yet, in the context of a company's daily operations, it is quite probable that you would want certain groups of employees to be granted access privileges to certain types of documents.
5. Workflow — the EDMS is capable of mapping a company's organizational rules in the form of access controls to the document databases. EDMS tool suites often provide the means to model their operational procedures in the form of workflow management utilities.
6. Security — protection of documents (e.g., IDs and passwords).
7. Search — An efficient EDMS will allow users to search documents via preset indices, keywords, full-text search, even via thesaurus

and synonym support. A majority of the time, filters can be applied, search criteria may be nested, and boolean and comparison operators may be used. We discuss this in more depth later.

8. Access — once you have identified the documents you wish to review, the EDMS must be capable of retrieving them fast and transparently, regardless of where they are located. Documents may be distributed in multiple databases, in multiple locations. An efficient access strategy will give the end user the impression that the documents are all stored in one location, on one computer.

9. Share — collaborative capabilities prevent end users from making duplicates of the retrieved documents.

The document management solution allows the user to deposit documents through multiple interfaces. Most users will access the DMS through a typical desktop configuration via a Web interface or an existing proprietary application. Access can also be obtained through imaging devices or through the organization's e-mail system, which archives e-mails as historical artifacts.

Search capabilities are typically built into the functionality of the DMS. Searches can be driven by a keyword search or through other designated parameters.

The Web content management interface depicts how documents within the DMS are published onto a Web site. Access through this Web content management interface would be independent of the access directly to a DMS, but defined accessibility and authentication would have to be established.

Originally, a DMS was a computer program (or set of programs) used to track and store images of paper documents. More recently, the term has been used to distinguish between imaging and RMSs that specialize in paper capture and records, respectively. DMSs commonly provide checkin, checkout, and storage and retrieval of electronic documents, often in the form of word processor files and the like.

Typical systems have the user scan-in the original paper document and store the image of the document in the DMS, although increasingly many documents start life in the digital format. The image is often given a name containing the date, and the user is often asked to type in additional tags to make finding the image easier. For instance, a user scanning-in an invoice might want to tag it with, "hardware, CompUSA invoice, 1/1/2002."

The United States Nuclear Regulatory Agency (www.nrc.gov) maintains a DMS for public use. The Agencywide Documents Access and Management System (ADAMS) is an information system that provides access to all image and text documents that the NRC has made public since

Figure 6.4   The U.S. Nuclear Regulatory Commission ADAMS CMS search interface.

November 1, 1999, as well as bibliographic records (some with abstracts and full text) that the NRC made public before November 1999. The NRC continues to add several hundred new documents daily. ADAMS permits full-text searching and enables users to view document images, download files, and print locally.

Two methods of using ADAMS are available, as shown in the following:

Web-based access enables users to search ADAMS with a Web-based search engine. New documents released during the day are added later that night. Most documents released before November 1999 are not available.

Citrix-based access enables users to access ADAMS using Citrix software, which must first be downloaded. Through the Citrix software, users may search for and retrieve documents using ADAMS features. This is different from browsing documents on the Internet and using a Web search engine. New documents are added throughout the day.

Figure 6.4 shows the ADAMS CMS interface.

A search for accidents returns a list of over 1000 documents, as shown in Figure 6.5.

ADAM and other document management systems have the look and feel of a typical Internet search engine. The methodology used to search

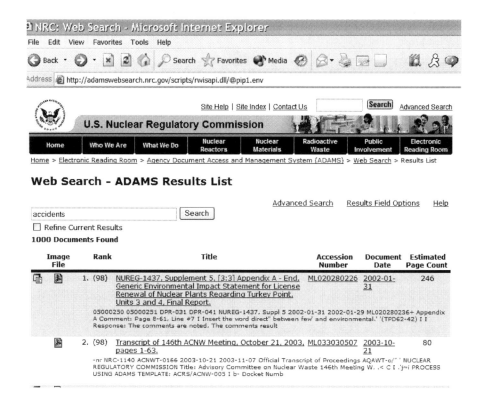

Figure 6.5   The search for accidents returns over 1000 documents.

and then display results will be of interest. The following discussion is based on the author's search for documents containing the terms "stock price" and "ethics."

Google, Vivisimo, and Metacrawler are three very different types of search tools. Google, which has indexed over 4 billion Web pages (Wong, 2004), primarily returns results based on popularity using its PageRank™ technology to calculate each page's ranking and importance. Metacrawler, on the other hand, does not search Web pages directly. Instead, it searches the results of its partners' (i.e., Google, Yahoo, Ask Jeeves, About.com, and Overture) Web directories and search engine databases and tries to provide the best results. Vivisimo is also a metasearch engine. Its "chief selling proposition" is its clustering engine, which organizes the results of the search into logical clusters or groupings.

For the researcher, the metasearch engine capability of Metacrawler and the clustering capability of Vivisimo provide superior search capabilities to Google. A researcher does not necessarily base his or her research on the popularity of a particular Web page (i.e., Google). Instead, the content and relevance of the site is of utmost importance. The value of Metacrawler is that it searches a wide variety of search engines, eliminates the duplicates, and attempts to display only the best results. It also provides a form of clustering, or categorization, although somewhat more limited than Vivisimo. In my opinion, Vivisimo's clustering technology provides its superior technical capabilities among the three search engines.

Google returns results based on importance. Vivisimo and Metacrawler are both metasearch facilities, meaning that they do not search the Internet and compile an index on their own, as does Google. Instead, they search the results of the search engine databases and Web directories of their search partners. Their goal is to improve the relevance of the search. Each of these two latter search facilities does this a bit differently.

Google's power is that it has the capability to speedily provide a wealth of related hits, although a high percentage of results will be on the fringe of what is desired. Because so many hits are returned, researchers seldom venture past the first three to five pages. As a result, it is quite possible that very relevant and important matches are overlooked. Metacrawler attempts to overcome this problem by searching multiple search engines and then uses its technology to eliminate duplicates and display the most relevant searches. Vivisimo, also a metasearch engine, has increased in popularity among users recently because of its clustering technology, which permits it to organize results by category grouping. One Vivisimo negative is that there is a timeout feature. Vivisimo will return the number of hits found within a set amount of time. It is possible to perform the same search twice, therefore, and receive a different number of hits, depending on the system load.

The three search engines' unique capabilities can be summarized as follows:

1. Google: creates its own index, primed for speed, most comprehensive.
2. Vivisimo: metasearch, clustering.
3. Metacrawler: metasearch, elimination of duplicates, attempts to find the most relevant matches, some categorization.

A comparative table appears in Table 6.1.

Vivisimo's clustering capabilities provided the best results for my research, followed by Metacrawler. Google did provide some sources worthy of note; however, I needed to spend an inordinate amount of time searching through the matches that were not of interest to me. My usual search strategy is to do a comprehensive search using multiple search engines.

The actual search rules for each search engine are proprietary and closely guarded. More than a few search engine optimization companies claim to have reengineered these search engines to discover these rules. Their goal is to sell this information to Web-site owners who desire to

Table 6.1 Search Engine Comparison

Feature	Google	Metacrawler	Vivisimo
Creates its own index	Yes	No	No
Metasearch	No	Yes	Yes
Advanced search	Yes	Yes	Yes
Boolean capability	Yes	Yes	Yes
Clustering results	No	Yes (categories on the left side of the page under the title "Are you looking for")	Yes
Ability to restrict domains	Yes	Yes	Yes
Stemming (searches for diet and dieting)	Yes	No	No
Wildcard	Yes	—	—
Search by category	Yes	No	No
Synonym search	Yes	No	No
Select search engine to search	No	No	Yes
Search within search	Yes	Yes, within clusters	Yes, by clicking on category

have their Web site placed at the top of the search results list. There was limited information available on this subject.

Table 6.2 summarizes some of the interesting special search capabilities of the three search engines.

6.1.3 Records Management Systems

RMSs manage both physical and electronic documents.

As of 2005, records management has increased interest among corporations due to new compliance regulations and statutes. Although government, legal, and healthcare entities have a strong, historical records management discipline, general record-keeping of corporate records has been poorly standardized and implemented. In addition, scandals such as the Enron and Andersen scandals, and more recently, the records-related mishaps at Morgan Stanley, have renewed interest in corporate records compliance, litigation preparedness, and issues. Statutes such as the U.S.

Table 6.2 Special Search Capabilities of Major Search Engines

Google	Vivisimo	Metacrawler
Automatic "and." A search of "Hawaii vacation" translates to "vacation and Hawaii"	Can select search from Web or directories	Can sort results by sort engine or relevance
Automatic exclusion of common words such as "where" and "how" to speed up search	link:URL can find pages that link to a specific URL	Freeform Boolean searches providing unlimited flexibility
~ Synonym search	Linktext can find pages that contain specified text on page in any place other than the image tag, link or URL	Date restrict
+ Includes essential terms	Title can find text in the title of a page	—
Numrange searches	—	—
Occurrences — can specify where to search on the page	—	—
Date restrict	—	—

Sarbanes–Oxley Act have created new concerns among corporate compliance officers that result in more standardization of records management practices within an organization.

The practice of records management involves all of the following activities:

1. Creating, approving, and enforcing records policies, including a classification system and a records retention policy
2. Developing a records storage plan, which includes the short- and long-term housing of physical records and digital information
3. Identifying existing and newly created records, classifying them, and then storing them according to standard operating procedures
4. Monitoring the access and circulation of records within and even outside of an organization
5. Executing a retention policy to archive and destroy records according to operational needs, operating procedures, statues, and regulations

Trustworthy records are essential for an organization to meet its legal and internal business needs. Reliability, authenticity, integrity, and usability are the characteristics used to describe trustworthy records from a records management perspective.

Creating and maintaining trustworthy records requires resources. Organizations need to conduct a risk analysis to balance the level of trustworthiness of records against costs and risks.

Because companies are moving quickly to Web-based DMSs, a discussion of trustworthy records would be beneficial. Who better to provide this information than the U.S. National Archives and Records Administration (http://www.archives.gov/records-mgmt/policy/managing-web-records. html)? Billions of letters, photographs, video and audio recordings, drawings, maps, treaties, posters, and other informative materials exist that tell the stories of America's history as a nation. From the Declaration of Independence, the Constitution, and the Bill of Rights to census records that account for every citizen — the preservation of important American documents helps illustrate what happened in the United States before and after we were born.

The National Archives and Records Administration (NARA) is America's record keeper. NARA is the government agency that not only preserves documents and materials related to the United States but also makes sure people can access the information.

The characteristics of trustworthy records include those given in the following subsections:

6.1.3.1 Reliability

A reliable Web site is one whose content can be trusted as a full and accurate representation of the transactions, activities, or facts to which it attests and, therefore, can be depended upon in the course of subsequent transactions or activities.

6.1.3.2 Authenticity

An authentic Web site is one that is proved what it purports to be and to have been created by the organization with which it is identified.

Web-site-related records should be created by individuals who have direct knowledge of the facts or by instruments routinely used within the business to conduct the transaction.

To demonstrate the authenticity of a Web site, organizations should implement and document policies and procedures that control the creation, transmission, receipt, and maintenance of Web-site records to ensure that records creators are authorized and identified and that records are protected against unauthorized addition, deletion, and alteration (e.g., via hacking).

6.1.3.3 Integrity

The integrity of a Web-content record refers to its being complete and unaltered.

Web management policies and procedures for updating and modifying Web sites should be created. The International Standards Organization (ISO) specifies that records systems maintain audit trails or other elements sufficient to demonstrate that records were effectively protected from unauthorized alteration or destruction. The Web management policies should prescribe how changes to the Web site are to be documented.

Another aspect of integrity is the structural integrity of a Web site's content-related records. The structure of a Web site, that is, its physical and logical format and the relationships between the pages and content elements composing the site should remain physically or logically intact. Failure to maintain the Web site's structural integrity may impair its reliability and authenticity.

6.1.3.4 Usability

A usable Web site is one that can be located, retrieved, presented, and interpreted. In retrieval and use, you should be able to directly connect the Web site to the business activity or transaction that produced it. You should be able to identify both the site and its content within the context of broader business activities and functions.

The links between content, contextual, and structural Web-site-related records that document organizational Web-site activities should be maintained. These contextual linkages should provide an understanding of the transactions that created and used them.

6.1.3.5 What Are the Records Management Risks Associated with Web Sites?

From a records management perspective, risk relates to: (1) challenge to the trustworthiness of the records (e.g., legal challenge) that can be expected over the life of the record and (2) unauthorized loss or destruction of records. Consequences are measured by the degree of loss that the agency or citizens would suffer if the trustworthiness of the Web-site-related records could not be verified or if there were unauthorized loss or destruction.

Examples of records management-related risks associated with Web sites are mainly technical risks. Loss of information could result from the following:

1. An inability to document or validate transactions that occur via a Web-site front end
2. An inability to reconstruct views of Web content that was created dynamically and existed only virtually for the time that they were viewed
3. Compromise of transactions
4. An inability to track Web-assisted policy development or document decisions relating to Web operations

A variety of negative programmatic consequences can result from any of the following technical risks:

1. Litigation or liability if an organization is unable to verify what was on its site at a given point in time
2. Impairment of program operations or an inability to detect or punish fraud, false statements, or other illegal behavior because of a lack of valid or probative records
3. An inability to produce records that document accountability and stewardship of materials posted to the Web site and dissemination of misinformation
4. Financial losses due to compromising rights
5. Compromise of the organization's mission
6. Negative reactions of stakeholders
7. Unfavorable media attention

6.1.3.6 How Can I Conduct a Records Management Risk Assessment?

A risk assessment should address the possible consequences of untrust-worthy, lost, or unrecoverable records, including the legal risk and financial costs of losses, the likelihood that a damaging event will occur, and the costs of taking corrective actions. Organizations should have formal risk assessment procedures that may be applied to Web-site operations.

The assessment factors may include the following:

1. *Records management threats* relate to the likelihood of experiencing technical risks (e.g., risks of unauthorized destruction of Web-site-related records, litigation risks associated with inability to reconstruct views of Web sites at specific points in time, risks associated with inability to document Web-site policy decisions, etc.).
2. *Visibility* is the level of active public awareness of the operations of a Web site.

3. *Consequences* describe the level of negative organizational, economic, or programmatic impact if Web records are untrustworthy, lost, or unrecoverable.
4. *Sensitivity* characterizes the organization's assessment of the importance of Web-site operations.

The results of an assessment will support programs by providing a basis for determining what types of Web-site records should be created, how they should be maintained, and for how long. The assessment will help organizations ensure that the level of risk is tolerable and that resources are properly allocated. Assessment results can also aid in the development of Web-site records schedules.

6.1.3.7 How Do I Track Changes to Web-Site Content Pages between Backups?

Four types of changes can occur to a Web site's content between backups, which are as follows:

1. Changes to the content of an individual page without changing its placement in the overall organization of the Web site
2. Wholesale replacement of an individual page (or sections of pages) without changing its placement in the overall organization of the Web site
3. Changes in location of a page (or groups of pages)
4. Combinations of changes of the first three types

Changes of the first two types (i.e., changes to content without changing the page's placement in the overall organization of the Web site) can be treated as a version-control issue. You must decide how to best keep track of the versions of content pages.

The most fundamental, nonautomated approach to tracking Web-site content, particularly for relatively stable sites, is to "print and file" a record-keeping copy in the manual recordkeeping system. Another nonautomated approach to version control is to annotate changes of content pages as a comment in the HTML coding. The comment, which will not appear when the page is displayed in a browser, could indicate when the page was changed (e.g., <!--Updated by MDG on 03/02/05-->) or could reference the page that was replaced wholesale (e.g., <!--This page replaced content page Introduction_1.html on 09/10/05-->). Another manual approach would be to maintain a log file of content changes of the first two types of changes. (Keep in mind that neither of these approaches would allow you to actually reconstruct views presented at a particular time. This may be found acceptable as per your risk assessment).

Alternatively, you may use CMS to track versions of Web content in the first two cases. CMS would also offer limited page view reconstruction capabilities — default settings for the databases that support most CMS software would retain only recent changes.

You can handle major changes to the site's directory structure by producing a new site map at the time of major revision. This could be accomplished in a manual or automated manner.

One tool is a type of search engine called *Web harvester*. Also called a *spider* or *crawler*, a *harvester* is a program that visits Web sites and reads their pages and other information to create entries for a search engine index. You can use harvester software to identify changes to Web-site content and to gather content related to specific site units.

6.1.3.8 When Preserving Long-Term Web Content Records, How Can I Treat Hyperlinks?

Web content pages use hyperlinks to: (1) jump to another location within the page, (2) jump to a location on other pages within the Web site, or (3) jump to a page on another Web site. Depending on the preservation strategy chosen, it is possible, and in many cases likely, that these hyperlinks will not continue to function in the preservation copy of the Web content records. If the site does not follow external link-liability-transference policies such as those employing pop-up window notifications, agencies might want to use the following suggestions, to enhance the usability of preservation copies of long-term Web content records. Table 6.3 provides some alternatives for handling this situation.

Another alternative would be to produce what is in effect a bibliography for all of the hyperlinks referenced within the content pages composing a site. List all of the URLs referenced by hyperlinks, along with a description of the hyperlinked page (much as in the comment used in the previously suggested method).

6.1.3.9 Digital Asset Management

DAM is similar to RMS but focused on multimedia resources such as images, audio, and video.

DAM is still a new market with rapid technical evolution; hence, many different types of systems will be labeled as DAM systems, although they are designed to address slightly different problems or were created for a specific industry. A variety of commercial systems for DAM are available, and numerous groups are trying to establish standards for DAM.

Table 6.3 Hyperlink Handling

Internal target hyperlinks	For hyperlinks that simply send the user to a different location within the same page (aka internal target), no additional work is required, as the link will continue to function when the content page is interpreted by a browser application.
Hyperlinks not under local records management control	For hyperlinks that send the user to either a different page or another Web site that is not under the organization's records management control, it will be necessary to require Web-site content developers to modify the HTML syntax of Web content pages containing such hyperlinks on a day-forward basis. This modification would include the insertion of an HTML comment after the hyperlink that described, in plain English, the name of the site (and perhaps portion of site) or the page to which the hyperlink transfers. For example, the hyperlink in the records management portion of the NARA Web site discussing DoD 5015.2-STD that links to the Joint Interoperability Test Command's Web site, expressed in HTML (emphasis added) as z <a href="http://jitc.fhu.disa.mil/recmgt/#standard">Do D Standard 5015.2</a> would be modified, inserting an appropriate title attribute, per accessibility requirements, that describes it as follows: <a href="/global_pages/exit.html?link=http://jitc.fhu.dis a.mil/recmgt/#standard" title="Joint Interoperability Test Command's 5015.2 - STD Records Management Application Design Criteria Standard">DoD Standard 5015.2</a>
Hyperlink to new page within same Web site	When a page includes a hyperlink that sends the user to another page *in the same Web site*, it would be necessary to insert comments describing the hyperlink only when the site was not being scheduled *in toto* for the same retention (and those comments could reference the series containing the destination of the hyperlink).

DAM systems generally support functions for ingesting, managing, searching, retrieving, and archiving of assets. DAM systems may also include version control and asset format-conversion capabilities (i.e., dynamically downsizing a large, high-resolution image for display on a Web site). DAM systems are related to and can be considered a superset of CMSs.

DAM is a combination of workflow, software, and hardware that organizes and retrieves a company's digital assets.

There are three categories of DAM systems which are as follows:

1. Brand asset management systems, with a focus on facilitation of content reuse within large organizations.
2. Library asset management systems, with a focus on storage and retrieval of large amounts of infrequently changing media assets, for example, in video or photo archiving.
3. Production asset management systems, with a focus on storage, organization, and revision control of frequently changing digital assets, for example, in digital media production.

From a technical perspective, DAM applications are divided into two basic categories, media catalogs and asset repositories (Ross, 1999).

The primary characteristic of media catalogs is the utilization of proxies, such as thumbnails, in an indexed database that can be quickly searched by keyword. The actual source files are left untouched and under control of the operating system. The benefits of media catalogs include low cost, ease of installation and administration, and scalability across multiple divisions of an enterprise.

Because media catalogs do not actually manage the content themselves, anyone with system access can typically view, change, move, or delete any content element. This usually precludes such features as checkin or checkout of content, rights management, and automatic versioning (for example, the latest version of a print). Media catalogs can also become sluggish with very large catalogs, especially if distributed across multiple servers or geographic locations.

In asset repositories, the content itself is physically stored inside a secure database. This results in a host of benefits, including security levels, replication, referential integrity, and centralized data management. Also included are the comforts of full hierarchical storage management and disaster recovery.

6.2 THE SEMANTIC WEB

Tim Berners-Lee, who invented the World Wide Web as well as HTML, also came up the idea of the Semantic Web, as shown in Figure 6.6. The *Semantic Web* is a synthesis of all corporate and external data, including results from data-mining activities, hypermedia, knowledge systems, etc., which use a common interface that makes data easily accessible by all (e.g., suppliers, customers, and employees).

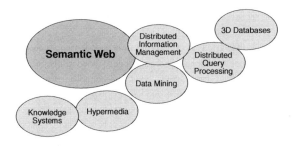

Figure 6.6   The Semantic Web.

The Semantic Web is sometimes called the "Defined Web" and is the ultimate repository of all content and knowledge on the Web. It uses XML (extensible markup language, a formalized version of HTML) to tag information on intranets, extranets, and the Internet.

Tim Berners-Lee explains the Semantic Web as follows:

> At the doctor's office, Lucy instructed her Semantic Web agent through her handheld Web browser. The agent promptly retrieved information about mom's prescribed treatment from the doctor's agent, looked up several lists of providers, and checked for the ones *in-plan* for mom's insurance within a 20-mi radius of her home and with a rating of excellent or very good on trusted rating services. It then began trying to find a match between available appointment times (supplied by the agents of individual providers through their Web sites) and Pete's and Lucy's busy schedules.

Hewlett-Packard's Semantic Web research group frequently circulates items of interest such as news articles, software tools, and links to Web sites. They call these *snippets*, or *information nuggets* (Cayzer, 2004). Because e-mail is not the ideal medium for this type of content, they needed to find a way to technique for decentralized, informal knowledge management. They began a research project to create a system that was capable of aggregating, annotating, indexing, and searching a community's snippets. The required characteristics of this system include the following:

1. Ease of use and capture.
2. Decentralized aggregation — snippets will be in a variety of locations and formats. It will be necessary to integrate them and perform a global search over the result.

3. Distributed knowledge — consumer should be able to add value to the information by enriching snippets at the point of use by adding ratings, annotations, etc.

4. Flexible data model — snippets are polymorphic. The system should be able to handle e-mail, Web pages, documents, text fragments, images, etc.

5. Extensible — it should be possible to extend the snippet data schema to model the changing world.

6. Inferencing — it should be possible to infer new metadata from old. For example, a machine should know that a snippet about a particular HP Photosmart model is about a digital camera.

Some have suggested that blogs make the ideal tools for this type of content and knowledge management. However, today's blogging tools offer only three of the six capabilities mentioned. Traditional blogging has many limitations, but the most important limitation is that metadata is used only for headline syndication in a blog. Metadata is not extensible, not linked to a risk, is a flexible data model, and not capable of supporting vocabulary mixing and inferencing.

The researchers, therefore, looked to the Semantic Web for a solution. As we have discussed, the premise of the Semantic Web is that data can be shared and reused across applications, enterprise, and community boundaries. RSS1.0 (web.resource.org/rss/1.0) is a Semantic Web vocabulary that provides a way to express and integrate with rich information models. The Semantic Web standard Resource Description Framework (RDF) specifies a Web-scale information modeling format (www.w3.org/RDF). Using these tools, they came up with a prototype (http://www.semanticblogging.org/blojsom-hp/blog/default/) for creating what they called a *Semantic Blog*. The prototype has some interesting searching capabilities. For example, snippets can be searched for either through their own attributes (e.g., "I am interested in snippets about HP.") or through the attributes of their attached blog entry (e.g., "I am interested in snippets captured by Bob.").

6.2.1 The eXtensible Rule Markup Language

The Semantic Web community has developed a language — the eXtensible Rule Markup Language (XRML) — to be able to process rules implicit in Web pages that cannot now be processed within XML (Lee and Sohn, 2003). Figure 6.7 provides a comparison between HTML, XML, and XRML.

XRML has the following three components:

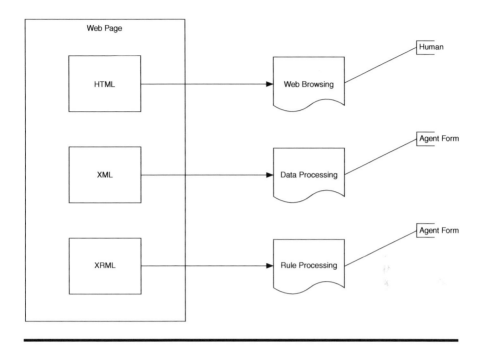

Figure 6.7 XRML and earlier technologies.

1. *Rule Identification Markup Language (RIML)* — the metaknowledge expressed in RIML should identify the existence of implicit rules in the hypertexts on the Web.
2. *Rule Structure Markup Language (RSML)* — rules in knowledge-based systems must be represented in a formal structure so they can be processed with inference engines.
3. *Rule Triggering Markup Language (RTML)* — RTML defines the conditions that trigger certain rules.

XRML provides a tool to assist the convergence of knowledge-based systems (artificial intelligence) and knowledge management systems. http://xrml.kaist.ac.kr/xrml_download/XRML-Ver1.doc represents a specification for XRML language design to achieve knowledge-sharing between humans and the software agent. This language will be used as a basis for concrete implementations of the functionality described in the XRML paper.

6.3 WHERE DO WE GO NEXT?

Chapter 1 through Chapter 6 took the reader through the paces of converting data to information. We also delved into the tenets and techniques of KM.

In Chapter 7, we are going to get into the nitty-gritty of business intelligence, which is the distillation of all the previous chapters.

References

Cayzer, S., Semantic blogging and decentralized knowledge management, *Communications of the ACM, 47*(12), December 2004.

Lee, J.K. and Sohn, M.M., The eXtensible Rule Markup Language, *Communications of the ACM, 46*(5), May 2003.

Ross, T., Digital Asset Management: The Art of Archiving, September 1999. Retrieved August 20, 2005 from http://www.techexchange.com/thelibrary/DAM.html.

Simplicity and Enterprise Search, 2003. Retrieved June 26, 2005 from http://www.google.com/enterprise/pdf/google_simplicity_enterprise_wp.pdf.

Wong, M., Company Must Now Focus on Competition, New Technology, *Monterey County Herald,* August 20, 2004. Retrieved August 20, 2005 from http://www.montereyherald.com/mld/montereyherald/business/9450718.htm.

7

BUSINESS INTELLIGENCE

Business intelligence (BI) is a set of methodologies and technologies for gathering, storing, analyzing, and providing access to data to help users make better business decisions. The goal of BI is to transform data into information and ultimately into knowledge and wisdom. BI is usually implemented to gain sustainable competitive advantage and is a valuable core competence in some instances.

In the first six chapters of this book, we addressed some of the categories of tools and techniques that commonly fall under the BI rubric. These include:

1. *OLAP (online analytical processing), sometimes simply called* analytics *(based on dimensional analysis and the hypercube or "cube")*
2. *Scorecarding, dashboarding, and data visualization*
3. *Data warehouses*
4. *DM — data mining*
5. *Document warehouses*
6. Text mining
7. *EIS — executive information systems*
8. *DSS — decision support systems*

In this chapter, we will delve a bit deeper into the nature and value of BI. First let us address where BI is going. Brunson (2005) lists ten trends in BI:

1. *Taking data quality very seriously.* Gartner predicted that the market for data quality software and services will grow 20 to 30 percent annually through 2007. Data quality is more than just entering the data correctly. Management now realizes that data quality must be "baked" into the processes that stage data for analysis.

2. *Infrastructure standardization and consolidation.* Companies tend not to know how much they spend on BI and data warehousing. The reason for this is that these efforts are usually undertaken in silos, where each business domain creates its own solution. Standardizing and consolidating BI and warehousing are easier said than done because it involves more than just technology. It also involves political and organizational issues.

3. *Offshore sourcing.* Sending BI and warehousing work offshore requires some careful planning because it requires more business knowledge and customization than other types of projects. In spite of significant cost savings, some companies are finding some disadvantages in this trend, including quality problems and communications issues. Most recently, onshore companies have begun developing capabilities that broaden the issues surrounding the on-site versus off-site versus offshore issue.

4. *Strategic approach to information.* Very few companies have embraced the "data as asset" philosophy although there will always be a small group of people within an organization that recognizes the strategic value of information. Although companies might not be implementing BI and data warehousing on an enterprisewide basis, they are being incorporated in — and have become a critical component of — other strategic systems.

5. *Regulatory compliance as a driver for BI and data warehousing.* Sarbanes–Oxley, environmental, and data-privacy legislative and regulatory directives have fundamentally shifted management's view on the need for high-quality data and the BI systems to analyze this data. Regulatory compliance, therefore, has become a major impetus driving BI efforts.

6. *Elevating the enterprise data integration discussion.* Many organizations have already made the decision on how to promote effective data integration. There are a variety of choices: ETL, which is an acronym for extract, transform, and load (Chapter 6 has a detailed discussion of this); and enterprise application integration (EAI) is the use of software and architectural principles to integrate two or more enterprise computer applications. EAI is related to middleware technologies such as message-oriented middleware (MOM), and data representation technologies such as eXtensible Makup Language (XML). Newer EAI technologies involve using Web services as part of service-oriented architecture as a means of integration.

7. *Educating the end user.* Gartner suggests that it is as important to train users in how to analyze the data as how to use the BI toolsets.

8. *Master data management.* Master or reference data defines core entities, such as customers, products, and suppliers. Because enterprise data is frequently siloed throughout the organization, master data may have become scattered across the enterprise. In addition, different domains may define *customer* in different ways. Organizational and political issues, such as who "owns" the master data, often get in the way of developing an enterprisewide "repository." It should be noted that this problem is similar to the one experienced in the 1980s when databases were first being integrated within the organization and the issue of centralized versus decentralized IT departments was being debated.

9. *Powerful new entrants to the BI and data warehousing market.* Enterprise resource planning (ERP) and customer relationship management (CRM) vendors such as SAP, Oracle, and Siebel see a profitable opportunity in providing what was missing from their original solutions.

10. *Actionable BI.* Organizations want more than strategy from their BI. They want to be able to use the information for more tactical decision-making purposes. For example, if they see a problem in their supply chain they want to know how they can fix the problem.

7.1 COMPETITIVE ADVANTAGE AND BI

How prepared are the workers of the future? Reports over the past few years on adult and student performance in math, geography, and other areas present a less-than-reassuring picture:

1. 75 percent of American adults cannot point to the Persian Gulf on a map.
2. 61 percent cannot find Massachusetts.
3. 60 percent of 13-year-old Americans can solve two-step math problems.

Each year, the United States graduates well over 700,000 high school students who cannot read at the fourth-grade level. It is no wonder that the nation repeatedly finishes dead last in comparative studies of math and science skills.

Foreign students now earn nearly half of all graduate degrees in the United States in science, technology, and engineering.

Saying that our scientific and technical capacity is beginning to atrophy even as other nations are developing their own human capital, 15 leading business organizations recently called for doubling the number of science, technology, engineering, and mathematics graduates by the year 2015. "The critical situation in American innovation threatens to undermine our standard of living at home and our leadership in the world," said John J. Castellani, president of Business Roundtable (http://www.businessroundtable.org.). Albert Shanker, former president of the American Federation of Teachers, says "we are as bad off as it seems. The evidence is very clear and is incontrovertible."

Welcome to the workplace of tomorrow. This book is certainly not a sociological treatise on what is wrong with American education. These sad statistics are mentioned only because a corporation's foundation rests on the skill of its workers. If the foundation is weak, the corporation will falter. And in spite of American industry's investment to the tune of billions a year for teaching employees the basic skills that should have been learned in school, the outlook is still bleak.

An antidote to this corporate woe is intelligent systems. Savvy organizations have long realized that technology could be used to assist white-collar workers in performing their functions more productively and more accurately. We need not dwell on the knowledge amplification abilities of computers to see that these systems have become more than a nicety in American corporations. It has become a necessity. But the coming dearth of talented and able workers will make it even more necessary to automate functions that have been deemed marginally automatable. These are the functions marked by reasoning and logic. As John Diebold, a well-known industry pundit, puts it: "You got a lot of people showing very elegant sets of figures all worked out in great plans, with the same sort of lack of judgment you would have had without the computers." Here are the workers that need to be assisted if American corporations are to stay their current competitive course.

But is it enough to stay the current course? With global competition intensifying and closing in rapidly, will we wind up, as *USA Today* so succinctly put it, as "an easy target in the slow lane"?

7.2 USING INFORMATION TECHNOLOGY TO GATHER INTELLIGENCE

The term *competitive intelligence* is very much on the tip of everyone's tongue in today's economic maelstrom. The majority, if not all, of American companies collect some sort of information about the direction that their competitors are taking. What few realize, though, is that competitive intelligence is really only part of a larger view of the business world we live in. This view is called *business intelligence*.

Competitive intelligence is a subset of BI and, as a subset, it is not the complete picture. Herbert E. Meyer, noted author and consultant, as well as past vice chairman of the U.S. National Intelligence Council, calls BI the corporate equivalent of radar (1987). As with radar, the business environment must be continually scanned to avoid danger and seize opportunities. Meyer describes BI as the other half of strategic planning. Once the plan is completed, BI monitors its implementation and assists in making strategic course corrections along the way.

BI is not just looking at your competition, but seeing all the changes around you — including those related to politics, consumer affairs, and even environmental issues. All these influence the long-term future of the company. The use of competitive intelligence transcends industry boundaries and, if used correctly, provides the organization with an immediate advantage.

No two companies will implement competitive intelligence system in the same way.

7.3 QUAKER OATS AND FRITO-LAY

Perhaps the department with the biggest need to digest huge amounts of information is corporate marketing. Aside from the product or service being marketed, it is the efforts of the marketing department that will make the biggest impact on the profitability of a company. It stands to reason that providing marketers with the appropriate tools and techniques will most certainly enhance their efforts and, in doing so, the bottom line.

Quaker Oats, acquired by PepsiCo in 2001, is a leading multibillion-dollar international food manufacturer of cereals, pancake mixes, snacks, frozen pizza, and pet foods. From a marketing perspective, this diversity of products makes it difficult to perform the necessary marketing analysis. All of these forces led Quaker Oats to build an automated decision-support tool. With its plethora of functions and uses, *Mikey* is a good example of that category of BI systems called the *executive information system.*

Mikey gets its name from the famous Quaker Oats commercial of a bygone era in which a finicky little boy tries a Quaker cereal and likes it. Mikey was developed for the ad hoc query capabilities of large corporate marketing bases and utilized a set of products from Information Resources (http://www.infores.com.). Due to its distributive nature, Mikey quickly became Quaker's central coordinating facility for the creation of distribution and marketing plans, production requirements, and financial estimates.

Quaker built a robust marketing system, the components of which include business review reporting, marketing planning, ad hoc reporting, general information, and utilities. The business review reporting component produces standard reports based on the company's historical sales and comparisons with competitors. The standard reports can be generated for an extensive range of market, brand, time and measure selections, or time aggregations.

The ad hoc reporting component allows marketing users to essentially write their own marketing analyses programs. This permits them to look at the data and create their own brand or market aggregates.

The market planning module permits the marketing department to review the marketing performance of any particular product. Data stored and able to be analyzed here include such things as package weight, cases, cost of the product to the company, price, and advertising budget. Mikey understands the relationships among all these items. In the planning mode, if marketing staff decide to alter one of these variables — for example, package weight — the system will automatically change the other relevant components in the mix.

Frito-Lay, another subsidiary of PepsiCo, makes corn chips, potato chips, and tortilla chips. This is an extremely competitive market, with much of the competition coming at the local and regional levels. With hundreds of product lines and thousands of stores, a mountain of data is produced on a daily basis. To get a leg up on the competition, Frito-Lay needed to be able to collect, digest, and then act on that mound of information quickly.

Frito-Lay's solution was a combination of advanced technologies. This included scanner data along with sales information from field staff, all combined on a sophisticated network, encompassing handheld computers and a private satellite communications network connecting the distribution sites, ultimately accessible through a decision-support system.

The idea of electronic data entry by the sales force dates back to the late 1970s, but it was not until 1989 that Frito-Lay saw their vision become reality. By then, the company had equipped more than 10,000 sales representatives with handheld computers developed with Fujitsu at a cost of more than $40 million.

These handheld computers, called *bricks* by Frito-Lay, are used to track inventories at retail stores as well as to enter orders. The bricks are connected to miniprinters in all delivery trucks. At the end of the day, all sales data collected at stores that day are sent to the central data center at the company's headquarters by way of distributed computers at the various distribution centers.

Frito-Lay built a total intelligence system that could be customized at every level in the company. As the network developed, the company realized it could shift from a national marketing strategy to one that targeted local consumers. This is known as *micromarketing*.

Employees using the system run the gamut, from marketing support to the CEO. On one occasion, the CEO noticed red numbers on his screen. This indicated that sales were down in the central region. Quickly calling up another screen, he located the source of the problem in Texas. Continuing on this hunt, he tracked the red numbers to a specific sales division and finally to a chain of stores. Apparently, a local company had successfully introduced a new white-corn chip that was eating into Frito-Lay's market share in the location. Frito-Lay immediately put a white-corn version of Tostitos into production, which appeared on shelves a few months later.

A typical sales manager is required to pull together sales information from a variety of sources. In some cases, this took weeks to assemble and had to be obtained from telephone calls. In other cases, the data was simply not available. With Frito-Lay's infomarketing system, this information is immediately available by brand, by type of store, or even by package size. The sales manager is able to obtain results from the best or the worst of sales representatives in his or her territory as well as information on pricing moves by competitors. The manager can compare the results of sales reps' performance with that of the previous week, the previous year, as well as with current targets. The sales manager can even compare products sales in different markets, such as supermarket versus convenience stores.

The significance of these systems is that they achieve positive returns on a multitude of levels. Frito-Lay's infomarketing system has affected every level of staff and every layer of the corporate hierarchy. What originally started out as a mechanism to reduce the overhead of the sales rep in the field has turned into a bonanza of information for the marketing staff back home, has cut down on administrative overhead at the home office, has fine-tuned the production cycle by providing timely information, and has even provided an EIS for the senior executives in the company. This system is pervasive.

7.4   THE VALUE OF EXECUTIVE INFORMATION SYSTEMS

Executive information systems are hands-on tools that focus, filter, and organize information to make more effective use of that information. The principle behind these systems is that by using information more effectively and strategically, a company can ultimately increase profitability. The goals of any EIS should be:

1. To reduce the amount of data bombarding the executive
2. To increase the relevance, timeliness, and usability of the information that reaches the executive
3. To focus a management team on critical success factors
4. To enhance executive follow-through and communication with others
5. To track the earliest of warning indicators: competitive moves, customer demands, and more

Many EIS systems are based on the paper-based briefing book, long a fixture in executive chambers. Its purpose is to advise senior executives of critical issues and the status of key projects within the organization. The problem with paper reports is that they usually arrive too late for preventive or corrective action and do not provide a format conducive to in-depth investigation. There is also no way that an executive can ask questions to get more detailed information. Thus, the briefing book is supplemented in most companies with monthly status meetings just to address these deficiencies.

This lack of information results in an organization's executives spending approximately 80 percent of their time in attending these status meetings. If one adds in the trickle-down requirement of rolling information down to the staff level, then these additional "one-on-ones" and roll-down meetings add overhead to a firm, forcing it to spend more time reading about being competitive that actually being competitive.

In many companies, at least part of the problem is being addressed by automating the briefing book. There are many advantages to an automated briefing book. Each executive can receive a personalized selection of reports and charts, reducing the amount of relevant information he or she sees. In addition, each executive can set up variables responding to acceptable tolerances. For example, an automobile executive wishes to flag any line of car for which the company's market share falls below 25 percent. Because executives often like to see facts in context, automated briefing books should have the capability of comparing information on a competitive or historical basis. For example, looking at current sales data as the latest event in a continuum indicates whether sales volume is heading up or down. Similarly, executives usually want to compare information with goals, budgets, and forecasts, as well as with information stored on the competition.

Perhaps the biggest obstacle to upward reporting is that the senior executive is only privy to information on a monthly basis. In an age of stiff competition but easy access to distribution channels, a fast reaction time to an event may make a major difference to the bottom line. This "information float" — the time it takes for information to wend its way up through the channels to senior management — can be nearly eliminated by use of this category of BI software.

Once a significant variance is identified within a briefing book report, the executive must be able to investigate the variance in much more detail and from multiple perspectives. It is not enough to know that profits have deviated from the goal by 7 percent at the consolidated level. Some business units might be over this goal, and others might be well under the goal. The executive must have some facility to answer questions such as: What makes up the deviation? Is it a faltering distribution channel? Are there competitive problems in an established product? Is it a failure in a particular geographic area, in a particular product line, or in one customer grouping? To do this, a multidimensional knowledge base designed to support the managerial perspective of financial performance must be made available.

Briefing book information is a synthesis of information gathered from the far-flung corners of an organization. Geac (www.geac.com.) refers to this as the *financial value chain*. This includes processes from payroll, inventory, procurement through process management and, ultimately, into the decision-making strategic planning and forecasting management set of processes.

Universal Studios Hollywood (USH), which is part of media and entertainment giant NBC Universal, is an example of a company that is taking advantage of software that enables automation of the financial value chain.

Universal comprises seven distinct businesses: operations, entertainment, ticketing, food service, merchandising, maintenance, and real estate management. They wanted to be able to easily do mission critical activities such as category and channel management, labor scheduling optimization, and providing real-time visibility into their key performance indicators (KPI). Similar to many companies, Universal was suffering from fragmented data sources and practices across different business units.

Their goal was to transform their organization from one based on spreadsheets and data gathering to one that spends 80 percent of its time on analysis and 20 percent on data gathering.

The company had already invested in a data warehouse solution to track ticketing information but wanted to add on robust budgeting functionality to quickly and successfully do scenario modeling for two hundred venues across seven businesses. Geac MPC was implemented in 2002, along with an ERP solution that would feed aggregated P&L performance data into Geac MPC for financial reporting. The Geac solution is also used to build daily budgets, which are then fed back into the data warehouse solution and to the ERP solution at the monthly level.

Geac MPC sits on Microsoft SQL Server and talks directly to their ERP and is well-integrated to their data warehouse. They use this synergy of BI systems for real-time KPI reporting and a complete focus on process management. Universal is also building KPI dashboards that will link directly to monthly or quarter-to-go analysis, show top-level and detailed department P&Ls, enable dynamic month-to-date and year-to-date calculations, and provide standard reporting templates. This solution has provided the company with real-time insights into both leading and lagging KPIs, as well as detailed category and sales channel penetration and scenario-enabled modeling, with detail on both risk management and variance analysis. The company's source systems are completely integrated with financial process controls.

7.5 THE SCIENCE OF GATHERING BUSINESS INTELLIGENCE

Frito-Lay, Quaker Oats, and Universal Hollywood use a first-class set of BI tools and procedures to collect, collate, and reassemble internal and external data to provide enough information to perform competitive decision making.

The systems, which have been refined to the point of providing these companies tailored, filtered, and usable information, required an intensive two-level effort to create. On the first level was the development of the underlying technological infrastructure, permitting the information to be distributed to, and analyzed by, the appropriate parties. On a higher level was the effort required to determine the depth and breadth of the information that would be required.

Sitting 100 people in a room with access to every newspaper, journal, magazine, and book that has ever been published will produce only disconnected tidbits of information. Virtually every piece of information in these journals, magazines, books, and newspapers is available online through any of a myriad of information vendors for a fee or free via the Internet.

With merely a PC and a modem, it is possible for farmers in Idaho to ascertain long-term weather conditions and for businessmen to download information on products, competitors, or trends.

Even with easy access to this wealth of information, however, you still do not have intelligence. Take the case of a major pharmaceutical company. Over a one-year period, they spent more than $10 million in online downloads. According to the CEO, virtually all of this information was worthless. That is because they did not have the ability or know-how to turn this plethora of information into intelligence. It is a capability that requires the use of tools and techniques to be able to coordinate and correlate discrete bits of information into intelligence.

Perhaps the biggest stumbling block in the process of creating BI is in deciding where it is to be done. Because the creation of this intelligence relies on the downloading of information, the task is often delegated to the information technology department. This was the case with the pharmaceutical company mentioned. It turned out to be an expensive mistake for them.

A profile of a department most likely to succeed in this endeavor will include the following abilities: being able to work with technology to gather the raw information, having the writing talent to present it in an understandable fashion to management, and possessing the sociopolitical skills to draw conclusions from the analyses that will be accepted by the diverse and often conflicting groups that make up a modern corporation.

This is the tactic that Herbert Meyer and his partner Mike Pincus take when advising their corporate clients on how to build an intelligence-gathering department. They look for people with library skills, technical skills, and familiarity with the company's business. They also look for someone who has an "in" with the CEO, so that the results do not get politicized.

Part of the problem with intelligence is that when it is done well it tends to offset the bad judgment that often comes from executive support people. According to Pincus, these executive support management people feel threatened by intelligence because it tends to offset their own bad opinions. Where you have bad management advice, you have to bring someone into the unit who has the social, political, and corporate capabilities to be able to move around in that environment without upsetting people and causing them to feel threatened.

The first step involved in building an intelligence unit is to develop a profile of the company. This is really a "needs analysis," which will document the products and services a company manufactures or performs, its goals and priorities, as well as the requirements for competitive intimation. Basically, this will be a comprehensive list of categories of information that the company must monitor to be competitive. Examples of categories are suppliers, markets, customers, and so on. The profile also exposes the irrelevant information that the company may be tracking. In addition to all of this, an assessment must be made of the cultural climate of a company. How is information passed up and down the corporate hierarchy? What political machinations are in place that could possibly affect, or even impede, the information flow?

With this profile in hand, the next step is to perform an intelligence audit. This is the process that determines if the right people are getting the right information. It is really a two-step process. First, as one would expect, the information needs uncovered during the process of developing the profile are satisfied by locating the proper online source that contains that piece of information. As already demonstrated, virtually anything ever written can be located via the Internet. The trick is in being able to first locate it, then being able to download it and, finally, to process it. This is where the second step of the intelligence audit comes in. The company's technological mentality should be assessed. What kind of technical expertise does the company have? What are they comfortable with? From the information collected in this process, it is possible to develop a technological solution that would best satisfy the needs and capabilities of a particular organization.

Probably the most crucial step in this entire process is in training selected personnel in how to convert the information obtained into BI. This is actually done on two levels. On the technical level, one or more people must be trained to develop skills in correlating intimation, which supports the staff who will ultimately turn this raw information into intelligence. This top-tier staff are the ones who will need to develop and hone skills to coordinate, correlate, analyze and, ultimately, convert raw streams of information into useful BI.

7.6 CHECKLIST FOR THE INFORMATION AUDIT

Information audits are tailored to specific companies and their individual needs. The goal of this process is to pinpoint the information requirements of a company and then to proceed to recommend solutions to satisfy these requirements. Basically, the process is composed of four steps:

1. Selecting what needs to be known
2. Collecting the information

3. Transforming this collected information into the finished product
4. Distribution of the finished product to appropriate staff

7.6.1 Selecting What Needs to Be Known

Figuring out the right things to know is one of the trickiest, least understood, and most underrated jobs. To perform this feat requires not so much an expertise in one or more fields, but the ability to recognize what factors will influence the particular issue or area of concern.

The process is begun by reviewing the objectives that have been outlined by the CEO or management committee. For example: the CEO of an aluminum manufacturing company wants to improve sales of the company's pop-top beverage cans. To do this requires an assessment of the prospects for growth in the beverage industry. This is the obvious information that would be required. A person experienced in performing these audits would most certainly look beyond the obvious to, say, assessing the prospects of third-world aluminum producers moving into the canning business. Even this might be obvious to some, so we need to go deeper into the assessment and evaluate producers of other materials that could replace aluminum cans (Meyer, 1987). In essence, this example demonstrates the need to think about issues in a multidimensional way.

7.6.2 Collecting the Information

Once it has been decided what needs to be known, one can begin to collect the appropriate information. There are several categories of information. First, there is *in-house-available information*, residing on some corporate database, on local PCs, on departmental distributed databases, or even on paper. The next category of information can be referred to as *public information*. This is information that is on the public record, available from magazines, newspapers, and from public agencies.

The next category is *private information*. This is information that is not publicly known but is available for a fee, such as from LexisNexis (http://www.lexisnexis.com/) and Thomson Research's Investext (http://research.thomsonib.com/).

The final category of information is what is known as *secret information*. This is information privately held by competitor companies. Unfortunately, most of this information is impossible to obtain legally, although some of it can be gleaned from discussions with former employees of competitors, sales people, customers, and vendors.

7.6.3 Transforming the Collected Information into Finished Products

Deciding upon and then collecting the information is only half the battle. For the information to be truly useful, it must be presented in analytic reports, which must provide the best judgments, conclusions, and projections based on this information.

Transforming this data into useful information is a multistep process. These steps require a team to study the material and then debate what the material actually means, whether it is accurate, and whether it harbors any inconsistencies. It is this first step in which all facts will be verified, experts consulted, and theses developed and tested.

Some approaches transform the collected information manually through the efforts of intelligence officers. These people argue over the facts and then make a decision as to the correct interpretation of the data to be delivered to the CEO or other staff members. Today's BI technology provides the ability to load all collected information into a knowledge base and then perform automatic analysis and distribution.

A good example of this is the combination of the data warehousing and data mining.

Wal-Mart's data warehouse is the world's largest nongovernmental database. Their current data warehouse has over 100 terabytes of sales information. It is run on an NCR Teradata massively parallel computer (MPP), which has 4096 processors. This machine houses all of the details from each cash register receipt for each sale at each of its over 4000 stores, supercenters, and Sam's Club stores for the past 16 months. One of Wal-Mart's tables has over two billion rows! Table scans are not a viable option for responding to a query on this table because the table is so massively large!

Wal-Mart uses its data warehouse for such things as its market basket analysis. Analyzing what is in each individual shopping cart (sales receipt), they were able to discover the correlation between cold medicine and Kleenex tissues. People who bought cold medicine usually also purchased tissues. In their stores, the Kleenex tissues were with the paper products, whereas their cold medicine was in the pharmacy department. When they stocked the tissues next to the cold medicine as well as in the paper products area, the sales of tissues increased dramatically. Perhaps cold sufferers did not know if they had tissues at home. Seeing the tissues enticed them to go ahead and purchase them just in case they did not have any at home.

Wal-Mart also discovered a relationship between bananas and cereal. Customers who bought cereal also were likely to purchase bananas. The cereal was often far removed from the fruit aisles. When they placed a banana display near the cereal, sales of bananas skyrocketed.

Wal-Mart also uses data mining to gather information about where its customers live. Using credit card information, they can determine how far its customers drove to shop at any given store. This data is utilized in the selection of locations for new stores.

The six steps of effective data mining are:

1. *Business understanding:* Understanding the specific business prob-lem's objectives and goals
2. *Data understanding:* Initial data collection and familiarization, identifying data quality problems, and identifying data subsets
3. *Data preparation:* Selecting and clearing final set of data
4. *Modeling:* Selecting and applying modeling techniques
5. *Evaluation:* Determining whether the result meets the business problem's specifications
6. *Deployment:* Presenting the data in a meaningful way so that an end user can use it

7.6.4 Distributing the Finished Product to Appropriate Staff

Information presented to the staff members should be appropriate to that staff member's level within the organization.

Robert E. Horn, while at Harvard and Columbia Universities, researched how people deal with large amounts of information. He created an approach called *Information Mapping* (www.infomap.com), which is based on learning theory, human factors engineering, and cognitive sci-ence. Horn's approach is quite similar to the Meyer and Pincus approach and is worth discussing in a bit more detail.

Information mapping is a research-based approach to the analysis, organization, and visual presentation of information. In the analysis com-ponent, it is necessary to determine the purpose, audience needs, and information types. In the organization component, the overall structure for the information will be created based on the analysis. In the presen-tation component, the information is formatted for clarity and accessibility depending on the audience. Table 7.1 demonstrates an information map that explains how to prepare data for an audit.

Information mapping has been used with success for the optimization of everything from content management systems to workflow analyses to ISO 9000 documentation.

7.7 LINCOLN NATIONAL CORPORATION

Lincoln National Corporation (www.lfg.com) is a 100-year-old company with $119 billion in consolidated assets under management. As is the case in any company of Lincoln's size, the process of collecting, interpreting, and disseminating information was time-consuming at best, and hit or miss at its worst.

One of the most demanding business problems Lincoln National was experiencing was a need to digest large amounts of information. In the past, this had been done by issuing a daily news digest. This paper report

Table 7.1　An Information Map

Introduction: One of the most important procedures in an audit is preparing the data. Careful preparation ensures that the data is correct and that each step of the preparation has been carried out.

Procedure: Follow these steps to prepare data for the audit:

Step	Action
1	For data items selected for audit, obtain the following: Source document samples Run data from the computer room
2	Verify the source document samples by comparing the samples to the original list
3	Record sufficient descriptive information on a worksheet to provide accurate identification for future audits. *Minimum Information Required*　*Examples* Attributes of the sample　　　　　Sales territory 　　　　　　　　　　　　　　　　Effective data Description of each data item　　　Account name 　　　　　　　　　　　　　　　　Account number 　　　　　　　　　　　　　　　　Type of business

formed the baseline of information around which Lincoln executives and managers made their strategic decisions.

Understanding that the method of creating this daily report left large chunks of BI unaccounted for, the company began developing a corporatewide information retrieval system, using information-auditing techniques.

Lincoln discovered that most executive needs were not for information on the corporate database. In general, the executives of Lincoln got their BI from various news sources. The technology group was able to create an automated morning report that retrieved, searched, and correlated textual external data to assist staff. The morning report's intelligence comes from a variety of external sources, including the *New York Times* and *Business Week*. It has given Lincoln the ability to analyze information from a wide variety of other sources as well.

The morning report is viewed by Lincoln as a BI-gathering tool that feeds information into their executive support systems. Lincoln has seen some significant productivity improvements. Prior to attending meetings, staff members can review the pertinent information, negating the need to brief meeting attendees, so that meetings can move forward more quickly. Perhaps the greatest benefit of all is improved communications within the company, permitting key executives to make better decisions and facilitating the company's avoidance of the inevitable filtering effect that so often happens as information makes its way through the corporate hierarchy.

Lincoln uses their executive support system for strategic planning and competitive analyses. Along with external information, Lincoln's management can analyze internal sales data, competitor activities, field reports from sales staff, as well as competitors' financial data to determine the best way to compete.

Competitive analysis is a major component of Lincoln's planning process. Using the information entered by the sales people in the field, Lincoln builds a profile of each competitor's strengths and weaknesses. This is done by identifying the factors that are considered critical for each line of business and then ranking each competitor's capabilities in the same area. Concurrently, the same criteria are used to rank Lincoln's own capabilities in these areas. Using a side-by-side comparison of the competitor versus itself, Lincoln can evaluate whether or not they are weak in the critical factors needed for success in any particular product line. If a perceived weakness is noted, Lincoln formulates a plan to strengthen the company in that particular area. At the same time, the marketing plan is modified to focus on the key strengths while minimizing the weaknesses. One of Lincoln's greatest strengths is the ability to track and process competitors' data and then relate it to their own data, further strengthening their own product and marketing plans. Being able to monitor what a competitor is up to requires a combination of smart technology and techniques.

7.8 THE COMPETITOR ANALYSIS

Competitive analysis serves a useful purpose. It helps organizations devise their strategic plans and gives them insight into how to craft their performance indicators.

The philosophy behind Combustion Engineering's technique (Conference Board, 1988) is that information coupled with the experience of a seasoned industry manager is more than adequate to take the place of expensive experts in the field of competitive analysis.

The goal behind Combustion Engineering's technique is to analyze one competitor at a time to identify strategies and predict future moves. The key difference between this technique and others is the level of involvement of senior managers of the firm. In most companies, research is delegated to staff who prepare a report on all competitors at the same time. Combustion Engineering's method is to gather the information on one competitor and then use senior managers to logically deduce the strategy of the competitor in question.

Combustion Engineering uses a five-step approach in performing competitive analyses:

7.8.1 Step 1: Preliminary Meeting

Once the competitor is chosen, a preliminary meeting is scheduled. It should be attended by all senior managers who might have information or insights to contribute concerning this competitor. This includes the CEO as well as the general manager and managers from sales, marketing, finance, and manufacturing. A broad array of staff attending these meetings is important to this technique because it serves to provide access to many diverse sources of information. This permits the merger of external information sources — as well as internal sources — collected by the organization, such as documents, observations, and personal experiences.

At this meeting, it is agreed that all attendees spend a specified amount of time collecting the most recent information about a competitor. At this time, a second meeting is scheduled in which to review this information.

7.8.2 Step 2: Information Meeting

At this meeting, each attendee will receive an allotment of time to present his or her information to the group.

The group will then perform a relative strengths–weaknesses analysis. This will be done for all areas of interest uncovered by the information obtained by the group. The analysis will seek to draw conclusions about two criteria. First, is a competitor stronger or weaker than their own company? Second, does the area have the potential to affect customer behavior?

Combustion Engineering's rules dictate that unless the area meets both of these criteria, it should not be pursued further, either in analysis or discussion. Because managers do not always agree on what areas to include or exclude, it is frequently necessary to appoint a moderator who is not part of the group.

7.8.3 Step 3: Cost Analysis

At this point, with areas of concern isolated, it is necessary to do a comparative cost analysis. The first step here is to prepare a breakdown of costs for each product. This includes labor, manufacturing, cost of goods, distribution, sales, administrative, as well as other relevant items of interest.

At this point, the competitor's cost for each of these factors is compared with Combustion Engineering, according to the following scale:

Significantly higher
Slightly higher
Slightly lower
Significantly lower

Now, these subjective ratings are translated to something a bit more tangible, e.g., slightly higher is equivalent to 15 percent. By weighting each of these factors by its relative contribution to the total product cost, it is now possible to calculate the competitor's total costs.

7.8.4 Step 4: Competitor Motivation

This is perhaps the most intangible of the steps. The group must now attempt to analyze their competitor's motivation by determining how the competitor measures success as well as what its objectives and strategies are.

During the research phase, the senior manager and his or her staff gathers considerable information on this topic. By using online databases and Web sites, it is possible to collect information from self-promotions, annual reports, press releases, etc. In addition, information from former employees, the sales force, investment analysts, suppliers, and mutual clients is extremely useful and serves to broaden the picture.

Based on the senior managers' understanding of the business, it is feasible to be able to deduce the competitor's motivation. Motivation can often be deduced by observing the way the competitor measures itself. Annual reports are good sources for this information. For example, a competitor that wants to reap the benefits of investment in a particular industry will most likely measure success in terms of return on investment.

7.8.5 Step 5: Total Picture

By reviewing information on the competitor's strengths and weaknesses, relative cost structure, goals, and strategies, the total picture of the firm can be created.

Using this information, the group should be able to use individual insights into the process of running a business in a similar industry to determine the competitor's next likely moves.

For example, analysis shows that a competitor is stronger in direct sales, has a cost advantage in labor, and is focused on growing from a regional to a national firm. The group would draw the conclusion that the competitor will attempt to assemble a direct sales effort nationwide, while positioning itself on the basis of low price.

Combustion Engineering also devised an approach for dealing with the situation in which an outsider enters the marketplace. Here, the strategy discussed earlier obviously would not work.

Using the same group of people gathered to analyze competitor strategy, this exercise demands that the group look at the market as an objective third party would. The task is to design a fictitious company that would be able to successfully penetrate the market. This fictitious company is compared with the competitor firms in the industry to see if any of the traditional competitors can easily adopt this approach.

When Combustion Engineering's phantom analysis uncovers a strategy that traditional competitors might easily adopt, they adopt this strategy themselves as a preemptive move. When this same analysis reveals that an outsider could penetrate the industry by following this strategy, Combustion Engineering attempts to create additional barriers to entry. This includes forming an alliance with an outside company to pursue the phantom strategy itself.

Hruby's (1989) missing piece analysis also attempts to anticipate competitor moves, but it does this by identifying key weaknesses in the competitor. By concentrating on a competitor's weakness, the great wealth of information on that competitor can be turned into usable, action-oriented intelligence.

The methodology for performing Hruby's missing piece analysis is to analyze the strengths and weaknesses of a competitor in six areas. In each of these areas, the competitor is compared to the company that is doing the analysis; the six areas are:

1. *Product* — Compare the strength of the competitor's product from a consumer's point of view.
2. *Manufacturing* — Compare capabilities, cost, and capacity.
3. *Sales and marketing* — How well does the competitor sell a product? Compare positioning, advertising, sales force, and so on.
4. *Finance* — Compare financial resources and the performance. How strong are these relative to requirements for launching a strong competitive thrust?
5. *Management* — How effective, aggressive, and qualified are the competitor's managers?
6. *Corporate culture* — Examine values and history to determine whether the competitor is likely to enter or to attempt to dominate a market.

The goal of this exercise is to identify weaknesses in each of these areas, as well as to see whether any one of these weaknesses stands out as a major vulnerability. According to Hruby, most companies have a key weakness — or missing piece — that can be exploited.

Table 7.2 Competitive Strengths Matrix

	Competitive Areas					
Competitor	*1*	*2*	*3*	*4*	*5*	*6*
Company A	5	3	4	**2**	4	3
Company B	4	4	3	**2**	3	4
Company C	1	3	3	5	2	3
Company D	4	4	4	4	5	4
Area 1 — Product						
Area 2 — Manufacturing						
Area 3 — Sales and marketing						
Area 4 — Finance						
Area 5 — Management						
Area 6 — Corporate culture						

Note: Key: 1 = Weak to 5 = Excellent

To perform this technique requires that the competitor be rated in each of the six areas listed. Ratings are done on a scale of 1 to 5 with 1 being very weak, 2 is weak or uncompetitive, 3 is adequate or average, 4 is very strong or competitive, and 5 is excellent or superior.

Hruby recommends summarizing the scores in a competitive strengths matrix as shown in Table 7.2. This matrix lists the names of the competitors down the left-hand side and the competitive areas of interest across the top. Scores are entered into the appropriate cells. The worst score for each competitor should be highlighted. This is their weakest point and should be monitored accordingly.

In our example, Company A and Company B are both weak in the finance area. This means that they do not have enough strength to launch a major advertising campaign to bolster a new product. What this means is that if the company doing this analysis is ready, willing, and able to spend a lot of money, a new product launch would most probably be successful.

Company C scored a 1 in the product category. This means that its product is not as good as the company doing the analysis. In this case, an advertising campaign emphasizing product differences would serve to grab some market share from Company C.

Company D, on the other hand, scored strongly in all matrix areas. Given a strong product and an aggressive management team, this company is likely to make an aggressive move — perhaps a new product launch or major advertising on an existing product. It might even reduce costs. Company D certainly bears watching.

Company C, on the other hand, has a weak product but a good financial position. It just might launch a new product. However, its weak management structure might defer any product launch.

In summary, upon analysis of the competitive strengths matrix, one would deduce that a combination of strong financial position and competent management are a mix that indicates a strong likelihood of aggressive action on the part of the competitor. By using this analysis on information obtained from various sources, it is quite possible to keep tabs on what the competition is up to as well as provide a wealth of performance indicators and measures that could be useful for performance management.

7.9 AUTOMATIC DISCOVERY PROGRAMS (AKA DATA MINING)

The number and size of operational databases are increasing at a progressively faster rate. Because of the number of these databases, their sizes, and complexity, there is a tremendous amount of valuable knowledge locked up in them that remains undiscovered. Because the tendency of most modern organizations is to cut back on staff, it follows that there will never be enough analysts to interpret the data in all the databases.

Over a decade ago, Kamran Parsaye (1990) coined the term *intelligent databases*. The goal of intelligent databases is to be able to manage information in a natural way, making the information stored within these databases easy to store, access, and use. The prototypical intelligent database would have some robust requirements. It would need to provide some high-level tools for data analysis, discovery, and integrity control. These tools would be used to allow users not only to extract knowledge from databases, but also to apply knowledge to data. So far, it is not possible to scan through the pages of a database as easily as it is to flip through the pages of a book. For the label of *intelligent database* to be valid, this feature is necessary. Users should be able to retrieve information from a computerized database as easily as from a helpful human expert. Finally, an intelligent database must be able to provide knowledge as opposed to data. To do this, it needs to use inferencing capabilities to determine what a user needs to know.

In developing the theory behind intelligent databases, Parsaye enumerated three basic levels in dealing with the database:

1. We collect data, e.g., we maintain records on clients, products, sales, etc.
2. We query data, e.g., "Which products had increasing sales last month?"
3. We try to understand data, e.g., "What makes a product successful?"

In general, most current database systems passively permit these functions. A database is a static repository of information that will provide answers when a human initiates a session and asks pertinent questions. Parsaye formed a company by the name of IntelligenceWare and put on the market an automatic discovery software. Induction on eXtremely Large (IXL) databases was a unique system that analyzed large databases and discovered patterns, rules, and, often, unexpected relationships. IXL used statistics and machine learning to generate easy-to-read rules, which characterize data providing insight and understanding. IXL attempted to change the view of databases from a static repository of information, which only provides answers when someone asks a specific question, to that of a more active repository, which automatically poses queries to the database, uncovering useful and sometimes unexpected information.

This was the case for a well-known computer manufacturer who suffered sporadic defect problems in their disk drive manufacturing process, the cause of which they just could not locate. Using the IXL program against a database that consisted of audit logs of the manufacturing process, this company was able to pinpoint the particular operator who was causing the problem. The defect was then traced back to lack of proper training.

An even more interesting case study deals with lead poisoning data from the University of Southern California's Cancer Registry. Analysis of this data, using the IXL program, uncovered a relationship between gender and the level of lead in the blood leading to kidney damage. Before IXL's analysis, this relationship was unknown and potentially deadly.

KnowledgeWare is long gone but the legacy of IXL lives on in the data-mining software that amplify our ability to navigate and analyze information so that it can be rapidly turned from discrete and disconnected pieces of data into real intelligence.

Data mining can help us not only in knowledge discovery (i.e., the identification of new phenomena) but also in enhancing our understanding of known phenomena. One of the key steps in data mining is pattern recognition, namely, the discovery and characterization of patterns in image and other high-dimensional data. A pattern is defined as an arrangement or an ordering in which some organization of underlying structure can be said to exist. Patterns in data are identified using measurable features or attributes that have been extracted from the data.

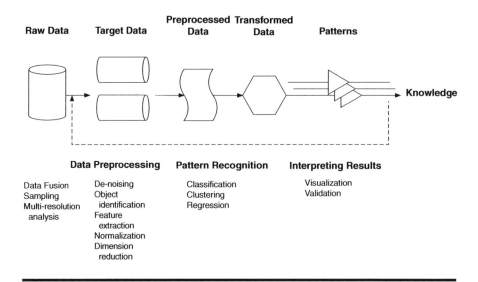

Raw Data   Target Data   Preprocessed Data   Transformed Data   Patterns

Knowledge

Data Preprocessing

Data Fusion
Sampling
Multi-resolution
  analysis

De-noising
Object
  identification
Feature
  extraction
Normalization
Dimension
  reduction

Pattern Recognition

Classification
Clustering
Regression

Interpreting Results

Visualization
Validation

Figure 7.1   The process of data mining.

Data mining is an interactive and iterative process involving data preprocessing, search for patterns, knowledge evaluation, and possible refinement of the process based on input from domain experts or feedback from one of the steps. See Figure 7.1. Wal-Mart, as discussed at the beginning of this chapter, champions data mining and has profited handsomely from its use.

The preprocessing of the data is a time-consuming but critical first step in the data-mining process. It is often domain and application dependent; however, several techniques developed in the context of one application or domain can be applied to other applications and domains as well. The pattern-recognition step is usually independent of the domain or application.

Data mining starts with the raw data, which usually takes the form of simulation data, observed signals, or images. These data are preprocessed using various techniques, such as sampling, multiresolution analysis, denoising, feature extraction, and normalization.

Sampling is a widely accepted technique to reduce the size of the dataset and make it easier to handle. However, in some cases, such as when looking for something that appears infrequently in the set, sampling may not be viable. Another technique to reduce the size of the dataset is multiresolution analysis. Data at a fine resolution can be "coarsened," which shrinks the dataset by removing some of the detail and extracts relevant features from the raw dataset. In credit card fraud, for instance, an important feature might be the location where a card is used. Thus, if a credit card is suddenly used in a country in which it has never been used before, fraudulence seems likely. Thus, the key to effective data mining is reducing the number of features used to mine data, so that only the features best at discriminating among the data items are retained.

Once the data is preprocessed or "transformed," pattern-recognition software is used to look for patterns. *Patterns* are defined as an ordering that contains some underlying structure. The results are processed back into a format familiar to the experts, who then can examine and interpret the results.

To be truly useful, data-mining techniques must be scalable. In other words, when the problem increases in size, we do not want the mining time to increase proportionally. Making the end-to-end process scalable can be very challenging, because it is not just a matter of scaling each step but of scaling the process as a whole.

Large-scale data mining is a field very much in its infancy, making it a source of several open research problems. To extend data-mining techniques to large-scale data, several barriers must be overcome. The extraction of key features from large, multidimensional, complex data is a critical issue that must be addressed first, prior to the application of the pattern-recognition algorithms. The features extracted must be relevant to the problem, insensitive to small changes in the data, and invariant to scaling, rotation, and translation. In addition, we need to select discriminating features through appropriate dimension reduction techniques. The pattern-recognition step poses several challenges as well. For example, is it possible to modify existing algorithms or design new ones that are scalable, robust, accurate, and interpretable? Further, can these algorithms be applied effectively and efficiently to complex, multidimensional data? And, is it possible to implement these algorithms efficiently on large-scale multiprocessor systems so that a scientist can interactively explore and analyze the data?

7.10 DATA VISUALIZATION

Data visualization is the attempt to display mined information in new ways. For instance, a map was once a "flat" (2D) piece of paper or parchment. As time went on, the map was overlaid onto a sphere, and we had our first globe. Data visualization hopes to take these concepts into the 21st century.

From a BI perspective, data visualization, called *information visualization* in this context, uses the computer to convert data into picture form. The most basic visualization is that of turning transaction data and summary information into charts and graphs. Visualization is used in computer-aided design (CAD) to render screen images into 3D models that can be viewed from all angles and can also be animated.

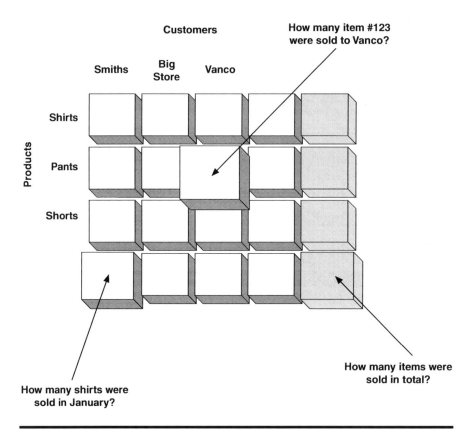

Figure 7.2 OLAP display information in the form of a cube so that analysts can "visualize" the information.

We briefly discussed OLAP in Chapter 5. OLAP places data into a cube structure that can be rotated by the user, which is particularly suited for financial summaries, as shown in Figure 7.2.

OLAP takes a snapshot of a relational database and restructures it into dimensional data. An OLAP structure created from the operational data is called an *OLAP cube*. The cube is created from a star schema of tables. At the centre is the fact table, which lists the core facts that make up the query. Numerous dimension tables are linked to the fact tables. These tables indicate how the aggregations of relational data can be analyzed. The number of possible aggregations is determined by every possible manner in which the original data can be hierarchically linked.

For example, a set of customers can be grouped by city, district, or country; hence, with 50 cities, 8 districts, and 2 countries, there are 3 hierarchical levels with 60 members. These customers can be considered in relation to products; if there are 250 products with 20 categories,

3 families, and 3 departments, then there are 276 product members. With just these 2 dimensions there are 16,560 possible aggregations. As the data considered increases, the number of aggregations can quickly total tens of millions or more.

7.11 WHERE DO WE GO NEXT?

Now that we are experts on all things related to knowledge management, it would be a good idea to discuss how we audit knowledge management systems. That is the focus of Chapter 8.

References

Brunson, D., Top 10 Trends in Business Intelligence and Data Warehousing for 2005 revisited, Business Intelligence Network, June 7, 2005. Retrieved June 15, 2005 from http://www.b-eye-network.com/print/969.

Conference Board, Calculating Competitor Action: Combustion Engineering's Strategy, *Management Briefing: Marketing*, October–November 1988.

Hruby, F.M., Missing Piece Analysis Targets the Competitor's Weakness, *Marketing News*, January 2, 1989.

Meyer, H.E., *Real-World Intelligence*, New York: Grove and Weidenfeld, 1987.

8

AUDITING KNOWLEDGE MANAGEMENT

It is no secret that computers make mistakes or, rather, that programs have been written with misconceptions and errors in the code. In very large systems, especially knowledge-based systems, in which the code is complex and the programs are very long, the possibility for error is very high. EDP (electronic data processing) auditors are charged with ensuring that the process of creating and running these advanced computer systems is consistent with recognized development practices.

8.1 COMPLEXITY

Knowledge-based systems are both harder and easier to audit than your garden-variety computer system. The wind can blow in either direction, depending on what building tools are used. When you build a log cabin, you clear the land and lay the foundation. Log after log is joined together, inching upward to the sky. When it is done, you can walk about, inside and out, rubbing your finger along the neatly stacked logs. You can see at a glance just how the log cabin was made.

Then there is the skyscraper. Acres of dirt are hauled away to lay the foundation, often as deep as a dungeon. Steel girders are hoisted heavenward by groaning cranes. Hundreds of hard-hatted workers scurry around on the high crossbeams. The skyscraper rises as does the log cabin — the difference is in the complexity. Many knowledge-based systems are built to be as easily understood as our log cabin, many are built to skyscraper levels of complexity, and many more are built to be somewhere between the two extremes. Three factors determine a system's complexity.

The first factor is tool complexity. There are hundreds of tools in use today: from programming languages to expert system shells to data-mining tools. Many of these tools are simple and self-documenting. But many more require great deal of training and expertise before they can be used to build effective systems.

The second factor is the level of expertise being snared in the fishing net. A system that makes wine selections is simpler than a system that determines when your false teeth will be ready, which is simpler than a system that makes recommendations about personal investment, which is simpler than a system that authorizes loans, which is simpler than a system that makes buy–sell decisions for foreign exchange deals, which is simpler than a system that authorizes the launch of the space shuttle, and so on.

Meyer and Curley (1989) studied many successful knowledge-based systems and the management tactics used in achieving these systems. Their goal was to identify these attributes and attempt to develop a usable methodology. They reviewed twelve different knowledge-based systems and found that it really boiled down to four different types.

A *knowledge-intensive system* is knowledge bound but uses a simple computing environment and usually acts in an advisory capacity. The other extreme is the *technology-intensive system*, which contains limited knowledge, or knowledge in a limited domain, but requires advanced computing prowess. This sort of system can usually be found in areas in which improvement in organizational productivity is envisioned. The most exotic type of system is a *strategic impact system,* in which not only is complex knowledge encoded but also the system is technologically complex. At the lower end of the totem pole are *personal productivity systems,* in which limited amounts of knowledge and simple technology are the characteristics. The higher end is exemplified by foreign exchange systems in which advanced workstations are used, massive data feeds are integrated, and complex rules of knowledge are encoded. Another example would be the massive Wal-Mart data-mining and warehousing system, discussed in earlier chapters.

The third factor is the most vital and the most problematic. Will we adhere to the decisions of the knowledge-based system, or will we not?

8.2 AUDIT QUESTIONS

Because knowledge-based systems have a level of complexity greater than a conventional system, the audit should also be a level of complexity greater than the conventional system audit.

8.2.1 Where Did You Get the Knowledge for this System?

Now if we are dealing with a medical expert system and the answer to the work question is Dr. Kildare, a televised medical show from the 1960s, the auditor should roll up those sleeves, because he or she is in for the duration. Expert knowledge should come from an expert. No compromises here, no "Let's use Mary because she's here." The audit process should check to ensure that the best possible candidate was chosen.

It is substance that is at the heart of the knowledge-based system. So how do we get it? Unfortunately, for many knowledge-based systems, the expert selected is the person who has the most free time. For other systems, the top guru in the department is selected, who is then taken offline for several weeks or months in an attempt to wrest the knowledge from its very roots. Some very smart systems use the combined expertise of several experts, which gives them the ability to incorporate differing or competing viewpoints. Perhaps the most brilliant of systems incorporate the views and opinions of experts external to the company itself. The degree of expertise selected should be proportional to the level of strategic competitiveness that the system is expected to display.

Functions within an organization are often graded proportionally to their worth to the organization. In a bank, those responsible for approving mortgage loans are a higher grade within the organization than those who authorize credit card purchases. The organization inherently recognizes the complexity of the mortgage authorization process as compared to the credit card authorization process. American Express, in the development of their own credit authorization knowledge-based system for their Green Card, appropriately used the senior authorizer as the basis for the rules governing their very successful system. The rules governing this sort of credit approval may be many but are noncomplex and based on a moderate number of variables. Mortgage approval is a horse of a different color. Many variables come into play here, some vague and fuzzy. This process must take into account such things as the amount of mortgage, down payment, security, primary income, secondary income, rate basis, rate spread, terms of loan, etc. There is obviously much more risk associated with this process. The inputs for this brand of knowledge-based system must come from a much more senior staffer and from more than one staffer to boot.

Most corporations have been quite perceptive about the failings of their own internal organizations and in certain areas of expertise. Many organizations compete for the most experienced personnel. Many hire big names, such as past members of presidential cabinets, for their unique perspectives of world events. It is the same with knowledge-based systems. Figure 8.1 makes it readily understandable that there is great risk in building a knowledge-based system that utilizes the wrong level of expertise.

Brilliant	Interest rate forecasting	Many high level outside experts
Expert	Mortgage processing	Multiple experts, some outside
Extremely knowledgeable	Pension check processing	Multiple inside experts
Smart	Credit card authorization	Single expert
Conventional	Payroll	Little expertise

Figure 8.1   Expertise-required continuum.

At one prestigious Wall Street firm, it was decided to build a trading system that would provide expertise in the time-honored tactic of hedging. Because hedging is more of an art than a science, the development team needed to gain the cooperation of the premier participants in this art form. Unfortunately these extraordinary folks were determined not to part with their knowledge. They felt it was what made them uniquely market-able, not an unusual position for an expert to take. Because the development team could not get the cooperation they needed, they turned to textbooks as substitute mentors. Textbooks contain the rules and procedures and not the gut instincts and rules of thumb that could make this sort of knowledge-based system expert or even brilliant.

As the expertise-required continuum in Figure 8.1 shows, there are many gradations of knowledge-based system types, the smarter-than-conventional systems to the very brilliant. In each of the systems, a certain level of expertise is required. If the systems are to be built, management should not look askance at the technology but should take an active interest in its success. The way this can be done is to become involved at the point at which the actual level of expertise is to be selected. The selection, which can appear trivial, is fraught with risk for those who take a *laissez-faire* attitude. The continuum in Figure 8.1 clearly shows that some systems are so complex, requiring as input the analysis of so many far-reaching variables, that defaulting to in-house staff as a total solution is not realistic. For these systems, which often reside in key areas of the company, including outside experts to gain a broader perspective is endorsed.

8.2.2   Did We Get All of the Knowledge?

Once the auditor is confident that a *bona fide* expert was chosen, a thorough analysis should be done to determine if all the knowledge was captured. How should this be done? One way would be to review the transcripts of the knowledge-engineering sessions, but this would be extremely time consuming. Probably the best way is to observe the use of the system in practice and look for the holes. A complete knowledge-based system should leave no question unanswered and no stone unturned. So, it should account for all situations that arise during a sample test period. For example, suppose we build a super-duper credit authorization system. During the system development process, the expert worked diligently to encode all the processing rules as well as the expert's gut instinct in approving credit. The system is put into the credit department amid much fanfare. Sixty people come to work on Monday morning ready, eager, and willing to work with their new electronic credit adviser. At 9:01 A.M. the phones start ringing off the hook. Real customers. Real credit decisions. The question is, can every situation be handled? And handled correctly?

The auditor should observe this process. A group of credit authorizers should be preselected to log all instances of variances and omissions between what the system does and what they would have done manually. Because this process should also have been a part of the original test plan, the auditors should find few problems, but given the enormity of the task of capturing the whole ball of wax, it is a sure thing that the auditors will find some discrepancies.

Auditors enjoy looking for discrepancies, and the most common way they find them is by using an audit trail. Now, audit trails are uncommon to most computer systems for a simple reason: They cost to build, and they cost to run. One of the niceties of using some of the expert system technologies is that an audit trail is almost a natural part of system design. So, it should be easy for an auditor to perform an after-the-fact audit when this type of technology is used. Here, the auditor examines a printed audit trail and compares the system decision to the decision a human credit authorizer would have given.

8.2.3   How Much Common Sense Does the Knowledge-Based System Exhibit?

Common sense is hard to systematize and easy to miss. Some experts get so caught up in the esoterics of what they do for a living that they miss the trivial common sensibilities of their daily tasks. In one case, a bank built a prototype knowledge-based system for determining the scope of

Table 8.1   Confusion Matrix

	Black Plague	Flu	Cold
Black plague	—	35 percent	45 percent
Flu	20 percent	—	15 percent
Cold	10 percent	5 percent	—

an internal audit. The prototype worked wonderfully in predicting the scope of a local audit for branch banks until it ran aground at one branch that did not have any loans.

8.2.4   Does the Knowledge-Based System Make Mistakes?

What happens if the system becomes confused? In the field of psychology, a confusion matrix is built to determine the ratios between correct responses and those responses that were close but not quite correct. We can use the same technique to determine just how right or wrong a system is. Let us look at an example. Based on patients' symptoms, we have just built a knowledge-based system to determine the type of disease. Our list of possible diseases is: the flu, a cold, and the black plague. Sitting in one room is a medical expert who examines several patients and makes diagnoses. Across the hall is a computer that also makes diagnoses. Table 8.1 shows a confusion matrix for the differences between the human doctor's diagnosis and the computer's diagnosis. Remember that in each instance the information given to the doctor is the same as that fed into the system. Presuming that our doctor is a *bona fide* expert, the responses of the knowledge-based system should exactly parallel those of the doctor. From the confusion matrix, you can see that this did happen. Each slot or entry in the matrix represents the percentage of times that the expert system differs from the human expert, which really means the percentage of times the knowledge-based system was confused. For example, when our doctor diagnosed the flu, the knowledge-based system diagnosed the black plague 20 percent of the time and a cold 15 percent of the time. These erroneous conclusions totaled 35 percent. This means that our knowledge-based system was correct 65 percent of the time. The average of these percentages will give us an error threshold that we must decide whether to consider acceptable or not. In the case of our medical experts system, the total error threshold was 57 percent, i.e., the system was correct only 57 percent of the time. This would be unacceptable in anybody's medical textbook.

8.2.5   Is the System Kept Up-to-Date?

By the sweat of everybody's brow, three years and 2000 hours later the system is complete. With great fanfare the system is presented to management followed by a champagne party and many press releases. While everyone is toasting each other and slapping each other on the back, something terrible is happening. The system is becoming obsolete.

You have all heard the old saw about books — as soon as it is in print, it is out of date. Will the same thing hold true for knowledge-based systems? Knowledge bases seldom stay static. They grow and expand beyond the developers' wildest dreams.

How do they grow? This is the question that the auditor should ask. Which department has a responsibility for ensuring new tidbits of knowledge? Is it the IT department? The experts? Those that use the knowledge-based system?

And the auditor should be on the lookout for adolescent sloppiness. When the system is new, there is usually adequate money, time, and enthusiasm to do the job right. After the fanfare is over and the spotlight fades, the system matures into adolescence. Gradually, the heavy hitters move away from the system to something a bit more exciting, leaving our little system alone, forlorn. When a change has to be made to the system, it will be made during maintenance mode rather than the development mode.

Maintenance is not the most interesting work. And those who are assigned to it usually manage to work up the same level of enthusiasm as they do for a weekend trip to the dentist. Changes made in this matter are usually sloppy or, if you are really lucky, just careless. The meticulousness exhibited during the development stage, when the team wanted everything to be just so, is usually never replicated. So the auditor would be wise to take a look at the procedures put into place to handle the maintenance of these systems.

8.2.6   Will the Users Actually Use the Knowledge-Based System?

Most knowledge-based systems are used in an advisory capacity. This means a real live human being will read the decision and do one of two things: Use it or ignore it. A well-designed system will track the adherence factor, which can then be used by the auditor to track whether the system is being used effectively. Of course, it is a pretty good idea for management to use this feature too.

The adherence factor is actually an audit trail of the system's recommendations. For each consultation, the system keeps track of the conclusion and advice. This conclusion can then be compared to the one the staff actually made. To simplify the process, some add an online justification feature that permits the user of the system to enter what was actually done. Those who would serve as auditors will most likely place this high on the list of features to consider.

8.3 AN AUDIT PLAN

Most people think of auditing as a necessary evil. Systems folk do not think kindly of auditors. No wonder auditors take a fine-tooth comb to every facet of the development process, from file design to documentation to user manuals. Knowledge-based system auditing will ask the following questions:

1. Can you recreate an expert system consultation?
2. Is the data captured during the consultation edited or verified in any way?
3. When an error is detected, which users receive immediate notification?
4. If an error is detected, does the knowledge base flag the error?
5. How rigorously are the answer fields constrained?
6. Are new releases of the knowledge base tracked?
7. What were the test cases used to verify the system?
8. Are new releases quality assured?
9. Are new releases endorsed by the expert?
10. How are differences between the system and the human expert handled?
11. Is documentation maintained?

The following are the basic steps in performing the audit:

1. Planning the audit
2. Evaluating internal controls
3. Audit procedures
4. Completing the audit

The auditor must plan and conduct the audit to ensure that the audit risk (reaching an incorrect conclusion based on the audit findings) will be limited to an acceptable level. To eliminate the possibility of assessing audit risk too low, the auditor should perform the following steps:

1. *Obtain an understanding of the organization and its environment:* This understanding is used to assess the risk of material misstatement or weakness and to set the scope of the audit. The auditor's

understanding should include information on the nature of the entity, management, governance, objectives and strategies, and business processes.

2. *Identify risks that may result in material misstatements:* The auditor must evaluate an organization's business risks (threats to the organization's ability to achieve its objectives). An organization's business risks can arise or change due to new personnel, new or restructured information systems, corporate restructuring, and rapid growth, to name a few.

3. *Evaluate the organization's response to those risks:* Once the auditor has evaluated the organization's response to the assessed risks, he or she should obtain evidence of management's actions toward those risks. The organization's response (or lack thereof) to any business risks will impact the auditor's assessed level of audit risk.

4. *Assess the risk of material misstatement:* Based on the knowledge obtained in evaluating the organization's responses to business risks, the auditor then assesses the risk of material misstatements and determines specific audit procedures that are necessary.

5. *Evaluate results and issue an audit report:* At this level, the auditor should determine if the assessments of risks were appropriate and whether sufficient evidence was obtained. The auditor will issue either an unqualified or qualified audit report based on their findings.

The auditor evaluates the organization's control structure by understanding the organization's five interrelated control components. They include:

1. The *control environment*, which provides the foundation for the other components. It encompasses such factors as management's philosophy and operating style.

2. The *risk assessment*, which consists of risk identification and analysis.

3. The *control activities*, which consist of the policies and procedures which ensure that employees carry out management's directions. Types of control activities an organization must implement are preventative controls (controls intended to stop an error from occurring), detective controls (controls intended to detect if an error has occurred), and mitigating controls (control activities that can mitigate the risks associated with a key control not operating effectively).

4. *Information and communication*, which ensures that the organization obtains pertinent information and then communicates it throughout the organization.

5. *Monitoring,* which involves reviewing the output generated by control activities and conducting special evaluations. In addition to understanding the organization's control components, the auditor must also evaluate the organization's general and application controls.

Controls that have an effect on knowledge management processes include:

1. *Organizational controls* — includes segregation-of-duties controls.
2. *Data center and network operations controls* — ensures the proper entry of data into an application system and proper oversight of error correction.
3. *Hardware and software acquisition and maintenance controls* — includes controls to compare data for accuracy when it is input twice by two separate components.
4. *Access security controls* — ensures the physical protection of computer equipment, software, and data, and is concerned with the loss of assets and information through theft or unauthorized use.
5. *Application system acquisition, development, and maintenance controls* — ensure the reliability of information processing.
6. *Application controls* — application controls apply to the processing of individual accounting applications and help ensure the completeness and accuracy of transaction processing, authorization, and validity. Types of application controls include:
   a. *Data capture controls* — ensures that all transactions are recorded in the application system, transactions are recorded only once, and rejected transactions are identified, controlled, corrected, and reentered into the system.
   b. *Data validation controls* — ensures that all transactions are properly valued.
   c. *Processing controls* — ensures the proper processing of transactions.
   d. *Output controls* — ensures that computer output is not distributed or displayed to unauthorized users.
   e. *Error controls* — ensures that errors are corrected and resubmitted to the application system at the correct point in processing.

Application controls may be compromised by the following application risks:

1. Weak security
2. Unauthorized access to data and unauthorized remote access

3. Inaccurate information and erroneous or falsified data input
4. Misuse by authorized end users
5. Incomplete processing and duplicate transactions
6. Untimely processing
7. Communication system failure
8. Inadequate training and support

8.4   RISK AND KNOWLEDGE MANAGEMENT

Hala (2002) stresses that effective knowledge management is crucial to enterprise risk management (ERM). ERM is based on the fact that business processes, risks, and controls across the organization are interrelated. Effective risk management can only emerge when the organization begins to share and control knowledge systematically across its functions and departments.

Effective ERM guidelines include:

1. Create a risk ownership focus for each employee.
2. Develop a corporate integrity program (as did Chicago's Memorial Hospital).
3. Develop a common risk language for the entire organization.
4. Develop a common process classification for the entire organization.
5. Develop a process for managing risks.
6. Internal auditing should become proactively involved in any organizational project or initiative, e.g., key business initiatives, mergers, new business systems, or project redesigns.
7. Develop business expertise within the internal audit department. Each auditor should be assigned one aspect of the business and this should become his or her focal point from a knowledge-gathering standpoint.
8. There should be a single focus point for managing the critical business knowledge within an organization. Some organizations have highly structured groups in charge of monitoring, managing, and facilitating the internal sharing of knowledge. Some organizations, however, do not have a group specifically devoted to this task. Many auditors believe that this should be the role of the audit function.

8.5   LINKING KNOWLEDGE MANAGEMENT TO BUSINESS PERFORMANCE

Carrillo, Robinson, Anumba, and Al-Ghassani (2003) have developed the IMPaKT framework for linking KM to business performance. Similar to most researchers and practitioners, they stress that to be able to assess the impact of KM, KM initiatives must be aligned to an organization's strategic objectives. IMPaKT organizes a KM initiative into three stages, which are then further explored through templates supported by detailed guidelines. For each stage, there are steps or thought processes required to structure business problems.

The aim of Stage 1 is to provide a structure for formulating a strategic business plan by identifying business drivers, defining strategic objectives or goals, identifying critical success factors, and developing measures for monitoring performance improvement. The outcome of Stage 1 is a business improvement plan with performance targets and measurable goals.

An abbreviated template for Stage 1 might consist of:

1. Choose a business problem with a knowledge dimension.
2. Place the business problem in a strategic context by relating it to your external business drivers, strategic objectives, and critical success factors.
3. Select an appropriate set of measures to monitor progress.
4. Identify previous, current, target, and benchmark scores for various performance measures.

Each of these four steps is supported by detailed guides, such as sample performance measures and various glossaries.

The purpose of Stage 2 is to determine whether the business problem has a knowledge dimension and to develop specific KM initiatives to address the business problem. A sample template for Stage 2 might consist of:

1. Clarifying the knowledge dimension of your business problem by identifying the KM processes involved
2. Developing specific KM initiatives
3. Selecting possible tools to support the KM processes identified
4. Identifying possible relationships between KM initiatives and performance measures. Use a cause-and-effect map for this purpose.
5. Preparing an action plan and identifying change management and resources required

Stage 2 steps are supported by detailed guides such as a questionnaire to identify the KM subprocesses involved, a matrix for the selection of the most appropriate tools, and a checklist to identify possible barriers and facilitators prior to implementation.

In Stage 3, a KM evaluation strategy and implementation plan are developed. The output of Stage 1 and Stage 2 of the IMPaKT framework is a business improvement strategy underpinned by KM.

A sample template for Stage 3 might consist of:

1 Use the cause-and-effect map developed in Step 4 of Stage 2 to assess the likely contribution of the KM initiatives to performance measures.
2. Assess the probability of success of the KM initiative.
3. Identify the cost components for implementing each KM initiative and the possible benefits.
4. Choose an appropriate method to assess the impact of each KM initiative on business performance.
5. Prioritize KM initiatives based on the measures of performance.

Several evaluation techniques may be used:

1. *Cost minimization analysis* involves a simple cost comparison of KM initiatives, as it is assumed that the outputs are identical or differences between the outputs are insignificant. This technique does not take account of the monetary value of the outputs.
2. *Cost–effectiveness analysis* involves the comparison of KM initiatives where the consequences are measured using the same units.
3. *Cost–utility analysis* involves a comparison of KM initiatives, which are measured in monetary units with the consequences measured using a preference scale, e.g., preferences of individuals, teams, or the organization.
4. *Cost–benefit analysis* approach provides a comparison of the value of input resources to be used by the KM initiative compared to the value of the output resources the KM initiative might save or create.

8.6 WHERE DO WE GO NEXT?

In Chapter 8, we concentrated on the audit of KM systems. In Chapter 9, we will start at the beginning and delve into project management concepts for the KM development manager.

References

Carrillo, P.M., Robinson, H.S., Anumba, C.J., and Al-Ghassani, A.M., IMPaKT: a framework for linking knowledge management to business performance, *Electronic Journal of Knowledge Management, 1*(1), 2003.
Hala, N., Unlock the potential, *The Internal Auditor, 59*(5), October 2002.
Meyer, M.H. and Curley, K.F., Expert system success models, *Datamation, 35*(17), pp. 35–37, 1989.

9

PROJECT MANAGEMENT TECHNIQUES

The goal of project management (PM) is to define and achieve targets while optimizing the use of resources (time, money, people, space, etc.). Implementing knowledge management (KM) systems follows a traditional software engineering paradigm, including project management. Because proper project planning is critical to the success of a KM project, it is worthwhile to spend a few pages covering the basics.

9.1 THE LINK BETWEEN KNOWLEDGE MANAGEMENT AND PRODUCT MANAGEMENT

Hernandez (2005) provides an excellent checklist of the organizational considerations and KM components to think about when making a KM decision:

1. *Strategic plan:* What are you doing and for whom? Are you improving search functionality for a specific type or user, or are you typing together all enterprise initiatives into a holistic vision?
2. *Executive and stakeholder commitment.*
3. *Type of knowledge required:* Will the users be dealing with reasonably predictable and routine questions that have known answers, or are the users working in a more unique research mode?
4. *Knowledge delivery approaches:* What are the intended delivery channels (bots, search, push, collaborative, browsing, portal, etc.), and what is the process to properly format the knowledge for the intended user?

5. *Required versus available enterprise resources:* Identify required resources early in the process. Compare required time, budget, subject matter experts, various IT staff, knowledge engineers, etc., that need to be available. Identify your gaps. It should be noted that content management and authoring requirements are routinely underestimated, which results in substantial content, data, or knowledge-related challenges.

6. *Business process redesign plan:* In the event that some changes are required to existing processes, it is best to define these early in the design phases.

7. *Organizational change management plan:* How do you implement the proposed KM vision while sustaining current requirements and operations?

8. *Understand KM components needed:* What type of users will you be supporting? What are the sources of data or content, and what are their formats? How will the source content be processed? Can any content be directly published from an automated content management system? Who will the knowledge authors and reviewers be? What is the content review process? Is workflow management a module of the proposed KM suite? Who owns the workflow design and oversight? What tools will be used to report on KM processes and performance? What metrics will be used? What hardware and software will need to be acquired? What are the requirements for knowledge base development and maintenance? How will the knowledge reach the end users — bots, self-help, live agent, machine-to-machine, etc.?

Each of the points on this checklist is related to systems development (aka software engineering) in some way. Some KM initiatives do not succeed simply because they fail to effectively manage the entire life cycle of the initiative (Davis, 2004). The systems development life cycle (SDLC) consists of several phases, including feasibility, project planning, systems analysis, systems design, implementation, coding, and installation.

Once the KM project has been deemed feasible by senior management, the very next SDLC phase is project planning. It is in this phase of systems development that the KM initiative is "fleshed out":

1. Provides the framework for the remainder of the development effort
2. Provides the blueprint or instructions for systems development
3. Determines business needs as well as technology needs
4. Determines resources required

9.2 THE PROJECT PLANNING DOCUMENT

The project planning document articulates what the system will do. Some developers are troubled by the fact that the project planning process is usually undertaken prior to the stages of systems analysis and design, when end-user requirements are typically captured. Whereas the systems analysis and design stages capture a "micro" view of the system, the project planning process is only required to capture a "macro" view of the system. This is usually sufficient for the purposes of planning, resource allocation, and budgeting.

9.2.1 Defining the Plan

9.2.1.1 What Will Be Done?

The goals and objectives section of the project plan provides a general statement of the scope of the project as well as a more detailed list of requirements, interfaces (i.e., data mining, data warehousing, etc.), and constraints (i.e., the system must have a response time of below 1 second).

9.2.1.2 When Will It Be Done?

Most organizations permit only the most experienced of personnel to tackle the difficult task of scheduling. These pros utilize a variety of methodologies (e.g., deterministic approach, stochastic approach, etc.) and toolsets (e.g., Microsoft Project) to apportion tasks to available personnel in the most optimum manner as shown in Figure 9.1.

9.2.1.3 How Much Will It Cost?

The project plan is bottom-line oriented and, therefore, must include the estimated costs of the project for review and approval by the various stakeholders.

Estimators may use a wide variety of techniques to perform the project cost effort. It is customary, in fact, for the estimator to use at least two techniques and then "triangulate" the two (i.e., discuss the reasons why the two estimates have differences). Often, the "true" estimate is the average of the results of the various estimation methods used.

One of the more popular estimation methodologies is COCOMO (Cost Construction Model II), devised by Barry Boehm in 1981 (see http://sunset. usc.edu/Research_Group/barry.html), which is both a formula and a software tool (http://sunset.usc.edu/research/COCOMOII/). Figure 9.2 shows its application to cost estimation in project planning.

ID	❶	Task Name	Duration	Start	Finish	Pred																
							Dec '04		Jan '05					Feb '05				Mar '05			Apr '05			May '05
							5	12	19	26	2	9	16	23	30	6	13	20	27	6	13	20	27	3	10	17	24	1	8
1		Implementation initiation	7 days	Sat 1/1/05	Tue 1/11/05																	
2		Determine team members	1 day	Mon 1/3/05	Mon 1/3/05		PM															
3		Training	3 days	Tue 1/4/05	Thu 1/6/05	2	PM															
4		Define & Secure additional resou	6 days	Tue 1/4/05	Tue 1/11/05	2	PM															
5		Review legal/copyright/digital rig	2 days	Mon 1/3/05	Tue 1/4/05		PM,CO															
6		Notify authors	1 day	Mon 1/3/05	Mon 1/3/05		PM															
7		Team creation complete	0 days	Sat 1/1/05	Sat 1/1/05																	
8		e-Commerce analysis	8.13 days	Wed 1/12/05	Mon 1/24/05	1																
9		Conduct needs analysis	3 days	Wed 1/12/05	Fri 1/14/05		DB,WB															
10		Draft preliminary software speci	2 days	Mon 1/17/05	Tue 1/18/05	9	DB,WB															
11		Develop preliminary budget	1 day	Wed 1/12/05	Wed 1/12/05	7	PM															
12		Review software/hardware spe	1 day	Wed 1/19/05	Wed 1/19/05	10	PM,DB,WB															
13		Incorporate feedback on specific	0.5 days	Thu 1/20/05	Thu 1/20/05	12	PM,DB,WB															
14		Develop delivery timeline	0.5 days	Thu 1/20/05	Thu 1/20/05	13	PM															
15		Obtain approvals to proceed (co	1 hr	Fri 1/21/05	Fri 1/21/05	14	PM															
16		Secure required resources	1 day	Fri 1/21/05	Mon 1/24/05	15	PM															
17		Analysis complete	0 days	Mon 1/24/05	Mon 1/24/05	16	1/24															
18		c-commerce design	14 days	Mon 1/24/05	Fri 2/11/05																	
19		Review preliminary specification	2 days	Mon 1/24/05	Wed 1/26/05	17	DB,WB															
20		Develop functional specifications	4 days	Wed 1/26/05	Tue 2/1/05	19	DB,WB															
21		Obtain hardware	4 days	Tue 2/1/05	Mon 2/7/05	20	DB,WB															
22		Review functional specifications	2 days	Mon 2/7/05	Wed 2/9/05	21	DB,WB,PM															
23		Incorporate feedback into functi	2 days	Wed 2/9/05	Fri 2/11/05	22	DB,WB															
24		Design complete	0 days	Fri 2/11/05	Fri 2/11/05	23	2/11															
25		e-commerce development	77 days	Fri 2/11/05	Tue 5/31/05	8																
26		Review functional specifications	1 day	Fri 2/11/05	Mon 2/14/05	24	PM,DB,WB															
27		Obtain servers	1 day	Mon 2/14/05	Tue 2/15/05	26	PM,DB,WB															
28		Develop Code -DB	40 days	Tue 2/15/05	Tue 4/12/05	27																PM

Figure 9.1 A typical schedule, created using Microsoft Project.

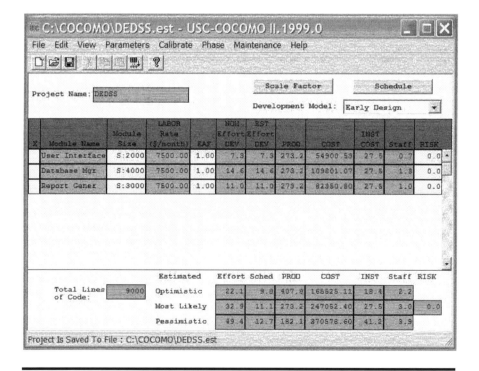

Figure 9.2 Using COCOMO to estimate project cost.

The true cost of a project must also include software and hardware required, time expended by outside personnel such as trainers, end users, and managers, as well as administrative overheads.

9.2.1.4 What Resources Will Be Needed?

The reader of the project plan should be able to easily ascertain the requirements in terms of people as well as other resources:

1. How much will the project cost?
2. How long will it take?
3. How many people are needed?
4. What will these people do?
5. What kinds of people (e.g., programmers, trainers, etc.) are needed?
6. What, if any, software will be required to be purchased?
7. What, if any, hardware will be required to be purchased?
8. What, if any, outside services will be required to be secured?
9. What business, project, or product risks might be encountered, and what resources are required to counter these risks?

9.2.2 Defining Project Goals

Project goals are always subsets of business goals. In a project plan, one or more project goals are described and tied back to the business goals of the organization.

For example, a company might decide to develop a Web-based executive information system. The goal of this project might be defined as: "The goal of EIS (executive information system) is to provide a dashboard of corporate and competitor analytics to our strategic personnel." We can then tie this project goal to one or more of the company's stated business goals, thus: "EIS is aligned to the corporate business goal of increasing competitive advantage by utilizing enhanced analytics."

9.2.3 Defining Project Scope

The project scope is a short description of the project, which includes the following:

1. Justification for project
2. What the system will do
3. How the system will generate revenue, if applicable

The project scope will flesh out the list of project goals. An example of a scope statement follows:

> Our company stores an enormous amount of data. Currently, data is distributed across multiple platforms. In addition, aside from some basic reports, there is no capability to sift through this data to find patterns in that data that might afford us competitive advantage. EIS will utilize data warehouse and data mining techniques and technologies to provide advanced analytics to our strategic staff.

9.2.4 Time Constraints

The project plan will usually determine the cost, resources, and time requirements for the proposed project. However, regulatory, legal, and competitive pressures might impose a specific deadline. This is referred to as *timeboxing*. It is interesting to note that many governmental contracts impose a financial penalty on a contracting company that delivers the project late.

9.2.5 Budget Constraints

If the project is to be constrained by a set amount of dollars, then this too is required to be clearly articulated. Many companies create a yearly business plan that allocates financial resources to each department. Project plans, therefore, will have to be managed within the constraints of this preallocated budget.

9.2.6 General Requirements

The requirements section is the heart of the project plan. The requirements usually take the form of a list of features that the system must have. For example, a sample of the general requirements that were specified for the EIS project include the following:

- A Web-based application allowing users easy access and use
- The ability to access customer and competitor data
- The ability to plot and chart data
- Natural language query capability
- Dashboard showing key performance indicators

This feature set was most likely collated during the feasibility phase of the SDLC. Many of the desired features might have been selected as a result of competitor analysis. Web sites such as Hoovers.com or governmental regulatory agencies such as the Securities and Exchange Commission provide a wealth of detail about the company's competitors. The competitor's Web site also provides a great deal of detail, including marketing brochures and even downloadable trial software.

The functionality of a system must be ascertained as scheduling and cost estimation are dependent on knowing what the system is going to do.

9.2.7 Technical Requirements

Most projects are built under a series of constraints. For example, a particular system must be built using the Oracle database. These constraints must be addressed in the project plan. This includes, but is not limited to, standards, existing systems, hardware, software, operating systems, networking, application software, security, disaster recovery, availability, scalability, and reliability.

9.2.8 Hardware

This section will describe the following:

1. Existing hardware that is required to be used
2. Proposed hardware that is desired to be used

All costs should be included.

9.2.9 Operating Systems

If one or more operating systems are required, it should be specified in this section.

9.2.10 Networking

Computer systems may be designed using a variety of physical architectures. A system may utilize a one-tier (e.g., PC only or mainframe only), two-tier (e.g., PC and mainframe or PC and server), or three-tier (e.g., PC, server or mainframe) architecture. Computer systems might use one server, two servers, or many servers. The system might have "hanging off of it" 1 PC or 10,000 PCs (usually called clients). The system might be Internet based, intranet based, or conventional (i.e., not connected to the Internet). The system might support wireless devices, PDAs, and even cell phones. If the new system is required to work within the constraints of a particular network, a diagram of the network should be included in the project plan.

All costs should be included.

9.2.11 Application Software

This section of the project plan specifies the software required to be used; e.g., artificial intelligence, data warehouse, etc. All costs should be included.

9.2.12 Security

Most organizations have security requirements that must be adhered to by all systems. This should be included in the project plan. A security statement might contain the following information:

The system will provide a number of different security features. First, all members must log into the system at member PCs and must provide a username and password before gaining access to the system. Second, remote users access the system via a gateway that provides a firewall. The firewall allows access to services designated as remote access services but blocks access to all other services, such as administrator services. Cookies will also be used to aid in identifying remote users.

The database management systems (DBMSs) and data warehouse provide a high level of security. Security profiles for the different user types will be created so that specific users have only the permissions (create, update, or delete) on selected data objects. For example, only the administrator will have create and delete permissions in the databases. Stored procedures will be used to maintain referential integrity in the databases.

9.2.13 Scalability

Scalability refers to how much a system can be expanded. A scalability statement might specify the following:

The system will be able to expand to 200 users without breaking down or requiring major changes in procedure.

9.2.14 Availability

Availability refers to the percentage of time that a system is available for use. It is also referred to as *uptime* — i.e., the amount of time "the system is up." Availability is an important component of information systems. An availability statement might specify the following:

System uptime will not be lower than 99 percent. Providing a reliable and continuous service to users is one of the key requirements of the system. When a failure occurs, system downtime will be kept to a minimum. The target is to have the system operational within 2 hours following a serious failure.

9.2.15   Reliability

Reliability refers to the accuracy, correctness, and quality of the system. Several IEEE standards were written with the objective of providing the software community with defined measures that can be used as indicators of reliability. By emphasizing early reliability assessment, this standard supports methods through measurement to improve product reliability. The most commonly used measures are described in the following text:

1. *Fault density.* This measure can be used to predict remaining faults by comparison with expected fault density, determine if sufficient testing has been completed, and establish standard fault densities for comparison and prediction. It is given by:

$$Fd = \frac{F}{KSLOC}$$

   where F is the total number of unique faults found in a given interval resulting in failures of a specified severity level, and KSLOC is the number of source lines of executable code and nonexecutable data declarations in thousands.

2. *Defect density.* This measure can be used after design and code inspections of new development or large block modifications. If the defect density is outside the norm after several inspections, it is an indication of a problem. It is given by:

$$DD = \sum_{i=1}^{I}\left(\frac{Di}{KSLOD}\right)$$

   where Di is the total number of unique defects detected during the ith design or code inspection process, I is the total number of inspections, and KSLOD is the number of source lines of executable code and nonexecutable data declarations in thousands (in the design phase).

3. *Cumulative failure profile.* This is a graphical method used to predict reliability, estimate additional testing time to reach an acceptable, reliable system, and identify modules and subsystems that require additional testing. A plot is drawn of cumulative failures versus a suitable time base.

4. *Fault-days number.* This measure represents the number of days that faults exist in the system from their creation to their removal. For each fault detected and removed during any phase, the number of days from its creation to its removal (fault days) is determined. The fault days are then summed for all faults detected and removed, to get the fault-days number at system level, including all faults detected and removed up to the delivery date. In those cases in which the creation date of the fault is not known, the fault is assumed to have been created at the middle of the phase in which it was introduced.

9.2.16 Maintenance

The maintenance statement should discuss policies and procedures that the company has put into place to handle the various types of maintenance. This should address any configuration management change control policies that the company already has in place. Alternatively, the maintenance statement might specify a requirement that those bidding on the RFP create a set of policies and procedures to deal with maintenance issues.

9.2.17 Disaster Recovery

For the purposes of the goals and objectives statement, all that is required is a brief statement such as the following:

> The DBMS software will provide a backup capability to ensure protection of the data in the database. In addition, the DBMS software provides a transaction recording feature that can be used to keep track of all transactions during normal daytime operation. If a failure occurs, the transaction record can be used to roll back to the last successful transaction so that the information lost is minimized.

9.3 WORK BREAKDOWN STRUCTURE (WBS): THE BASIS FOR PROJECT ESTIMATES

Project managers develop project plans in three dimensions: resources, time, and budget, each a constraint on what he or she can do. This is why this trio is often called the *triple constraint*:

1. *Resources* — This answers the question, "what kinds of human and nonhuman resources, including hardware and software, are required.
2. *Time* — This answers the question, "how much time needs to be allocated to the project in its entirety, and specifically to each individual task."
3. *Money* — This answers the question, "how much will the project cost in its entirety and, specifically, how much does each individual task cost."

The left-hand side of Figure 9.1 shows the WBS for the EIS system. Once a project is broken down into manageable tasks, it becomes possible to begin the estimation process.

9.3.1 The Process of Human Resource Estimation: An Example

Project managers use a wide variety of techniques to perform the project cost estimation effort. It is customary, in fact, for the estimator to use at least two techniques and then triangulate the two (i.e., discuss the reasons why the two estimates have differences). Often, the best estimate is the average of the results of the various estimation methods used.

A real-world example of this methodology follows. Notice that all three dimensions of the triple constraint are accounted for.

9.3.1.1 Project Estimates

This portion of the document provides cost, effort, and time estimates for the project using various estimation techniques.

9.3.1.2 Historical Data Used for Estimates

Local data was collected to determine the average salaries for IT professionals in Roanoke, Virginia. Table 9.1 summarizes this data.

Table 9.1 shows the average salary for IT professionals. The average salary values do not include the administrative costs associated with the employee. These administrative costs are typically 40 percent of the employee's salary. Therefore, the real cost of the employee is 1.4 times the average salary. This adjusted salary value is shown in the second to last column of the table. The last column adjusts the salary to a per month basis.

To utilize for this project, we have a well-rounded group of programmers who have several years of experience in IT-related fields. Therefore, the adjusted average salary from Table 9.1 will be used for estimation purposes.

Table 9.1 Average Salaries

Profession	Average Salary ($)	Adjusted Salary[a] ($)	Per Month ($)
Computer programmer 2	50,328	70,459	5,871
Computer programmer 3	44,949	62,928	5,244
Database administrator	53,923	75,492	6,291
Database analyst	48,406	67,768	5,647
Software design manager	77,619	108,666	9,055
Software design supervisor	58,325	81,655	6,804
Software engineer	58,395	81,753	6,812

[a] Average salary + overheads @ 40 percent.

It is important that current real-world data is always used. All too often, estimates are based on "gut" feelings about what the true cost of development is. Many IT Web sites provide comparative cost data. In addition, the human resources department presumably has accurate cost information.

9.3.1.3 Estimation Techniques Applied and Results

Two estimation techniques were used for planning purposes, so that the results could be compared and contrasted to ensure that the plan is as accurate as possible:

- Process based
- COCOMO II model

The project manager selected these two techniques from a wide variety of estimation techniques. (Read on through this chapter for information on other estimation techniques.)

9.3.1.3.1 Process-Based Estimation

This technique is based on the project to be implemented. It is accomplished by breaking (decomposing) the project down into a relatively small set of tasks. The time required to accomplish each task is then estimated. These are the major functions for this system:

- User interface and control engineering (UICE)
- Search interface and algorithm engineering (SIAE)
- Database design and management (DDM)
- Automated notification algorithms (ANA)
- Digital camera system (DCS)
- Credit card transaction (CCT)
- Automated backup recovery system (ABRS)

This is where the WBS comes in handy. These structures enable the estimator to successively decompose a system into multiple levels of subtasks. This makes it easier to provide an accurate cost estimate.

The process-based estimation results show that the project will require 9.15 person-months of time to complete.

Estimation is one part science and one part "guestimation." Table 9.2 represents a series of time estimates based on months for each task. For example, the project manager who created this estimate decided that it would take about a quarter of a month (.25) to complete the analysis of the UICE. Where did she get that quarter of a month from?

The project team will be made up of three software engineers, one database analyst and one software design manager. The software design manager will be shared between this and four other projects. Therefore, one fifth of the cost of the software design manager will be applied to this project.

Table 9.2 shows that the project requires 9.15 person-months of work. However, this does not mean that four developers can complete the project in one fourth of the time. There are two reasons for this. The more developers on a project, the more the lines of communication that must be maintained.

Communications can dominate productivity. Most project problems arise as the result of poor communications between workers. If there are n workers on the team, then there are $n(n - 1)/2$ interfaces across which there may be communications problems.

Maintaining these lines of communication takes project resources away from the actual development work. Also, the critical path may not be completed in one fourth of the time. Therefore, the actual amount of time required to complete the project will be estimated at 35 percent higher than the time shown in Table 9.2. The amount of time required to complete the project will be $(9.15 \times 1.35)/4 = 3.08$ months.

The critical path is the longest path through a project. This path determines the earliest date a project may be completed.

The cost of the project team will be $84,795. See table on page 211.

Table 9.2 Process-Based Human Resources Estimation

Activity (Task / Function)	Customer Communication	Planning	Risk Analysis	Engineering — Analysis	Engineering — Design	Construction Release — Code	Construction Release — Test	Customer Evaluation	Total
UICE	0.38	0.08	0.03	0.25	0.38	0.38	0.38	0.15	2.03
SIAE	0.23	0.03	0.02	0.13	0.25	0.15	0.25	0.08	1.14
DDM	0.08	0.03	0.05	0.38	0.5	0.13	0.25	0.03	1.45
ANA	0.15	0.03	0.03	0.13	0.15	0.13	0.13	0.03	0.78
DCS	0.08	0.03	0.02	0.13	0.38	0.5	0.38	0.03	1.55
CCT	0.08	0.02	0.02	0.13	0.25	0.25	0.25	0.03	1.03
ABRS	0.08	0.03	0.02	0.13	0.25	0.25	0.38	0.03	1.17
Total	1.08	0.25	0.19	1.28	2.16	1.79	2.02	0.38	**9.15**
Percentage effort	12	3	2	14	24	19	22	4	100

Software engineer 1	$20,708	(From Table 9.1, a software engineer is costed at $6,812. Multiply this by 3.04 months, and you get $20,708)
Software engineer 2	$20,708	
Software engineer 3	$20,708	
Database analyst	$17,166	
Software design manager	$5,505	
Total	$84,795	

9.3.1.3.1 FP-Based Estimation

All project plans should be estimated using a minimum of two estimation techniques. To help ensure the accuracy of the estimation, the COCOMO II estimation model was used in conjunction with the process-based estimation technique discussed in Subsection 9.3.1.3.1.

COCOMO is an abbreviation for *COst COnstruction MOdel*. Developed by Barry Boehm and popularized by his book entitled *Software Engineering Economics* (1981), it is a formula that describes factors that affect the ultimate cost of computer software. The factors fall into four broad categories: product, computer, personnel, and project.

The COCOMO II model uses either LOC (lines of code) or FPs (function points) for the analysis. For this project, FPs were defined for the major software functions:

- User interface and control engineering (UICE)
- Search interface and algorithm engineering (SIAE)
- Database design and management (DDM)
- Automated notification algorithms (ANA)
- Digital camera system (DCS)
- Credit card transaction (CCT)
- Automated backup recovery system (ABRS)

The FPs for each major software function are shown in Table 9.3. These FPs were plugged into the COCOMO II model. Figure 9.3 shows the results. Notice that, while FPs were used for the estimation, the COCOMO outputted its results in lines of code. The COCOMO II toolset will convert this automatically.

The COCOMO II Estimation Model results show that the project will require 31.8 person-months of time to complete at a cost of $254,000. This is significantly different from the 9.02 person-months of time estimated using process-based estimation. Part of the reason for the wide difference in results is the fact that the project is still in the very early phases. This document, as well as the estimation models, will be updated throughout

Table 9.3 Function Points for the Major Software Functions

	Inputs	Outputs	Files	Interfaces	Queries
UICE	1	1	0	0	0
SIAE	0	0	0	0	1
DDM	0	0	0	1	0
ANA	0	1	0	0	1
DCS	0	0	0	1	0
CCT	0	0	0	1	0
ABRS	1	0	0	0	0

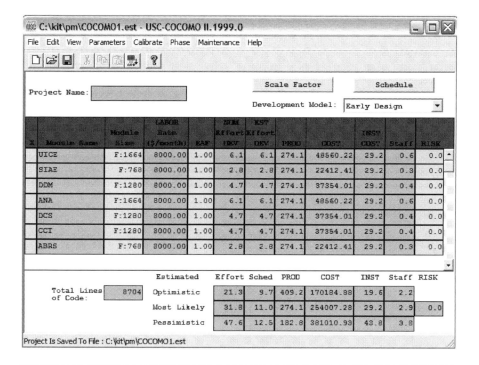

Figure 9.3 COCOMO II project estimation.

the project to ensure that accurate estimation data always exists. This will ensure that any issues with the project will be found as early as possible.

Notice that a reason was given for the discrepancy between the two estimations. This is referred to as *triangulation*. At this point, the estimator will either select one of the two estimates or utilize the average of the two. This final determination, therefore, will become the cost estimation for the human resource component of the project plan.

9.3.2 Other Estimation Techniques

The most important thing for you to understand about project estimation is that uncertainty is inherent in most estimation endeavors; so you need to plan for it. Using a variety of estimation techniques will ensure that your estimate is as accurate as possible.

Estimating by analogy relates the cost of a system to the cost of a known similar system through comparisons of key technical and management characteristics.

An assessment of the technique is presented:

Advantages
- Estimates when little data is available
- Requires limited data collection
- Based on "actual" costs (depending on adjustments)

Disadvantages
- Based on limited data
- Subjective adjustments — may be difficult to validate
- Accuracy highly dependent on similarity between items
- Does not identify cost drivers
- Difficult to assess impact of design changes

Uses
- When little data is available
- Quick, rough order of magnitude
- Check on other techniques

Bottom-up (grass roots) estimating builds up an estimate of a system using detailed information (i.e., you start from the lowest-level tasks and build your system upwards. It is analogous to bottom-up design versus top-down design when designing software systems).

An appraisal of this technique follows:

Advantages
- Sensitive to changes in design
- Provides visibility into cost drivers
- The most precise cost estimating methodology

Disadvantages
- Requires detailed design information
- Time consuming
- Difficult to perform cost trade-offs
- Accuracy depends on stability of design and skill of team

Uses
- Production estimating
- Estimate development of firm designs

Parametric estimation relates the cost of a system to one or more parameters of the system such as physical or performance characteristics utilizing a mathematical model. Parametric cost modeling techniques were first developed in the 1950s by the Rand Corporation. Here is a brief analysis of this technique:

Advantages
- Sensitive to significant design changes
- Quantifies effects of cost drivers
- Based on real-world experience of many systems
- Gives quick, reproducible results

Disadvantages
- Subjective inputs
- Results not as precise as bottom-up
- Requires skilled analyst to develop

Uses
- Cost estimates and trade-offs for systems in early development
- Quick reaction estimates
- Independent check on other estimates

9.3.2.1 *Estimating Nonhuman Resources*

The scope of the project plan should detail the nonhuman resources required by the project. This includes all hardware, software, office supplies, training, and even travel-related expenses necessitated by the project. The cost of these resources must be estimated as well. These costs may be ascertained by researching the Internet or directly from various vendors. The total estimated project cost, therefore, is the sum of the human resource estimate and nonhuman resource estimate.

9.3.3 Managing Project Resources

A variety of human resources may be assigned to a project. These people have a variety of titles and pay scales. The project plan's section on estimation will contain historical data for these various pay scales, which is then used to calculate the project's cost. The project plan will also contain extensive information that describes the people involved in the project as well as the equipment (i.e., nonhuman resources) that are needed for the project.

9.3.3.1 Human Resources

An excerpt of a typical project plan that deals with this requirement follows:

> This project will require four developers. Three of them are software engineers, and one is a database analyst. A software design manager will manage the project. The team is well rounded, and each team member has several years of experience in the IT field. As the team members have a wide range of expertise, this project should require very little additional training.

The one part of the project that may require some minimum training is the digital camera system. One of the software engineers will be sent to a two-day training course on the system that will be purchased. This will ensure that the risks involved with the most technically challenging aspect of the project will be limited. The cost of the training class and travel will be $2000.

There will also be a group of five end users who will be paid for their testing of the system. They will provide feedback from the users' perspectives. Their feedback will be solicited during regular dinner sessions. They will be served dinner while the latest changes to the system are discussed. After dinner, they will be allowed to test out the system for about 1 hr. They will each be paid $20 for each testing session (five sessions).

9.3.3.2 Nonhuman Resources

This includes costs for resources such as hardware (e.g., personal computers, servers, etc.), software (e.g., operating system, database management system, etc.), and even office supplies (e.g., desks). The project manager determines the nonhuman resources for each low-level task by asking, "what does the human resource require to perform this task?"

9.3.4 Budgeting

All projects have budgets. A *budget* is the total sum of all the costs of a project. This includes the following:

1. Salaries
2. Hardware
3. Software
4. Training, as applicable
5. Other equipment such as telephones, stamps, paper, etc.

One talks about costs from two perspectives:

1. *Fixed costs* are those costs that never vary. For example, let us say that a proposed system requires the company to purchase Microsoft Visual Basic. The price of Visual Basic is fixed; therefore, this can be identified as a fixed cost.
2. *Overhead costs* are costs not directly related to the project. For example, the project team's office space is considered overhead. Most project estimations will include overhead as a factor of salaries. This is referred to as administrative overhead and is generally estimated to be 30 to 40 percent of the salary. For example, if $50 is the amount we are using for a typical programmer's hourly cost, then the project manager will craft a budget using an hourly rate of $65 (i.e., $50 + [30 percent of $50]).

There are several different methods of preparing a budget: top-down, bottom-up, and iterative. In all cases, the main goal of the budgetary process is to craft an accurate assessment of the costs of completing the project without overburdening the budget with extraneous costs.

9.3.4.1 Top-Down

Budgeting within organizations is multi-tiered. The organization itself prepares a budget (strategic) as do the departments within the organization (tactical). The organization's master budget is the result of long-range planning, whereas each department prepares a budget based on short-range planning.

Top-down budgeting requires the project planner to be constrained by whatever dollar allocations are made available via the long-range plan. Problems with this methodology include the inevitable competition for scarce budget dollars and a lack of understanding on the part of senior management of the specifics of the project.

9.3.4.2 Bottom-Up

Bottom-up is the preferred budgeting approach from the project manager's perspective. In this scenario, each project manager prepares a budget proposal for each project under his or her direction. The advantages to this approach are a granular level of detail for each project's budget, making the budgeting process far more accurate.

A disadvantage of this methodology is loss of control by senior management. Once the many project budgets are aggregated, it is very likely that the gap between the resultant tactically created budget and the organization plan and budget is quite wide.

9.3.4.3 Iterative

An iterative approach to budgeting tries to combine the advantages of both bottom-up and top-down budgeting while avoiding their respective disadvantages.

The iterative approach starts with management's crafting of a strategic budgetary framework, which is then passed down to the lower levels of the organization. Project managers use the guidance from the framework to develop their respective project budgets. These project budgets are then aggregated at the departmental (i.e., functional) level and then, finally, into an organizational budget. Senior management then reviews this budget based on organizational goals, schedule, available resources, and cost; makes its comments; and returns the budget to the functional areas for revision. Once revised, the project budgets are then reaggregated at the functional level and resubmitted to senior management. This process is iterative and, at times, quite time consuming.

9.3.5 Budget Analysis

Prior to the inception of a project, the feasibility of the project is analyzed. Aside from whether the project is technologically feasible, the costs of the system versus the benefits of the system are also examined to determine economic feasibility. This is called *budget analysis*.

9.3.5.1 Cost-Benefit Analysis

This analysis is quite easy to understand. The process involves comparing the costs of the system to its benefits. We all do this on a daily basis. For example, if we go out to buy a new $1000 PC, we weigh the cost of expending that $1000 against the benefits of owning the PC. For example, these might be the benefits:

1. No longer have to rent a computer — cost savings $75 per month
2. Possible to earn extra money by typing term papers for students — potential earnings $300 per month

We can summarize this as shown in Table 9.4:

Table 9.4 Break-Even Analysis

Costs (Onetime)		Benefits per Year	
	$1000	1. Rental computer savings ($75 × 12)	$900
		2. Typing income ($300 × 12)	$3,600
Total	**$1000**	**Total**	**$4,500**
Potential savings/earnings		$3,500 first year; $4,500 subsequent years	

Onetime capital costs such as computers are usually amortized over a certain period of time. For example, a computer costing $1000 can be amortized over five years, which means that instead of comparing a onetime cost of $1000 to the benefits of purchasing the PC, we can compare a monthly cost.

Not all cost-benefit analyses are so clear-cut, however. In our example, the benefits were both financially based. Not all benefits are so easily quantifiable. Benefits that cannot be quantified are called *intangible benefits*. The following are examples:

1. Reduced turnaround time
2. Improved customer satisfaction
3. Compliance with mandates
4. Enhanced interagency communication

Aside from having to deal with both tangible and intangible benefits, most cost-benefit analyses also need to deal with several alternatives. For example, let us say that a bank uses a loan processing system that is old and often has problems. There might be several alternative solutions:

1. Rewrite the system from scratch
2. Modify the existing system
3. Outsource the system

In each case, a spreadsheet should be created that details one time costs as well as continuing costs. These should then be compared to the benefits of each alternative, both tangible as well as nontangible.

9.3.5.2 Break-Even Analysis

All projects have associated costs. All projects will also have associated benefits. At the outset of a project, costs will far exceed benefits. However, the benefits will start outweighing the costs at some point. This is called the *breakeven point*. The analysis that is done to figure out when this breakeven point will occur is called *breakeven analysis*. In Table 9.4, we see that the breakeven point comes during the first year.

Calculating the breakeven point in a project with multiple alternatives enables the project manager to select the optimum solution. The project manager will generally select the alternative with the shortest breakeven point.

9.3.5.3 Return on Investment

Most organizations select projects that have a positive *return on investment* (ROI), which is the additional amount earned after costs are earned back. In our "buy-versus-rent" PC decision discussed in Subsection 9.3.5.1, we can see that the ROI is quite positive during the first and, especially, during subsequent years of ownership.

The formula for ROI is:

$$ROI = (Benefit - Cost)/Cost$$

Thus, for the first year:

$$ROI = (4500 - 1000)/1000 = 3.5$$

9.4 THE TASK NETWORK

A project is composed of one or more tasks, which have interdependencies, usually based on their sequence. Most projects have more than one person involved in the engineering process, so it is likely that some tasks will be done in parallel; for example, Task A and Task B are developed concurrently. It is very important that tasks be carefully coordinated so that, for example, if Task C depends on Task D, then Task D has available to it on a timely basis the work product outputted by Task C.

To create a WBS, a great deal of information will need to be elicited about the project to be tasked. In general, the steps required to create a WBS include the following:

1. Start with the project statement of work (SOW). Place a task at the top of the list.
2. Define the inputs, outputs, resources, and milestones for the task.

3. If the task as defined can be achieved as a stand-alone task, then go to Step 5, otherwise go to Step 4.
4. Create subtasks for the task, and repeat Step 2 and Step 3 for each subtask.
5. Return to Step 2 to work on the next task until all tasks are accounted for.

9.4.1 Task Identification and Descriptions

Generating a WBS will require a great deal of information about each task to be collected and understood. At a minimum, information should be available about the purpose or objective of the task, as well as the deliverables.

The task description should consist of the following, as shown in Table 9.5:

1. *Number.* This is done according to "task numbering," as explained later.
2. *Task title.* The title should be descriptive. A combination of a noun and a verb is recommended such that the task is described actively rather than passively.
3. *Deliverables.* Each task will have one or more deliverables associated with it; e.g., training manual, meeting notes, and specification.
4. *Subtasks.* Some systems developers equate deliverables with subtasks.

Once a preliminary schedule is articulated, it can be fine-tuned as the project manager gains a better understanding of tasks, dependencies, and specific milestone and due date requirements. At this point, the project manager will usually start using the functionality of Microsoft Project for schedule revision.

Many systems developers use a top-down approach to task identification. Using this methodology, a complex project is decomposed (i.e., divided up) into less complex subprojects, or tasks. Top-down design is a tenet of good software engineering, so it follows that the top-down approach to task identification would offer similar quality attributes. Top-down methodologies promote usability, efficiency, reliability, maintainability, and reusability.

When using a top-down approach, we proceed from top to bottom. We conceptualize the highest-order tasks and then break these down into subtasks. For example, the following might be two high-order tasks:

Develop modifications to system
Produce faculty training

Next, we proceed to identify the subtasks for each of the higher-order tasks that we have already identified:

Develop modifications to system
　　Clean up and finalize for delivery
　　Develop additional perks

Produce faculty training
　　Create in-house training
　　Create campus training

An alternative to the top-down methodology is the bottom-up ("grass-roots") methodology. In a bottom-up approach you start by defining the low-level tasks, such as "develop additional perks," and then figure out how these will be put together to create successively higher-level tasks (i.e., develop modifications to system) and, ultimately, the entire system.

There are many advantages to using a bottom-up methodology. The most important advantage is that we are assured that we will conform to requirements, each of which is tasked at a low level, thus satisfying our end users. Therefore, it can be said that bottom-up estimating is the most precise of all methodologies.

The system developer creating Table 9.5 could have created this task list using a bottom-up approach. He or she would have done this by listing the deliverables, grouping these deliverables (i.e., subtasks), and, finally, creating the major tasks.

Creating a bottom-up task list requires the developer to have detailed information and, as a result, can be quite time consuming.

Accurate task identification is critical to the successful development and implementation of a project. Guidelines should be developed and published such that the methodology deployed to create the WBS is a repeatable process within the organization.

Configuration management is the recommended repeatable process by which task identification is managed.

9.4.2　Task Sequence

Tasks will be performed in a particular sequence. The WBS diagram does a good job of visualizing task sequence. A Gantt chart is another task

Table 9.5   A Typical Systems Development Task List

Number	Task	Deliverable	Dates/Days	Precedence	Milestone
A0000	Start of project	Agreement/contact	04/02/05		
A9999	Project ends	Delivery			10/05/05
A0010	Hold meetings	Weekly meetings	02/04/05		07/05/05
A0101	Develop requirements	Assess functional requirements; demonstrate system; evaluate testing needs; assess nonfunctional requirements; final requirements specification	4	A0102, A0103, A0104	01/03/05
A0102			8		
A0103			2		
A0104			9		
A0105			4		
A0201	Develop documentation	Quality assurance plan; project plan; requirements document; design document; user guide; final project notebook; maintenance plan	2		03/05/05
A0202			8		
A0203			13		
A0204			11		
A0205			5		
A0206			4		
A0207			4		

ID	Task	Description	Duration	Predecessors	Date
A0301 A0302	Produce programmer training	Web design training; database design training	6 4	A0202, A0204	12/03/05
A0401 A0402	Create preliminary design	Brainstorming; architectural layout	1 5	A0203, A0204 A0204, A0401	20/03/05
A0501 A0502	Create detailed design	Design user interface; database design	10 10		04/01/05
A0602 A0603 A0604	Perform coding	Build database; user interface of campus version; user interface of in-house version	0 14 14		19/04/05
A0701 A0702	Perform integration testing	In-house testing; necessary modifications	4 3	A0104	26/04/05
A0801 A0802	Perform posttest	On-campus testing; necessary modifications	4 4	A0701, A0702	03/05/05
A0901 A0902	Develop modification	"Clean up" and finalize for delivery; additional "perks"	1		07/05/05
A1001 A1002	Produce faculty training	In-house training; campus training	0 1	A0901, A0205	10/05/05

modeling technique that is frequently used to show task relationships as well as scheduling and resource requirements.

9.4.3 Task Precedence

Precedence is an indicator of task interdependency. In other words, it tells us when each task can start.

The following list of tasks clearly indicates tasks and their subtasks:

A2000: Develop modifications to system
  A2010: Clean up and finalize for delivery
  A2020: Develop additional perks

A3000: Produce faculty training
  A3010: Create in-house training
  A3020: Create campus training

However, it does not really tell us whether it is necessary for A2000 to begin and end before A3000 or whether A2000 and A3000 can be performed concurrently.

Task preference, therefore, is an indicator of the interrelationship between task start and stop times. Time intervals can be evaluated using several methodologies:

1. *Start-to-finish time of each task.* This is the most common of precedence relationships between tasks. It requires that a task can start only after its predecessor has been completed.
2. *Start-to-start time of two tasks.* In this relationship, an activity can start only after a specified activity has already begun.
3. *Finish-to-finish time of two tasks.* In this relationship, a task cannot end until a specified task has been completed.
4. *Overlap between tasks.* In this relationship, start and end times of tasks are permitted to overlap.
5. *The gap between tasks.* In any of these relationships, a time delay or gap may be added. This is usually done to allow for uncertainty.

9.4.4 The Task List

Generating a WBS will require a significant amount of information about each task to be collected and understood. At a minimum, the following information should be available for each task:

1. The purpose or objective of the task. An example of this would be "training end users to use the new system."
2. Deliverables for each task. In the case of our end-user training objective, several deliverables might be required; e.g., development of training materials, development of online training modules, etc.
3. Scheduled start and completion time for each task.
4. Budget.
5. Responsibility. Each task should have an owner, i.e., the person responsible for getting the task done.
6. Metrics. Whether or not a task has been successfully completed should be made quantifiable. Metrics can be in this form: number of days overdue, cost overrun amount, user acceptance ratio, etc.

9.4.5 Project Scheduling

People who perform project scheduling are often referred to as *estimators*. These employees are usually senior members of the staff, who have years of experience working on a wide variety of projects and an in-depth knowledge of the organization and its systems.

After a WBS has been developed, each of the tasks must be scheduled.

Just how long will it take to perform a particular task? There are several estimation approaches to choose from:

1. *Stochastic approach:* It is unlikely that one can ever calculate the duration of a task with certainty. The stochastic approach takes this uncertainty into consideration by estimating task duration along with variance.
2. *Deterministic approach:* Most project schedulers do not want to deal with uncertainty; so, the deterministic approach is the preferred method. A deterministic estimate is based on past experiences, in which the number used is the average time it took to perform the task in the past.
3. *Modular approach:* This technique is similar to the top-down method of task identification. A task is first decomposed into its subtasks. Each subtask is then estimated. The sum of the estimates is "rolled up" to provide an estimate for the major task. For example, A2000 (develop modifications to system) referred to in Subsection 9.4.3 has two subtasks. If we estimate A2010 to take 20 days and A2020 to take 30 days, then the duration for task A2000 is calculated to be 50 days.
4. *Benchmark job technique:* This technique is best used for repetitive tasks in which task duration has proved to be consistent over time

(i.e., benchmark). For example, let us say it takes 20 min to install anti-virus software on a PC. The company has 100 PCs. Given that each PC is similar and that the process of installing the software is the same for each PC, we can estimate the duration for the complete task to be 33.33 hr (20 min × 100 PCs).

5. *Experience is best:* The very best estimators are those with years of experience in the organization and with in-depth knowledge of the systems, policies, and procedures used by the organization.

The most prevalent unit of measure for a schedule is *days*. In a time-critical system (i.e., man-rated where life and death is often at stake), it is quite possible that hours and even minutes might need to be used. When summarizing the project schedule, it is customary to roll-up the schedule to provide an overview. In this case, time spans longer than days are permissible.

9.5 THE PROACTIVE RISK STRATEGY

A proactive risk strategy should always be adopted. It is better to plan for possible risk than have to react to it in a crisis. The first thing that needs to be done is to identify risks. One method is to create a risk item checklist. A typical project plan might list the following risks:

1. Customer will change or modify requirements.
2. Lack of sophistication of end users.
3. Delivery deadline will be tightened.
4. End users resist system.
5. Server may not be able to handle larger number of users simultaneously.
6. Technology will not meet expectations.
7. Larger number of users than planned.
8. Lack of training of end users.
9. Inexperienced project team.
10. System (security and firewall) will be hacked.

Software risks generally include project risks, technical risks, and business risks.

Project risks can include budgetary, staffing, scheduling, customer, requirement, and resource problems. For example, a key stakeholder may leave the company, taking his knowledge base with him.

Technical risks can include design, implementation, interface, ambiguity, technical obsolescence, and leading-edge problems. An example of this is the development of a project around a leading-edge technology that has not yet been proved.

Table 9.6 A Typical Risk Table

Risks	Category	Percentage Probability	Impact
Risk 1	PS	70	2
Risk 2	CU	60	3

Notes: Impact values: 1 = catastrophic, 2 = critical, 3 = marginal, 4 = negligible; category abbreviations: BU = business impact risk, CU = customer characteristics risk, PS = process definition risk, ST = staff size and experience risk, TE = technology risk.

Business risks include building a product or system no one wants (market risk), losing support of senior management (management risk), building a product that no longer fits into the strategic plan (strategic risk), losing budgetary support (budget risks), and building a product that the sales staff does not know how to sell.

Risks can also be categorized as known, predictable, or unpredictable. *Known risks* are those that can be uncovered upon careful review of the project plan and the environment in which the project is being developed (e.g., lack of development tools, unrealistic delivery date, or lack of knowledge in the problem domain). *Predictable risks* can be extrapolated from past experience. For example, if your past experience with the end users has not been good, it is reasonable to assume that the current project will suffer from the same problem. *Unpredictable risks* are hard, if not impossible, to identify in advance. For example, no one could have predicted the events of September 11, but this one event affected computers worldwide.

Once risks have been identified, most managers project these risks in two dimensions: likelihood and consequences. As shown in Table 9.6, a risk table is a simple tool for risk projection. First, based on the risk item checklist, list all risks in the first column of the table. Then, in the following columns fill in each risk's category, probability of occurrence, and assessed impact. Afterwards, sort the table by probability and then by impact, study it, and define a cutoff line (i.e., the line demarking the threshold of acceptable risk). All risks above the cutoff line must be managed and discussed. Factors influencing their probability and impact should be specified.

A risk mitigation, monitoring, and management (RMMM) plan is the tool to help avoid risks. Causes of the risks must be identified and mitigated. Risk monitoring activities take place as the project proceeds and should be planned early.

9.5.1 Sample Risk Plan

An excerpt of a typical RMMM plan is presented in this subsection.

9.5.1.1 Scope and Intent of RMMM Activities

This project will be uploaded to a server, which will be exposed to the outside world; hence, we need to develop security protection. We will need to configure a firewall and restrict access to only "authorized users" through the linked data warehouse. We will have to know how to deal with load balance if the number of visits to the site is very large at one time.

We will need to know how to maintain the databases and data warehouse to make it more efficient, what type of database we should use, who should have the responsibility to maintain it, and who should be the administrator. Proper training of the aforementioned personnel is very important, so that the database and the system contain accurate information.

9.5.1.2 Risk Management Organizational Role

The software project manager must maintain track of the efforts and schedules of the team. They must anticipate any "unwelcome" event that may occur during the development or maintenance stages and establish plans to avoid these events or minimize their consequences.

It is the responsibility of everyone on the project team with regular input from the customer to assess potential risks throughout the project. Communication among everyone involved is very important for the success of the project. In this way, it is possible to mitigate and eliminate possible risks before they occur. This is known as a *proactive approach* or *strategy for risk management.*

9.5.1.3 Risk Description

This section describes the risks that may occur during this project:

Business impact risk (BU): This risk would entail that the software produced does not meet the needs of the client who requested the product. It would also have a business impact if the product no longer fits into the overall business strategy of the company.

Customer characteristics risks (CU): This risk is the customer's lack of involvement in the project and their nonavailability for meetings with the developers from time to time. Also the customer's sophistication regarding the product being developed and ability to use it form part of this risk.

Development risks (DE): Risks associated with the availability and quality of the tools to be used to build the product. The equipment and software provided by the client on which to run the product must be compatible with the software project being developed.

Process definition risks (PS): Does the software being developed meet the requirements as originally defined by the developer and client? Did the development team follow the correct design throughout the project? These are examples of process risks.

Product size (PR): The product size risk involves the overall size of the software being built or modified. Risks involved would include the customer not providing the proper size of the product to be developed and the software development team misjudging the size or scope of the project. The latter problem could create a product that is too small (rarely) or too large for the client and could result in a loss of money to the development team because the cost of developing a larger product cannot be recouped from the client.

Staff size and experience risk (ST): This would include appropriate and knowledgeable programmers to code the product as well as the cooperation of the entire software project team. It would also mean that the team has enough members who are competent and able to complete the project.

Technology risk (TE): Technology risk could occur if the product being developed is obsolete by the time it is ready to be sold. The opposite effect could also be a factor, if the product is so "new" that the end users would have problems using the system and resist the changes made. A new technological product could also be so new that there may be problems using it. It would also include the complexity of the design of the system being developed.

9.5.1.4   Risk Table

The risk table provides a simple technique to view and analyze the risks associated with the project. The probability of each risk was then estimated and its impact on the development process assessed. A key to the impact values and categories appear at the end of the table. A sorted version of the risk table is presented in Table 9.7.

The table was sorted first by probability and then by impact value.

9.5.2   RMMM Strategy

Each risk or group of risks should have a corresponding strategy associated with it. The RMMM strategy discusses how risks will be monitored and dealt with. Risk plans (i.e., contingency plans) are usually created in tandem with end users and managers. An excerpt of an RMMM strategy is given in the following subsections.

Table 9.7 Risks Table (Sorted)

Risks	Category	Percentage Probability	Impact
Customer will change or modify requirements	PS	70%	2
Lack of sophistication of end users	CU	60%	3
Users will not attend training	CU	50%	2
Delivery deadline will be tightened	BU	50%	2
End users resist system	BU	40%	3
Server may not be able to handle larger number of users simultaneously	PS	30%	1
Technology will not meet expectations	TE	30%	1
Larger number of users than planned	PS	30%	3
Lack of training of end users	CU	30%	3
Inexperienced project team	ST	20%	2
System (security and firewall) will be hacked	BU	15%	2

Notes: Impact values: 1 = catastrophic, 2 = critical, 3 = marginal, 4 = negligible; category abbreviations: BU = business impact risk, CU = customer characteristics risk, PS = process definition risk, ST = staff size and experience risk, TE = technology risk.

9.5.2.1 Project Risk RMMM Strategy

The area of design and development that contributes the largest percentage to the overall project cost is the database and data warehouse subsystems. Our estimate for this portion does provide a small degree of buffer for unexpected difficulties (as do all estimates). This effort will be closely monitored and coordinated with the customer to ensure that any impact, either positive or negative, is quickly identified. Schedules and personnel resources will be adjusted accordingly to minimize the effect or maximize the advantage, as appropriate.

Schedule and milestone progress will be monitored as part of the routine project management with appropriate emphasis on meeting target dates. Adjustments to parallel efforts will be made as appropriate, should the need arise. Personnel turnover will be managed through use of internal personnel matrix capacity. Our organization has a large software engineering base with sufficient numbers to support our potential demand.

9.5.2.2 Technical Risk RMMM Strategy

We are planning for two senior software engineers to be assigned to this project, both of whom have significant experience in designing and developing Web-based applications. The project progress will be monitored as part of the routine project management with appropriate emphasis on meeting target dates and adjusted as appropriate.

Prior to implementing any core operating software upgrades, full parallel testing will be conducted to ensure compatibility with the system as developed. The application will be developed using only public application programming interfaces (APIs), and no "hidden" hooks. Although this does not guarantee compatibility, it should minimize any potential conflicts. Any problems identified will be quantified using cost-benefit and trade-off analysis, and then coordinated with the customer prior to implementation.

The database/data warehouse subsystem is expected to be the most complex portion of the application; however, it is still a relatively routine implementation. Efforts to minimize potential problems include the abstraction of the interface from the implementation of the database code to allow changing the underlying database with minimum impact. Additionally, only industry-standard SQL calls will be used, avoiding all proprietary extensions available.

9.5.2.3 Business Risk RMMM Strategy

The first business risk, lower-than-expected success, is beyond the control of the development team. Our only potential impact is to use the current state-of-the-art tools to ensure that the system performs (in particular, that database access meets user expectations) and that graphics are designed using industry-standard look-and-feel styles.

Similarly, the second business risk, loss of senior management support, is really beyond the direct control of the development team. However, to help manage this risk, we will strive to impart a positive attitude during meetings with the customer, as well as present very professional work products throughout the development period. Many advocate the use of a risk information sheet, an example of which appears in Table 9.8.

9.6 WHERE DO WE GO NEXT?

That just about wraps it up. In Chapter 1 through Chapter 9, we covered the entirety of KM topics, from content management to business intelligence. In Chapter 10, you will find a lengthy list of KM tools, which might be of interest to you. Good luck!

Table 9.8   A Sample Risk Information Sheet

Risk Information Sheet
Risk id: PO2-4-32 Date: March 4, 2004 Probability: 80 percent Impact: high
Description: Over 70 percent of the software components scheduled for reuse will be integrated into the application. The remaining functionality will have to be custom-developed.
Refinement/context: 1. Certain reusable components were developed by a third party with no knowledge of internal design standards 2. Certain reusable components have been implemented in a language that is not supported on the target environment
Mitigation/monitoring: 1. Contact third party to determine conformance to design standards 2. Check to see if language support can be acquired
Management/contingency plan/trigger: Develop a revised schedule assuming that 18 additional components will have to be built Trigger: Mitigation steps unproductive as of March 30, 2004
Current status: In process
Originator: Jane Manager

References

Boehm, B., *Software Engineering Economics,* Prentice Hall, 1981.

Davis, C., A roadmap for long-term knowledge management success, *AIIM E-Doc Magazine, 18*(1), January–February 2004.

Hernandez, H., Knowledge management doesn't come in a box, *Customer Inter@actions Solutions, 23*(7), January 2005.

Appendix A

LESSONS LEARNED FORM

Project name or work unit:	Date:
Division or unit:	Sponsor name:
Project or work unit manager:	Facilitator:
Project team or work unit members:	

Objective: Customer expectations are met	How well we did		
	Fell short of expectations	Met expectations	Exceeded expectations
Explanation (what helped/what hindered):			

Objective: All specifications are achieved	How well we did		
	Fell short of expectations	Met expectations	Exceeded expectations
Explanation (what helped/what hindered):			

Objective: Completed on time	How well we did		
	Fell short of expectations	Met expectations	Exceeded expectations
Explanation (what helped/what hindered):			

Objective: Completed within budget	How well we did		
	Fell short of expectations	Met expectations	Exceeded expectations
Explanation (what helped/what hindered):			

Objective: Return on investment achieved	How well we did		
	Fell short of expectations	Met expectations	Exceeded expectations
Explanation (what helped/what hindered):			

Objective: Organizational goals met	How well we did		
	Fell short of expectations	Met expectations	Exceeded expectations
Explanation (What helped/what hindered?):			

Objective: Positive experience for project team or work unit	How well we did		
	Fell short of expectations	Met expectations	Exceeded expectations
Explanation (what helped/what hindered):			

Objective:	How well we did		
	Fell short of expectations	Met expectations	Exceeded expectations
Explanation (what helped/what hindered):			

Note: Use additional sheets for more objectives or areas.

Appendix B

METRICS GUIDE
FOR KNOWLEDGE
MANAGEMENT INITIATIVES

B.1   OVERVIEW

Knowledge management (KM) initiatives should be continually gauged for their progress in achieving their objectives to ensure success. Given the complex and dynamic nature of modern organizations, KM, as well as all other organizational initiatives, cannot guarantee that plans and strategies will succeed. However, well-designed performance measures will yield insight to help managers understand and adapt their organizations.

This guide, adapted from the U.S. Department of the Navy (2005) presents a practical framework for measuring the value of investments in KM initiatives. Because the value of KM depends on each organization's goals and people, it is not a "cookbook" of standard procedures but rather an aid to help you identify and apply appropriate metrics for your initiative.

The measurement process is composed of several steps to clearly identify what should be measured, how to measure it, and how to use the measures. This process is built as a series of questions that help guide you through the decisions of defining, choosing, and using the metrics. However, you should have first identified the business purpose of the KM project, and have an understanding how the KM project will enhance your objectives. The questions are as follows:

1. What is the business objective? (Answered prior to developing a metrics plan.)
2. What KM methods and tools will we use? (Answered prior to developing a metrics plan.)

3. Who are the stakeholders and what do they need to know?
4. Which framework is best?
5. What should we measure?
6. How should we collect and analyze the measures?
7. What do the measures tell us and how should we change?

The knowledge-centric organization (KCO) model uses three types of specific measures to monitor the KM initiative from different perspectives. *Outcome metrics* concern the overall organization and measure large-scale characteristics such as increased productivity or revenue for the enterprise. *Output metrics* measure project-level characteristics such as the effectiveness of lessons learned information to capturing new business. *System metrics* monitor the usefulness and responsiveness of the supporting technology tools.

Three primary classes of business objectives are used to characterize KM initiatives and to help design the proper mix of performance measures, which are as follows:

- *Program and process management:* This class includes strategic organizational objectives such as leveraging best practices and transferring lessons learned. Some of the business problems that program and process management initiatives are designed to solve include issues such as ensuring consistency across the organization and proactively preventing duplication of effort.
- *Program execution and operations:* This class includes objectives such as connecting people with experts, transferring expertise instantaneously, and getting the right operational knowledge to people in the field when they need it.
- *Personnel and training:* This class includes personnel and learning issues such as acquiring and retaining talent and improving quality of life for employees.

B.2 INTRODUCTION

KM provides a methodology for creating and modifying processes to promote knowledge creation and sharing. These processes are not new and independent KM business processes but processes developed by applying the KM methodology to core organizational applications. KM, implemented by and at the organizational level and supporting empowerment and responsibility at the individual level, focuses on understanding the knowledge needs of an organization and the sharing and creation of knowledge by becoming part of the fabric of the organization.

Connecting people is the primary focus of KM initiatives. Indeed, it is essential to understand that KM is not about simply increasing access to information. On the contrary, access to large amounts of information is good when there is ample time to peruse it, but this access does not provide quick answers. KM seeks to provide these answers through a balance between stored, succinct, and directly pertinent information and links to other people who are likely to know how to help.

KM provides two following major benefits to an organization:

- It improves the organization's performance through increased effectiveness, productivity, quality, and innovation
- It increases the financial value of the organization by treating people's knowledge as an asset similar to traditional assets such as inventory and capital facilities

Each of these benefits has distinct qualities that can be measured, such as the effectiveness of sharing and the intrinsic value of knowledge assets. This guide focuses on determining effective performance measures to assess the organization's current status in becoming a KCO. At every stage in the journey, metrics provide a valuable means of focusing attention on desired behaviors and results.

Many of the organizational changes will be intangible characteristics, such as how quickly people adapt to new situations, morale, camaraderie, and other important factors that cannot easily be quantified. Performance measures for KM build on the experience in accounting and management for other types of intangible initiatives such as learning and training. Metrics are particularly important to KM because a return on investment (ROI) for KM often takes significant time to appear. Putting a KM program into effect will impact other business processes as the organization learns to use and leverage the new KM capabilities. This "acculturation" to KM can take 18 to 36 months in some cases. According to the Gartner Group, "in no case should a KM program (at the enterprise level) be expected to show ROI in less than 12 months."*

B.2.1 Building a Knowledge-Centric Organization: The Role of Metrics

Performance measures for KM have several objectives:

- To help make a business case for implementation
- To help guide and tune the implementation process by providing feedback

---

* F. Caldwell. "CEO Update: Measuring the Success of Enterprise Knowledge Management," *Gartner Group.* December 13, 2000.

- To provide a target or goal
- To measure, retrospectively, the value of the initial investment decision and the lessons learned
- To develop benchmarks for future comparisons and for others to use
- To aid learning from the effort and develop lessons learned

Performance measures should be designed and implemented to reflect organizational goals and objectives. KM is a strategic business process that enables other critical business processes. Therefore, it is important to focus measures (and the entire initiative) on factors that affect the ability to achieve strategic objectives.

The KCO model uses three types of metrics to assess different levels of KM impact, namely, outcome (enterprise or overall value), output (project or task), and system (technology tool). These are defined and explained in Subsection B.3.4.4. However, care must be taken to "pick the right measure" similar to "picking the right tool," as outlined in the National Performance Review report on performance measures.*¹ Based on a review of many high-performing organizations, this report identified several key factors in designing and using performance measures that are just as important to building a KCO, and which we will emphasize throughout this guide. These factors include: (1) using a few focused measures aligned to strategic objectives, (2) measuring critical characteristics of the business processes, and (3) recognizing measures as being only valuable tools and not the products of the project.

The perspectives of the customer, department, organization, and individual in an enterprise are critical to its success and need to be incorporated into that success. The implication of this for KM metrics is critical — when thinking about metrics, it is important to identify who is likely to use the performance measurement information. Potential users include strategic decision makers, special project decision makers, funding and approval stakeholders, or customers. Measures should be in terms that are familiar to the stakeholder. For this reason, you may find that there are several different metrics that need to be captured for your initiative. There is no one "right" set of measures for KM initiatives, and most KM initiatives will require a combination of measurement types and classes to effectively communicate with the key stakeholders. The measures must reflect the overall mission and strategy of the organization.

---

* Serving the American Public: Best Practices in Performance Measurements from National Performance Review, 1997.

B.2.2   What Is the Metrics Guide?

This guide describes several types of metrics that have been effectively used in previous KM and other business projects, along with suggested applications. These applications differ in how people perceive knowledge and the timeliness with which they need to access and act upon the knowledge. Three primary classes of business objectives that are used to characterize KM initiatives and to help design the proper mix of performance measures include: (1) program and project management, (2) program execution and operations, and (3) personnel and training.

B.3   DESIGNING ACTIONABLE KM PERFORMANCE MEASURES

Performance measures support decision making and communication throughout an organization to understand the progress, efficiency, value, and strategic alignment of KM projects. One of the most important things to keep in mind about KM initiatives is that performance measures are just a starting point; it takes a far more serious, strategic commitment to make organizations truly effective. To achieve the objectives of a KCO, the KM initiative must be continuously assessed at all levels of the organization to ensure that the required actions and changes are being made, and redefined if necessary. This is a continuous process.

This section presents general techniques to develop measures that are actionable — measures that provide a basis for making decisions, changing behaviors, or taking action. The remaining sections of this guide present specific information on applying these techniques to the three primary classes of business objectives, such as program and project management, program execution and operations, and personnel and training.

B.3.1   The KM Measurement Process

The measurement process is composed of several steps to clearly identify what should be measured, how to measure it, and how to use the measures. This process is a series of questions that help guide you through the decisions of defining, choosing, and using the metrics. You should have already identified the business purpose of the KM project and have an understanding of how the KM project will enhance your objectives. Each step of the measurement process will be discussed separately in this section.

B.3.2   Who Are the Stakeholders and What Do They Need to Know?

The first step in the measurement process is to identify who will use the measures. This can be a KM project champion, officers and managers, participants, funding and approval officials, internal customers, supply industries, and other stakeholders. A useful technique is to brainstorm a list of all possible audiences for the measures and then review the list to remove duplicates and add any positions or organizations not included previously.

However, be careful not to include such a large number or a wide range of people that it will be too difficult to accommodate all of their concerns and needs. A key part of defining the business objective and KM methods (steps done before the metrics process begins) is to focus the KM initiative on specific organizational needs. These activities should have identified the primary stakeholders, even if only in a general sense, and this list can help consolidate the final list into stakeholders who are substantially connected to the initiative.

Next, identify the stakeholders' most important questions and the decisions they will make to determine exactly what information they need to glean from the measures. They may want to determine how valuable the knowledge assets are to the organization in practice, how effective the KM system is in enabling knowledge sharing and reuse, or both. Thus, measures have to be tailored to each need.

B.3.3   Which Framework Is Best?

A framework helps ensure the metrics are aligned to the project objectives and the organization's strategic goals. A framework is a more useful way to convey the measures than merely listing them. A framework can show how actions contribute to overall goals, the mechanisms by which actions produce benefits, the rationale for conducting the KM project, and, in some cases, provide an analytical tool for making investment trade-offs.

There are several ways to construct a framework using organization schemes such as a balanced set of measures, benchmarking, target-setting, matrices, hierarchies, flow diagrams, and even management systems. The best choice for your initiative depends on which one, or ones, makes it easy for your team to gauge and understand the costs, benefits, relationships, and impacts of the KM processes and measures to each other, and to your business objectives.

The key characteristics of some of these schemes relating to KM initiatives are described as follows.

- *Flow:* A flow framework traces KM activities to impacts and related measures and is good for showing how KM activities produce benefits.
- *Matrix:* A matrix is good for showing the rationale for prioritizing and selecting from among a group of KM projects, and is often

used in portfolio management. Matrices are effective for condensing many interdependent factors into a readable format. For example, one matrix can show the relationship among KM activities, points of contact, expected results, measures used, actual results, stakeholders, and resource costs.

■ *Causal diagrams: Causal loop* diagrams show the cause-and-effect structure of a system through the relationships between its key parts. These diagrams can help you understand complicated relationships in which many factors interact and there are few, if any, simple linear cause–effect relationships. Causal loop diagrams were popularized by the systems thinking field, in which they are an important component of viewing an organization as a total entity rather than as independent units.

■ *Balanced scorecard:* This provides a view of business performance by combining financial measures, which tell the results of actions already taken, with operational measures of customer satisfaction, internal processes, and the enterprise's innovation and improvement activities — the drivers of future performance. A balanced scorecard aligns measures with strategies to track progress, reinforce accountability, and prioritize improvement opportunities. A traditional balanced scorecard integrates four related perspectives, as shown in Figure B.1. These are as follows:

1. *Customer perspective:* How do customers see us? General mission statements need to be made concrete with specific measures of what matters to customers, namely time, quality, performance or service, and cost.

2. *Internal perspective:* What must we excel at? To achieve goals on cycle time, quality, performance and cost, managers must devise measures that are influenced by subordinates' actions. Because much of the action takes place at the division and workstation levels, managers need to decompose overall cycle time, quality, product, and cost measures to local levels. That way, the measures link top management's judgment about key internal processes and competencies to the actions taken by individuals that affect overall command objectives.

3. *Innovation and learning perspective:* Can we continue to improve and create value? An organization's ability to innovate, improve, and learn ties directly to that organization's value. That is, only through adapting to evolving new missions, creating more value for customers, and improving operating efficiencies can a command maximize the use of existing mission capabilities while meeting the personal and developmental needs of its people.

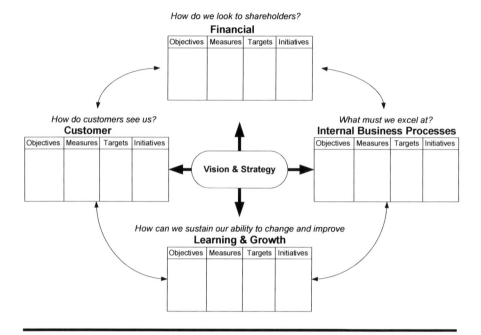

Figure B.1   Balanced scorecard.

4. *Financial perspective:* How do we look to stakeholders? Ideally, organizations should specify how improvements in quality of life, cycle time, mission readiness, training opportunities, equipment, and new mission directives lead to improved near-term readiness, increased retention, progress in modernization and recapitalization programs, reduced manpower requirements, increased personal or training time, faster skills acquisition, or to reduced operating expenses. The challenge is to learn how to make such an explicit linkage between operations and finance. Financial performance measures indicate whether the organization's strategy, implementation, and execution are contributing to bottom-line improvement. (Typical financial goals have to do with profitability, growth, and stakeholder value.)

These measures can be tailored to your KM initiative. An example of a modified balanced scorecard is shown in Figure B.2, in which new measures are defined for strategic management of information systems.

B.3.4   What Should Be Measured?

The most important characteristic to consider when choosing or defining a KM performance measure is whether the metric tells if knowledge is

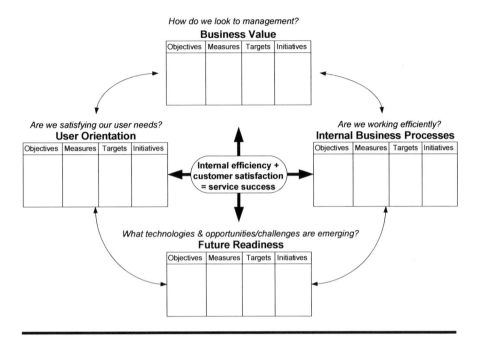

How do we look to management?
Business Value

Objectives	Measures	Targets	Initiatives

Are we satisfying our user needs?
User Orientation

Objectives	Measures	Targets	Initiatives

Are we working efficiently?
Internal Business Processes

Objectives	Measures	Targets	Initiatives

Internal efficiency + customer satisfaction = service success

What technologies & opportunities/challenges are emerging?
Future Readiness

Objectives	Measures	Targets	Initiatives

Figure B.2   IT balanced scorecard.

being shared and used. For example, a metric for a best practices database might be the number of times the database has been accessed. A large number of accesses or "hits" suggest that people are reading the document, but this does not definitively indicate whether it was useful to anyone or whether it improved operational efficiency or quality. A better metric would be to track database usage and ask a sampling of the users if and how it helped them.

Measures should be tied to the maturity of the KM initiative, which has a life cycle that progresses through a series of phases: preplanning, start-up, pilot project, and growth and expansion. In 2001, the American Productivity and Quality Center (APQC) published the results of a benchmarking study on measurement for knowledge management that discusses how metrics differ through a life cycle. In the preplanning phase, an integrated product team can use its complementary mix of expertise to do process and risk analysis, develop strategies, and predict results. The goals of the start-up phase are to generate interest and support for KM, which creates a higher value on measures that convince people that KM is worthwhile, such as anecdotes, comparisons to other organizations, and levels of funding and participation. The pilot-project phase concentrates on developing evidence of success and lessons learned that can be transferred to other initiatives. In this phase, more definitive measures are needed, such as changes in business costs (e.g., reduced support and resources), cultural changes (e.g., increased sharing among groups), and the currency and usage of collected knowledge bases. For the growth and expansion stage, KM is institutionalized across the corporation, and measures that reflect enterprisewide benefits are therefore needed. These include KM proficiency gauged against best practices, formal KM elements in performance evaluations, and sophisticated capital-valuation calculations.

B.3.4.1 Qualitative and Quantitative Measures

Measurements for KM initiatives can be quantitative or qualitative and, in general, a measurement program should include both types of measures. Quantitative measures use numbers and typically provide hard data to evaluate performance between points (such as last month to this month) or to spot trends. For example, you can collect quantitative data on Website statistics, the number of hours spent on a particular task, or the percentage of equipment removed from operational status for repairs. Qualitative measures use the situation's context to provide a sense of value and are referred to as *soft data*. These measures include stories, anecdotes, and future scenarios. When it is difficult to capture meaningful quantitative measures, such as the value to the individual for being a member of a community of practice, a story from a member about how the community helped him solve a critical problem can have as much or more impact on stakeholders. Qualitative measures can augment quantitative measures with additional context and meaning.

A closely related concept to the need for qualitative measures is the notion of tangible and intangible benefits. A *tangible benefit* is concrete and can have a direct measurement of its value. In contrast, an *intangible benefit* cannot be definitively described by a quantitative value. For example, the value of a machine can be computed from its production rate compared to its operating costs, although the value of a company's brand image to its profitability cannot easily be computed. As we will discuss in a later section, quantitative measures can provide an indirect (although uncertain) indication of intangible value.

Despite the difficulty of quantifying intangible benefits, many organizations need to evaluate programs and choose strategic directions based on their values. For a KM initiative, people's unspoken know-how is one of the largest potential sources of value. This tacit knowledge is an example of an intellectual asset whose value is only realized when it is actually shared and reused effectively. Determining its value and effectiveness is hampered by many unknown factors, such as how people really use knowledge to make decisions, when knowledge sharing is and is not useful to specific tasks, and if people require a prior personal relationship before accepting knowledge as trustworthy. Several new techniques have been developed that attempt to measure the value of intellectual assets and other intangibles. We have already discussed one in detail in Subsection B.3.3, the balanced scorecard method, which used a balanced set of tangible and intangible factors to describe performance. Examples of a few other well-known measurement techniques are summarized as follows:

- *Intangible assets monitor:* This model defines three types of intangible assets that account for the book-to-market discrepancy in the value of many companies: individual competence, internal structure, and external structure. People are the only true agents in business and all assets and structures, whether tangible or intangible, are a result of human actions. You need to have a very good understanding of your corporate goals and objectives to apply the intangible assets monitor because the indicators are specifically chosen to have the maximum impact (good or bad) on those goals.

- *Skandia navigator:* Developed by Leif Edvinsson at Skandia Assurance and Financial Services in Sweden, it combines the balanced scorecard approach with the theory behind the intangible assets monitor. In 1994, Skandia published the results of this framework as the first supplement to their annual report, for the first time using the term *intellectual assets* instead of *intangible assets*. The Skandia Navigator defines two components of intellectual capital: human capital plus structural capital.

- *Intellectual capital index:* Developed by Johan and Goran Roos, this approach emphasizes the flows of intellectual capital. The Roos index provides a framework for measures in two general categories: human capital (competence, attitude, intellectual agility, knowledge capital, and skill capital) and structural capital (external relationships, internal organization, renewal and development, strategic processes, and flow of products and services).

Another important technique uses modeling and simulation to extract the effect of process changes on an organization. Actual business processes are modeled as thoroughly as possible using quantitative measures and then the effects of a change — such as a lessons learned database, a collaboration Web site, or informal knowledge-sharing events — are simulated as new portions of the business process. The intangible benefit is assessed by the improvement or deterioration of the organization's overall performance.

B.3.4.2   A Key Qualitative Measurement Strategy: Storytelling

One of the most popular ways to communicate qualitative measures is through storytelling or "serious anecdote management." The storytelling approach was originally identified by Tom Davenport and Larry Prusak (authors of *Working Knowledge*) and popularized by Stephen Denning (formally of the World Bank) and David Snowden (IBM Global Services). *Serious anecdotes* (a term coined by Davenport) are stories with a measurement "punch line." Stories capture context, which gives them meaning and makes them powerful. In addition, stories are how human beings make sense of things. A story about how knowledge was leveraged in the organization to achieve value does two things. First, it creates an interesting context around which to remember the measure being described. Second, it educates the reader or listener about alternative methods that they themselves might employ to achieve similar results, thus helping to "spread the word" about the KM program and speed up the cultural change. Consider this example from a professional services firm:

> I joined the organization on March 16, 1998, without previous experience. After one week of training, I joined a project team. After one day of training on the project, I was assigned a task to learn a particular technology that was new to everyone on the team. I was given a bunch of books and told that I had three days to learn how to create a project using this technology.
>
> In my first week of training, I remembered learning about the company's expertise database. I sent an e-mail to four people I found in the database, asking for their help. One of them sent me a document containing exactly what I wanted. Instead of three days, my task was completed in half a day.

This story is compelling for several reasons. First, we can all empathize with the author's struggle. Everyone can identify a situation in which they felt completely overwhelmed and were not sure they could complete the assignment given to them. Second, we can also sympathize with the employee's distress at being told to figure out what was needed from a stack of manuals! In practice, people rely on a network of relationships for information and advice.

We can also relate to this story because we can see that the KM initiative complemented the natural work pattern rather than requiring a new set of behaviors or tools. Finally, we "get" the value of the KM initiative immediately with the punch line of the story — "I completed a three-day task in half a day." Imagine the value of completing all three-day tasks in one-half a day, and you can start to envision the very large value a KM initiative can provide.

B.3.4.3 Future Scenarios

There is a special type of storytelling that is particularly useful at the early stages of a KM project. This type of story creates a future vision for the enterprise, a vision that describes how life will be different when the KM initiative is fully implemented. These stories, often called *future scenarios*, provide a qualitative way of describing the value of a KM investment even before the project starts. The following example presents a future scenario for a research organization in a manufacturing firm:

> On May 19, 2001, Angela, a senior scientist in the Image Science Laboratory, is working on a complex technology problem. She reaches a stumbling point in her analysis and wonders if someone else at the company might have some insights that would help her with this problem. Angela is new to the firm, having only just joined in March, and she has a limited personal network. Looking for insight into the key areas of resistance, she logs on to "Knowledge-Zone," the company's knowledge portal. Although Angela had previously defined her areas of interest, her personal page, My K-Zone, includes links to two recently published scientific papers and an upcoming conference. She also sees that several other scientists with similar interests are also logged in to the system, but she has got no time for that now — she is on a mission.
>
> Angela begins her search by entering a simple, English-language question to find out if there is any relevant work in the company document repository. She comes across a few papers written on her topic that have four-star ratings from other imaging scientists. She also identifies a community of interest within the firm on a related subject.
>
> Angela gets a list of the community members from within K-Zone and sees that one of the members works in an office in her building. She also sees that he is online, and she sends him an instant message with her question. He has some information that can help her but suggests that she also launch a question in the expertise profiler. Angela's question is routed automatically, in e-mail, to the ten scientists who are most likely to be able to answer her question based on their expertise. As

it turns out, only five of the scientists work inside the firm. The other five are part of an extended community that includes some ex-company employees and industry experts. She receives four replies that help her solve the problem, and the entire interaction is stored in the knowledge repository, so that if a similar question comes up in the future, the answer can be automatically retrieved.

When she completes the analysis she is working on, Angela saves the results back to K-Zone so that it can be shared with the rest of the company. Notification of her contribution to K-Zone is immediately pushed to those employees who have registered an interest in the topic covered by her analysis.

In this future scenario, Angela is able to capitalize on the opportunity to improve the way the company leverages intellectual assets. She shares the best practices of her colleagues; finds information quickly, enabling her to spend more time effectively executing and analyzing her work and end results; easily creates assets for others to leverage; becomes part of a community of practice in her field, and benefits from the knowledge exchanged in a community of practice outside her area of expertise. In short, Angela is part of a knowledge-centric organization, a company in which knowledge management is not something extra that she does — it is what she does.

B.3.4.4 KCO-Specific Measures

The KCO model uses three types of specific measures to monitor the KM initiative from different perspectives:

- System metrics relate the performance of the supporting information technologies to the KM initiative. They give an indirect indication of knowledge sharing and reuse but can highlight which assets are the most popular and any usability problems that might exist and limit participation. For example, the Virtual Naval Hospital uses measures of the number of successful accesses, pages read, and visitors to monitor the viability of the information provided.
- Output metrics measure direct process output for users and give a picture of the extent to which personnel are drawn to and actually using the knowledge system. For example, some companies evaluate "lesson reuse" to ensure that the lessons they are maintaining are valuable to users.

- Outcome metrics determine the impact of the KM project on the organization and help determine if the knowledge base and knowledge-transfer processes are working to create a more effective organization. Outcome measures are often the hardest measures to evaluate, particularly because of the intangible nature of knowledge assets. Some of the best examples of outcome measures are in the private sector. For example, energy giant Royal Dutch/Shell Group reports that ideas exchanged in their community of practice for engineers saved the company $200 million in 2000 alone. In one example, communication on the community message board led to approximately $5 million in new revenue when the engineering teams in Europe and the Far East helped a crew in Africa solve a problem they had previously attempted to resolve.*

B.3.5   How Should We Collect and Analyze the Measures?

As you identify the measures that you will use for your KM initiative, you will also need to identify a process for collecting these measures. The important element is to structure information gathering and to probe deep enough to understand how decisions are made and the information that measures can provide to help decisions.

For system measures, look for automated data collection systems, such as tools that measure Web-site accesses and "wait times." System-performance logs will also provide valuable system measures.

For output and outcome measures, you may end up relying on manual counts, estimates, or surveys. Although surveys are considered a source of soft data because they measure perceptions and reactions, they can be quantitative. For example, a survey might ask the user to respond to a statement using a 1-to-5 Likert scale (in which 1 means "strongly disagree" and 5 means "strongly agree"). Survey data can also be useful to capture and summarize qualitative information such as comments and anecdotes. One consulting firm used contests with prizes to encourage members of communities of practice to contribute anecdotes describing how being a member of the community helped them accomplish a measurable objective for the firm (such as saving time or money or generating new revenue). Surveys can be conducted in person, by telephone, or in written form. Written surveys can be transmitted by mail, e-mail, or through a Web site. Surveys can have a dual purpose: they not only collect useful information but they also help educate the survey takers by raising their awareness of key issues or critical success factors for the initiative.

Other techniques that can be useful include the following:

---

* Caulfield, Brian, Talk is Cheap, and Good for Sales, Too, *eCompany Now*, April 2000.

- Interviews or workshops: Stakeholders can be interviewed individually or through a group setting in a facilitated workshop to draw out opinions and generate group consensus. The best choice depends on the people, organizational culture, the information needed, and people's availability. In each case, it is important to structure the sessions proactively. Merely asking people what information they would like is unlikely to yield useful results. Facilitation of any session is recommended to urge managers to talk about the type of decisions they commonly make and what decision-making information would be useful by asking "what-if" questions.
- Structured program flows: Tracing the flow of the program capabilities, the uses of these capabilities by direct users, and the benefits to the end user is another way to identify the information desired from performance measures. This flow-tracking technique is particularly useful for programs for which it is difficult to directly identify or calculate measures for the ultimate end-user benefits.
- Organization documents: Documents contain useful information regarding an organization's goals, priorities, measures, problems, and business operations.
- Meetings involving the performing organization and stakeholders: Many organizations have steering committees comprised of representative internal and external stakeholders. Observing the interchange at meetings can yield the priorities and issues that the stakeholders believe are important.

Once the measures have been collected, they should be analyzed within the framework chosen earlier. This will ensure that the measures are correlated to the objectives of the initiative and aligned with the strategic goals of the organization. In particular, explicitly note whether the measures give a direct or indirect indication of effects so that your team and stakeholders do not misconstrue or have unrealistic expectations of performance.

B.3.6 What Do the Measures Tell Us? How Should We Change?

This is one of the most critical steps in the measurement process as well as in the entire KCO implementation process. The complex and dynamic nature of KM makes it extremely difficult to devise a plan in the preplanning phase that will not later need to be changed. Use the framework to help elucidate what you can discover about the effectiveness and participation of stakeholders in the KM project. Are they using the knowledge? Are people sharing meaningful knowledge openly? Have people participated during the rollout while there was a great deal of fanfare and then stopped? Are there any anecdotes showing that people became more efficient or solved a problem faster because of the knowledge?

For all of these questions and your other indicators, ask why it happened or had that response. Even without a firm answer, the search for an answer will most likely yield valuable insights and ideas on how to improve your KM project. Collect and prioritize these new ideas and go back to your original plans and assumptions to see if they need to be changed. It is normal that several measures will need to be modified. This is a good time to assemble your team and build a consensus on what should be changed, how to change it, and when to introduce the changes. Also, you should update the measures and framework to make sure they are tightly coupled to your new KM plans.

B.4 GETTING STARTED

The remaining sections are organized by the general classes of business objectives and problems that KM initiatives are designed to address. These business objectives are grouped in the following categories:

- Program and process management (Section B.5): This class includes strategic organizational objectives such as leveraging best practices and transferring lessons learned. Some of the business problems that program and process management initiatives are designed to solve include issues such as ensuring consistency across the organization and proactively preventing duplication of effort.
- Program execution and operations (Section B.6): This class includes objectives such as connecting people with experts, transferring expertise instantaneously, and getting the right operational knowledge to people in the field when they need it.
- Personnel and training (Section B.7): This class includes personnel and learning issues such as acquiring and retaining talent and improving quality of life for employees.

The matrix in Section B.8 is a comprehensive summary of potential measures (which have all been "field tested") for KM initiatives. There is no guarantee that these measures are the most appropriate for your project. Remember, these metrics describe what you can do, not what you must do or even what you should do.

B.5 PROGRAM AND PROCESS MANAGEMENT

This section discusses classes of business objectives that share a common need for understanding the current and future performance of programs relating to their requirements. These requirements span a range of development objectives and milestone dates, financial constraints, resource needs and usage, alignment with organizational strategic plans, and adherence to legal, environmental, and safety regulations and laws.

B.5.1 Business Applications

The program and process management business area is concerned with monitoring and guiding business tasks to ensure that they achieve development, financial, and resource objectives. In addition, this area includes business development activities in which people need to identify and assess opportunities, determine their customers' key interests and funding levels, and obtain business intelligence on competitor capabilities and plans. You should read this section if you are applying KM to the following or similar activities:

- Program management
- Project control
- Business process reengineering
- Quality management
- Strategic planning
- Policy and standards definition
- Integrated product teams
- Architecture design and review
- Plan of action and milestones (POAM)
- Budgeting
- Business development
- Business intelligence
- Enterprise resource planning (ERP)
- Customer relationship management (CRM)

The primary KM objectives of these types of activities are the following:

- Create a consistent understanding across the organization of key issues, such as standardized methods, policies, and goals and objectives.
- Improve business development.
- Increase effectiveness, productivity, and quality.
- Implement best practices.
- Share and reuse lessons learned.

Some examples of KM initiatives for program and process management are as follows:

- Experienced program managers have learned how to substantially reduce the time they spend reporting their programs to different sponsors, each of which has a different format and set of regulations. This knowledge can help junior program managers be more efficient and provide a higher level of service to their customers. A community of practice is established to enable junior and senior program managers to informally interact and share information on their projects and methods. A special component is the "Mentor's Corner," which includes a series of video interviews in which the experienced managers explain their key insights and methods.

■ Near the end of every fiscal year, key leaders must stop working on their daily projects for five days to answer urgent requests for consolidated status reports by Congress. Most of this time is spent finding the proper people who can explain current and projected data. This serious disruption to operations can be reduced to one half day with a current listing of points of contact for key projects. Thus, an experts directory that is validated and kept up-to-date is developed.

B.5.2 Performance Measures

KM metrics should be extensively correlated to as many factors influencing the results as possible. Although there are many forces within an organization that affect people's learning, sharing, and efficiency, it is difficult to separate the effects of the KM processes from others. The KM measures should be used as a body of evidence to support analysis and decision making. As much as possible, the KM measures should be related to, or the same as, existing measures in the organization that are used to monitor the success of performing mission objectives.

B.5.2.1 Outcome Measures

Examples of possible outcome measures include the following:

■ Measure the change in resource costs (funds, time, and personnel) used in a business process over time. To tie to the KM initiative, gauge this change against when the KM asset was made available and its usage, and to other business processes that are not part of the KM initiative. Also, include surveys of user attitudes and practices. For example, do the groups who regularly use and maintain a lessons learned database spend less overhead funds than other groups? Do they say the lessons learned helped them?

■ Measure the success and failure rates of programs linked to the KM assets over time. For example, has the number of programs completed on time and within cost increased? For all groups, or mostly for groups actively engaged in the KM initiative?

■ Determine the number of groups meeting best practices criteria, and how long it took them to achieve this status versus the existence and use of the KM system. For example, did any groups entering a new business area reach an expert level much faster than usual by using the collected best practices and associated corporate learning from the beginning of their project?

■ Gauge the "smartness" of the organization, i.e., are more customers commenting on the high level of expertise of different groups, or are more industry awards being won? Are these comments based on the ability of individual workgroups presenting the capabilities of their colleagues as well as their own? How did these groups get the information?

B.5.2.2 Output Measures

Examples of possible output measures include the following:

■ Conduct a survey to find out how useful people find the KM initiative. How have people used the collected knowledge? Was it valuable? Did it answer their questions and help solve their problems, or was it merely another set of information to read and digest? How do they suggest improving the KM system?

■ Find examples of specific mistakes or problems that were avoided or quickly solved because of KM. These are typically uncovered by talking to people and collecting anecdotes. For example, did the lessons learned database help someone immediately find out how to compute future-estimated resource costs according to new regulations?

■ Determine how much new business is connected to using the sharing of expertise. For example, did someone win a new contract with a new customer because they watched the video interviews of business development experts in the Mentor's Corner of the community of practice?

■ Measure the decrease in time required to develop program-status reports. For example, do all managers of cross-functional programs have the same information on resource usage and development progress, as well as all problems encountered, with the responsible point of contact and its resolution?

B.5.2.3 System Measures

Examples of possible system measures include the following:

- Measure the statistics from the KM system. For example, how many times has the Web site been accessed? How many times have lessons learned or best practice files been downloaded?
- Measure the activity of a community of practice. For example, how many members are in the community, and how often do they interact? How long has it been since the last contribution to a shared repository or threaded discussion? What percentage of the total members are active contributors?
- How easy is it for people to find the information they want? Conduct a survey and test the site yourself. Find out how many responses are typically generated from a search. If this number is too high (greater than 50), people may be giving up the search and not making use of the knowledge assets. Are the responses what the user wants to see? Check to see if the site is easy to navigate with an organizational structure consistent with the way users work and think about the information. What is the system latency, i.e., the wait time between a user requesting something and when the system delivers it?
- Measure how frequently the knowledge assets are updated. Are the best practices outdated and superseded by new versions? Are the points of contact no longer working on the project? Is there a listed update time that has been exceeded? Are a large number of links to experts no longer valid?

B.6 PROGRAM EXECUTION AND OPERATIONS

This section discusses classes of business objectives that share a common need for efficiently performing work tasks in a timely manner. These tasks commonly require extensive training and experience, are complex, and can be dangerous.

B.6.1 Business Applications

The program execution and operations business area concerns the activities involved in performing a program's statement of work; designing, building, testing, evaluating, installing, and maintaining systems; controlling real-time operations; and other tasks focused on developing and deploying tangible products and services. This knowledge must be useful and practical, and typically includes highly detailed procedures, facts, and analyses. Consequently, this business area involves a substantial amount of tacit knowledge — that is, the unspoken knowledge people build through experience, which is not always easy to articulate. For example, a master electrician knows many characteristics of power systems that a novice electrician does not, making the master electrician many times more productive and efficient on complex tasks. This knowledge is commonly transferred during apprentice, mentoring, and educational relationships. You should read this section if you are applying KM to the following or similar activities:

- Maintenance
- Engineering design
- Research and development
- Manufacturing
- Test and evaluation
- Logistics
- Operations management
- Software development
- Hardware and software installation
- Construction
- Demolition

The primary KM objectives of these types of activities are to accomplish the following:

- Increase effectiveness, productivity, and quality
- Implement best practices
- Share and reuse lessons learned
- Accelerate learning
- Maintain, share, and leverage expertise
- Facilitate team collaboration

Some examples of KM initiatives for program execution and operations are as follows:

- An engineering design team includes members from many different contractors and government organizations located throughout the United States. The entire team is able to meet in person only twice a year at the formal program reviews. To avoid redundant efforts and wasting the team's high level of complementary expertise, a distributed collaborative Web-based work environment is created in which all project information is posted and informal online work sessions occur with file sharing, whiteboards, video, and speech. Although this is the team's official news source and work center, everyone is confident that they will find valuable information whenever they enter the environment.
- A construction organization is faced with many of their senior members retiring in the next couple of years. A great deal of the organization's expertise and success depends on the workers' knowledge built over their long careers. A lessons learned database

is created in which the senior experts are asked to describe their key thoughts on doing their work. The lessons learned are collected in both text and video formats and posted on the organization's intranet.

B.6.2   Performance Measures

See B.5.2.

B.6.2.1   Outcome Measures

See B.5.2.1.

B.6.2.2   Output Measures

See B.5.2.2.

B.6.2.3   System Measures

See B.5.2.3.

B.7   PERSONNEL AND TRAINING

This section describes classes of business objectives that share a common focus on helping people coordinate and decide professional and personal issues that affect their income, jobs, careers, retirement, education, families, and other quality-of-life topics.

B.7.1   Business Applications

The personnel and training business area is concerned with activities for human resources, continuing education, personal life issues, and quality of life. These applications focus on helping people improve the effectiveness or quality of their work life and helping organizations attract and retain talent. These activities share a common need for people to determine what options are available from various programs, how they impact their personal finances and families, what experiences other people have had (good and bad) with these options, whom to contact to make arrangements, and what they are required to do for the programs. You should read this section if you are applying KM to the following or similar activities:

- Human resources
- Distance or E-learning and continuing education

- Fringe benefits management
- Career planning
- Employee retention
- Relocation

The primary KM objectives of these types of activities are as follows:

- Provide retirement, health, and financial services.
- Arrange for moving jobs and families to new locations.
- Plan career growth.
- Enhance learning opportunities.
- Improve quality of life.
- Retain and attract employees.

Some examples of KM initiatives for personnel and training are as follows:

- An employee is relocating to a new area. Without an opportunity to visit the new location, the employee's family has to find a home, change banks, arrange for daycare and school, and notify the utility, telephone, and cable companies in both locations. Logging into the relocation community of practice Web site, the employee finds links to local information and directories at the new base, and suggestions from people who live there on the best places to live, local daycare centers, how to enroll children for school, and how to sign up for utilities.
- Employees are encouraged to take continuing education courses through the Internet offered by several authorized institutions. They can access their personnel records to see what courses they need for various job positions and promotions. As they take an online course, their progress is automatically noted in their personnel records and sent to their supervisor to be included in their performance reviews.
- Employees can access their fringe-benefit plans through the human resources department's Web site. They can change their options during open season and compare the cost and benefits offered by retirement and health plans using the Web site's interactive feature-comparison application. In addition, a lessons learned database includes key issues discussed by experts on these plans.

B.7.2 Performance Measures

See B.5.2.

B.7.2.1   Outcome Measures

See B.5.2.1.

Measure retention rates and the cost of attracting new people. Are fewer people leaving the organization for other jobs? Are starting salaries stable or are they and other benefits rising to compete with other organizations?

B.7.2.2   Output Measures

See B.5.2.2.

Measure the usage of the distance learning system. Are employees taking only required courses or courses for career advancement as well?

B.7.2.3   System Measures

See B.5.2.3.

B.8 SUMMARY OF KM PERFORMANCE MEASURES

Common measures: These measures can be used for all KM initiatives.

Outcome
Time, money, or personnel time saved as a result of implementing initiative
Percentage of successful programs compared to those before KM implementation

Output
Usefulness surveys where users evaluate how useful initiatives have been in helping them accomplish their objectives
Usage anecdotes where users describe (in quantitative terms) how the initiative has contributed to business objectives

System
Latency (response times)
Number of downloads
Number of site accesses
Dwell time per page or section
Usability survey
Frequency of use
Navigation path analysis
Number of help desk calls
Number of users
Frequency of use
Percentage of total employees using system

KM Initiative	Key System Measures	Key Output Measures	Key Outcome Measures
Best practice directory	Number of downloads Dwell time Usability survey Number of users Total number of contributions Contribution rate over time	Usefulness survey Anecdotes User ratings of contribution value	Time, money, or personnel time saved by implementing best practices Number of groups certified in the use of the best practice Rate of change in operating costs

Lessons learned database	Number of downloads Dwell time Usability survey Number of users Total number of contributions Contribution rate over time	Time to solve problems Usefulness survey Anecdotes User ratings of contribution value	Time, money, or personnel time saved by applying lessons learned from others Rate of change in operating costs
Communities of practice or special interest groups	Number of contributions Frequency of update Number of members Ratio of the number of members to the number of contributors (conversion rate)	Number of apprentices mentored by colleagues Number of problems solved	Savings or improvement in organizational quality and efficiency Captured organizational memory Attrition rate of community members versus nonmember cohort
Expert or expertise directory	Number of site accesses Frequency of use Number of contributions Contribution or update rate over time Navigation path analysis Number of help desk calls	Time to solve problems Number of problems solved Time to find expert	Savings or improvement in organizational quality and efficiency Time, money, or personnel time saved by leveraging experts' knowledge or expertise knowledge base

Common measures: These measures can be used for all KM initiatives.

KM Initiative	Key System Measures	Key Output Measures	Key Outcome Measures
Portal	Searching precision and recall Dwell time Latency Usability survey	Common awareness within teams Time spent gathering information Time spent analyzing information	Time, money, or personnel time saved as a result of portal use Reduced training time or learning curve as a result of single access to multiple information sources Customer satisfaction (based on the value of self-service or improved ability for employees to respond to customer needs)
Lead tracking system	Number of contributions Frequency of update Number of users Frequency of use Navigation path analysis	Number of successful leads Number of new customers and value from these customers Value of new work from existing customers Proposal response times Proposal "win" rates Percentage of business developers who report finding value in the use of the system	Revenue and overhead costs Customer demographics Cost and time to produce proposals Alignment of programs with strategic plans

Collaborative systems	Latency during collaborative process Number of users Number of patents or trademarks produced Number of articles published plus number of conference presentations per employee	Number of projects collaborated on Time lost due to program delays Number of new products developed Value of sales from products created in the last 3–5 years (a measure of innovation) Average learning curve per employee Proposal response times Proposal "win" rates	Reduced cost of product development, acquisition, or maintenance Reduction in the number of program delays Faster response to proposals Reduced learning curve for new employees
Yellow pages	Number of users Frequency of use Latency Searching precision and recall	Time to find people Time to solve problems	Time, money, or personnel time saved as a result of the use of yellow pages Savings or improvement in organizational quality and efficiency
E-learning systems	Latency Number of users Number of courses taken per user	Training costs	Savings or improvement in organizational quality and efficiency Improved employee satisfaction Reduced cost of training Reduced learning curve for new employees

References

U.S. Department of the Navy. Retrieved June 22, 2005, from http://openacademy. mindef.gov.sg/OpenAcademy/Central/HTML%20Folder/KM/bcp/downloads/ KM_Metrics_Guide_Final_15AUG01.doc.

Appendix C

WEB RESOURCES

Business Intelligence
    Business Intelligence Forum:
        http://www.managementlogs.com/business_intelligence.html
    TechWeb's Intelligent Enterprise BI Channel:
        http://www.intelligententerprise.com/channels/bi/
    TechWeb's Business Intelligence Pipeline:
        http://www.bizintelligencepipeline.com/
    The resource for business intelligence:
        http://www.businessintelligence.com/
    Ganthead project management — BI portal:
        http://www.gantthead.com/departments/departmentPage.
        cfm?ID=1
    Business Intelligence Network:
        http://www.b-eye-network.com/channels/?filter_channel=1127

Content Management
    TechWeb's Intelligent Enterprise Content Management Channel:
        http://www.intelligententerprise.com/channels/content_
        management/

Knowledge Management
    Knowledge Management Knowledge Base:
        http://knowledgemanagement.ittoolbox.com/documents/
        document.asp?i=1237
    KMNetwork and the WWW Virtual Library on Knowledge
        Management: http://www.brint.com/km/
    Harvard Business School Working Knowledge Report:
        http://hbswk.hbs.edu

Global Development Research Center KM Portal:
http://www.gdrc.org/kmgmt/index.html

APQC Knowledge Management:
http://www.apqc.org/portal/apqc/site/generic2?path=/site/
splash_pages/km_whitepapers.jhtml&campaignSource=GLkmWP

Global Community for Knowledge:
http://www.knowledgeboard.com/

Knowledge Management networks:
http://www.knowledgeboard.com/networks/index.html

Knowledge Management Organizations and Gateways:
http://km.gov/QuickPlace/km/Main.nsf/
h_516E61451D172AB785256C7E007A1AD4/
16930f894fae3c6f85256c7e007a23f1/?OpenDocument

Appendix D

SELECTING A CONTENT MANAGEMENT SYSTEM CHECKLIST

D.1 BEFORE YOU START

1. Consider the time required to select an appropriate product.
2. Consider the range of products available in the marketplace.
3. Build content management knowledge.
4. Consider risks and risk-mitigation strategies.
5. Redesign the site if necessary.

D.2 DETERMINING PROJECT GOALS AND TARGETS

1. Focus on business outcomes.
2. Specify targets and how their achievement will be measured.

D.3 DETERMINING AND DOCUMENTING BUSINESS REQUIREMENTS

1. Focus on business needs rather than technical solutions.
2. Address compliance needs.
3. Provide descriptions and examples to clarify meaning.
4. Avoid specifying too many requirements.
5. Make use of existing resources.
6. Consider gaining an external review of requirements.
7. Consider the use of scenarios to help document requirements.

D.4 PRODUCING DOCUMENTATION

1. Include background information.
2. Include any new site design.
3. Specify technical infrastructure.

D.5 EVALUATING AND SELECTING A CMS

1. Use scenarios during demonstrations.
2. Visit reference sites.
3. Focus on usability and simplicity.
4. Assess the vendor's implementation methodology.
5. Consider the total cost of ownership.

References

Selecting a Content Management System (2005), Australian Government. Retrieved June 26, 2005, from http://www.agimo.gov.au/practice/delivery/checklists/select_cms.

Appendix E

CHECKLIST FOR MANAGING ONLINE CONTENT

E.1 GENERAL

1. Consider what type of content needs to be managed.
2. Review how content is currently managed and the adequacy of these processes.
3. Consider whether existing processes will be adequate in the foreseeable future.
4. Evaluate the particular challenges the agency may have in managing content.
5. Ensure that the organization has clearly documented and updated processes for managing all types of Web content.
6. Consider the challenges in managing intranets.

E.2 CONTENT MANAGEMENT ISSUES

1. Identify information and services to be provided on the Web site.
2. Determine end-user information needs.
3. Allocate roles and responsibilities.
4. Maintain a list of content owners.
5. Focus on establishing viable content management processes.
6. Assist content creators to create suitable resources for online delivery.
7. Establish testing processes.
8. Review and remove or amend Web-site content as necessary.
9. Meet archiving and storage requirements.
10. Assess and manage any legal implications of Web site content.
11. Track content approval.

12. Manage user feedback regarding the Web site and other online customer services.
13. Select appropriate content management tools.

REFERENCES

Managing Online Content (2004). Retrieved June 26, 2005, from http://www.agimo.gov.au/__data/assets/file/33918/BPC8.pdf.

Appendix F

CHECKLIST FOR KM PROFESSIONAL SERVICES

The Gartner Group (Harris and Bair, 1998) recommends that the search for a KM service provider include a search for competencies other than project management skills and business trend rhetoric. They stress that when evaluating an external services provider (ESP), KM-specific performance, skills, and expertise also be evaluated.

1. Strength of the ESP's internal KM implementation. How does the ESP manage its own intellectual assets? If the ESP has no program for this, then Gartner recommends going no further. Ask how long the program has been in place, its scope, the metrics established to gauge performance, and the infrastructure supporting the program.
2. Completeness of KM vision. The KM vision should go well beyond information management. The KM vision should span KM subprocesses and activities (e.g., knowledge creation, sharing, and application).
3. Reference cases. The ESP should provide reference cases or clients. Enterprises should request references with demographics similar to their own.
4. KM-technology-specific expertise. ESPs should demonstrate expertise on three levels, as follows:
    a. An understanding of the technical components of KM architecture and its deployment of integrated semantic, collaborative, and visualization technologies
    b. An understanding of the foundation technologies of KM
    c. Proficiency at assessing the needs of knowledge workers to communicate, capture, and retrieve explicit knowledge, as well as to manage relationships

5. KM-program-specific expertise. ESPs should have a formal methodology for KM program development and should demonstrate proficiency in six KM-specific techniques such as the following:
   a. Defining a KM strategy
   b. Identifying the explicit and tacit intellectual assets required
   c. Designing a knowledge map of the business usage of knowledge assets
   d. Organizing and completing a knowledge audit
   e. Designing the KM administration function (roles, responsibilities, and jobs) including program ownership and knowledge content ownership
   f. Managing the enterprise transition to a culture of collaboration and knowledge sharing
6. KM cultural and organizational skills transfer. Ask the provided references the following question: If the ESP walks away, will the KM team, program, and culture survive and continue to gain momentum?

References

Harris, J. and Bair, J., The Gartner Group Checklist for KM Professional Services, June 30, 1998. Retrieved June 26, 2005, from http://www.providersedge.com/docs/km_articles/Checklist_for_KM_Prof_Svcs_-_Gartner.pdf.

Appendix G

KNOWLEDGE MANAGEMENT CAPACITY CHECKLIST

This survey can be used to assess organizations' KM capacities alongside generally accepted best practices. The information gathered will be used for the following:

- Integrating the full range of capabilities necessary to implement improved information management (IM)
- Gauging compliance with existing IM or KM policies
- Providing information to improve KM
- Prioritizing KM initiatives and developing a plan of action
- Highlighting risk areas
- Increasing awareness and understanding of KM issues across the organization

The survey brings together key elements of IM practice and assesses the level of capability within the organization in support each of those elements.

G.1 FORMAT OF THE SURVEY

In the following pages, each capacity is shown in the far-left column. The maturity levels to be measured are outlined in the adjacent five columns. The capabilities are depicted within each criterion and represent the different plateaus that the organization may seek to achieve. The descriptions are incremental. The organization should identify which level of maturity is most appropriate to support its business needs and priorities.

A rating system of 1 to 5 is used. A rating of 5 does not necessarily indicate "goodness" but rather maturity of capability. The ideal maturity rating for any area is dependent upon the requirements of the organization.

G.2 HOW TO COMPLETE THE SURVEY

It will take around 20 min to complete the survey.

Below each capacity criteria (1 to 5), indicate with a "C" where you believe the organization's current capability is, in relation to the criteria. In the same row, insert an "F" under the criterion you feel the organization should strive to be in the future.

This survey is confidential, but respondents are asked to identify their group or division so that the results pinpoint specific group KM issues.

Knowledge Management Capacity Check Survey

In Which Group or Division Do You Work?

1. Culture

Capacity	1	2	3	4	5	
Does the organization recognize information as a strategic corporate asset requiring stewardship? What level of support is there within the organization to support and reinforce behavior that is consistent with these values?	Information is not recognized as an asset. There is no clear stewardship of information. Focus is primarily on managing data, not on information management.	KM concepts are intuitively understood and practiced on an *ad hoc* basis. Stewardship of the information is informal. Information is recognized by some as being of strategic importance to the organization. This has not been effectively communicated across the organization.	Many parts of the organization value information as a strategic asset. Internal information experts maintain clear lines of responsibility, and stewardship of the information takes place at all senior levels.	Information is recognized as a strategic asset in most parts of the organization and throughout most levels from operations to senior management. Resources are committed to ensuring effective stewardship and management of knowledge both at the senior management and expert levels.	Information is treated at all levels throughout the organization as a strategic asset to be leveraged and reused. All staff are empowered and equipped to take stewardship of information and are seen as "knowledge workers."	
Current or future status						

Capacity	1	2	3	4	5	
			2. Change Management			
Does the organization have mechanisms to facilitate the adoption of KM change?	No consideration is given to the way in which changes within IM are planned, coordinated, and implemented.	Management is aware of the need to manage change when implementing new IM processes. Key change-management implications are identified for new projects. The implementation of new methods is occasionally coordinated with other changes taking place.	A formal change-management process exists within the organization to manage change related to IM. Sufficient resources are available to guide change management for IM initiatives. A communication plan is established that supports the change initiative. Mechanisms exist to identify stakeholders affected by change and their particular needs.	Staff and stakeholder collaboration is sought in developing the change-management process. Management plays an active part in leading change. Changes are implemented consistently and in an integrated fashion. There is little disruption to core services and processes during periods of significant change. Evolving to a learning organization.	Senior management has committed resources to facilitate ongoing change within a learning organization. The organization has established methods for continuous improvement of redesigned IM processes. IM change initiatives are fully integrated with organizationwide change management processes.	
Current or future status						

3. External Environment

Does the organization conduct environmental scans and assess their possible impacts on KM?	No formal environmental scanning is done regarding new IM sources, technologies, processes, etc.	Environmental scanning is done on a limited basis. There is little or no aggregation of results. Assessment of external opportunities and threats is done on an informal, *ad hoc* basis.	The organization is using current methodologies and tools for environmental scanning. Staff are aware of their role in environmental intelligence gathering. Results are shared with key stakeholders.	Results of environmental scans are shared and tracked over time. Analysis is made of trends and patterns to determine potential opportunities, emerging IM enablers, and new sources of information. Comprehensive, flexible tools exist to enable effective scanning.	Environmental scanning is done on a regular basis in support of IM. Results of environmental scans are integrated into strategic and tactical planning, and are used by the management to drive change and continuous development.	
Current or future status						

4. KM Community

Capacity	1	2	3	4	5
Has the organization identified the competencies required to implement its KM strategies and plans? Have staff received training appropriate for their responsibilities?	There is no understanding of KM competencies (knowledge, skills, and behaviors). KM-competency-building programs are not available. There is no KM specialist capacity within the organization.	Required KM competencies for KM specialists have been identified; however, the current organizational competencies are assessed in an *ad hoc* manner. There is limited KM specialist capacity.	Organizational competencies have been assessed at the position level, and KM competency gaps have been determined. Sufficient resources with the required skills are in place to support delivery of KM services.	The workforce demonstrates the requisite knowledge, skills, and behaviors to successfully manage knowledge. Staffing and training in KM competencies are high priorities.	KM competencies are an integral part of the organization's performance management process. There are no significant capacity or competency gaps within the organization.
Current or future status					

5. Expert Advice

To what extent are expert KM advisors available and utilized for objective commentary and independent advice?	Specialists and expert advice are not available or utilized to support initiatives.	Specialists respond to requests from employees for both process and strategic advice on an *ad hoc* basis. IM specialists are not always familiar with the operations. The quality of IM service and expert advice varies between branches or areas.	Advice is readily available when required; is technically competent; and works with operational managers in providing strategic and tactical advice. Seen as partners in analysis and decision making. Proactive in suggesting new tools and techniques.	Specialists work closely with employees by providing value-added information, technical and user-responsive advice. Familiar with operations, and knowledgeable of the analytical techniques to support the operational manager. Maintain a current knowledge of related policy areas.	The expert advisory role is valued by all levels. Seen as key enablers in helping initiate change. Called upon by their peers to provide advice and support, or to speak at conferences on new trends or best practices. Anticipate emerging needs, issues, and opportunities and act on them.
Current or future status					

6. Tools for Managing Information

Capacity	1	2	3	4	5
To what extent are tools for managing information and knowledge available to staff? Do staff have the skills and knowledge to use them effectively? (Tools include policies, standards, guidelines, procedures, classifications, structure, document management systems, etc.)	There are no tools and techniques available to assist employees in the life-cycle management of information. There is no awareness of tool availability. Managers tend to use their own individual approaches.	Basic tools are in place to support data and document management initiatives but are used inconsistently across the organization. Staff do not have the skills or knowledge to use the tools effectively. Requirements for new tools have been identified, and are being developed or acquired.	Staff have access to flexible tools, and techniques to support information management life cycle. Employees at all levels are exposed to tools and techniques. Staff have been provided training on the use of these tools and are actively using them.	A consistent suite of flexible and versatile internal and corporate tools is available and used across the organization to support the IM life cycle management of information. Expertise on the application of key KM tools and techniques is uniform and widespread across the organization.	Tools are assessed on a continual basis and updated based on evolving KM requirements and most recent relevant business and technology research. Users have online access to information through sophisticated and flexible KM support tools and models.
Current or future status					

7. Technology Integration

To what degree are KM-enabling technologies integrated across the organization to support the delivery of information, programs, and services?	There is no technology-integration strategy or plan to support KM initiatives. There is no consistent definition of technology standards or business processes in use within the organization. Business functions are supported via a diverse and nonstandardized set of technologies.	An overall technology architecture to enable KM is being developed but is not yet complete and up-to-date. Currently, technology integration is being adapted to support KM at the business unit level. Minimal standardization exists for some application areas.	A technology integration architecture has been defined for supporting organizationwide KM initiatives. Technology standards have been defined, and new applications adhere to these standards. Older applications do not adhere to the overall technology integration strategy or plan. Information is not integrated across KM platforms.	An organizationwide technology architecture exists to support KM initiatives, and all existing applications conform to the technology integration standards across the organization. Technology support staff have a broad range of expertise in technology functionality and integration. Information needs and systems are periodically reassessed based on changing business needs and identified gaps.	Driven by strategic and operational plans, an integrated KM-enabling-technology architecture is in place. The architecture facilitates rapid adaptive technology integration across KM platforms and organization boundaries. Supporting integration standards are in place to facilitate interoperability with clients, suppliers, and business partners, and integrated information is readily accessible through executive information systems (EISs).
Current or future status					

8. Project Management

Capacity	1	2	3	4	5	
To what extent do mechanisms exist to manage projects in the organization to ensure optimal design, development, and deployment of KM initiatives?	No project management processes, standards, and tools exist in the organization to help in managing KM projects. No capability to lead or manage KM initiatives exists in-house.	Project management processes, standards, and tools exist within the organization but are not consistently applied to KM projects. Less-than-rigorous management of requirements, scope, cost, schedule, quality, risk, and communications leads to project performance shortfalls.	Organizationwide project management processes, standards, and tools exist to support KM initiatives. The majority of projects fall within acceptable performance limits and are facilitated by a project management function.	KM project teams are highly productive and deliver the optimal balance between cost, schedule, and quality. Stakeholder expectations are well managed.	KM projects are effectively managed with a balance between technical, business, and social issues. Project management techniques contribute to open communication and collaboration among team members. Project lessons learned are always collected and used to improve future project efforts.	
Current or future status						

9. Relationship Management

To what extent are mechanisms in place to access updated information in support of stakeholder relationship management?	There is no formal relationship management process in the organization and no information available to support roles involved in managing relations with external stakeholders.	Staff from a number of functional groups are starting to work together to manage significant organization relationships. Distributed databases of stakeholder contact details exist.	The organization recognizes the value of strategic stakeholder relationships, and mechanisms exist to support relationship management. There is not yet a single view of stakeholder information.	There is an organizationwide approach to managing strategic stakeholder relationships and a single view of stakeholder information.	The organization has an in-depth knowledge of stakeholder needs and interests. The organizationwide repository of stakeholder information is actively used to add value to stakeholder interactions.
Current or future status					

10. Leadership

Capacity	1	2	3	4	5
To what extent have senior management demonstrated their understanding and commitment to KM?	Senior management has no understanding of, nor commitment to, modern KM practices. No communication of a KM vision or direction occurs.	Senior management has some understanding of the concept of modern KM practices, and recognizes the need for change. Senior management is somewhat supportive of improving KM capabilities.	Senior management is highly committed to, and supportive of, KM and improving KM practices. The organization has committed sufficient resources to promote these practices.	Senior management has created a climate wherein KM is highly valued by the organization. A clearly defined vision has been established, communicated, and implemented and is periodically adjusted, based on experiences.	The organization is recognized amongst peers for leadership in implementing KM management practices. Senior management has earned a high level of trust from other agencies that have high levels of confidence in the effectiveness and integrity KM systems.
Current or future status					

11. Strategic Planning

What is the quality of strategic, business, and operational plans for KM, and the linkages between plans, costs, benefits, resources, and controls?				
Strategic and operational plans do not integrate any KM concepts, processes, or planning. KM planning is not a priority in the organization. No effort is made to develop KM strategies or devote resources to improving KM capabilities.	Strategic and business plans are prepared independently of a KM strategy or plan. A KM strategy and plans are documented. Some effort is made to link the KM functional plan and the organizationwide strategic plan.	Desired results, strategic priorities, and resources are clearly stated in KM functional plans. Strong linkages exist between strategic objectives and priorities, and the KM functional plans, operational plans, and budgets. Resources are adjusted annually to reflect priorities in KM. Results achieved in the KM function are monitored against strategic priorities.	Strategic business plans and organization business models are integrated with the KM strategy. Plans highlight organizationwide KM issues, major risks, and the resource implications. Plans reflect KM needs of clients or stakeholders, who are consulted as part of the process.	KM planning is a key component of organizationwide planning and links the organization's vision and strategic objectives to its overall management of information. The KM strategy and associated KM plans are developed in collaboration with users and stakeholders; they are approved by senior management and communicated to managers, staff, and stakeholders.
Current or future status				

Capacity	1	2	3	4	5
			12. Principles, Policies and Standards		
To what extent do principles, policies, and standards address requirements for managing information and knowledge?	There are no principles, policies, and standards in the organization for managing information and knowledge.	There are some policies and standards for managing information and knowledge. These are being applied in an ad hoc manner. Other informal principles and practices are employed to varying degrees.	Sufficient policies and standards for managing information and knowledge exist within the organization. Most staff are aware of, and follow the principles and standards, and formal documentation and communication are provided.	Employees have a high level of awareness and have put into practice formal principles, policies, and standards for managing information and knowledge. The policy and management framework is documented and periodically improved.	Principles, policies, and standards for managing information and knowledge are fully accessible and utilized throughout the organization. They are updated continuously to ensure relevance.
Current or future status					

13. Roles and Responsibilities

Are roles, responsibilities, and accountabilities for managing information and knowledge clearly defined, understood, accepted, and integrated into staff's daily work?	KM roles and responsibilities are not well defined. The organization and governance structures are not appropriate for the management of information and knowledge.	KM roles and responsibilities are generally defined but not well understood. Minimal governance structures exist in support of KM. Responsibility for managing information and knowledge is limited to small functional groups.	KM roles and responsibilities are clearly defined and understood, and generally aligned with the organization's objectives. The governance structure is appropriately positioned within the organization.	KM roles and responsibilities are defined, understood, and aligned with the organization's objectives. Each staff member takes responsibility for managing knowledge in day-to-day work, and there is an effectively functioning specialist KM team.	KM champions are responsible for ensuring the integration of KM practices across the organization. KM roles, responsibilities, and governance structures are continuously updated to reflect changing business and technology environments.
Current or future status					

Capacity	1	2	3	4	5
			14. Program Integration		
To what extent do the organizations, programs, and projects proactively and efficiently integrate KM principles, policies, and standards?	KM is not a consideration when designing or delivering services or programs.	KM practices are included in some program planning and design exercises. KM practices are not consistently followed in program or service delivery.	KM is integrated into most program planning and delivery. The level of impact or improvement varies. Most employees are aware of organization-level KM policies, principles, and standards; however, the integration of KM practices is typically initiated by KM specialists.	The organization includes KM principles, policies, and standards in all project and program design and management. KM is contributing to increased impact of program delivery. Program staff recognize the value of KM and actively seek the involvement of KM in program planning and delivery. Employees are continuously updated on KM practices.	The organization is recognized as a leader in utilizing KM for superior program delivery. Program staff actively share best practices and lessons learned and collaborate on evolving KM practices. KM best practices guide both strategic and tactical program design and delivery.	
Current or future status					

15. Risk Management

Does the organization have mechanisms in place for identifying, measuring, and monitoring KM risks, including options for risk allocation and mitigation?	No formal KM risk management measures are in place. Concept of KM risk management is not understood.	Risk management policies and guidelines are in place for specific KM areas. KM risk management is applied primarily to major initiatives involving significant resources. The organization is beginning to use a common KM risk management language.	An integrated KM risk management framework is in place. The organization maintains a corporate KM risk profile. Management direction on risk management and organization-level risk tolerance is communicated, and senior managers champion KM risk management. Major KM risks are identified and plans developed to manage risks.	Integrated KM risk management is embedded in the organization's corporate strategy and shapes the organization's risk culture. The results of KM risk management are integrated in organization-level policies, plans, and practices. Various tools, training, and methods are used for managing risk (e.g., risk maps, modeling tools). The organization reviews its risk tolerance over time.	KM risk management supports a cultural shift to a risk-smart workforce and environment. The organization embraces innovation and responsible risk-taking. Results of KM risk management are used to support innovation, learning, and continuous improvement. The KM team is seen as a leader in KM risk management.	
Current or future status						

16. Performance Management

Capacity	1	2	3	4	5
To what extent is the achievement of financial and operating results embedded into the performance management framework for KM?	No organization-level performance measures exist for KM.	KM performance is measured independently. KM priority areas to be measured have been identified. Some project KM performance measures have been organized on an *ad hoc* basis. The methods of collecting the information and sources of information have generally been identified but not consistently implemented.	High-level strategic measures for KM are in place in the organization. Linkages between KM measures are evident. KM performance measures have been communicated, and agreed upon. KM measures follow a balanced-scorecard approach and include financial, learning, client, and business process measures.	Integrated organization-level KM performance results are captured and reported. Results are monitored against targets and the organization's strategic KM objectives. Results are used to make trade-offs in organizationwide priorities. Organization-level measures are refined on an ongoing basis and provide historical and future-oriented views.	KM performance results indicate positive improvement. Strategic and business plans are continuously modified, based on KM results achieved. Information is readily accessible through EIS. People and process and technology requirements are continuously reassessed, based on changing KM needs and identified gaps.
Current or future status					

17. Information Quality

Are mechanisms in place for monitoring the quality of the organization's information assets and for ensuring that the information is accurate, consistent, complete, and current?	The organization lacks the resources to ascertain the quality of its information. Information quality issues are dealt with in a reactive and *ad hoc* manner.	Information quality assurance processes and controls are limited. The organization does not have a formal information quality program. Very little focus is placed on preventative measures to mitigate information quality issues. Information quality is uneven across the organization.	Management has embraced information quality principles and has publicly shown commitment. A formal information quality program has been established. Organization-level information is generally accurate, consistent, complete, and current.	Remedial processes are in place to quickly resolve information quality issues. Information users are confident that the organization-level information is of high quality. Information quality is viewed as a corporate responsibility.	The organization's KM systems are recognized as a source of authentic information by both internal and external users. The organization has a proactive information quality program that is often cited as a best practice.	
Current or future status						

Capacity	1	2	3	4	5	
			18. Security			
Are mechanisms in place to ensure information is protected from unauthorized access, use, and destruction?	The organization does not have a security architecture or mechanism to effectively support IM.	IM security systems and controls have not been consistently implemented across the organization. IM security audits and assessments are conducted on an *ad hoc* basis. Basic awareness of security and security-related issues exist.	IM security architecture, systems, controls, and procedures are in place. The organization can demonstrate compliance with all aspects of IM security and privacy requirements. Threat and risk assessments (TRA) are conducted for the IM infrastructure. Most systems have controls and ongoing monitoring.	Systems, controls, and procedures are regularly reviewed (e.g., security audits) to assess risk (potential benefit or amount of exposure to loss), and immediate corrective action is taken. All IM security requirements are communicated throughout the organization and are consistently applied to IM initiatives. TRAs are conducted on all IM systems, appropriate IM safeguards, and security architecture. IM is supported by real-time intrusion detection and incident response.	Areas of potential security vulnerability are continuously researched, and mitigation plans are developed. Clients and partners have full confidence that security has been integrated into the development of all IM initiatives. TRAs are continuously improved; IM safeguards anticipate new risks-adaptive architecture. Full detection and response to incidents.	
Current or future status						

19. Business Continuity

Are contingency plans and mechanisms in place to ensure timely information recovery, the restoration of essential records, and business resumption in the event of information corruption or loss?	The organization has no business continuity strategy to deal with information corruption or loss.	Different business units within the organization have developed and implemented contingency plans and mechanisms. No mechanisms have been developed at the organizationwide level.	The organization has a defined business continuity strategy and high-level contingency plans. Infrastructure to support business continuity is in place. Adequate awareness has been provided, and training has been conducted.	The organization has successfully tested business resumption plans and mechanisms. The organization-level business resumption plans and infrastructure are refreshed in light of changing business requirements. Ongoing training and awareness is provided to employees.	Investment in business-resumption strategies, plans, and infrastructure is optimized to allow undisrupted program delivery in the event of critical information corruption or loss.
Current or future status					

Capacity	1	2	3	4	5
		20. Compliance			
Are effective processes in place to ensure awareness of and compliance with applicable legislations, policies, and standards?	The organization does not have any audit and review process in place, ensuring compliance with specific KM legislations, policies, and standards for managing information.	The organization has initiated a program for compliance to some of the relevant legislations, policies, and standards for KM initiatives. The audit and review process has not been fully implemented across the organization.	The audit and review process of KM ensures an adequate level of awareness and compliance with applicable legislations, policies, and standards.	Corrective actions are undertaken in a systematic and timely fashion. All KM-compliance requirements are communicated throughout the organization and are consistently applied to KM initiatives. Compliance audits are performed throughout the life cycle of all KM initiatives.	Clients and stakeholders have full confidence that the organization is compliant with the relevant legislations, policies, and standards. Corrective actions typically address the root causes of noncompliance.
Current or future status					

21. Planning

| To what extent are information life-cycle requirements incorporated into the development of policies, services, and systems? | KM considerations are not incorporated in the planning cycle for policies, programs, services, and systems. | Some consideration is given to the KM requirements of policies, services, and systems but is not formally incorporated into the planning process. Planning is done for some paper-based information, but not electronic information. Little or no consideration is given to governance and accountability structures nor on how to maximize the interoperability of KM systems. | Requirements are formally incorporated in the planning process of policies, services, and systems. Planning applies to all information, regardless of format (paper or electronic). The need for KM governance and accountability structures has been appropriately addressed. Some consideration is given to maximizing the interoperability of KM systems. | Planning applies to all information across organizational boundaries. To the extent that is practical, opportunities to maximize KM system interoperability with external partners is regularly identified. | In addition to explicit information, some planning also applies to tacit knowledge. The planning includes not only information but also the entire life cycle of information. Optimal interorganizational governance and accountability structures are appropriately planned for. KM system interoperability is highly valued and continuously sought after. | |
| *Current or future status* | | | | | | |

Capacity	1	2	3	4	5
			22. Collection, Creation, Use, and Sharing		
How does the organization ensure that it collects, creates, uses, and shares information that will be useful?	Information is collected in an *ad hoc* fashion, with no consideration given to sharing and reuse or the requirements for documenting decisions and the decision-making process. No consideration is given to what information is really necessary to be collected and the impact on those who collect and provide it.	Some consideration is given to what and how information needs to be collected to improve sharing and reuse internally, as well as documenting decisions and the decision-making process. Some attempts are made to reduce the information collection burden.	Information collection is planned and undertaken efficiently and effectively, in accordance with legal and policy obligations. Opportunities for sharing and reuse are identified, as is information that already exists within the organization, and, therefore, does not need to be collected or created again.	The organization has a formal set of principles, policies, and standards for information collection that optimizes sharing and reuse internally and externally and reduces duplication. Stakeholders are aware of the organization's information-collection principles, policies, and standards.	Principles, policies, and standards exist for both explicit information and tacit knowledge collection. The organization places significant emphasis on sharing relevant information as a basis for collaboration and action.
Current or future status					

23. Business Process Alignment

To what extent is information identified, categorized, catalogued, and stored to effectively and efficiently support the business processes?	Information is not organized, categorized, catalogued, or stored effectively.	Some consideration is given to how the organization's information should be organized as evidenced by classification structures or other methods and tools. Some parts of the organization are organizing their information according to these methods.	The organization has formally accepted methods and tools for organizing, using, and disseminating its information. To a large extent, these methods and tools are used within the organization.	Standard methods and tools for organizing information are in widespread use within the organization. The business requirements of information owners and users are consistently met. The processes for organization of information resources are continuously assessed and revised in light of world-class practices.	Stakeholders are consulted on an ongoing basis to ensure alignment between their business requirements and the organization of information. Tools and models are assessed on a continual basis and updated based on ongoing business requirements and technology availability.
Current or future status					

24. Use and Dissemination

Capacity	1	2	3	4	5
To what extent is the organization's information able to be located, retrieved, and delivered to provide users with timely and convenient access?	No consideration is given to providing users with timely and convenient access to the organization's information.	Provisions for ensuring the availability of the organization's information exist but are being applied inconsistently across the organization. The administration of information use and dissemination is inconsistent across the organization.	Effective mechanisms exist for administering the information use and dissemination within the context of the organizational mandate and policy framework. Users are generally able to access the information they require, although there may be some delays and inconvenience.	Standard methods and tools for using and disseminating information are in widespread use within the organization. Information assets are available to users and in a timely and convenient fashion. Information is consistently accessible across all channels. Provisions have been made to accommodate the special needs of users.	Information assets are fully integrated across the organization and are accessible through a variety of access channels. Tools can be personalized to meet individual needs and preferences.
Current or future status					

25. Archiving and Preservation of the Public Record

To what extent can the organization ensure the long-term usability and safeguarding of its information assets?	No consideration has been given to ensure the long-term usability and safeguarding of information.	Consideration has been given and some methods put in place to safeguard information from improper disclosure, use, disposition, or destruction. Communication of maintenance procedures is internal only.	The organization has developed an approach that incorporates established principles for maintaining and preserving information, regardless of format. Information of enduring value to the organization and people of New Zealand has been identified and steps taken to ensure its long-term availability.	The organization has a formal set of principles, policies, and standards for maintaining and preserving information. These principles, policies, and standards are in widespread use throughout the organization. External stakeholders and clients are aware of and comply with this framework.	The organization regularly collaborates with stakeholders and reviews its information assets and associated legal and policy obligations to determine if current maintenance and preservation principles and standards are appropriate. Corrective actions are taken as necessary.
Current or future status					

Capacity	1	2	3	4	5
26. Retention and Disposal					
Do organization-level retention and disposal plans exist, and are they followed to ensure the timely disposition of information, subject to legal and policy obligations?	No consideration has been given to retention and disposal of information.	Consideration has been given and some methods put in place for the appropriate retention and disposal of information.	The organization has developed an approach to information disposal that adheres to retention schedules and other legal and policy obligations. Information of historic value is transferred to Archives NZ.	The organization has a formal set of policies and standards for disposing of information. These policies and standards are in widespread use throughout the organization and with key stakeholders. The organization has comprehensive coverage of retention schedules for all records under its control.	The organization regularly collaborates with stakeholders and reviews its information assets and associated legal and policy obligations to determine if current information disposal principles, policies, and standards are appropriate. Corrective actions are taken as necessary.	
Current or future status					

27. Staff Training and Support

What mechanisms exist to help train and support the staff in accessing and using information?	No staff-specific training is available or provided to support access and use of information. No explicit staff support (i.e., help desk) is available to help staff improve their access and use of information.	Some ad hoc training is provided to staff, usually through external courses, when new KM technologies and information resources are made available. No corporate staff-training strategy or program has been developed to support the training needs.	A formal training program has been developed and implemented. Training requirements for the use of KM technologies and information resources have been developed. KM specialists develop the training. A formal staff support help desk is widely utilized by staff.	User training on all aspects of relevant information technologies, information access, and appropriate use are provided and made available through a variety of delivery mechanisms. The training is based on staff feedback and requirements. Self-learning training is provided online and is actively utilized by staff.	Multiple lines of staff training are provided (e.g., online, classroom, computer-based, "how-to" booklets, etc.). Customized training, geared toward the training needs of individuals, is provided online. Continual staff feedback shapes the direction of the KM training programs.
Current or future status					

Capacity	1	2	3	4	5	
			28. Staff Satisfaction			
Is staff satisfaction measured regularly? Are staff expectations, needs, and wants considered in the planning and delivery of KM tools, systems, and support mechanisms?	There are no clearly established mechanisms to collect and review staff satisfaction for available KM tools, systems, and support mechanisms.	Staff satisfaction surveys are occasionally conducted to measure satisfaction on KM tools, systems, and support mechanisms. Survey results are evaluated but rarely lead to any corrective measures.	Formal mechanisms have been developed at the organization level to measure staff satisfaction on KM tools, systems, and support mechanisms. Staff feedback and suggestions are collected and generally incorporated into the refinement of KM tools, systems, and support mechanisms.	KM specialists consult with users as part of the normal development and refinement process to tailor KM tools, systems, and support mechanisms to the needs of individuals and communities of interest. Staff feedback is systematically incorporated.	KM tools, systems, and support mechanisms are recognized as being "user centric." Information offerings are continually molded to meet anticipated needs of the users.	
Current or future status						

References

Creating a Management Capacity Checklist, Ministry of Justice, New Zealand. Retrieved June 29, 2005, from http://www.justice.govt.nz/jsis/knowledge-management-guide/chapter-8a.html.

Appendix H

KNOWLEDGE AND INFORMATION MANAGEMENT COMPETENCIES

This competencies survey is specifically related to knowledge and information management (K&IM). They are required at some level by everyone in knowledge-sharing organizations, but the depth and level required is dependent on their role. They are defined in three team levels (strategic leader, team leader, and team member) together with a fourth level that covers the K&IM competencies required by everyone working in such an organization.

The description of each competency match from A to I with the team and employee levels 1 to 4 (e.g., A3 and C4) is given in Table H.1.

General leadership and management competencies are summarized as J to U in Table H.2.

Table H.1 Knowledge and Information Management (K&IM) Competencies Framework

	Strategic Leader	Team Leader	Team Member	All Employees
	1	2	3	4
A	Engages with thought leaders within and outside the organization to identify the value of knowledge and information to the organization and develop a knowledge-based vision	Demonstrates awareness of K&IM market trends, developments, experience, and good practice	Scans and reviews K&IM market opportunities/developments	Aware of the knowledge and information relevant to their roles and the value this brings to the organization
B	Identifies, develops and articulates K&IM strategies that will add value to the organization	Identifies business opportunities to deliver value through improved K&IM	Researches opportunities, methods, and approaches for delivering value through improved K&IM	Reviews and communicates gaps in knowledge and information that hinder the achievement of objectives
C	Ensures that K&IM strategies are embedded within corporate strategies and key business processes	Develops K&IM processes that can be embedded in key business processes and ensures that K&IM activities are coordinated across the organization	Supports and facilitates the development and implementation of K&IM processes across organizational silos	Uses K&IM processes to help achieve objectives
D	Identifies and develops strategies to encourage and enable collaborative working for the organization and partners	Identifies, develops, and nurtures networks and communities	Supports and develops networked and community working	Participates in and learns from networked and community approaches

E	Fosters a knowledge- and information-rich culture and ensures that K&IM competencies are recognized as core competencies of the organization to develop individual and organizational capability	a. Develops K&IM competencies throughout the organization b. Inspires knowledge sharing and capture to enable continuous learning and knowledge creation c. Champions collaborative working d. Develops motivational approaches	a. Trains, or facilitates the training of, all employees in appropriate K&IM competencies b. Supports and facilitates knowledge and information sharing c. Develops appropriate reward and recognition systems	a. Develops and uses appropriate K&IM competencies b. Shares knowledge and information and participates in activities to facilitate sharing c. Works collaboratively d. Understands and appreciates reward and recognition systems
F	Fosters the development of appropriate knowledge and information assets and the adoption of effective K&IM processes, tools, and standards	a. Identifies and develops knowledge and information assets and introduces processes to improve their leverage b. Identifies and builds on social networks that enable knowledge and information flow c. Facilitates the acquisition or development of appropriate K&IM processes, tools, and standards	a. Audits, maps, and monitors knowledge and information assets and their use b. Audits, maps, and monitors knowledge and information flows c. Develops and supports processes, tools, and standards for knowledge sharing and capture d. Trains staff at all levels in the use of K&IM tools, standards, and processes e. Develops tailored K&IM approaches aligned to specific business processes	a. Builds and manages appropriate knowledge and information assets b. Understands the knowledge and information flows relevant to their role c. Uses the K&IM processes, tools, and standards provided d. Contributes to the development of K&IM processes, tools, and standards

Table H.1 Knowledge and Information Management (K&IM) Competencies Framework (continued)

	Strategic Leader	Team Leader	Team Member	All Employees
	1	2	3	4
G	Enables an effective K&IM architecture	a. Develops and implements information and communications technology (ICT) policies b. Develops and implements information management policies c. Develops and implements content management policies d. Develops and implements document and records management policies e. Develops and implements access and dissemination policies	a. Incorporates Web-enabled opportunities b. Develops software programs in appropriate languages and levels c. Develops information management standards and guidelines d. Identifies and acquires external sources e. Identifies and acquires internal knowledge and information sources f. Develops tools and protocols for creation, integration, and publishing g. Develops corporate coding and tagging tools h. Plans and manages records centers and document management storage i. Develops retrieval capabilities j. Designs processes and systems for effective knowledge and information dissemination	a. Is aware of internal and external Web developments b. Understands and complies with information management standards and guidelines c. Understands the scope and relevance of internal and external sources d. Complies with records and document management policies e. Effectively uses standard retrieval and dissemination tools f. Complies with knowledge and information dissemination policies

H	Enables knowledge and information services	a. Designs and implements knowledge and information services b. Designs and implements content creation services c. Enables utilization of knowledge and information sources	a. Ensures the availability of selected resources b. Enables staff members to find relevant knowledge and information c. Provides journalistic services d. Applies markup languages e. Undertakes knowledge analysis and evaluation f. Uses most appropriate mix of knowledge and information sources g. Delivers relevant knowledge and information in appropriate forms	a. Uses appropriate knowledge and information resources b. Utilizes tools and processes provided to enable content creation c. Understands and communicates the need for knowledge and information services d. Uses a variety of knowledge and information formats
I	Drives value and constantly reviews the impact of K&IM strategies	a. Incorporates measurement systems b. Benchmarks K&IM strategies	a. Collects, monitors, and analyzes appropriate data b. Benchmarks knowledge and information activities	Complies with feedback requirements

Table H.2 General Leadership and Management Competencies Framework

	K&IM Strategic Leader	K&IM Team Leader	K&IM Team Member	All Employees
	1	2	3	4
J	Demonstrates breadth of vision	Demonstrates analysis and judgment	Uses information effectively	Uses appropriate information sources
K	Generates ideas	Innovates	Demonstrates creativity and solutions orientation	Demonstrates innovative problem solving
L	Generates options for change	a. Develops and delivers change b. Demonstrates commercial awareness	a. Adapts to change b. Scans and reviews market opportunities	Adapts to new and changing circumstances and commits to lifelong learning
M	Demonstrates a high level of interpersonal skills	Demonstrates customer/colleague focus	Works with others	Supports colleagues
N	Facilitates team working	Develops the team	Takes responsibility for team tasks	Contributes to team objectives
O	Develops people	Develops team members	Develops self	Supports training and development objectives
P	Influences	a. Manages relationships b. Negotiates	a. Demonstrates impact b. Values others	Builds positive relationships

Q	Inspires others	Builds confidence in decisions	Engenders support	Takes the lead when appropriate
R	Communicates direction of the organization	Communicates direction to the team	Interprets and presents the key messages	Communicates effectively
S	Leads implementation	a. Undertakes effective resource and business planning b. Achieves results c. Manages projects effectively	a. Undertakes task planning b. Pays attention to detail	Undertakes personal planning
T	Seeks continuous improvement	Achieves quality outcomes	Introduces improvements	Demonstrates quality awareness
U	Secures resources	a. Identifies resource requirements b. Develops budgets and financial business cases c. Plans and makes a case for human resources	Ensures productive utilization of resources	Demonstrates awareness of resource planning

Source: Knowledge and information management competencies (n.d.), Ministry of Justice, New Zealand. Retrieved June 29, 2005, http://www.justice.govt.nz/jsis/ knowledge-management-guide/chapter-8k.html.

Appendix I

KNOWLEDGE DISCOVERY TECHNIQUES

Knowledge can be transmitted between or among people, but this does not mean that it can only be copied. People learn rather than are taught, and the transferred knowledge is recreated by the recipient. So, it can change as it replicates and will not always take the same form. The key concept in this regard is to understand the extent to which useful knowledge can actually be codified. One of the simpler concepts to grasp is the difference between "explicit" and "tacit" knowledge.

A large number of organizations have seized on this concept as a way of capturing knowledge that resides inside their organizations and which they hope will prove to be a valuable asset. Sometimes, this is limited to programs of managing the firm's intellectual property. This form of knowledge management (KM) has been characterized as *defensive*, that is, concerned with protecting some aspect of the organization's activity.

There are, however, other forms of knowledge that are not so easily amenable to being codified. Typically, these are skills or abilities (sometimes physical in nature) that resist easy replication. Sports stars are the example most often cited to explain this difference, but the concept can also be illustrated by examples from what are often referred to as creative occupations or even from design and engineering work. At the root of this is an understanding that some forms of knowledge do not exist outside their context and that some forms of knowledge are created socially.

Because some forms of knowledge or experience cannot easily be codified, the experience of one person or a group of people cannot always be written down and passed on in book form for another group to replicate. Learning from the experience of others may require additional approaches and other skills. Table I.1 lists some of the techniques discussed in this appendix.

Innovation is one of the key drivers of knowledge management and other collaborative activities in commercial organizations. It is very strongly

315

Table I.1 Knowledge Discovery Techniques

Technique	Basic or Advanced	Whether Cultural Change Is Required
Exit interviews	B	N
Speed dating	B	N
Mind mapping	B	N
After-action reviews	B	N
Project reviews	B	N
Baton passing	B	Y
Virtual teams	B	Y
Coaching and mentoring	B	N
Intellectual capital	B	Y
Communities of practice	B	Y
Social network analysis	A	N
Complex adaptive systems	A	Y
Knowledge audits	A	N
Design of space	A	Y
Knowledge harvesting	A	Y
Domain knowledge mapping	A	Y
Storytelling	A	Y

Note: B = basic, A = advanced, Y = yes, N = no.

marked in research-based industries, such as pharmaceuticals, particularly in those cases in which new developments can be converted into major financial assets such as patents. However, there are other forms of innovation, such as improved internal processes or new services to offer.

I.1 SOURCES OF KNOWLEDGE

Knowledge management is a collection of approaches designed to answer two questions:

How do we know what we know?

How do we get to know what we need to know?

Although understanding the sources of existing knowledge is not the only component of a successful knowledge management strategy and creating new knowledge is, in the longer term, even more important, it is vital to understand the sources of knowledge to support service improvement activities.

There are a wide and diverse set of sources that can be categorized into thee main areas: your customers, your own organization, and others.

I.1.1   Learning from Customers

Customers are a major source of knowledge about areas of service improvement. The skill, however, lies in understanding what to ask and in interpreting the answer. Many organizations have put in place customer complaints systems, but it is not always clear how these are used to derive lessons that can feed service improvement.

This is where the technology of customer relationship management can fit in. However, it is not just the recording of the customer interactions that is important. It is also the mining of the data. This is the knowledge management dimension — the need to combine insights from a number of sources to gain a better understanding of the sources of innovation.

I.1.2   Learning from Your Organization

In almost all organizations, the chief source of expertise and the wellspring of innovation come from within the organization itself. Although every organization produces some of its "organizational capital" in the form of manuals and procedure documents, most of it is actually contained in the minds and the behaviors of its employees. The chief issues in trying to liberate this capital are about getting buy-in from the staff that control access to this learning. They may need to get some value from this in terms of material reward or recognition. However, it should be understood that this expertise may be contained in parts of the organization other than the ones that provide the specific service.

The management of the organization may be the biggest problem in opening up this source either because of a distrust on the part of the individuals or groups with access to this capability or because new ways of working may threaten existing power structures. Knowing actually where the expertise lies in your organization is the other major inhibitor to effective organizational learning. The ways of addressing this are to adopt some of the methods identified as being useful ways of capturing tacit knowledge.

I.1.3 Learning from Other Organizations

This is easily the largest, most complex, and most diffuse source of knowledge. Organizations can usually learn a considerable amount from other comparable organizations. These other organizations do not need to be the same type of organization. Sometimes, very dissimilar organizations can be the greatest source of learning. However, to take advantage of this learning, organizations must be able to learn from the experience of others.

I.2 KM TECHNIQUES

I.2.1 Problem Solving

An important area for sharing knowledge and expertise is in solving specific problems. A number of basic techniques have been developed for this.

I.2.1.1 Exit Interviews

This is normally seen as a basic HR activity. Its specific relevance to knowledge sharing and collaboration is the link to retaining specialist knowledge within the organization. In a number of commercial organizations, this is linked to retaining the intellectual property of the company. Exit interviews are a long-standing and well-known technique in human resources management. From the HR perspective, they are a way of gaining insights into how employees see the organization and identifying potential areas for improvement.

Interest has grown more recently, however, in the potential of exit interviews as a knowledge management tool. Put simply, a number of organizations have begun to realize that a store of valuable information and knowledge about the way jobs are done or about customer expectations are locked inside the heads of employees (i.e., tacit rather than explicit knowledge) and can easily be lost if they leave the organization without recording or passing on their understanding and expertise.

The traditional, HR-focused exit interviews can be conducted in a number of ways, including by telephone, by questionnaire, or even via the Internet. However, for knowledge management objectives, a face-to-face interview is the only realistic approach.

There is no single agreed approach to conducting knowledge-focused exit interviews.

Each organization can develop its own approach that fits its particular circumstances.

The principal value of exit interviews lies in their simplicity. However, their successful use depends on how well the process is integrated with other knowledge-sharing activities. The results from the interviews need to be fed back into other developmental processes to ensure that the value of any knowledge or information gained is immediately accessible to other parts of the organization.

Exit interviews are, therefore, a spectrum that includes other forms of "knowledge elicitation." These include support for "blogging" and more elaborate forms of "knowledge harvesting," discussed later in this chapter.

I.2.1.2 Speed Dating

The purpose of "speed dating" is to elicit the largest number of potential solutions to a problem. The person with the problem will then be able to sift the responses to see if any offer potential solutions. It is possible to organize the "speed dating" in any way that is convenient, but one basic approach is as follows:

1. A range of people from different backgrounds are arranged into groups.
2. Those people with a problem looking for a potential solution then go around each group in turn.
3. The person with the problem has a short period (say, 5 to 10 min) to explain the problem.
4. The group offering solutions then has a short period (say, 10 to 15 min) to suggest as many solutions as they can.

The chief benefit of this technique is that, apart from the cost of bringing people together, it is comparatively cheap. It does allow a range of different people to contribute to identifying potential solutions.

At its simplest, it involves someone with a specific problem presenting it briefly to a group of individuals from different backgrounds. The group listening then has a short period of time to suggest possible answers. To be effective, the process needs to be repeated several times with other groups.

I.2.1.3 Mind Mapping

Mind mapping is a well-established technique developed in the 1960s by Tony Buzan. It is a graphic technique that allows one individual or a group to visualize the relationships among a range of related topics and to represent them in the form of a diagram. Its primary purpose is to clarify thinking and understanding. Tony Buzan (http://www.mind-map.com/EN/mindmaps/how_to.htm) has written extensively on mind mapping, and there are various printed guides available that document the processes.

Successful mind maps help visualize the relationship between different components of an issue. They can be very personal, but they can also be used to reveal and discuss differences in understanding between people who need to collaborate on a specific issue.

The potential application of mind mapping to organizational improvement activities lies in the structure it offers that allows groups of people to explore or clarify thinking — and thus access or share knowledge — particularly in identifying linkages across different components. In this regard, it offers some interesting links to Ishikawa (or "fishbone") diagrams used in quality improvement activities. It also provides a linkage of corporate objectives to detailed performance measures that form the core for the use of the Balanced Scorecard to support strategic management.

I.2.2 Organizational Learning Approaches

Organizational learning is a key component of any knowledge management strategy or any attempt to harness the experience of an organization to improve its performance.

There is a major area of overlap between organizational learning approaches and collaboration. A number of the techniques developed to support organizational learning are, therefore, of direct interest or use to knowledge management approaches.

I.2.2.1 After-Action Reviews

This is one of the simplest approaches to learning from doing. It was originally developed by the U.S. military to learn the lessons from combat.

An *after-action review* (AAR) is a professional discussion of an event, focused on performance standards, that enables soldiers to discover for themselves what happened, why it happened, and how to sustain strengths and improve on weaknesses. There are several important features of this definition. First of all, the emphasis is on a professional discussion. The discussion is structured and is based on the assumption that there existed a plan to be followed as well as preexisting standards that were to have been observed in carrying out the tasks. Finally, and most importantly, the use of AARs needs to feed into performance management and service improvement activities. It is not a stand-alone activity.

An AAR is both an art and a science. The art lies in the obtainment of mutual trust so that people will speak freely. Innovative behavior should be the norm. Problem solving should be pragmatic, and employees should not be preoccupied with status, territory, or second-guessing "what the leader will think." There is a fine line between encouraging informality (but not so much that the meeting becomes chaotic and nothing gets done) and retaining some atmosphere of formality and politeness (but not to the point that issues are masked — especially with the boss — and nothing really gets done).

It raises several basic questions:

1. What was supposed to happen?
2. What actually happened?
3. Why was there a difference?
4. What did we learn?

The important thing to notice from this approach is that to be effective it needs to be removed from any attempt to assign blame. The major advantage of AAR is its independence from any technology and its ability to be used in a variety of situations from very minor reviews to quite elaborate ones.

I.2.2.2 Project Reviews

Project reviews are in some ways a more sophisticated version of the AARs. In general, they are used to review larger areas of work than those for which AARs are employed. They are often linked to more complex methodologies for large-scale project management.

It is a major technique for codifying knowledge, because it attempts to capture learning points from the experience of delivering projects. It can be linked to a number of performance management activities.

I.2.2.3 Baton Passing

Baton passing is a more sophisticated approach to passing on the lessons from a recently experienced process to another team that is about to undergo the same process. It is a technique developed by Victor Newman of European Pfizer Research University. It is a more sophisticated technique than the two review methods outlined earlier for passing on lessons learned.

The key elements in baton passing are that the team that has just successfully completed the process should record their experiences immediately after the process is completed. So, the key feature is the "just-in-time" knowledge transfer. The specific requirement of project teams that had just successfully completed a project review to pass on the lessons to the next project team about to embark on a similar phase of activity led to its development. The reason for adopting a just-in-time approach was to capture the experience of a group that had successfully completed a rarely encountered process. It becomes important then to capture the knowledge and experience before it is lost, because it is unlikely to be of use to the successful team, at least for some time.

The following are the key phases in the process:

1. Build, identify, and capture experience.
2. Review and exchange experience between outgoing and incoming teams to connect learning and questions.
3. Produce an action plan to be able to mobilize the lessons.
4. Commit the plan to action.

The applicability of this technique to service improvement is in using the learning gained in one area to prepare the next area for the same test.

I.2.3 Organizational Design Approaches

A number of approaches to collaboration and sharing knowledge have a strong component of organizational change and redesign. These are more formal than those in the earlier section.

I.2.3.1 Virtual Teams

The distinguishing characteristic of virtual teams is that they are collections of individuals or groups who are located apart physically but need to collaborate across physical boundaries. This is often because they are working on a specific project, but there are other circumstances in which this kind of approach is productive. In research-based activities, such as in pharmaceutical companies, it may be important to get research teams to collaborate. This may to be maximize scarce resources or, more usually, to try to generate new areas of knowledge from existing ones.

Virtual teams offer a way of bringing together the distributed resources to work on a number of projects. They offer greater flexibility in the use of resources and the ability to produce new expertise from old.

These are key issues for the successful use of virtual teams:

1. The need to have occasional physical contact at the outset of the project. Some basic degree of physical contact is important for communication and building trust. This has been confirmed by a number of research studies.
2. The need to address cultural differences among the various members of the team. In multinational firms, this is usually a problem of different national cultures.

Direct physical contact and a degree of socialization can contribute to breaking down these barriers. The effective use of technology can also be a key determinant of the success or failure of virtual teams. Effective information systems can allow collaboration, whereas ineffective ones can hinder effective communications. E-mail tends to be the simplest of methods that are employed, but more elaborate technologies include collaboration software or the use of videoconferencing technologies.

The potential contribution of virtual teams to performance improvement is in the direction of resources toward the solution of particular tasks. It is quite a common experience in organizations that experience or expertise is restricted to one organizational unit and cannot easily be released to another one if the only way to do this is to transfer the member of staff.

Virtual teams offer the opportunity for individuals or groups to collaborate without changing organizational boundaries. They also differ from many matrix management structures in that they do not necessitate changes in formal reporting structures. However, creating and maintaining virtual teams are not without their challenges. Several key areas need to be addressed:

1. *Job design.* Team working methods and expectations need to be dealt with explicitly. This also includes designing job accountability and decision-making authority.
2. *Team design.* As virtual teams are meant to overcome the limitations of traditional organization boundaries, they need new criteria. These include identifying the purpose of the team and selecting members who fit. More important, the team needs to have a clear identity and a defined statement of purpose.
3. *Communication methods* are essential to the success of virtual teams because physical contact is kept to a minimum. Communications need to be comprehensive (i.e., everyone should be fully informed), frequent, but preferably with short messages. Quality of communication is the most important aspect.
4. *Leadership* appears to have a key impact on the success of virtual teams. This includes setting clear goals and providing continuous feedback on performance.
5. *Trust.* This is at the heart of almost all successful knowledge management practices. Trust is best established by social interaction, particularly at the start of the project.
6. *Cultural awareness.* The cultural dimension should be tackled at the outset to improve coherence and minimize misunderstanding.
7. *Technology.* Once again, this is a key enabler; relatively advanced technology will be required to support collaboration, and not merely to ensure frequent contact.

I.2.3.2 Coaching and Mentoring

Coaching and mentoring are well-known techniques from human resources and organizational development work. Their relevance to knowledge-based work is the opportunities they provide for direct person-to-person assimilation. In this regard, they are similar to the way that apprentices have traditionally learned their craft.

Not all useful information can be conveyed by capturing tacit knowledge and codifying it, for example, in the form of guides or handbooks. Certain types of knowledge are best provided by observing someone else at work and, if possible, copying and asking questions. The principal advantages of mentoring and coaching are the following:

1. The personal contact and, therefore, the opportunities for socialization and internalizing knowledge are available.
2. It can strongly reinforce cultural aspects of work. It offers opportunities for feedback and development.

However, there are corresponding disadvantages, too:

1. It can be very intensive and time consuming. This may, in some cases, interfere with normal work activities.
2. Although it is strong at imparting existing knowledge, it can hinder the development of new knowledge or expertise.

For these reasons, coaching and mentoring are often restricted to very highly regarded areas such as senior management development.

I.2.4 Cultural Approaches

Many of the most effective knowledge management approaches have their basis in understanding the cultural aspects of organizational behavior and in concentrating on improving the cultural bias toward sharing knowledge or other information.

I.2.4.1 Identifying Intellectual Capital

Intellectual capital is a concept that has been gaining acceptance in commercial organizations but is not yet used extensively or understood in the public sector — except, perhaps, for people who concentrate on organizational development activities.

The concept can be traced back to work carried out for the Skandia Corporation by Leif Edvinsson. The model developed there was intended to demonstrate the importance of assets other than financial ones to the value and performance of a company.

The nonfinancial forms of capital are, for the most part, intangible assets but they represent things of value to the organization. *Customer capital* represents the value of the customers to the organization and, in particular, their contribution to future income and profits. Customer capital can also be represented in terms of the feedback or ideas that can be obtained from consultations, surveys, or reviews of complaints.

Structural capital represents all the nonhuman, nonfinancial aspects. It includes all the processes and procedures that an organization has developed. In the commercial world, the processes and procedures are often the source of competitive advantage. Human capital is a rather easier concept to explain. In its most basic form, it consists of all those intangible assets contributed by employees: their skills, experience, knowledge, and abilities (current and potential). In service-based organizations, human capital is often the key source of improvement and innovation. It is capable of being increased or renewed, either by staff turnover or by education, development, and the acquisition of new skills. There are a number of issues with the measurement of either the level of human capital in an organization or its financial valuation. Some progress has been made on including valuations for human capital in areas such as transfer fees for sportsmen and women and in the market valuation of companies whose intellectual assets far outweigh their tangible ones. This has long been true of consultancy firms, for instance, and companies such as Microsoft.

Social capital is the name given to a set of processes that attempt to stress the importance of the relationships built and developed by individuals who work together to provide goods or services. Most people will recognize this in the strength of working relationships and goodwill that exists among effective teams. Although intangible, it is real. Social capital covers the value that is generated by the interaction between people in organizations.

Social capital is essential to exploiting intellectual capital. This is because much of the knowledge created by individuals is created in social contexts rather than by them acting alone. Social capital is one of the major contributions made by teams to the efficiency and effectiveness of organizations.

Intellectual capital is less of a technique that can be applied directly than a way of analyzing and interpreting the basic capacity of an organization. It helps identify the assets that an organization has and can be used to improve its effectiveness and ability to change and innovate. The key to opening up intellectual capital is, therefore, developing a measurement and reporting system that can account for these assets in a reasonably objective fashion.

I.2.4.2 Building Communities of Practice (CoP)

CoPs are a comparatively new but very powerful way of developing links among individuals and groups that can, in turn, develop links across wider groups to share experiences. A CoP is essentially a social network, a group of individuals who have recognized and expressed a need to share knowledge (and information) or collaborate in a specific and usually work-related area. The term is of relatively recent coinage, but the concept is a very old one. It is, however, an idea that has begun to take off.

The strength of CoPs is that they can be formed around any topic of interest or concern. Communities can also be short lived or long lived, depending on the nature of the area of interest. Although the typical CoP is formed by people from similar backgrounds, it is also potentially a very powerful approach for bringing together a range of disparate people to share knowledge and experience to tackle a new problem, when questions are still to be formulated and the answers are not yet clear.

CoPs differ from teams or workgroups in a number of quite significant ways.

Teams tend to have very specific goals with targets or demonstrable objectives. CoPs tend to concentrate on wider areas of interest that can develop over time. Teams are usually a formal part of the organizational structure, whereas CoPs are more amorphous and often voluntary.

Although CoPs are not dependent on technology, there is no doubt that increased availability of IT has offered the opportunity to boost their importance. The key technologies in this area are e-mail, bulletin boards, and collaboration software.

The experience in commercial organizations is that managerial organization of CoPs is unlikely to lead to their being successful. Most successful CoPs tend to be self-organizing, and this offers challenges to organizations, particularly very hierarchical or highly structured ones.

The potential contribution of CoPs to performance improvement is quite easy to see.

CoPs offer the opportunity not only to learn directly from more experienced individuals but also can provide a space in which ideas can be put forward and explored without being put directly into practice.

I.2.5 Advanced Techniques

I.2.5.1 Social Network Analysis

This is at the same time a specific academic technique and a useful way of analyzing the way that communications flow through an organization. As an analytical activity, it does help illuminate the way social relationships can improve or impede the flow of knowledge. However, there is no preferred model; the analysis demonstrates the situation.

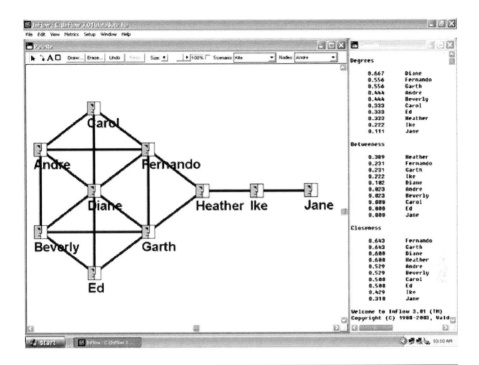

Figure I.1   Social network analysis.

KM staff who wish to design a preferred outcome need to mold the organizational structure. Social network analysis is essentially an analytical technique but one that can be used diagnostically. However, the key skill required for its successful application is in the design of the questionnaires required to elicit the basic data. Accurate and relevant data is the key to properly mapping the network. The resulting network map is a strongly visual description, as shown in Figure I.1.

I.2.5.2   Knowledge Audits

Knowledge audits are quite complex but potentially very effective in identifying and describing the way in which knowledge is created and stored in organizations. The audits cannot be open ended and need to be prepared and, in particular, need to be based on a fundamental analysis of knowledge types and knowledge flows.

I.2.5.3   Design of Space

The design of working space is a very powerful aspect of the use of knowledge management techniques to improve effective working. There is a whole body of research in a range of different settings that demonstrate the impact of working-space design on working relationships and collaboration. In general, working space should be created to allow individuals a degree of freedom in meeting so that spontaneous conversations can develop. This is often referred to as the "water cooler" approach. Key aspects of design include the provision for neutral spaces and wide corridors that enable chance meetings to occur without any feeling on the part of the individuals that they are interrupting someone else's work.

A particular analysis of the approach to designing office space can be found in *The New Office* by Francis Duffy, who divides office space into four kinds:

1. The hive — open place humming with activity
2. The club — 18th-century coffeehouse style, for deals and ideas and bonding
3. The den — for intense communicative work among a small number of people
4. The cell — where an individual works in a contemplative sort of way

I.2.5.4 Knowledge Harvesting

Knowledge harvesting covers a range of techniques that aim to recover knowledge assets from many forms of tacit knowledge contained within an organization. Several of the approaches are concerned with capturing tacit knowledge and codifying it, i.e., turning it into explicit knowledge. The principal techniques include developing communities of interest, which are functionally parallel to CoPs and encourage activities such as Web logging ("blogging"). Another technique is to use resources such as internal directories as guides to likely sources of expertise.

I.2.5.5 Domain Knowledge Mapping

This is a rather more complicated approach to identifying knowledge that is recognized as important but not well defined. It is often useful for beginning the recording of knowledge in newly developed fields.

Domain knowledge mapping often concentrates on developing high-level knowledge models. This is often a helpful way of providing an overview of available and missing knowledge in core business areas. Knowledge mapping is a good example of a useful knowledge management activity with existing knowledge acquisition and modeling techniques at its foundations. It particularly concentrates on the visualization of relationships, particularly in newly evolving or complex areas of study.

I.2.5.6   Storytelling

Storytelling is quite simply the use of stories in organizations as a communication tool to share knowledge. It is a deceptively simple approach, but it has been put in the category of advanced techniques because its effective use is quite a complex matter.

Although virtually all people are attracted to stories, not everyone is good at telling them. Stories have to be well selected for the appropriateness and content as well as their presentation. This is a skill well understood by traditional storytellers, and the skills often require years to acquire and be developed into a useful activity.

A rare example of storytelling in the public sector — the National Health Service (United Kingdom), in this case — is provided on this Web site: http://www.affinitymc.com/The-Power-of-Storytelling.htm.

I.3   TOOLS FOR ORGANIZING KNOWLEDGE ASSETS

There is a very wide range of software available for organizing knowledge assets.

I.3.1   Tools Based on Database Technologies

These are very heavily influenced by computing theories and rely frequently on relational database models. They are optimized for highly structured data but have more difficulty in dealing with unstructured data. However, newer RDBMS often have support for other structures.

I.3.2   Electronic Document Management Systems (EDMS)

These are increasingly touted as being the answer to all knowledge management problems, largely because they work with unstructured information as well as highly structured information.

I.3.3   Metadata Management Systems

Metadata is the key component of all comprehensive management systems. However, there is a dearth of metadata schemes that relate to service improvement or performance management. One area, however, in which something similar has been developed is in the metadata layer of business intelligence or other reporting tools. In addition to allowing the mapping between object names used in the service areas with the usually less-meaningful table names and views, these metadata layers also frequently support the creation of new objects derived from underlying values in the base data. This allows the creation of standard approaches for deriving or calculating performance indicators or other values in a consistent fashion.

I.3.4   Generalized Retrieval Systems

These use a variety of technologies, but there is an increasing preference for very sophisticated probabilistic searching methods, often based on Bayesian inference.

A popular area for the deployment of the searching tools is in support of CRM systems, to allow multiskilled agents to access organizational information. These developments are managed in a variety of ways. Increasingly, suppliers of CRM and help-desk software are including software often described as *knowledge management software*. This is often used to extend the capability of the basic system by allowing agents to record how new or unusual problems were dealt with and making the resulting knowledge available to colleagues who might face the same problem in future.

I.3.5   Tools for Collaboration

These constitute the other main category of tools. This is an area that is less structured and, therefore, less highly developed in some ways than the tools for organizing knowledge. There are two main categories of collaboration software: systems written for specific groups or for specific purposes. These include a whole range of different software types.

There are a wide variety of collaborative tools, from development tools such as Lotus Notes/Domino to systems designed to provide enterprise information portals. The recent concentration on portals provides a good example of the issues that need to be addressed in providing generic solutions to knowledge work and collaboration. Portals offer a range of services intended to allow information services simply to be "plugged in" to the portal and then made available to desktops throughout the organization. In reality, however, portals can be extremely complex software environments that require considerable programming resources to utilize properly. The choice of the basic platform is, therefore, one of the critical success factors for any portal project.

The other significant IT component that relates to both the organization of knowledge assets and collaboration areas is intranets. *Intranet* is an increasingly loose term; its strict meaning applies to the deployment of Internet technologies within a single organization. In practice, however, it is used as a kind of shorthand for a collection of information management and collaboration tools delivered to a set of desktops.

Many organizations have encountered difficulties with the effective deployment of intranets. The main problems have been the following:

1. Poor information management, where duplication has been permitted and information has been allowed to get out of date.
2. Similar to the Internet, intranets are subject to Gresham's law of information and knowledge, where the less useful material is all too easy to find but the genuinely useful material is not in regular circulation.
3. A proliferation of intranets, each based on an organizational unit, thereby reinforcing internal barriers instead of trying to help break them down; problems of cultural fit between the opportunities offered by the technology and the wider organizational culture. The latter needs to support a degree of openness in the use of the technology; effective collaboration is otherwise unlikely to result.

I.4 FRAMEWORKS

The literature on knowledge management is replete with proposed frameworks of varying degrees of complexity. Although there are competing models, there are basically two major approaches:

1. Maturity models
2. Strategy or implementation frameworks

The maturity models, common in other areas too, purport to describe a journey that is possible to be made from less sophisticated to more sophisticated approaches.

A good example of the maturity model is the Siemens KMMM model (http://w4.siemens.de/ct/en/technologies/ic/beispiele/kmmm.html). Based on the well-known Capability Maturity Model (CMM) from the Software Engineering Institute, KMMM includes an analysis model and a development model.

Implementation frameworks can be simple or complex, often depending on the sophistication of the organization. One well-regarded framework is that devised by British Petroleum, which consists of three steps:

1. Create awareness.
2. Build knowledge assets.
3. Leverage knowledge assets.

When considering the application of knowledge management to process improvement, managers should look to the simplest possible approach that is congruent with organizational goals. That predisposes them to frameworks such as the BP model.

I.5   PRODUCING CORPORATE KM STRATEGIES

Knowledge management strategies are highly problematic. They tend to imply that there is a well-defined path to achieving knowledge management. That is an arguable concept. A very useful model is that of George von Krogh et al. (2000), who suggest the following "enablers":

1. Instill a knowledge vision.
2. Manage conversations.
3. Mobilize knowledge activists.
4. Create the right context.
5. Globalize local knowledge.

I.6   THEORIES OF KNOWLEDGE

Theories of knowledge — *epistemologies*, to give them their formal name — provide a huge area of debate that covers philosophy, psychology, and, more recently, areas of information theory. The span of this work also reaches from the ancient world to the present and across a range of different cultures. There are two basic approaches to understanding the nature of knowledge and, in particular, of knowledge creation, which may be of use in planning the introduction of knowledge management initiatives.

The *Cognitive model*, which regards knowledge as essentially something objective and transferable, stresses the capturing of tacit knowledge and embedding it into more explicit forms. The resulting knowledge can therefore be shared and reused. This model is very strongly linked to approaches that stress the importance of explicit knowledge as a form of intellectual property. It is also the model that lies behind most of the IT systems that are sold as knowledge management systems. These are very heavily reliant on regarding knowledge management as being essentially a more complex form of information processing, in which cognitive abilities are seen as the major inputs that the technology can transform into the desired outputs.

The *Social model*, which is sometimes called the *Community* or *Connectiveness model*, stresses that knowledge creation is essentially a social process. This model emphasizes the importance of social interaction both to the creation and dissemination of knowledge. It is naturally a view held very strongly in the social sciences and by professionals and researchers who concentrate on organizational development and human resources processes. The most important formulation of the theory, however, is probably that of Nonaka and Takeuchi in their book, *The Knowledge-Creating Company* (1995). The theoretical basis of this book also relies on far-eastern philosophies as well as modern business practices. The principal idea expounded in the work is that the kinds of knowledge that need to be created to drive innovation are essentially social. The Nonaka and Takeuchi model sees knowledge management as an iterative process, whereby tacit knowledge is often shared in social contexts before being made explicit and explicit knowledge is often internalized before being used to help create new forms of tacit knowledge.

The *autopoietic model* is a more recent development but one that has excited a lot of interest. The word *autopoiesis* (self-creation) was coined by two biologists, Humberto Maturano and Francisco Varela, to explain a theory about the development of organisms. They developed these findings in their book *The Tree of Knowledge* (1987), which proposed a theory of knowledge creation based on the interaction of individual organisms with their environment. In this model, knowledge does not exist independently of the organism (as it does in the cognitive model), and it is created by the individual organism and not by the interaction with other organisms (as in the social model). There are considerable implications in this model for any systematic view of knowledge management. The model has, however, been criticized for a number of reasons, perhaps the most significant in this context being the assumption that what may hold for simple organisms may not hold for complex, self-aware higher organisms.

Knowledge management needs to be undertaken for some practical reason. The two main reasons are the following:

1. To provide some degree of protection for current intellectual property or assets. These approaches tend to concentrate more on turning tacit knowledge into explicit knowledge, or *knowledge harvesting*. They have been characterized as *survival strategy*.
2. To provide a source for future or continuing competitive advantage. This focuses on the creation of new knowledge or on new ways of exploiting existing knowledge. This approach is characterized by emphasis on collaboration. This is sometimes referred to as an *advancement strategy*.

Innovation is a critical issue for commercial organizations. In some industries, such as pharmaceuticals, this is a major reason for investing in knowledge management initiatives. The knowledge proposition is that significant additional stakeholder value and competitive advantage will be derived if the expertise, information, and ideas of employees, partners, and customers are continually developed and used in all business and decision-making processes.

NOTE

This chapter is based on "Knowledge Management and Service Improvement: Cookbook A." Retrieved July 6, 2005, from http://www.localegov. gov.uk.

References

Duffy, Francis, *The New Office,* London: Conran Octopus, 1997.
Maturana, H. and Varela, F., *The Tree of Knowledge,* Boston: Shambhala Press, 1992.
Nonaka, I. and Takeuchi, H., The Knowledge-Creating Company, New York: Oxford University Press, 1995.
Van Krogh, G., Ichijo, K., and Nonaka, I., *Enabling Knowledge Creation: How to Unlock the Mystery of Tacit Knowledge and Release the Power of Innovation,* Oxford: Oxford University Press, 2000.

Appendix J

SELECTING AND INTEGRATING A METADATA REPOSITORY

There are many roads to productivity. The one least traveled, but perhaps most profitable, is the one in which software tools are integrated in a manner that produces accessible and timely information.

The three keywords here are *information, tools,* and *integration.* Information is really the most important asset a company owns. With its proper utilization, information becomes a potent competitive force. And in today's very global (and very competitive) economy, information may, in fact, be the deciding factor in determining the color of the organization's bottom line.

Understanding that information is a resource to be valued, organizations made a heavy investment in information technology. This investment, to the tune of billions of dollars, included development of new systems as well as purchase of a variety of software tools.

Software tools are decidedly of two flavors. On the one hand, there are the end-user-oriented tools that include report writers and 4GLs, and, on the other hand, there are tools that specifically target the development function. These tools run the gamut from compilers to data administration tools to visual development tools. What was common among all of these tools was the decided lack of interconnectiveness — or integration.

Lack of integration is a subtle defect with a powerful negative impact on the productivity — and competitiveness — of an organization. It translates to the inability of information to be managed in a consistent and nonredundant fashion. Because software tools have seams, information cannot flow easily from one tool to another, forcing organizations to either manually move the information between tools — or worse, to create redundant and conflicting information stores.

The industry, recognizing the ramifications of these problems, began to move in the direction of development frameworks. The goal of these frameworks is to provide a boundaryless environment to spur the free flow of information, through the use of standards and guidelines, for the development of software tools.

Metadata repositories, the focus of this chapter, have historically focused on application development and data warehousing. Recently, this mission has been extended to support component middleware frameworks and business objects. In the near future, knowledge management and enterprise information portal environments will be supported as well.

Metadata repositories, which I will henceforth call *repository work-benches*, have three functions. They are a repository. They provide tools. And they form the "connecting glue" of the development framework — in other words, integration.

A short and standard definition of a *repository* is "an organized reference to the data content of something. That something could be a system, a database, or a collection of all the files, program's databases, and manual records maintained by a large organization." Although the definition of tools should be self-evident, in this context it is not. Tools in a repository workbench environment encompass a broad spectrum of functionality that goes beyond what is commonly available. The last component of the repository workbench equation is integration. It is this component that meshes the repository and the repository-based tools into an organization's environment. The net sum of the repository equation is the ability to better leverage the skillset of a wide range of the organization's staff — from data administrators to programmers to analysts and to the end users themselves. And, it is this leveraging of skillsets that leads to a dramatic increase in productivity.

The remainder of this chapter assists the reader in three areas: evaluating the benefits of a repository workbench solution, planning for its implementation, and measuring it.

J.1 HOW TO USE THIS APPENDIX

In Subsection J.1.1, a quantitative approach is taken to assist the reader in understanding the features of a repository workbench and compare these features across competitive products. Twenty-three distinct criteria are divided into three categories — repository, integration, and tools. Each criteria is presented in the form of a set of features. To quantify the assessment, each criteria should be rated in terms of its importance to the organization. A rating or weight of 1 to 3 should be used (1 = not important to the organization, 2 = required by the organization, and 3 = of high importance to the organization).

Each of the features describing the criteria should next be rated according to how well the vendor fulfills the requirement. A scale of 1 through 5 should be used (1 = fails, 2 = weak, 3 = adequate, 4 = good, and 5 = excellent).

After you finish rating all 23 criteria, your scores can be transferred to the charts at the end of this chapter. These charts allow you to add up repository scores and to make overall evaluations and comparisons.

In Subsection J.1.2, a series of checklists is provided to assist the reader in deciding whether or not a repository workbench solution is desirable and in developing a plan for repository workbench implementation.

In Subsection J.1.3, a series of measurements are provided to assist the reader in determining how well the repository is being utilized.

J.1.1 Evaluating the Repository Workbench

Selecting a repository workbench is not a simple process. Repository workbench software is quite complex, and the selection process mirrors this complexity. Because a repository workbench offers a composite of functionality, the evaluation team needs to review three discrete levels of functionality: the repository component, the workbench component, and the integrative component. What follows is a set of categories that will assist in this process. Each category represents a different level of functionality that a product of this type should have.

J.1.1.1 Repository

The repository is the heart of the repository workbench. It is much more than a data dictionary or a data warehouse. It stores information about objects — whether those objects be file definitions or process rules. The sections below itemize the major attributes of a repository. An effective and robust repository should meet the objectives presented in the following section.

J.1.1.1.1 Initial Data Capture (Criterion 1)

For the most part, objects that will be required to be entered into the repository are objects that already reside in catalogs, files, databases, computer-aided software engineering (CASE) encyclopedias, or as part of a program (i.e., working storage as well as the procedure divisions). Scanning enables an organization to quickly populate the repository through the importation of objects from a preexisting source. Among the facilities that a robust repository product provides are the following:

Weightage	Rating
Scan program source — file sections	1 2 3 4 5
Scan program source — working storage sections	1 2 3 4 5
Scan program source — procedure divisions	1 2 3 4 5
Scan copybooks	1 2 3 4 5
Scan multiple copybooks	1 2 3 4 5
Scan database catalogs	1 2 3 4 5
Scan CASE encyclopedias	1 2 3 4 5
Scan databases	1 2 3 4 5
Provide the ability to repopulate the repository as many times as necessary through versioning	1 2 3 4 5
Provide collision resolution	1 2 3 4 5
Multilevel impact analysis	1 2 3 4 5
Scan data dictionaries	1 2 3 4 5
Scan class dictionaries	1 2 3 4 5

J.1.1.1.2   Tracking (Criterion 2)

A repository should have the ability to keep detailed information about objects. The repository defines an object as more than the traditional data definition. An *object* may be a field, a file, a procedure, or a system. Because the repository maintains detailed information about objects, the organization has an excellent opportunity to track the status of many of the formal processes that form the underpinnings of IT. A robust repository should be able to do the following:

Weightage	*Rating*
Keep track of jobs	1 2 3 4 5
Keep track of programs or objects	1 2 3 4 5
Document data content of files and databases	1 2 3 4 5
Document data processed by programs, jobs, systems	1 2 3 4 5
Document reports and screens	1 2 3 4 5
Document schedules	1 2 3 4 5
Document backup and retention	1 2 3 4 5
Document maintenance responsibilities	1 2 3 4 5

J.1.1.1.3   Source and Use (Criterion 3)

All organizations have different policies, methods, and procedures for their IT processes. The repository workbench must integrate itself as well as act as an integrator of these policies, methods, and procedures. The repository workbench must be flexible enough to assist in the following:

Weightage	Rating
Support data model	1 2 3 4 5
Support object model	1 2 3 4 5
Support information center usage	1 2 3 4 5
Support application generator	1 2 3 4 5
Support life-cycle methodology	1 2 3 4 5
Support distributed processing	1 2 3 4 5
Document communications network	1 2 3 4 5
Maintain hardware inventory	1 2 3 4 5
Support data security planning	1 2 3 4 5
Support forms control	1 2 3 4 5
Support change and problem control	1 2 3 4 5
Support procedures and standards for repository update and maintenance	1 2 3 4 5

J.1.1.1.4 User Access (Criterion 4)

Studies on productivity have shown that it is the user interface that has the greatest impact on the usability of the system. For the function of data administration, a flexible user interface is mandatory if the organization is to leverage the resources of skilled professionals. The repository workbench product should offer the following features:

Weightage	Rating
Mainframe based:	
Easy to use	1 2 3 4 5
Contextual help facility	1 2 3 4 5
SAA/CUA compliant	1 2 3 4 5
Customizable	1 2 3 4 5
Pull-down menus	1 2 3 4 5
Popup windows	1 2 3 4 5
Fast path commands	1 2 3 4 5
Client/server based:	
GUI	1 2 3 4 5
Graphical representation of E-R model	1 2 3 4 5
Point and click	1 2 3 4 5
Multiple platforms	1 2 3 4 5
CPI-C	1 2 3 4 5
XML	1 2 3 4 5
Online	1 2 3 4 5
Batch	1 2 3 4 5
Internet or intranet	1 2 3 4 5

J.1.1.1.5   Dialog (Criterion 5)

A robust repository dialog should provide a simple, intuitive means for maintaining and querying information assets as well as accessing tools. Features should include the following:

Weightage	*Rating*
Contextual menus	1 2 3 4 5
Menus rebuilt automatically as tools added	1 2 3 4 5
Self-maintaining	1 2 3 4 5
E-R-rule-based data entry screens	1 2 3 4 5
Project-based menus	1 2 3 4 5
Context-sensitive feedback	1 2 3 4 5
Reusable panels	1 2 3 4 5
Scrollable panels	1 2 3 4 5
Spreadsheet-like displays	1 2 3 4 5
Customize forms	1 2 3 4 5
End-user SQL queries	1 2 3 4 5
Project-defined SQL queries	1 2 3 4 5
Multilevel impact analysis	1 2 3 4 5
Attribute anchoring	1 2 3 4 5
Meaningful labels for DB names	1 2 3 4 5
Multiple text types	1 2 3 4 5

J.1.1.1.6   Extensibility (Criterion 6)

A robust repository workbench is not rigid. It should support growth. This growth should not be limited to merely data definitions. In an object-based environment, a repository workbench should have the flexibility to add new sources of information as well as new tools, reports, and procedures. Each of these is defined as an object. Extensibility features should include the following:

Weightage	Rating
Dialog assistance	1 2 3 4 5
Automatic rebinding	1 2 3 4 5
Automatic creation of repository table spaces	1 2 3 4 5
Recreation of repository indices	1 2 3 4 5
Reorg	1 2 3 4 5
Error handling and correction	1 2 3 4 5
Regranting of table privileges	1 2 3 4 5
Integration with repository tools	1 2 3 4 5
Ability to "add on" in-house tools	1 2 3 4 5
Ability to "add on" third-party tools	1 2 3 4 5
Ease in defining migration rules	1 2 3 4 5
Ease in defining security	1 2 3 4 5
Ease in defining validation rules	1 2 3 4 5
Ease in defining integrity rules	1 2 3 4 5
Ease in defining derivation rules	1 2 3 4 5
Ease in defining domain constraints	1 2 3 4 5

J.1.1.1.7   Project Control (Criterion 7)

A repository workbench must provide facilities to automate the enforcement of corporate and project standards and procedures, and control distribution of repository resources. Capabilities should include the following:

Weightage	Rating
Project-oriented security requirements	1 2 3 4 5
Clone function for rapid project definition	1 2 3 4 5
Access or update or migrate privileges	1 2 3 4 5
Ability to subset E-R types	1 2 3 4 5
Life-cycle phase authorization	1 2 3 4 5
Project parameterization	1 2 3 4 5

J.1.1.1.8   Versioning (Criterion 8)

The repository workbench must provide a comprehensive set of facilities for supporting, monitoring, and auditing the evolution of repository definitions. This feature makes it possible to plan and implement the maintenance procedures that become necessary as systems mature and require modifications. A robust repository workbench provides the following capabilities:

Weightage	Rating
Use of variation name attribute	1 2 3 4 5
Unlimited number of variations	1 2 3 4 5
Support of revision number attribute	1 2 3 4 5
Ability to perform set-level operations	
Set rename	1 2 3 4 5
Set delete	1 2 3 4 5
Set copy	1 2 3 4 5
ANSI IRDS support	1 2 3 4 5
Alias support	1 2 3 4 5

J.1.1.1.9   Life-Cycle Phase Management (Criterion 9)

Supporting an organization's methodologies is an essential role of a repository. A robust repository workbench provides an organization extensible means of defining the various stages of object evolution. These stages are referred to as *life-cycle phases*. Transition rules define the movement of an object from one phase to another. Relationships between entities based on their respective life-cycle phases should be verified to ensure proper migration results. Managing life-cycle phases and object migration is a vital function within a repository if it is to control and participate in an organization's development and maintenance methodology. Features should include the following:

Weightage	Rating
Customizable controls	1 2 3 4 5
Ability to add or remove life-cycle definitions	1 2 3 4 5
Transition rules	1 2 3 4 5
Migration paths	1 2 3 4 5
Relationship-state rules	1 2 3 4 5
Project controlled life-cycle phases	1 2 3 4 5
Versioning within life-cycle phase	1 2 3 4 5

J.1.1.2   Integration

Developmental frameworks such as AD/Cycle are philosophies. For the most part, software engineering tools such as CASE maintain key positions within this framework but do little to integrate themselves effectively to other tools in other quadrants of the framework — or even to other tools within the same quadrant. The objectives in this section, if met by the tool being evaluated, will assure the organization that the repository will be seamlessly integrated with repository tools as well as in-house developed and third-party tools.

J.1.1.2.1   Architecture

A repository workbench is a unique hybrid of repository, tools, and an integrative vehicle. To support this threefold functionality, the underlying architecture of a repository workbench product must provide both openness and an extensible framework. The organization must be able to easily integrate into and expand upon the framework. The architectural features of a robust architectural framework include the following:

Weightage	Rating
Object-based approach	1 2 3 4 5
Extensible	1 2 3 4 5
Easily configurable	1 2 3 4 5
Easily modifiable	1 2 3 4 5
Easy integration	1 2 3 4 5
Underlying metametamodel	1 2 3 4 5
Vendor supplied metamodel	1 2 3 4 5
Security, backup, and recovery	1 2 3 4 5
Referential integrity	1 2 3 4 5

J.1.1.2.2 Standards (Criterion 11)

The basis of any open framework is the standards it rests on. For this framework to be fully integrative with an organization's environment, the framework must conform to and support the standards and guidelines that the industry has embraced. Additionally, the repository workbench must provide the organization with the ability to support the standards that it has developed as a part of its policy and procedures. This includes, where applicable, the following:

Weightage	Rating
XML	1 2 3 4 5
Web services	1 2 3 4 5
ANSI SQL	1 2 3 4 5
UML	1 2 3 4 5
Java community process	1 2 3 4 5
Internet Engineering Task Force	1 2 3 4 5
OAG (Open Applications Group)	1 2 3 4 5
OMG (Object Management Group)	1 2 3 4 5
Business objects	1 2 3 4 5
Organizational naming conventions	1 2 3 4 5
Organizational keywords and abbreviations	1 2 3 4 5
Organizational custom rules	1 2 3 4 5
Other	1 2 3 4 5

J.1.1.2.3   Gateways (Criterion 12)

The basis of a repository product is information. Information, however, is not confined to a single source. A repository product must provide the organization with a series of gateways that allow the organization to export and import information between these information sources (e.g., application development tools, various databases, and files). Because it is expected that the organization will have multiple requirements for gateways, the most robust of repository workbenches will generically define a gateway bridge that provides a commonality of approach across diverse products. Features should include the following:

Weightage	Rating
Generic bridge architecture	1 2 3 4 5
Bidirectional bridge	1 2 3 4 5
Upload or download facilities	1 2 3 4 5
Check-in/checkout	1 2 3 4 5
Collision resolution	1 2 3 4 5
Impact analysis	1 2 3 4 5
Import or export capabilities	1 2 3 4 5
Bulk population ability	1 2 3 4 5
Repopulate through versioning	1 2 3 4 5
Default rules	1 2 3 4 5
Variable name mapping	1 2 3 4 5
Catalog import	1 2 3 4 5
Source import from multiple catalogs	1 2 3 4 5
Flat file import	1 2 3 4 5
Obsolete file import	1 2 3 4 5
IMS bridge	
Store and manage IMS objects	1 2 3 4 5
Generate copybooks, PSBs, DBDs	1 2 3 4 5
Impact analysis across objects	1 2 3 4 5
IMS SQL report writing	1 2 3 4 5

J.1.1.2.4 CASE Bridge (Criterion 13)

A very specific gateway is the one required by CASE (application development) tools.

The gateway allows CASE objects to be integrated into the repository with the goal of permitting CASE users to have a more efficient way of controlling, securing, reporting, and distributing specifications captured in their workstations. A robust repository can be thought of as a clearinghouse between workstations and CASE products. The repository workbench should provide management tools that enable the organization to share data resources. This includes the following:

Weightage	Rating
Shared model between different tools	1 2 3 4 5
Support change control	1 2 3 4 5
Report on design and analysis	1 2 3 4 5
Upload CASE product encyclopedia	
Reporting	1 2 3 4 5
Rehearsal	1 2 3 4 5
Extend the definition of CASE objects	1 2 3 4 5
Reusability	1 2 3 4 5

J.1.1.2.5 Services (Criterion 14)

A product is only as good as the service provided by the product vendor. Towards this end, the following features should be evaluated:

Weightage	Rating
Continuous support	1 2 3 4 5
Toll-free hotline	1 2 3 4 5
Timely assistance	1 2 3 4 5
Trial period provided	1 2 3 4 5
Customer references provided	1 2 3 4 5
Support during trial	1 2 3 4 5
Quality of staff	1 2 3 4 5
Maintenance program	1 2 3 4 5
Product improvement schedule	1 2 3 4 5
Responsiveness	1 2 3 4 5
Track record	1 2 3 4 5
Tailored training program	1 2 3 4 5
Online documentation	1 2 3 4 5
Manuals	1 2 3 4 5
Newsletter	1 2 3 4 5
User groups	1 2 3 4 5

J.1.1.2.6 Workbench Integration (Criterion 15)

The repository workbench creates a productive environment in which repository information is integrated with an extensible toolset. This approach offers you the flexibility to incorporate both your existing tools and those that you may consider in the future. Tool integration capabilities include the following:

Weightage	Rating
Ability to integrate user-defined tools	1 2 3 4 5
Ability to integrate third-party packages	1 2 3 4 5
All tools accessible through online dialog	1 2 3 4 5
Extensible end-user interface	1 2 3 4 5
Well-documented API	1 2 3 4 5
Easy incorporation into menu system	1 2 3 4 5
User security	1 2 3 4 5
Customizable help dialogs and messages	1 2 3 4 5

J.1.1.3   Tools

A robust repository workbench needs to supply a series of tools that takes advantage both of the repository and its integrative prowess. The features described in this section are those of a robust environment.

J.1.1.3.1   Tool Integration (Criterion 16)

Being able to integrate tools to the workbench is only one side of the coin. The other side is in being provided with the facilities to develop in-house tools. A tool development environment should possess the following capabilities:

Weightage	Rating
Vendor-supplied shell programs	1 2 3 4 5
Vendor-supplied subroutine libraries	1 2 3 4 5
Comprehensive assistance	1 2 3 4 5
Encapsulation	1 2 3 4 5
In-house tools developed invoked through dialog	1 2 3 4 5
Vendor-supplied tools reusable	1 2 3 4 5

J.1.1.3.2 Groupware (Criterion 17)

Productivity is greatly enhanced when a facility is provided for project teams and users to communicate with each other. This is often referred to as *groupware*. Within a repository environment, this can be accomplished through the use of e-mail. Features available should include the following:

Weightage	Rating
E-mail available	1 2 3 4 5
Messaging to project members	1 2 3 4 5
Messaging to users	1 2 3 4 5
Batch output messaging	1 2 3 4 5
Edit output and resend	1 2 3 4 5
Reusable method	1 2 3 4 5

J.1.1.3.3   Reporting (Criterion 18)

Various levels of the organization require access to the repository for reporting. On one level, the end users require access to the repository to find information about the types of information available within the organization. On the other hand, data administration staff has a real need to control the transition of information within the repository. Both levels of user access need to be supported. Reporting features include the following:

Weightage	Rating
QMF reporting interface	1 2 3 4 5
FOCUS reporting interface	1 2 3 4 5
Canned reports should include:	
Repository detail	1 2 3 4 5
Catalog detail	1 2 3 4 5
Repository/catalog comparison	1 2 3 4 5
Table column cross reference	1 2 3 4 5
Table structure/element cross reference	1 2 3 4 5
Logical/physical element reference	1 2 3 4 5
Logical entity cross reference	1 2 3 4 5
Structure circular references	1 2 3 4 5
Catalog statistical and action summary	1 2 3 4 5
Repository/catalog comparison	1 2 3 4 5
Repository-content detail	1 2 3 4 5
Catalog-content detail	1 2 3 4 5

J.1.1.3.4   Impact Analysis (Criterion 19)

In nonrepository systems, a large percentage of nonproductive time is spent in determining the impact of change. Analysts and programmers must manually review documentation and program source listings to evaluate the extent of change necessary as well as the length of time it will require to make those changes. This can be a lengthy process. A repository-based system automates this process through the function of impact analysis. Automatic impact analysis deconstructs the repository to determine the level of change required.

The impact analysis function should include the following capabilities:

Weightage	Rating
Multiple level	1 2 3 4 5
Nested impact analysis	1 2 3 4 5
Interactive as well as batch	1 2 3 4 5
Immediate maintenance capabilities	1 2 3 4 5
"Uses" and "where-used" displayed concurrently	1 2 3 4 5

J.1.1.3.5   Scripting (Criterion 20)

Database administrative procedures are extraordinarily complex. The complexity of many of these tasks implies that the staff member involved must have the highest degree of skill and exercise the utmost level of care. In organizations that wish to leverage the skill set of the average user, increase the speed at which a task may be completed, or deploy vast functionality across differing layers of the organization, what is required is the means to decrease the complexity level of the activity and, thereby, reduce the risk of error. A repository-based scripting facility provides this functionality. Capabilities should include:

Weightage	Rating
Recursive script development	1 2 3 4 5
Ability to invoke any vendor-supplied tool	1 2 3 4 5
Ability to invoke any vendor-supplied report	1 2 3 4 5
Ability to invoke any vendor-supplied script	1 2 3 4 5
Ability to invoke any in-house tool	1 2 3 4 5
Ability to invoke any in-house report	1 2 3 4 5
Ability to invoke any in-house script	1 2 3 4 5
Batch mode	1 2 3 4 5
Commit points and breakpoints	1 2 3 4 5
Script status feedback	1 2 3 4 5
Parameterized	1 2 3 4 5
Vendor-supplied base start-up scripts	1 2 3 4 5
Cut and paste facility	1 2 3 4 5
Invoked by e-mail	1 2 3 4 5

J.1.1.3.6 Forms (Criterion 21)

Forms provide the ability to establish external layout definitions that serve to present a modified view of the objects within the repository without altering the object itself. Although the definitions of objects in the repository are not altered, the user view can be modified to afford the greatest expediency in utilization of the repository without having to write code. Features should include the following:

Weightage	Rating
Project-level modification	1 2 3 4 5
Order of presentation	1 2 3 4 5
Alteration of the prompt label	1 2 3 4 5
Alteration of the annotation	1 2 3 4 5
Modification display rules	1 2 3 4 5
Modification of item length	1 2 3 4 5
Customization of the default values	1 2 3 4 5
Object-orientation of form	1 2 3 4 5
Maintainable via a method	1 2 3 4 5
Accessible through dialog menus	1 2 3 4 5
Accessible via scripting	1 2 3 4 5

J.1.1.3.7   Generation (Criterion 22)

Although the repository acts as the central clearinghouse for corporate information resource management, the repository must have the ability to act in concert with definitions used by application development and end-user tools. To enhance productivity, consistency, and security, the repository workbench must have the ability to generate syntax. This includes the ability to do the following:

Weightage	Rating
DDL, DML syntax including:	
Create	1 2 3 4 5
Drop	1 2 3 4 5
Grant	1 2 3 4 5
Revoke	1 2 3 4 5
Bind	1 2 3 4 5
Rebind	1 2 3 4 5
Free	1 2 3 4 5
Generate and execute mode	1 2 3 4 5
Generate and save mode	1 2 3 4 5
Copybook generation	1 2 3 4 5
DBD, PSB for IMS	1 2 3 4 5
DCLGENs	1 2 3 4 5

J.1.1.3.8 Managing Relational Tables (Criterion 23)

A repository workbench needs to be more than just a repository. Facilities to manage the underlying database should be fully integrated into the toolset. These tools should provide the ability to do the following:

Weightage	Rating
Unload/reload databases	1 2 3 4 5
Create and drop objects	1 2 3 4 5
Referential integrity support	1 2 3 4 5
Grant and revoke commands	1 2 3 4 5
Bind, rebind, and free commands	1 2 3 4 5
Reorg, runstats, and copy commands	1 2 3 4 5

J.1.2 Preparing for the Repository Workbench

Preparing for any software implementation requires careful planning and control. In the case of a repository workbench, where information, systems, and integration factors must be considered, even more care is urged for a successful implementation. A series of checklists is provided for this purpose.

Preplanning includes action items:

1. Standardize the names, definitions, and physical descriptions of data elements used in all programs.
2. Document which data is kept in which files, databases, or schemas.
3. Document which reports and screens are produced by which programs, jobs, and systems.
4. Document which programs, jobs, and systems access and update which data elements in which files, databases, or schemas.
5. Document which modules and subprograms are included in which programs.
6. Document processing schedules, file backup, and retention and responsibilities for program and jobstream maintenance.

Questions to ask for sizing of data collection efforts:

1. How many systems are there?
2. What is the quality of system documentation?

3. If documentation is inadequate, can the required data be obtained from the original developers or from users?
4. How many programs are in each system?
5. How good are the run books and program documentation?
6. Have these been kept up to date as changes have been made?
7. Are job control statements kept in a single file or library?
8. Are program source statements kept in a single file or library?
9. Is some sort of source library maintenance system in use?
10. Is library content really kept up to date?
11. How many files, databases, and schemas are there in each system?
12. How many different record types are there?
13. How many different relational tables are there?
14. Are standard record descriptions used?
15. Are they kept in a central library?
16. Are data element names standardized?
17. Are the names meaningful?
18. Are good definitions available?
19. Is there documentation of coding structures?
20. How well are reports, display screens, and input transactions documented?
21. Can the data content be obtained from user manuals?
22. If the above information is not readily available, how will it be obtained? Who will compile it?
23. Who will do the actual work of preparing repository inputs?
24. How will it be done?
25. Can part of the data be obtained by scanning source programs or copy libraries?
26. Who will review edit lists and resolve naming discrepancies and other problems?

Questions to ask concerning technical and operational issues:

1. Will the repository always be running? System initialization must be amended to include this.
2. Will reports be produced automatically on some predetermined schedule? Will they be triggered by specific events, such as the implementation of a new system? Will they be on a run-on request basis? Who will initiate the jobs to produce the reports? How will they be distributed? How will special requests be handled?
3. How will repository problems be reported and resolved?

4. Will computer operations think of the repository as a production system?
5. Will procedures for the turnover of new systems or system changes incorporate steps that will ensure that the repository has been correctly updated?

Questions to ask about security:

1. Who should be allowed to access what? Can project teams alter data that they think of as their own?
2. Will passwords be controlled and changed from time to time? Will they be changed when employees leave or are discharged?
3. Does repository software provide a mechanism to prevent access to repository via means other than the repository software?

Questions to ask concerning redundant and inconsistent data:

1. Can you identify all occurrences of the same information?
2. Can you determine which elements are calculated or derived? How?
3. Will you know the original sources of all elements?
4. Will you know the uses of the elements?
5. Can the repository implementation help to determine whether there are procedures or programs to ensure consistency?
6. Will the repository implementation provide for validation rules and criteria?
7. Does it provide for data consistency and integrity rules?
8. What about procedures to ensure that such rules are actually entered in the repository?

Questions to ask about complexity and interdependence:

1. Does the repository help us determine who actually uses the reports or screens?
2. Does it help identify screens and reports that really contain the same information?
3. Does it help use of the tasks and procedures that require the information contained in the reports and screens?
4. Will it help improve documentation?
5. Will it decrease complexity by providing reusability?

J.1.3 Repository Metrics

These criteria measure how well a repository collects, maintains, and retrieves information about data. The objectives of these measures are to offer users cost-effective means of retrieving relevant information and reducing information overload. Five criteria are proposed to evaluate data dictionaries or repositories: relevance, consistency, common use among information systems, degree of automation, and degree of security.

J.1.3.1 DBA Objective Metrics

The following criteria measure how well each commercial repository or repository product fulfills the DBA's objectives.

J.1.3.1.1 Relevance

This criterion measures the effectiveness of retrieving correct information in response to a request. It is measured by two factors: recall and precision.

$$\text{Recall} = \frac{\text{Number of matching data elements retrieved by a product}}{\text{Maximum number of matches possible}}$$

$$\text{Precision} = \frac{\text{Number of matching data elements retrieved by a product}}{\text{Number of data elements retrieved by a product}}$$

J.1.3.1.2 Consistency

This criterion measures the performance of the product in removing redundancies and storing the minimum number of elements from which all other elements can be derived. The result will be what James Martin (1989) refers to as a canonical data repository — a minimal and nonredundant representation of data elements in an enterprise.

$$\text{Consistency} = \frac{\text{Number of elements in the final repository}}{\text{Number of elements in the original data dictionaries}}$$

J.1.3.1.3 Common Use among Different Information System Organizations

This criterion measures whether the product can be consistently applied to standardize ISs in different departments and operations within an IS organization. Current trends toward integrating networks and information systems to build integrated repository-network management environments make it important that repositories handle multiple environments. Deciding which repository to use as the central repository may depend on a repository's flexibility in handling a variety of software and hardware. The common use criterion measures this flexibility:

$$\text{Common use} = \frac{\text{Number of elements standardized using particular product}}{\text{Number of elements standardized in the organization}}$$

J.1.3.1.4   Degree of Automation

An active repository uses substantially less manpower than a passive repository. In response to an enquiry, an active repository can locate the elements and find out who has access to them. The repository then directs the database management system to obtain those data elements. On the other hand, passive data dictionaries have no tie-ins to the operating system and require the user to write programs to gain access to the elements. This criterion measures the extent to which a product makes it easy for a DBA to standardize and store elements.

$$\text{Degree of automation} = \frac{\text{Time spent in training and using product}}{\text{Total time available}}$$

J.1.3.1.5   Degree of Security

Overall security depends on managing the access controls to the various data elements. Access control limits have to be defined for each user and violations acted upon.

$$\text{Degree of security} = \frac{\text{Number of security failures}}{\text{Number of attempts to breach security}}$$

J.1.3.2   Repository Workbench Metrics

The following metrics measure additional attributes of the repository workbench.

J.1.3.2.1 Redundancy

One of the objects of a repository solution is to act as the single source for all information flows. To measure how successful the repository implementation is, one requires knowledge concerning the number of objects stored in the repository versus the total number of objects stored, simultaneously, in different sources.

$$\text{Redundancy} = \frac{\text{Number of redundant objects}}{\text{Total number of objects}}$$

J.1.3.2.2 Intuitive Access

One of the most important, but underrated, features of a repository workbench is its user interface. The more intuitive the dialog, the more the repository workbench will be used. Frequency of use translates into higher productivity. A low rating implies need for tuning or training.

$$\text{Intuitiveness} = \frac{\text{Number of users requiring manual}}{\text{Total number of users}}$$

J.1.3.2.3 Level-of-Impact Analysis

This metric measures how well the impact analysis function is being utilized.

$$\text{Level of impact analysis} = \frac{\text{Number of levels being accessed}}{\text{Total number of levels in E-R model}}$$

J.1.3.2.4 Integration

This metric determines the progress of the tool-integration effort. Although a repository workbench enables complete tool integration, the level of integration implies progress, or lack of it.

$$\text{Integration} = \frac{\text{Number of tools integrated}}{\text{Total number of tools to use}}$$

J.1.4 Scoring the Repository Workbench

The following list provides a means to conduct a quantitative evaluation of several repository products. To use this chart, simply transfer the scores from each of the rating scales under the 23 criteria. To transfer the score, multiply the rating (1 through 5) by the weighting (1 through 3).

	Product A	*Product B*
1. Initial data capture		
2. Tracking		
3. Source and use		
4. User access		
5. Dialog		
6. Extensibility		
7. Project control		
8. Versioning		
9. Life cycle		
10. Architecture		
11. Standards		
12. Gateways		
13. CASE bridges		
14. Services		
15. Workbench integration		
16. Tool development		
17. Groupware		
18. Reporting		
19. Impact analysis		
20. Scripting		
21. Forms		
22. Generation		
23. Table management		

References

Martin, J., *Information Engineering, Book I: Introduction*, Englewood Cliffs, NJ: Prentice Hall, 1989.

Martin, J., *Information Engineering, Book II: Planning and Analysis*, Englewood Cliffs, NJ: Prentice Hall, 1990.

Appendix K

SAMPLE USE CASES

Use cases is a software engineering technique used during requirements elicitation. The goal of a use case is to provide the "who, what, where, when, and how" for one or more business processes. Essentially, a use case captures the expertise of the individual performing the business process. Therefore, use cases are particularly relevant and useful in knowledge engineering.

K.1 USE CASES

K.1.1 Client

The following use cases outline the client scenarios based on the client system.

K.1.1.1 Free Tour

Primary actor: Client
Stakeholders and interests:
- Client: Wants to see what the Web site has to offer.
- Administration: Wants to attract new clients.
Preconditions: The client has accessed the Web site.
Success guarantee (post conditions): The client has completed the tour and returned to the main page.
Main success scenario:
1. Client clicks on the "Free Tour" link located on the main page of the Web site.
2. System conducts virtual tour of the Web site.
3. Client returns to the main page.

K.1.1.2   Client Registration

Primary actor: Client

Stakeholders and interests:

- Client: Wants to register so that they can use the service provided.
- Administration: Wants client to register for service to increase profit.

Preconditions: The client has accessed the Web site and has the information needed to register.

Success guarantee (post conditions): The client has registered and is ready to use the system with the username and password provided. The client's billing information has been collected.

Main success scenario:

1. Client clicks on the "Register" link located on the main page of the Web site.
2. Client fills out the registration form (including what level of service is desired and their profile).
3. Client submits the registration.
4. System collects the client information and sets up an account for the client.

K.1.1.3   Searching the Database

Primary actor: Client

Stakeholders and interests:

- Client wants to search for potential breeding matches.
- Administration wants to provide a quality product.

Preconditions: User has logged into the system.

Success guarantee (post conditions): Search results have been displayed.

Main success scenario:

1. Person clicks on "Search" link on the main Web page.
2. Person enters search criteria.
3. System looks for potential matches.
4. System displays potential matches.

K.1.1.4   Using the Discussion Board

Primary actor: Client

Stakeholders and interests:

- Client wants to discuss information with other registered members.
- Administration wants to provide clients with communication tools.

Preconditions: Client has registered as preferred or premium and has logged into the system.

Success guarantee (post conditions): Client has ability to read and post messages.

Main success scenario:

1. Client clicks on "Discussion Board" link on the main Web page.
2. Client selects the appropriate discussion board to enter.
3. System displays all of the currently posted message titles.
4. Client selects the message to read, based on the title of the message.
5. System displays the message.
6. Client selects "Reply" to reply to the message.
7. Client fills in the reply criteria.
8. Client selects "Submit" to post the message.
9. System posts the message to the discussion board.

K.1.1.5 Accessing Billing History

Primary actor: Client

Stakeholders and Interests:

- Client wants to review past and current charges and accounts.
- Staff wants to assist customers in answering their own questions.
- Administration wants to provide a good-quality product.

Preconditions: Client has logged into the system.

Success guarantee (post conditions): Client has reviewed their account of interest.

Main success scenario:

1. Person selects "View Account."
2. System displays the account summary.

K.1.1.6 Submitting Feedback

Primary actor: Client

Stakeholders and interests:

- Client wants to provide feedback to the company, based on personal experience.
- Administration wants to provide a product that the customer enjoys using.

Preconditions: Client has logged into the system.

Success guarantee (post conditions): System has collected feedback.

Main success scenario:

1. Client clicks on the "Submit Feedback" link.
2. System displays the submit feedback form.

3. Client fills out the feedback form.
4. Client clicks "Submit" button.
5. System collects the information.

K.1.1.7 Accessing Help

Primary actor: Client
Stakeholders and interests:
- Client wants help with an issue they are having with the service.
- Administration wants to provide help to customers.

Preconditions: Client has logged into the system.
Success guarantee (post conditions): System has displayed the help resources.
Main success scenario:
1. Client clicks on the "Help" link.
2. System displays the "Help frequently asked questions" along with a link that the customer can click on to e-mail the company.

K.1.2 Staff

The following use cases outline the staff scenarios based on the staff system context.

K.1.2.1 Accessing Database Information

Primary actor: Staff
Stakeholders and interests:
- Staff wants to provide answers to clients based on this information.
- Administration wants to allow staff to assist customers in a timely fashion.

Preconditions: Staff has logged into the staff Web page.
Success guarantee (post conditions): System has displayed the client's information.
Main success scenario:
1. Staff clicks on the "Access Client Information" link on the staff Web page.
2. System requests client's full name.
3. Staff enters the name and selects "Access."
4. System displays the client's information.

K.1.2.2 Accessing Billing History

Primary actor: Staff

Stakeholders and interests:

- Staff wants to assist customers with questions regarding their account.
- Administration wants to allow staff to handle questions about billing.

Preconditions: Staff has logged into the staff Web page.

Success guarantee (post conditions): System has displayed the client's billing history.

Main success scenario:

Staff has accessed the database information for the client.

Staff selects "Billing History" link.

System displays a summary of the client's account, including past and current charges and payments.

K.1.3 Administration

The following use cases outline the administrative scenarios based on the administration system context as outlined in Section 1.3.3.

K.1.3.1 Grant Access Level

Primary actor: Administration

Stakeholders and interests:

- Administration wants to allow new staff to assist customers.
- Administration wants to remove privileges from an employee who no longer works for the company.

Preconditions: Administrator has logged into the administrative Web page.

Success guarantee (post conditions): System has granted access rights to the person.

Main success scenario:

1. Administrator selects "Change User Access Level" on the Web page.
2. System prompts for user information.
3. Administrator fills in the required fields.
4. System shows current access level.
5. Administrator selects the new level of access for the person.
6. System updates the person's access level privileges.

K.1.3.2 Generate Reports

Primary actor: Administration
Stakeholders and interests:
- Administration wants to generate numerous types of reports.

Preconditions: Administrator has logged into the administrative Web page.
Success guarantee (post conditions): System has generated reports.
Main success scenario:
1. Administrator selects the "Report Generation" link on the Web page.
2. System displays the available types of reports.
3. Administrator selects the type of report that he wants.
4. System prompts user if more information is needed (e.g., client's name).
5. Administrator fills in the required information, if needed.
6. System displays the requested report.

K.1.3.3 Update the Web Site

Primary actor: Administration
Stakeholders and interests:
- Administrator wants to keep the Web site current.
- Administrator wants to fix errors in the Web site.
- Client wants an updated Web site.

Preconditions: Administrator has logged into the administrative Web page.
Success guarantee (post conditions): System has updated the Web site.
Main success scenario:
1. Administrator selects "Update Web site" link on the Web page.
2. System displays current Web site code.
3. Administrator changes the code and selects "Preview."
4. System shows the administrator a preview of how the Web page was affected.
5. Administrator selects "Save" to save the code changes.
6. System updates the Web page.

K.1.3.4 Review Feedback

Primary actor: Administration
Stakeholders and interests:
- Administrator wants to keep the Web site current.
- Administrator wants prepare for future enhancements.
- Client wants to let the company know how they feel about the service.

Preconditions: Administrator has logged into the administrative Web page.

Success guarantee (post conditions): System has displayed the feedback report.

Main success scenario:

1. Administrator selects "Review Feedback" link on the Web page.
2. System displays a summary of the feedback reports.
3. Administrator selects the summary of the report they want to look at.
4. System displays the feedback.

Appendix L

COMMUNITY OF PRACTICE: A PRACTITIONER'S GUIDE

L.1 INTRODUCTION

The community of practice (CoP) practitioner's guide presents information in the same order that you should follow as you roll out CoPs.

L.2 GETTING STARTED: HOW TO CREATE A COMMUNITY

PURPOSE	OK, so how do you start? How do you translate the concept of a community into a functioning body that provides value to its members and the enterprise? How do you mold a group of individuals, possibly from different organizations, backgrounds, and locations, into a viable living source of relevant knowledge that members can tap into? To facilitate this transformation — from concept to a working reality — is the goal of this section.
EXPECTED OUTCOMES	A clear understanding of the roles and responsibilities involved in a community A community identity A foundation for community activities
PRODUCTS	An established collaborative work environment (instant messenger, chat, e-mail, corporate document management system [CDMS] work space, facilities, community experience locator, etc.) An orientation workshop for community members An assessment of community viability

KEY TASKS	1. Conduct core planning 2. Prepare for initial community workshop 3. Host initial community workshop 4. Check community progress 5. Build community experience locator
Key task 1: **Conduct core** **planning**	The core group (working group of key community members) needs to conduct a meeting to determine what building blocks must be in place to launch a community. This section identifies the following building blocks as agenda items for a core group planning meeting: ■ Community identity ■ Community type ■ Community roles and responsibilities ■ Community membership ■ Collaborative work environment Each of these areas is discussed in detail. Additionally, a sample core planning agenda is provided as a tool at the end of this section. It is essential that those individuals who participated in the community's originating sessions — sessions that identified the community's critical knowledge needs — attend this planning meeting as well. The community's functional sponsor, community leader, and facilitator should also be in attendance, if not included in the originating group. (See "Community and Corporate Roles and Responsibilities" at the end of this section for a detailed description of the functional sponsor and community leader).
	Agenda Item: Create Community Identity
Lay the *groundwork*	One building block for working together is a collective understanding, or identity, for the community. The identity should address the community's purpose, how the community supports the company's mission and goals, how the community determines whether it is adding value, what members need from the community, and what cultural norms or conventions will be followed.

	To save community member time, the core group may choose to develop a strawman model that addresses community identity and purpose. By investing some time up front, the core group develops the community identity, which will be used during the initial community workshop. Conversely, the community may best be served by fleshing out these ideas itself; the exercise of "thinking collaboratively" may begin to form a shared sense of community among members.
	In either approach, the collective identity will be a useful tool when trying to induce interest and membership in the community.
	Tip: If the core group chooses a strawman model approach, it must be open to a change in direction when presented to the community; try to avoid "pride of ownership."
	Agenda Item: Types of Communities
Understanding the intent of the community	A collective understanding of the intent of the community is useful in further clarifying the identity and purpose of the community. There are four types of communities:
	1. Helping communities provide a forum for community members to help each other solve everyday work problems.
	2. Best practice communities develop and disseminate best practices, guidelines, and procedures for members' use.
	3. Knowledge-stewarding communities organize, manage, and steward a body of knowledge from which community members can draw.
	4. Innovation communities create breakthrough ideas, knowledge, and practices.
	Determining a community's primary intent will help decide how it will be organized in terms of the key activities that it will undertake, its structure, and leadership roles. Although they may serve more than one of these purposes, most communities focus on one type and develop their structure with that specific intent in mind.

	Agenda Item: Clarify Roles and Responsibilities
What roles are played in a community?	Communities may be supported by "corporate" roles that provide resources and infrastructure support, or the community may itself provide these roles internally. Useful community roles include a functional sponsor, a core group, a community leader, a facilitator, and a logistics coordinator. These roles are useful when getting a community up and running, creating and maintaining tools to foster collaboration, planning community events, creating or capturing knowledge, sharing knowledge, and providing continued focus and support. Typical community and corporate roles and responsibilities are presented at the end of this section.
	Agenda Item: Identify Community Members
Who should be included in the community?	Anyone who wants to participate should be welcome at community events. However, it is recommended that prospective community members — individuals who could learn from each other and have a stake in the community's success — be identified and cultivated. Consider positions in the organization that could contribute and benefit from sharing knowledge about their roles.
Without members, there is no community	The essence of a community is its members. Membership is voluntary rather than prescribed. Members are self-organizing and participate because they get value from their participation.
Participation should not be mandated	The core group and the community leader should personally invite prospective members to the initial community workshop and subsequent forums until the community takes on momentum. When encouraging participation, emphasize that this is not another task force or project team. Communities do not have task plans or deliverables. Stress that membership is voluntary and individuals are encouraged to participate only if they see the community purpose to be meaningful and believe they could gain from or contribute to the community.

What makes a good member?	Good members embrace and appreciate diversity of thought and perspective and are key thought leaders. *Tip: A technique for identifying those individuals in your organization that "connect" the informal networks already operating in your organization is social networking and knowledge flow diagramming. Looking at a network of relationships can help you to identify the integrators, or the employees who are seen by many as experts or who are trusted as an information source. Recruiting such individuals for your community will make your communication effort easier, as these people have a wide reach in the informal communication network of the organization.* *Tip: An alternative technique would be to use the knowledge needs supply mapping technique to identify thought and opinion leaders in your organization. A discussion of this technique is provided as a tool at the end of this section.*
Publicize commencement of new communities; stress benefits for members	*Tip: The core group could write a short article for publication in internal magazines or bulletins, describing the outcomes of community interaction and what the community sees as the next milestone in its development. This public declaration can build up a creative tension that will help motivate the community to further advances.*
	Agenda Item: Define Collaborative Work Environment
	The community will need an operational environment for collaborative work. The core group will need to identify what mechanisms are available and can be put in place.
How will members work together?	Some companies use a corporate document management system (CDMS) as the standard for document management, workflow, and shared workspace. Another possibility is the use of chat room and instant messaging capabilities. The community leader will also need to arrange for meeting rooms. Depending on membership, video conferencing may also be required.

Key task 2: Prepare for initial community workshop	First and foremost, the goal of the initial community workshop should be to engage member interest and stimulate continued involvement — not to increase their workload. The first workshop should also serve to begin building relationships among members. Careful planning can help ensure the success of the initial community workshop.
	Develop Agenda for Orientation Workshop
	A sample agenda is provided as a tool at the end of this section. The agenda for the initial workshop should include at least the following: ■ Solidify community identity. ■ Clarify community intent. ■ Begin building relationships (exercise). ■ Clarify roles. ■ Provide overview of methods to create, capture, and share knowledge. ■ Provide overview of how selected tools, such as CDMS, may be used to further community goals. ■ Identify highest-priority knowledge needs. ■ Identify future steps to satisfy specific knowledge needs. The functional sponsor should join the workshop to welcome members, encourage participation, and spark dialogue.
Let core group establish themselves as members — not directors	*Tip: Consider facilitator services for at least the initial community workshop; the facilitator should be involved in planning this community orientation and should assist in developing the agenda.*
An e-mail invitation could easily be lost in the shuffle	*Tip: Just sending an e-mail invitation to prospective members is not enough. The core group and the community leader must reach out, in person or by telephone, to begin building personal relationships. Personal invitations provide an opportunity to distinguish the community from other requests for time — to stress what the individual can gain from the experience.*
Do not burden members with "administrivia"	*Tip: The community should be free to focus on its purpose — building its knowledge base. This cannot be overstated. What you do not want is for the community to get "turned off" by procedural or administrative duties before it even starts.*

Give them a reason to keep coming	*Tip: To jump-start the community, invite a guest speaker to share a best practice or innovation in an area of particular interest to the community.*
Optimum location is critical	The optimum location for a workshop is off site so that interruptions can be controlled. The most successful arrangements for the room include a U-shaped table for participants with a facilitator table in front for projection equipment and facilitator supplies. The room size should reflect the number of team members. If the room is too small, people will feel cramped and trapped. If the room is too large, intimacy will be difficult to establish. If using flip charts, solid, smooth walls are required for posting and maintaining group memory — discussions and decisions made by the group and documented on flip chart paper. Electronic means, for example, electronic whiteboards, to capture group memory would also be useful.
What supplies will you need?	■ Three or four easel boards with extra pads of paper, one for each possible subgroup ■ Markers ■ Masking tape ■ Name tents ■ Access to a copier or printer ■ Laptop
Key task 3: Host initial community workshop	The initial community workshop presents a one-time opportunity to engage member interest. As they say, "first impressions are the most lasting." This orientation should convince members that leadership is ready to invest in the community. A sample agenda is provided as a tool at the end of this section. The following tips for a successful workshop are cross-referenced to the appropriate agenda item.
	Agenda Item: Provide a Guest Speaker
An interview may generate more interest than a canned briefing	Consider conducting an interview with your guest speaker rather than having a formal briefing delivered. Not only will this approach to knowledge exchange more closely resemble the desired "give and take" of community interactions, it will also demonstrate a useful community technique for gathering knowledge.

	Members of the core group should serve as provocateurs. Interview questions designed to stimulate interesting dialogue should be prepared. *Tip: Have some questions on hand to spark dialogue during the question-and-answer session.* *Tip: A good learning technique is for the group to collectively list the key or salient points surfaced during the guest speaker's presentation or interview. This serves to reinforce concepts. Key points should be posted on a flip chart and recorded as a possible new knowledge nugget for posting in the shared workspace. A variation might be to hold this exercise until the end of the workshop and summarize key points learned throughout the workshop.*
	Agenda Item: Solidify Community Identity
	Community identity has several components, including common purpose, relationships, success criteria, and norms for interacting, and each needs to be clarified and agreed upon.
A community is a network of relationships	The first workshop is a good opportunity to begin the process of building person-to-person relationships among members. It is the human relationships that will sustain the community over time and provide a sense of reciprocity and obligation among each other. To foster this, it is suggested that a relationship-building exercise be included in the initial and subsequent workshops. A sample exercise is provided as a tool at the end of this section. Additional exercises can be found as tools in Section L.3, "Creating Knowledge."
A common purpose unifies and creates a sense of urgency	The best way to unify a community is for its members to share a common purpose. A community's purpose should be centered around knowledge areas that carry a sense of urgency and incite people's passion. The purpose should be directly connected to the challenges its members face in their work.
Success criteria guide community evolution	It is essential that the community realizes that it is responsible for determining its success — not that of enterprise leaders. Members must set their own success criteria for two reasons: it raises the sense of ownership in the CoP, and when individuals develop their own performance measures, more demanding targets are set.

	Some general success criteria include the following: ■ Sustained mutual relationships ■ Quick mobilization for discussion ■ Shared methodology ■ Rapid flow of information and fostering of innovation ■ Acknowledged participant base ■ Knowledge of what others know, what they do, and how they contribute ■ Mutually defined identities ■ Ability to assess appropriateness of actions and products ■ Tools, language, and definitions developed (or sustained) by the CoP ■ Open communication channels Here are some other possible success criteria: ■ Satisfaction of specific knowledge goals ■ Reduction in time needed to solve problems ■ Drop in rework ■ Number of innovative/breakthrough ideas ■ Results of surveys on member satisfaction ■ Transfer of best practices from one member to another ■ Adoption of best practices or innovations that were "not invented here" ■ Less redundancy of effort among members ■ Avoidance of costly mistakes ■ Quantitative measures ■ Success stories
A word on quantitative measures	Quantitative measures are most valuable when they are tracked over time and compared against a baseline recorded at the start of the initiative. For this reason, it is advisable to try to leverage existing measures if possible. Metrics are particularly important to knowledge management (KM) because a KM return on investment often takes significant time to appear. Putting a KM program in effect will impact other business processes as the organization learns to use and leverage the new KM capabilities. This "acculturation" to KM can take 18 to 36 months in some cases. In no case should a KM program be expected to show a return on investment in less than 12 months.

Leverage existing metrics; use available baseline data	For example, if one of the organizational goals is to improve customer satisfaction, there should already be an existing baseline metric for customer satisfaction. The KM initiative should leverage the process to track customer satisfaction already in place to monitor progress towards the goal.
Anecdotes or stories can be more powerful than numbers	A story about how knowledge was leveraged in the organization to achieve value does two things. First, it creates an interesting context around which to remember the measure being described. Second, it educates the reader or listener about the alternative methods that they themselves might employ to achieve similar results, thus helping to "spread the word" about the KM program and speed up the cultural change. Qualitative measures such as stories, anecdotes, and lessons learned often fulfill one of the primary benefits of KM measurement: allocation of resources and support to your KM pilot project.
Link to business objectives	It is critical that a community be able to link its purpose to specific business drivers or objectives of the organization. By establishing this link, the community can demonstrate direct value to the organization.
Norms help keep a community connected	When people work together or sit close enough to interact daily, they naturally establish a connection; they find commonality in the problems they face, see the value of each other's ideas, build trust, and create a common etiquette or set of norms on how to interact. It simply emerges from their regular contact. When building more "intentional" communities, it is tempting to jump right to "official community business" before the community has had time to form. During community events, allow some time for "technical schmoozing" allowing members to share immediate work problems and to begin helping each other.
	Although norms will evolve over time, some initial conventions can easily be discussed and possibly adopted by the community in the initial workshop. Here are some examples:
	■ Relevant information will be shared as soon as possible.
	■ One conversation at a time during discussions.

	■ Member preferences regarding time, place, etc., for regular meetings. ■ Frequency of events (schedule or standard, for example, second Wednesday of every month). ■ An "open meeting" policy; anyone can attend any meeting — with few exceptions. ■ All planned workshops should have an agenda; each agenda should provide for standard points of discussion; e.g., action item assignment and tracking. ■ How to identify areas of interest for evolving agenda items. ■ Use of facilitators. ■ When documentation is desired and how the community will ensure its preparation; perhaps, a role that rotates among members. *Tip: Once the community agrees to its "identity," this message should be posted in the workspace as a "welcome" to prospective members.* *Tip: Attendees at the workshop should be polled to identify individuals who could benefit from and contribute to the community's knowledge base.*
	Agenda Item: Prioritize Knowledge Needs
Member agreement on knowledge needs is key to continued involvement	The community must have a shared understanding about what knowledge it needs. Although the proceeding analyses identified knowledge, skills, and information (KSI) needed, it is wise to build consensus about which KSIs are most critical to community members. The community should prioritize its knowledge needs. *Tip: In a large group, an effective prioritization method is multivoting. Allow each member to cast five votes based on what they believe to be the five highest priorities (not allowed to cast more than one vote on any one item). This will quickly identify where there is the most energy and urgency.* *Tip: Another prioritization technique is to build consensus on decision criteria; e.g., mission, need, safety, cost, and risk. Once consensus is reached on the criteria, the prioritization of knowledge against criteria mutually agreed to will foster commitment and build ownership of the community process.*

	Agenda Item: Plan of Action
How will we transform a knowledge need into a knowledge nugget?	Once the top knowledge needs have been agreed to, the community should decide how it wishes to approach satisfying these needs. For example, "will the community conduct a search to acquire needed knowledge? Would a 'problem-solving session' produce the needed knowledge?" (See Section L.3, Creating Knowledge, for suggested techniques.) A plan of action should address the "who, what, when, and how" of the satisfaction of knowledge needs.
	Agenda Item: Collaborative Environment
Open members' minds to the possibilities of collaborative work tools	This agenda item is intended to provide members with an overview of available collaborative technology. The goal is not to provide hands-on training, but rather, to explore collaborative tools and how they can be used to promote member interactions with each other and the knowledge base.
	Agenda Item: Wrap Up
Schedule the next community forum before you wrap up for the day	To close the session, the community should agree on some future steps — at least a confirmed date for the next session as well as suggested agenda items. *Tip: If action items are identified, the core group should volunteer for as many as possible; the core group should be seen as a resource for the community, not the other way around.* *Tip: At this end, conduct a roundtable (in which all participants share their thoughts — whatever is on their minds) to solicit gut reaction, initial reservations, enthusiasm, etc. Be sure to listen rather than defend.*
Key task 4: Check community progress	The community leader and core group should do a quick progress check after the community's first event to ensure the community is on the road to success. The answer to each of the following questions should be "yes": 1. Does the community have a common purpose? Is the purpose compelling to leadership, prospective members, and their functional managers? 2. Is the common purpose aligned with the organizational strategy? 3. Is the right sponsorship in place — a respected leader who is willing to contribute to the community?

	4. Do the functional sponsors agree with the community's scope, purpose, and membership?
	5. Are core group members and the community leader strong content experts, enthusiastic, and able to develop the community?
	6. Do members' functional managers agree that "time away from the job" is valuable?
	7. Do we have the right content experts to provide perspective and meaning to our membership?
	8. Is there a shared space and context for dialogue, advice, and work?
	9. Do we have enough members to keep the community alive?
	10. Are collaborative tools in place? Are members "set" to use them?
	11. Are the required resources, for example, meeting rooms, VTC, travel dollars, conference fees, etc., available?
	The list is provided as a tool at the end of this section. Questions to which the answer is "no" present a potential barrier to the community's success. For each identified barrier, a solution should be developed and implemented.
Lessons learned provide valuable insight	A second valuable exercise for the core group or community leader would be to have a "lessons learned" discussion to evaluate how well the initial workshop went. This information will be useful in improving the community's next event; it will also be beneficial next time a new community is initiated. A sample form for collecting lessons learned is provided as a tool at the end of this section.
	Tip: A variation might be for the community to complete this exercise in lieu of a roundtable.
Key task 5: Build community experience locator	Another useful tool for rapidly getting the right information to the right person at the right time is to create a community "experience locator." The locator could be resident on a community's shared workspace and could include key information about members' experience, for example, top three jobs held and significant experience. A keyword search capability might be a feature of this tool. A sample CoP/experience locator template is provided as a tool at the end of this section.
	Tip: Consider developing your experience locator and hosting it in CDMS.

Tools	■ Sample core group planning meeting agenda ■ Community and corporate roles and responsibilities ■ Social networks and knowledge flow technique ■ Knowledge needs/supply map ■ Sample community workshop agenda (orientation) ■ Suggested exercise: building relationships ■ CoP early progress checklist ■ Lessons learned report template ■ CoP/experience locator template

Sample Core Group Planning Meeting Agenda

1. Set up
   1.1 Welcome
   1.2 Introductions (if applicable)
   1.3 Review objectives/agenda
2. Create community identity
   2.1 Clarify purpose
   2.2 Review prioritized knowledge needs
   2.3 Consider success criteria
   2.4 Consider community norms
3. Clarify community intent
   3.1 Review types of communities
   3.2 Determine the intent and focus of the community
4. Clarify roles and responsibilities
   4.1 Review functional sponsor role
   4.2 Review community leader role
   4.3 Review core group role
   4.4 Review logistics coordinator role
   4.5 Review facilitator role
5. Identify community members
   5.1 Review personnel identified in preceding analysis
   5.2 Brainstorm additional prospective contributors
   5.3 Devise methods to "get the word out"
6. Define collaborative work environment
   6.1 Explore the potential for a shared workspace (electronic)
   6.2 Evaluate chat room/discussion tools
   6.3 Identify meeting rooms with VTC capabilities
7. Wrap up
   7.1 Review future steps or action items
   7.2 Review meeting objectives

Objectives

- Clarify community origination and purpose
- Identify prospective community members
- Determine best methods for community collaboration

Community and Corporate Roles and Responsibilities

Within the context of KM there are two categories of roles: (1) those associated with a specific CoP and (2) those that support and link multiple CoPs or other KM initiatives, for example, building infrastructure for knowledge transfer. Corporate roles are not specific to a particular community. As the KM strategy evolves and communities are rolled out, corporate roles, for example, infomediaries, may gain more prominence. It is recognized that some communities will form as a grassroots movement and will not use any corporate resources; some may already be in place and successful. Roles, in this context, do not equate with job positions; they can be viewed as the different hats people wear to accomplish a task. These role descriptions are provided as a guide and should be tailored to suit your community's needs and resources.

CoP Roles and Responsibilities	
Functional sponsors pave the way for community success	Every community must have a functional sponsor. The functional sponsor is typically someone who can pave the way for community success. A community's sponsor believes in the value of knowledge sharing and commends participation in community activities. Further, sponsors promote the value of membership across an organization thereby encouraging community growth and commitment of organizational resources. Sponsorship may be shared by more than one person; this may be important if community membership spans multiple organizations. ■ Makes community participation a priority for its members ■ Builds support for the community among commanding officers, functional managers, and opinion leaders ■ Bolsters community membership — spreads the word ■ Plans and coordinates allocation of resources; (ensures funding for awards, etc., is in place) ■ Acts as champion for the community ■ Sets direction and provides guidance ■ Resolves issues ■ Works with community leader to track progress of community

A core group is instrumental in establishing effective work methods for the community	The core group, a subset of the community, is a working group that initially performs start-up activities, for example, planning. The core group is made up of knowledgeable and experienced members of the community, members who are super subject matter experts. Once the community is established, the core group will continue to provide ongoing organizational support.
	For example, core group members may use their knowledge of the discipline to judge what is important, groundbreaking, and useful and to enrich information by summarizing, combining, contrasting, and integrating it into the existing knowledge base.
	■ Participates in community ■ Gains support of functional managers ■ Ensures that the infrastructure is in place to meet the knowledge objectives of the community ■ Builds community experience locator ■ Creates collaborative environment ■ Harvests or creates new knowledge ■ Establishes taxonomy ■ Prescribes tool usage/functionality
Community leaders provide day-to-day support while serving as a contributing member	The community leader, an active member of the community, serves an integral role in the community's success. The leader energizes the process and provides continuous nourishment for the community. The leader must continuously strive to further the community's goals.
	■ Serves as a subject matter expert on the focus of the community ■ Plans and schedules community activities ■ Connects members with each other ■ Brings in new ideas when the community starts to lose energy ■ Interfaces with the functional sponsor ■ Bolsters community membership — spreads the word ■ Represents the community at briefings ■ Acts as liaison with other communities ■ Recognizes contributions ■ Manages day-to-day activities of the community (collateral duty) ■ Tracks budget expenditures (if applicable)

Without members, there is no community	The essence of a community is its members. Membership is voluntary rather than prescribed. Members are self-organizing and participate because they get value from their participation:
	■ Enjoys continuous learning as a result of participation ■ Bolsters community membership — spreads the word ■ Populates community experience locator, if applicable ■ Works in relevant business process; acts as a subject matter expert on data, process, or both ■ Looks outside community to identify relevant information ■ Conducts interviews to capture knowledge ■ Presents new information to community to determine added value ■ Acts as content owner by updating, creating, replenishing, and owning data in repository ■ Scans best practice materials ■ Performs benchmarking ■ Develops rules governing assets; ensures documentation consistency ■ Participates in face-to-face knowledge sharing experiences ■ May be a core group member ■ May document community proceedings
A facilitator can serve as a resource for a community	A facilitator can ensure community forums are productive for all members by acting as an independent, CoP process expert.
	■ Helps create and foster collaborative environment ■ Provides process analysis expertise ■ Provides tool expertise ■ Provides expertise about group dynamics and techniques to help community solve problems and evolve over time
Functional support provides the backbone	The role of functional support provides the backbone for storing knowledge in the collaborative environment.
	■ Provides on-the-spot expertise on the CoP building process: ■ Provides help desk services on CoP building process and specific tool support ■ May document community proceedings

Corporate Knowledge Management Infrastructure Roles	
Logistics coordinator	The role of logistics coordinator provides the administrative workload for a community:
	■ Coordinates calendars; schedules meetings or events ■ Coordinates facilities ■ Arranges for equipment
Infomediary	The infomediary acts as an information broker:
	■ Gleans data across communities for relevance ■ Possibly "connects" data across communities ■ Acts as liaison to related projects and CoPs
Project historian	The project historian is not part of a CoP. The role of the project historian is to document project decisions and events so that this information is not lost and can be reused by the corporation. Captures project history (main events, major discussions/decisions, sources of information, contacts, etc.) from information provided or generated by individual project teams, business process reengineering or enterprise resource planning efforts, or other types of teams or activities

Sample Community Orientation Workshop Agenda

1. Set up
    1.1 Welcome (by functional sponsor)
    1.2 Introductions
    1.3 Review objectives/agenda
2. Guest speaker
    2.1 Presentation
    2.2 Questions and answers
3. Relationship-building exercise
4. Community identity
    4.1 Clarify purpose
    4.2 Consider success criteria
    4.3 Consider community norms
    4.4 Identify additional prospective members
5. Clarify community intent
    5.1 Review types of communities
    5.2 Determine the intent and focus of the community

6. Knowledge needs
   6.1 Review prioritized knowledge needs
   6.2 Build consensus on prioritization technique
   6.3 Determine top knowledge needs
7. Plan of action
8. Collaborative environment
   8.1 Describe tools available for community use
   8.2 Determine member needs for installation, training, or access
9. Wrap up
   9.1 Review action items/next steps
   9.2 Review meeting objectives
   9.3 Plan next get-together

Objectives

- Solidify community identity
- Prioritize knowledge needs
- Develop plan to satisfy highest-priority knowledge need

Relationship-Building Exercise

Title	Connect with Community Members
Purpose	This exercise is designed to help build personal relationships between members and to begin to answer the questions, "What do we know, what do we need to know, and who knows it?"
Group size	5–40
Estimated time	20–60 minutes depending on group size
Props	A set of blank, individual, member index cards strung together on a loose ring — perhaps a community key ring! Each member should have a blank set.
Instructions	1. Organize participants into groups of four to six (adjust according to group size). 2. Explain that the goal of this activity is to learn about each other's unique backgrounds and perspectives as well as getting to know each other better. 3. Give each participant a set of blank index cards. 4. Explain the directions:

	■ Each subgroup should convene for 10 minutes to complete the index cards. ■ Complete the factoid card for each member. ■ After 10 minutes disperse and form new subgroups; make sure that everyone speaks with each member in one of the subgroup sessions. (Note: Rotations should last just long enough for members to gather information, but still want more time — whet their appetite!) 5. Repeat subgroup formation until each member has completed a card for each member.
Tips	1. *Provide complete set of blank cards to new members as they join, and encourage them to complete them, one-on-one, for each member* 2. *As new members join, provide new index cards to existing members and encourage them to complete new cards informally and add them to their rings.*

Community of Practice
Early Progress Checklist

1. Does the community have a common purpose? Is the purpose compelling to leadership, prospective members, and their functional managers?
2. Is the common purpose aligned with the enterprise strategy?
3. Is the right sponsorship in place — a respected leader who is willing to contribute to the community?
4. Does the functional sponsor agree with the community's scope, purpose, and membership?
5. Are core group members and the community leader strong content experts, enthusiastic, and able to develop the community?
6. Do members' functional managers agree that "time away from the job" is valuable?
7. Do we have the right content experts to provide perspective and meaning to our membership?
8. Is there a shared space and context for dialogue, advice, and work?
9. Do we have enough members to keep the community alive?
10. Are collaborative tools in place and easily accessible? Are members "set" to use them?
11. Are needed resources, for example, meeting rooms, VTC, travel dollars, conference fees, etc., available?

Lessons Learned Report	
Situation	
Observer	
Date	
What was done right?	
What went wrong?	
Suggestions	

CoP/Experience Locator Template

With today's technologies (e.g., e-mail and the Internet) knowledge can be rapidly transferred. Only, how does someone know whom to contact if they want to learn more about a specific topic? Consider the following true anecdote:

> I joined the organization on March 16, 1998, without previous experience. After one week of training, I joined a project team. After one day of training on the project, I was assigned a task: to learn a particular technology that was new to everyone on the team. I was given a bunch of books and told that I had three days to learn how to create a project using this technology.
>
> I remembered learning about the company's expertise database in my first week of training. I sent an e-mail to four people I found in the database asking for their help. One of them sent me a document containing exactly what I wanted. Instead of three days, my task was completed in half a day.

So how do you connect knowledge seekers with knowledge holders and facilitate knowledge exchange? One method seen in the industry today is the use of experience locators or "corporate yellow pages." Each community should post a CoP descriptor on the corporate Web site. The descriptor should be easily accessible to employees and should provide the following information:

- Name of community
- Purpose and scope of community
- Name of functional sponsor (organization, location, phone number, and e-mail)
- Name of community leader (organization, location, phone number, and e-mail)
- Name of core group members (organization, location, phone number, and e-mail)
- Membership contact information (organization, location, phone number, and e-mail, or direct link to members)
- Membership profiles (could include key information about members' experience; e.g., top three jobs held, fields of expertise, project experience, education, training, certifications, and publications)
- A listing of, or link to, community knowledge assets

Some interactive play could enhance the usefulness of a CoP/experience locator, including key word search capabilities and the facility to conduct an instant messaging session with a community member identified as a subject matter expert or, alternatively, contact experts via e-mail if that person is not online at that moment.

L.3 CREATING KNOWLEDGE

Purpose	The purpose of this section is to provide your community with suggested tools to help it create, capture, and share knowledge. This section consists primarily of tools. A tool, in this instance, does not refer to automated systems for transferring information. Rather, these tools are techniques or forums for thinking (e.g., techniques for generating ideas and building relationships) or forums that promote knowledge flow and transfer. The following is a list of tools discussed in this section: ■ Ad hoc sessions ■ Roadmap to generating new knowledge (problem solving and brainstorming) ■ Learning history ■ Interviews ■ Action learning ■ Learn from others ■ Guest speakers ■ Relationship building ■ Systems thinking The inventory, storage, and migration of explicit knowledge (e.g., publications, documents, and patents) are addressed in Section L.4.
Although resource intensive, efforts to create and transfer knowledge cannot be neglected	Converting tacit knowledge to commonly held community knowledge can be resource intensive, but the gains can be extraordinary. To cite some industry examples, companies have saved millions by transferring knowledge from one part of the organization to another: Ford claims that $34 million was saved in just one year by transferring ideas between vehicle operations plants; Texas Instruments saved enough by transferring knowledge between wafer fabrication plants to pay for building a whole new facility; Chevron reduced its costs on capital projects alone by $186 million. In fact, neither transferring common knowledge nor creating new knowledge can be neglected; the first is critical for current viability, the second for future viability.

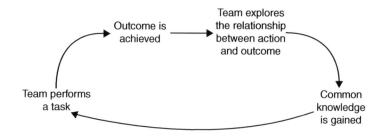

Figure L.1   Common knowledge.

	Communities offer a mechanism to continuously grow and transfer knowledge, as illustrated in Figure L.1.
	Once common knowledge is gained, a second cycle would be to leverage this knowledge across an organization; take the gained knowledge, translate it into usable forms, and transfer it to others who can adapt it for their own use.
Expected outcomes	▪ Designs for community forums for critical thinking and knowledge flow ▪ Practical techniques for knowledge creation, capture, and transfer
What technique should I use?	This section introduces each tool and provides a brief description. Where noted, supplemental information or templates are provided as tools at the end of this section.
	As an introduction to the subsection "Tools" at the end of this section, a matrix is presented with possible learning need scenarios. For example, a community member would like to learn how to perform a particular task. The matrix would suggest two techniques: conducting interviews or an action learning set.
	A possible success criteria discussed earlier was the ability of the community to rapidly mobilize in response to a member's "call for help." Being able to quickly pull together a group for a 30-minute brainstorming or just as a sounding board is a priceless resource. Instant messaging is a great device for calling together a quick session. Instant messaging, e-mail, conference calls, VTC, or chat rooms can also be used in lieu of a face-to-face sessions for rapid input. In general, any or all of these technologies can be used inside a single network security domain without any

***Ad hoc* sessions**	problem. However if, for example, the instant messaging or chat room protocols must traverse one or more firewalls to include all desired participants, this situation needs to be investigated ahead of time to ensure that the firewall is already configured to pass the required protocols. If the firewall blocks these signals, further analysis is required to ensure that opening a firewall port will not create unacceptable security vulnerabilities in the network. Under such circumstances a prior consultation with the local information system security manager (ISSM) is strongly recommended. *Tip: the community's experience locator would serve as a useful tool when a member needs to quickly reach out to someone who "has done this before."*
Roadmap to generating new knowledge	An excellent approach to creating and sharing knowledge about best practices is to host facilitated, collaborative problem-solving meetings. These forums serve many purposes: (1) solving relevant, day-to-day problems, (2) building trust among community members by actually helping each other, and (3) solving problems in a public forum, thereby creating a common understanding of tools, approaches, and solutions. Often during problem-solving discussions, communities will discover areas in which they need to create common standards or guidelines. These discoveries may lead to the creation of smaller, more focused workgroups to develop detailed standards for incorporation into best practice recommendations. This is an example of how communities naturally trigger continuous process improvement. A five-step roadmap for problem solving as a means to generate new knowledge is provided as a tool at the end of this section. This roadmap works well for best practices that can easily be reused; e.g., methodologies, analytical models, diagnostic approaches, case studies, and benchmark data.
Learning history	A learning history is a very useful tool to capture tacit knowledge resident in the minds of individuals. A learning history is a retrospective account of significant events in an organization's recent past, described in the voices of people who took part in them. Researched through a series of reflective interviews, the learning history uses feedback from employees at all levels to help an organization evaluate its progress.

A technique to capture tacit knowledge resident in individual minds	Organizations can learn by reviewing their successes and failures, assessing them systematically, and recording the lessons in a form that employees find open and accessible. To quote the famous philosopher George Santanya, "Those who cannot remember the past are condemned to repeat it." Learning from our mistakes can lead to subsequent success — failure is the ultimate teacher.
	Recording staff members' experience with technical projects, wartime operations, change programs, technical conferences or symposia, leadership conferences, workshops, site visits, etc., can help ensure that useful knowledge is shared and mistakes are not repeated. In debriefings, interviewees recall their experience in their own words in a manner that reflects their collective learning experience.
	The interview can be transcribed into a question-and-answer format, a standardized document format, or preserved as a video. Regardless of the medium, the important feature is to ensure that a record is made while events are still fresh in the mind and, ideally, before a project's conclusion. In effect, this allows access to accumulated hindsight, as opposed to hindsight tempered by poor memory recall and defensive reasoning.
	At Ford, learning histories are used by a car parts division, an assembly plant, and in product design and development. In the assembly plant, Ford has accomplished quality improvements of 25 percent per year since 1995, compared to less than 10 percent achieved by two comparable factories.
	A six-step approach to creating a learning history is provided as a tool at the end of this section.
Storytelling	*Storytelling*, the construction of fictional examples to illustrate a point, can be used to effectively transfer knowledge. An organizational story is a detailed narrative of management actions, employee interactions, or other intraorganizational events that are communicated informally within the organization.

	Conveying information in a story provides a rich context, remaining in the conscious memory longer and creating more memory traces than information not in context. Therefore a story is more likely to be acted upon than normal means of communications. Storytelling, whether in a personal or organizational setting, connects people, develops creativity, and increases confidence. The use of stories in organizations can build descriptive capabilities, increase organizational learning, convey complex meaning, and communicate common values and rule sets.
Conduct interviews	Conducting interviews with subject matter experts, stakeholders, process performers, customers — anyone who can shed new light on a topic or issue — is an excellent method to gather knowledge for the community and its knowledge base. These guidelines are provided as a tool at the end of this section.
Action learning	*Action learning* is a new way to approach learning. It is a very simple concept revolving around the fact that people learn by doing. Put simply, action learning involves the formation of a small group of people who share common issues, goals, or learning needs. This group, called an *action learning set*, works to resolve issues and achieve these goals together, meeting regularly, about once a month, to reflect on progress, issues, and solutions and refine the way forward. The team is able to brainstorm on alternative approaches or offer advice to an individual on how to proceed in achieving specific goals. Emphasis is on trying new things and evaluating the results. A methodology for action learning is provided as a tool at the end of this section. Action learning is task oriented and may be useful for approaching narrowly focused issues. However, a community is not expected, nor is it encouraged, to undertake large, task-oriented projects; e.g., reengineering, systems requirements definition, or policy overhauls. When the community recognizes the need for a major project, it should route the candidate project to leadership for direction. The community may wish to volunteer its subject expertise to a subsequent project team, if appropriate.

Learn from others; share relentlessly	Not all learning is derived from reflection and analysis. Sometimes, the most powerful insights come from looking outside your realm or industry to get a new perspective. Organizations stop changing when people stop learning and get stuck in the knowing.
	Consider benchmarking to identify better ways of doing business, site visits, or tours to "see" how a practice is applied in a specific environment, and interactions with customers to better understand their problems, preferences, and feedback on service or products.
	Tip: The American Productivity and Quality Center offers a benchmarking methodology as well as a wealth of information about best practices on its Web site (http://www.apqc.org).
	Not only should your community learn from external sources, but it should also leverage existing knowledge resident in the organization. Seek out existing sources of knowledge; e.g., work products from other departments and communities, exhibitors at knowledge fairs, or commissioned studies. One of the objectives of KM is to make these resources easily available to both the individual and the community.
Guest speakers	Inviting guest speakers to community forums is an opportunity to bring a fresh perspective or point of view into the community. Speakers should be selected based on relevance to community purpose or targeted areas of interest:
	■ Solicit ideas for speakers or topic areas from community members.
	■ Consider internal and external sources for relevant speakers. Possible sources include professional associations, sister organizations, supplier/partner organizations, project historians, etc.
	■ When appropriate, consider inviting representatives from other communities to speak and to begin building links across communities.
Relationship-building exercises	The strongest communities are built upon strong relationships. Relationships typically form naturally while working together over a period of time. It would not hurt to occasionally work a relationship-building exercise into community forums. Several exercises are provided as tools at the end of this section.

Systems thinking	Systems thinking provides an approach for managing complexity. It is a tool to help decision makers understand the cause and effect relationships among data, information, and people. It identifies archetypes (or patterns) that occur over and over again in decision making. In short, it expands individual thinking skills and improves both individual and group/team decision making. Additional information on systems thinking is provided at the end of this section.
Tools	■ Suggested techniques for scenarios ■ A roadmap to generating new knowledge ■ Learning history — overview ■ Storytelling — white paper ■ Interview guidelines ■ Action learning ■ Relationship-building exercises ■ Systems thinking

	Suggested Techniques for Scenarios									
Scenario	Ad Hoc Sessions	Roadmap	Learning	Storytelling	Interviews	Action Learning	Learn from Others	Guest Speakers	Relationship Building	Systems Thinking
No information is available on a subject					✔	✔	✔	✔		
A practice performed differently by many with varying levels of success — seeking a best practice for adoption by all	✔	✔		✔		✔	✔			
A common problem with many alternatives — seeking a best practice		✔	✔	✔	✔					✔

Suggested Techniques for Scenarios (continued)										
Scenario	Ad Hoc Sessions	Roadmap	Learning	Storytelling	Interviews	Action Learning	Learn from Others	Guest Speakers	Relationship Building	Systems Thinking
You want to energize the community with new ideas				✔				✔		✔
A method to test or prototype alternatives to determine a best practice		✔				✔				
One or more members need to learn how to perform a specific task					✔	✔				
A new tasking from command leadership — how best to implement?		✔				✔				✔
A problem has been identified but is not yet clearly understood — root cause?		✔	✔			✔				✔
You need an answer in a hurry or you need to bounce an idea off colleagues	✔					✔				
An exercise or event has occurred; was it successful?			✔	✔	✔			✔		
Build consensus on a topic with high levels of conflict or controversy		✔							Brain writing	✔
Need to generate and evaluate ideas									Brain writing	

Suggested Techniques for Scenarios (continued)									
Scenario	Ad Hoc Sessions	Roadmap	Learning	Storytelling	Interviews	Action Learning	Learn from Others	Guest Speakers	Relationship Building	Systems Thinking
To prepare a group to derive lessons learned — think beyond the obvious	✔		✔						What is the moral of the story?	
Think creatively; see the same thing in a new light		✔		✔			✔		New product offering	✔

A Roadmap to Generating New Knowledge

This roadmap is a variation on an approach commonly used for problem solving. It may be useful to a community if it is trying to solve a problem shared by many members or to develop a best practice that can be adopted by members. The roadmap leads the community through a series of steps: define a problem, conduct analysis, generate ideas, select a best practice or solution, and capture the knowledge in an explicit form. A group or an individual can use this approach. The steps remain the same.

Problem Exploration and Definition

Explore the problem and determine if additional information is needed. For example, members may decide to observe specific practices or research existing information on a topic. Other methods to collect more information might be to conduct interviews with impacted individuals or subject matter experts.

Jumping to a conclusion without understanding a problem can save time, but it could also waste time if you solve the wrong problem. Before jumping to the conclusions, consider the following:

- Examine the problem from all angles; try to see it from the perspective of an employee, a customer, or a supplier.
- Separate fact from fiction; perception is important but it must be distinguished from fact.

- Identify key players; who is affected by the problem, who is responsible for solving the problem, and who has the authority to accept a solution.
- Dissect or decompose the situation; break the problem down into pieces.
- Determine the plan for gathering information — survey, interviews, observations, brainstorm sessions, or benchmark reviews — if needed.

Clearly defining a problem, using clear, plain English, is like having your finger on its pulse. A clear definition builds a strong foundation for subsequent fact finding, communication, and analysis. A good definition does more:

- Distills the situation into a brief, concise statement
- Uses key words to get to the bottom of the situation
- States what a problem is rather than what it is not
- States a problem in terms of needs — not solutions

Analysis

Typically, what you see is only the tip of the iceberg — or the symptoms of a problem rather than its root cause. It is important to distinguish cause from effect to ensure that you are actually solving the source of the problem, not just addressing its symptoms. Consider a medical analogy. You have many symptoms of the common cold, but in fact, you have a sinus infection that can only be cured with an antibiotic. Even as you use over-the-counter cold medicines to alleviate your symptoms, your original infection continues to worsen. This is also true of an organization. By addressing only the symptoms, you miss the root cause, and the condition persists and may even worsen.

Discovering the root cause of a problem can be tricky. Sound questioning techniques are a good start. Using your problem definition statement, answer the following questions:

- Why does the problem persist?
- Where did it start and where did it come from?
- Why does it not resolve itself or just go away?
- What caused it in the first place?
- What changed just before it started?
- Why do we keep getting sucked back into the situation?
- Why will things not improve no matter what we try?

Still not sure? Do not move to the solution phase until you are sure you have found the root cause. Test your tentative conclusion using the following evaluations. The proposed root cause must pass the entire test to be the true root cause. If the results of these evaluations are not conclusive, continue analysis until you can answer "yes" to each question.

How to Know You Have Found the Root Cause		
Desired Response	Scenario	Yes/No
Dead end	You ran into a dead end when you asked, "What led to the proposed root cause?"	_____
Conversation ends	All conversation has come to a positive end.	_____
Feels good	Everyone involved feels good, motivated, and emotionally uplifted.	_____
Agreement	All agree it is the root cause that keeps the problem from resolving.	_____
Explains	The root cause fully explains from all points of view why the problem exists.	_____
Beginnings	The earliest beginnings of the situation have been explored and are understood.	_____
Logical	The root cause is logical, makes sense, and dispels all confusion.	_____
Control	The root cause is something you can influence, control, and deal with realistically.	_____
Hope	Finding the root cause has returned hope that something constructive can be done about the situation.	_____
Workable solution	Suddenly, workable solutions, not outrageous demands, begin to appear.	_____
Stable resolution	A stable, long-term, once-and-for-all resolution of the situation now appears feasible.	_____

Use of analytic techniques, for example, diagramming and process modeling, can also be applied during the analysis stage. A few additional techniques for analyzing a problem are suggested:

- Napoleon — imagine you are someone else to gain new perspectives.
- Morphological analysis — systematically examine each attribute of the problem.

- Create a deadline.
- Sleep on it.

Idea Generation

Once the root cause is identified, it is time to generate possible solutions. This is the time to be creative. One useful way to generate a storm of ideas with a group is a facilitation technique called *brainstorming.* The brainstorming process is useful in two ways: it enhances the flow of ideas and innovations, and it builds consensus and commitment via a participative process. There are four rules that must be followed for a truly effective brainstorming session:

- Quantity versus quality — the more ideas, the greater the likelihood of a useful one.
- Freewheeling — open the gate and allow ideas to freely flow; build on the ideas of others even if they seem wild or outrageous.
- Defer judgment — the surest way to shut down creative thinking is to judge each idea as it occurs. You are not deciding on ideas at this point, but simply thinking imaginatively.
- Hitchhike — if there is a lull in the flow, try making more out of what has already been said, changing it a little, or adding to it. For example, if a client meeting was suggested, add ideas on how to structure the meeting. *Voila,* a new idea!

A useful brainstorming process is presented in the following:

- Frame a session with an idea-seeking question; e.g., what are all the ways...or a general topic; display the question or topic where everyone can see it.
- Clearly state the purpose (to generate a storm of ideas) and brainstorming rules.
- Establish a time limit — 20 to 30 minutes.
- Try a round-robin to encourage participation, allowing members to pass or "green light" participants to speak out in any order that naturally occurs.
- Encourage participants to build on others' ideas.
- Post all ideas.
- Allow no evaluation, criticism, or discussion while ideas are being generated; look out for "killing phrases."
- Allow participants time to think; do not let a lull in the storm stop the session.
- After all ideas have been generated, reduce the list by questioning, categorizing, and consolidating.

Remember, the goal is to think creatively and view the problem from a new perspective. To quote Nobel-Prize-winning physician Albert Szent-Gyorgyi, "Discovery consists of looking at the same thing as everyone else and thinking something different." Another creative genius, Albert Einstein, once said, "Problems cannot be solved at the same level of consciousness that created them." Before generating ideas, try some creativity exercises.

When generating ideas, avoid mental locks; e.g., "I already have the answer." The following table provides a listing of common mental locks and possible techniques to overcome them.

Mental Locks	Consider
The right answer	There is often more than one right answer.
That is not logical	Excessive logical thinking can short-circuit your creative process; be curious, look for surprises.
Follow the rules	Challenge the rules. "Slaying sacred cows makes great steaks" — Dick Nicolosi, philosopher.
Be practical	Ask "what if" questions. Use them as stepping stones.
Play is frivolous	Use play to fertilize your thinking. Make a game of it.
That is not my idea	Specialization limits you. Develop an explorer's attitude. Leave your own turf.
Do not be foolish	Foolish thinking can get you out of a rut.
Avoid ambiguity	Too much specificity can stifle your imagination.
To err is wrong	Do not be afraid to fail. "A ship in port is safe, but that's not what ships are built for" — Grace Hopper, inventor.
I am not creative	Believe in the worth of your ideas.
I do not have time	You do not have time not to.

Solution Selection

The goal at this point is to narrow the list of ideas into feasible, creative, and win-win alternatives. By using an objective, criterion-based method to select ideas, you will coincidentally make the decision-making process much easier in that you have defined the terms for reaching a consensus. The process, therefore, becomes fact-based and less emotionally charged.

Establishing objective criteria is similar to judging a sporting event. Olympic judges use consistent, objective criteria to evaluate the performance of athletes to select winners. In addition to establishing criteria, you may want to prioritize criteria. For example, some criteria may be mandatory whereas others are optional. Another technique might be to set acceptable ranges. For example, if an idea meets less than 80 percent of the criteria, it will be removed from the running.

If a clear winner does not emerge, identify the best and worst outcomes for each idea or the pros and cons of each idea. Another step might be to validate the practice with stakeholders or peers. For a final check, ask yourself the following questions:

- Is the best practice, or alternative, based upon good, sound reasoning and data?
- Were the right people involved in the problem solving process?

Following this roadmap will serve to create new knowledge that can improve not only your own job, but also the overall performance of your organization as well as the jobs of sailors and peers in other organizations.

Knowledge Capture

It is recommended that all new knowledge, or best practices, generated by the community, be presented with at least the following pieces of information. Readers should be encouraged to call either the point of contact (originator) or members to gain more understanding of the topic.

- Date prepared.
- Point of contact — include name, organization, and contact information.
- Members who participated in development of best practice and contact information.
- Problem statement.
- Background — note any research that was conducted during the exploration phase and a summary of significant findings. Include findings from root cause analysis.
- Alternatives considered — list significant ideas that were considered and explain reasons for nonselection.
- Best practice — provide sufficient information to clearly express best practice. If additional materials, e.g., models, business rules, etc., were developed, include them. Consider how graphics could be used to enhance knowledge transfer.

LEARNING HISTORY — OVERVIEW

A *learning history* is a retrospective history of significant events in an organization's recent past, described in the voices of people who took part in them. Researched through a series of reflective interviews, the learning history uses feedback from employees at all levels to help an organization evaluate its progress.

A learning history goes beyond simply gathering best practices and other lessons learned. A learning history is categorized by the following:

- Provides the time and space for participants to openly reflect on the learning from the initiative or exercise
- Enhances the reflection process so that team members begin to make new connections and see how their actions ultimately produce final outcomes
- Gathers information from a variety of perspectives to reduce bias
- Analyzes data to draw out key themes
- Contains accurate, validated information
- Is written in the words of those involved — not paraphrased in the words of consultants
- Provides a vehicle to promote discussion among participants in the initiative

Approach

A learning history is a structured process for gathering information related to a project, mission, or initiative. The steps to create a learning history are depicted in Figure L.2.

Figure L.2   The process of gathering information for a learning history.

Step 1: Select Interview Candidates

Interview candidates are selected to give a variety of perspectives on the process. The selection of interview candidates in a thorough learning history should include those who initiated, participated in, or were affected by the project in some manner.

Step 2: Conduct Interviews

Interviews can be conducted in person, or by telephone when in-person interviews are not possible. The interviews generally average about 45 min in length and are conducted by the same interviewers whenever possible to maintain consistency. The interviews are designed to be reflective, to allow the interview candidate to speak freely without the constraints of a structured interview. No more than six general questions are prepared in advance. Additional questions are asked during the interview based on the responses of the interview candidates to gather more specific information. General interview questions might include the following:

- What was your role in the exercise/initiative?
- How would you judge the success of the initiative?
- What would you do differently if you could?
- What recommendations do you have for other people who might go through a similar process?
- What innovative things were done or could have been done?

Step 3: Record and Transcribe Interviews

Interviews are recorded to ensure that quotes used in the learning history are accurate. The recorded interviews are transcribed to enable analysis of interview data.

Step 4: Analyze Data

The interview data is analyzed and sorted to identify similar themes and subthemes. Quotes are identified to support the major themes from a balance of perspectives.

Step 5: Document Key Themes and Supporting Quotes

In this step, assemble and record the themes and supporting quotes into the right-hand column of the document (see section titled Format of Document). The quotes should be in no particular order but are designed to provide a picture of the theme from the different perspectives of the interview candidates.

Now develop the left-hand column of each section, which includes commentary and potential questions for consideration that relate to the adjacent quotes. The left-hand column commentary does not reflect the questions asked during the interview process but rather comments, questions, and conclusions posed by the author to the reader for further reflection.

Step 6: Validate Quotes

In the final step of the process, validate the quotes that are used in the learning history document with the interview candidates. Although interviews were recorded and quotes are anonymous, quotes are validated to ensure they were not taken out of context and truly represent the intent of the speaker. Quotes are sent to each interview candidate for correction and a signature of approval.

Format of Document

Part 1: In this section, describe the theme and any related practices of successful organizations.

Part 2: In this section, present the quotes that describe the theme in the right column. The quotes presented in the learning history are not inclusive of all the quotes received; rather, the quotes selected are designed to be representative of the various perspectives of interview candidates and representative of the information gathered throughout the interview process.

The left column of the document does not list questions asked during the interview but records commentary and questions posed to the reader by the author for further consideration when reading the document. The commentary on the left relates to the adjacent quote or quotes. The commentary is presented to provide the reader with ideas for reflection. The reader is encouraged to record their own thoughts and questions as they read.

Part 3: The final section of the theme is a summary of the key points from the quotes in Part 2. Questions for further consideration relating to the theme are presented at the end of this section.

The format of each section is depicted in the following table:

Theme Title	
Part 1 Overview of the theme.	
Part 2 *Commentary, conclusions, and potential questions to be asked that relate to the adjacent quotes.*	Quotes from interviewing process. The quotes represent key responses to questions posed by the learning consultant during the interview process.
Part 3 Brief summary of quotes, as heard by the learning consultant. Additional questions for the purpose of providing more clarity to the theme.	

The Use of Storytelling

Storytelling, the construction of fictional examples to illustrate a point, can be used to effectively transfer knowledge. An organizational story is a detailed narrative of management actions, employee interactions, or other intraorganizational events that are communicated informally within the organization.

A variety of story forms exist naturally throughout organizations, including scenarios and anecdotes. *Scenarios* are the articulation of possible future states, constructed within the imaginative limits of the author. Although scenarios provide an awareness of alternatives — of value in and of itself — they are often used as planning tools for possible future situations. The plan becomes a vehicle to respond to recognized objectives in each scenario. An *anecdote* is a brief sequence captured in the field or arising from a brainstorming session. To reinforce positive behavior, sensitive managers can seek out and disseminate true anecdotes that embody the value desired in the organization. The capture and distribution of anecdotes across organizations carries a high value. Once a critical number of anecdotes are captured from a community, the value set or rules underlying the behavior of that community can be determined. Understanding these values has allowed the utilization of informal as well as formal aspects of the organization.

Conveying information in a story provides a rich context, remaining in the conscious memory longer and creating more memory traces than information not in context. Therefore, a story is more likely to be acted upon than normal means of communications. Storytelling, whether in a personal or organizational setting, connects people, develops creativity, and increases confidence. The use of stories in organizations can build descriptive capabilities, increase organizational learning, convey complex meaning, and communicate common values and rule sets.

First, stories have the ability to increase our descriptive capabilities, a strength in this age of uncertainty where we must be able to describe our environment and have the self-awareness to describe our individual capabilities. Description capabilities are essential in strategic thinking and planning and create a greater awareness of what we could achieve. Fictional stories can be powerful because they provide a mechanism by which an organization can learn from failure without attributing blame. Some organizations actually create characters from archetypes taken from a large number of organizational anecdotes. These characters are used over and over again. Once established, they become a natural vehicle for organizational learning and a repository for organizational memory.

When well constructed, stories can convey a high level of complex meaning. The use of subtext can convey this meaning without making it obvious. *Subtext* is a term that refers to an unstated message, not explicit in the dialogue of the story. Analogies are often used to aid in the transfer of particularly complex information and knowledge to give the human mind something to relate to. This form of learning has been used throughout human history to transfer complex concepts and core values.

Finally, because stories communicate common values and rule systems, they provide a mechanism to build organic response to emerging requirements. This means that as new situations and new challenges arise in response to an ever-changing world, a common set of values will drive that response at every level of the organization. Snowden explains that to operate in a highly uncertain environment, we must have common values and rule systems that support networks of communities self-organizing around a common purpose. Stories provide such a catalyst. Snowden states that in this world, old skills, such as stories and other models drawn from organic rather than mechanical thinking, are survival skills, not just nice-to-haves.

The World Bank has used what they call a *springboard story* over the past several years to move that organization to a knowledge organization. The springboard story (a powerful method of communicating knowledge about norms and values) is a transformational story that enables the listener to take a personal leap in understanding how an organization, community, or complex system may change. The intent of this type of story is not to transfer information, but to serve as a catalyst for creating understanding within the listener. These stories enable listeners to easily and quickly grasp the ideas as a whole in a nonthreatening manner. In effect, they invite the listener to see analogies from their own histories, contexts, and fields of expertise.

These springboard stories were told from the perspective of a single protagonist who was known to the audience and actually in the predicament being told in the story; there was an element of strangeness or incongruity to the listeners, which could capture their attention and imagination; the story had a degree of plausibility and a premonition of what the future might be like; and there was a happy ending. Happy endings make it easier for listeners to take the imaginative leap from the explicit story to the implicit meaning.

With the advent of the Internet and intranet, there is a larger opportunity to use stories to bring about change. Electronic media adds moving images and sound as context setters. Hypertext capabilities and collaboration software invite groups, teams, and communities to cocreate their stories. New multiprocessing skills are required to navigate this new world, skills that include the quick and sure assimilation of and response to fast-flowing, sounds, and sensory assaults.

Interview Guidelines

The interview guidelines are a reference for conducting interviews to gather information.

Steps in Conducting Effective Interviews

Prepare for the Interview:

1. Determine the purpose of the interview and the associated types of information that will be collected.
2. Identify the categories of questions to be asked during the interview (e.g., knowledge requirements, knowledge sharing and interaction, and knowledge exchange).
3. Specify the areas of data necessary to meet the objectives of the interview.
   - Attempt to conduct the interview in their workspace in case you need to access info/data located in their office.
   - You should notify them in advance of the interview and your data requirements.
4. State questions utilizing the following techniques:
   - Ask open-ended questions. (e.g., How can the process be improved?)
   - Ensure clarity of meaning by eliminating ambiguity. (e.g., How would you rate the professionalism of your staff? Professionalism can have various meanings to different people.)
   - Keep questions simple. (e.g., "Our staff was both fast and friendly" — rate "agree" or "disagree.")
   - Watch out for biased questions, which can be difficult to detect and hinder obtaining insight. (e.g., Do you wish me to pass on any complements to the CEO?)

During the Interview:

5. Introduce yourself, your objective, and the agenda of the interview, specifically as follows:
   - Find out if interviewees have any objectives of their own for either the KCO implementation or the interview. Their objectives are important, because you can use this information to motivate or enable the implementation of the KCO in the organization.
   - Ask if they have any general questions pertaining to the project.
   - Explain how information will be used.
6. Put the interviewee at ease about the note-taking by explaining that the notes are to be used for reference as to what was discussed.

Try to capture their exact words, particularly if you think it may be of high importance. Ensure understanding throughout the interview and paraphrase back to them what you understood from their words.

7. Utilize the funnel technique to move from general ideas to detail. For example:
   - Initially, broad ("Tell me about...," "Describe...")
   - Later, more detail ("Who? What? When? Where? How?")
   - Finally, very detailed ("Yes"/"No" to verify information)

After the Interview:

8. Document your findings as soon as possible, and follow up on areas of uncertainty with interviewees.
9. Send them a summary of their comments (if relevant) to confirm what you heard and how you interpreted their statements.

Ladder of Inference

The *ladder of inference* is a model that describes an individual's mental process of observing situations, drawing conclusions, and taking action. When we say, "the fact is," what we are actually saying is the fact, as we understand it, based upon our data selection process, cultural and personal background, judgments, beliefs, and assumptions. Why is this important? This is important as there are a lot of steps in between the data and the actions we take based upon that data. By allowing others to explore our thinking process, we may reveal more effective and higher-leverage solutions.

After an event takes place, our mental processing immediately screens out a certain percentage of the data. In other words, our vision is naturally blurred and only absorbs a certain amount of the data that represents the life events.

When we look at the data we have collected, we attach our own personal meaning and cultural biases to the data that we observe. No data, therefore, is pure — it is influenced by whoever analyzes the data. Based on the meaning we attach to the data collected, we make inferences or judgments and arrive at conclusions, which influence our behavior. Therefore, one piece of data could lead to as many different conclusions as there are people analyzing that particular piece of data. Over time, the conclusions we reach from an event or pattern of events develop our belief system. We become fixated on certain ways of viewing how the world works, creating our own mental models that reoccur each time an event takes place.

All too often, people fall into what may be termed *competency traps* — a routine of problem solving that provided initial success and is used over and over with little regard to how accurately it fits with the current problem. The ladder of inference helps us break out of that trap by providing us an easy tool to ask, "What assumptions am I making about this particular situation that may limit my deeper understanding of the problem?" As we work to more clearly understand the problem, we may actually be able to reframe the problem.

The ladder of inference helps us understand why it is important to make our reasoning steps explicit. By consciously reviewing the data that supports our conclusions, we can improve our ability to explore complex problems and reduce those instances in which we jump to conclusions based upon data that is incomplete.

People often employ defensive behaviors such as trying to control situations that we have little control over, always acting as if we are in control, and never saying "I don't know." By having a tool that provides us an opportunity to say, "As I understand what you are saying, x leads to y, which results in z, ... am I on track with your thinking?", we do not have to resort to trying to defuse complex issues on our own, or end up attempting to cover up the fact that we do not have a clue.

When people in organizations jointly practice skilled incompetence, the result is the formation of defensive routines. By having a mutually acceptable tool, we can enquire into each other's thinking without resorting to rudeness.

A very powerful application of the ladder of inference is to introduce it at the beginning of a project. When team members commit to individually and collectively examining their beliefs and assumptions and making them explicit, a great deal of time spent in arguing and going around in circles can be eliminated.

Left-Hand Column

The left-hand column is the basic premise that during conversations there are actually two conversations taking place. One conversation is explicit. This conversation consists of the words that are actually spoken throughout the exchange between two or more persons. The other conversation consists of what the individuals are thinking and feeling but not saying. The term *left-hand column* is derived from an exercise designed to explore what is not said, but thought about, during the course of a conversation. This tool offers a way to actually study our conversations so that we can redesign them to be more effective in creating the results that we wish to create.

People need an introduction to this tool before you can begin using it effectively as a team. Here is an exercise that you can use to introduce the team to.

Step 1: Choosing a Problem

Select a difficult problem you have been involved with during the last month or two. Write a brief paragraph describing the situation. What are you trying to accomplish? Who or what is blocking you? What might happen? Examples include the following:

- The rest of the organization is resisting, or you believe they will resist, a change you want to implement.
- You believe your team is not paying much attention to the most crucial problem.

Step 2: The Right-Hand Column (What Was Said)

Now, recall a frustrating conversation you had over this. Take a piece of paper and draw a line down the center. In the right-hand column, write out the conversation that actually occurred. Or write the conversation you are pretty sure would occur if you were to raise this issue. The discussion may go on for several pages. Leave the left-hand column blank, until you are finished.

Step 3: The Left-Hand Column (What You Were Thinking)

Now, in the left-hand column, write out what you were thinking and feeling, but not saying.

Step 4: Individual Reflection: Using Your Left-Hand Column as a Resource

You can learn a great deal just from the act of writing out a case, putting it away for a week, and then looking at it again. As you reflect, ask yourself the following questions:

- What has really led me to think and feel this way?
- How might my comments have contributed to the difficulties?
- Why did I not say what was in my left-hand column?
- What assumptions am I making about the other person or people?
- How can I use my left-hand column as a resource to improve our communications?

Step 5: Discuss in Pairs or a Small Group

The pairs or small groups review one or more of the left-hand columns written in Step 3. The conversation should focus on exploring the assumptions behind both speakers' words, discussing alternative ways in which the participant could have conducted the conversation so that he or she would have been more satisfied with the outcome.

Action Learning

Overview

Action learning is a new way of approaching learning. It is a very simple concept revolving around the fact that people learn by doing. Put simply, it involves the formation of a small group of people who share common issues, goals, or learning needs. This group, called an *action learning set*, works to resolve issues and achieve these goals together, meeting regularly, about once a month, to reflect on progress, issues, and solutions, and refine the way forward. The team is able to brainstorm on alternative approaches or offer advice to an individual on how to proceed in achieving specific goals. Emphasis is on trying new things and evaluating the results.

Method

Action learning is cyclical. It consists of the following steps:

1. Identify task and learning opportunity
2. Planning together
3. Doing
4. Reflecting
5. Sharing the learning
6. Closing out

Identify Task and Learning Opportunity

Determine the objectives of the action learning program. Form the action learning set. Discuss with the team the development needs and job challenges that might be addressed by action learning. Not all of the members of the set will necessarily have the same development need, but these should be similar. It is important for the group to understand the development needs of the individuals within the group and any development needs of the group as a whole. An action learning set is ideally five to eight people in size to allow for good discussion within the sessions. Assign somebody to facilitate the group meeting sessions, asking questions of the participants, to draw out the key learning points. Define how often the group will meet and some ground rules for the meetings. Identify subject matter experts who might be able to come and talk to the group.

Planning Together

The official start of an action learning program should be in the form of a start-up workshop. Ideally, the workshop should be held off site to allow the participants to spend time away from the usual distractions of the workplace. Included in the agenda for the workshop should be time for the following activities:

- Developing personal learning plans and a common view of the purpose of the action learning set.
- Declaring individual objectives for membership of this action learning set and identifying medium- and short-term actions that can be taken to progress towards these objectives. In addition, set members should be asked how they will know when objectives have been reached, or how will they be able to measure their progress?
- Identifying opportunities to apply new ideas and learning points in the workplace.
- Introduction to the practice of reflection and keeping a learning log to capture key learning and progress.
- Reviewing, at the end of the section, what went well, and what could be done to improve the format for future sessions.

Doing

This is time spent working on a task. The members of the action learning set spend time experimenting with new approaches and testing new ideas developed during the action learning set meetings, all with the aim of making progress on a problem, project, or issue of importance to them. The following should be referred to as instructions during this phase:

- Refer back to the action plans developed during the planning workshop.
- Before taking action, reflect on what you think the outcome of the action will be. If possible, record this in the learning log.
- Take action. Try out the approach as planned. This is where you do the work you do every day but with the benefit of advanced planning and documenting your expectations before you act.

- Look for evidence of how effective you have been. What did you observe?
- Write down your observations in the learning log. This is where you create the opportunities to learn, by reflecting on your observations, both by yourself and with the benefit of the perspective of others, at the next set meeting.

Reflecting

This is a regular session in which members of the action learning set come together to reflect on the progress they have made on their work issues. It is a time for challenging assumptions, exploring new ways of thinking about problems, and planning what to do next in the workplace. It is also an opportunity for set members to bring up specific issues of their work that they would like others to think through with them, as well as offer their thinking support to explore the issues and problems raised by others.

The following points can be noted for conduction of effective reflecting sessions:

- Plan reflection sessions on a regular basis and as far in advance as possible; ensure maximum attendance.
- Book enough time to allow the thorough exploration of issues of importance. Try 30 minutes per person plus an extra 30 minutes as an estimate, when planning reflection sessions.
- Make sure that participants have prepared for the reflection session by updating learning logs and notifying the facilitator of any key issues they wish to discuss.
- The facilitator should ensure that each individual declares what actions they intend to take once they leave the reflection session and what outcomes they expect from these actions.

Sharing

This is where new knowledge, skills, and experiences can be shared outside of the action learning set to allow other individuals and teams to benefit from the experiences. Capturing the knowledge that grows out of the action learning experience contributes to the intellectual capital of the organization. As new knowledge is added to the KCO Web site over time, users will find more and more content that is timely and applicable to their current learning needs.

The following features can be included in the KCO Web site:

- Newsgroup and threaded discussion features can be included to allow action learning set members to collaborate online. This can open up the set so that others can see what is being achieved.
- The KCO Web site should keep a running list of all action learning sets. Each entry should list basic information about the members, the set's objectives, and the timing of the set's meetings, as well as the contact details of the set facilitator.
- Some action learning sets may decide to create a *learning history* — a document that describes the day-to-day work of the team and also attempts to capture how the set's learning evolved and changed during the project.
- At the conclusion of the action learning set, the team members, with the help of their facilitator, can select the information from their experience that others would probably find valuable, and post it to the KCO Web site. Suggested topics would include objectives, conclusions, recommendations, etc., as well as a list of experts who were consulted, and planning documents such as agendas.

Closing Out

The purpose of a close-out event is to ensure that the action learning set reflects on the time spent together and reviews the progress made against the original objectives. The close-out session is facilitated in the same way as the regular reflection sessions and includes the administrative tasks associated with disbanding the set. The most important of these tasks is to decide which resources and learning points are to be shared with the rest of the organization.

The following points can be borne in mind in the event of organizing a close-out session:

- Plan the event to allow time to reflect on both the task that the set has been working on between sessions as well as the individual and team learning that has occurred through the process.
- In advance of the close-out session, all set members should be asked to prepare their reflections. The facilitator may choose to issue a structured form to focus this preparation. Suggested questions include: What has become clearer to you since the start of the action learning program? How has your perspective of the task or problem changed during the time you have spent as a member of this action learning set? What were the defining moments of the set — at what points did major breakthroughs take place?

Relationship-Building Exercises

Title	Brain writing
Purpose	Collaborate on an idea or issue when sensitivities or conflict are anticipated; gather ideas and opinions in a nonthreatening manner.
Group size	Having 4 to 8 people is important for focused issue or ideas and wording.
	Up to 20 people if intent is to gather ideas and opinions.
Estimated time	For a group of 4–8 people, 10 minutes.
	For a group of up to 20 people, 20 minutes to write and 10 minutes to discuss.
Props	Blank paper and writing tool for each participant.
Instructions	1. Pose or frame the question, issue, or problem facing the group. Ask each person to write the following on the top of the paper: ■ An answer (if a question is posed) ■ A resolution (if an issue is presented) ■ An idea (if a problem is confronted) ■ Proposed wording (if a statement is being crafted, e.g., a mission) 2. Ask each person to pass their paper to the person on their left. 3. Each person should then comment on the paper in front of him or her by either writing a rewording of the suggestion below the original or commenting on his or her opinion of the suggestion. When complete, pass the paper on. 4. This should continue until the papers return to their originators. 5. Discuss the findings. Most often, consensus will have built around a small number of suggestions, narrowing the discussion field.
Variations	If ideas have already been generated, post each one on a sheet of flip chart paper, and post them around the room. Give people a marker, and have them travel around the room commenting on as many items as desired, as many times as desired. When the activity dies down, review each chart to determine if the comments lead to a common conclusion.

Tips	Suggest people use a checkmark to indicate agreement.
	This technique may be used to assess group opinion and to narrow the field prior to voting.
Title	What is the moral of the story?
Purpose	To practice sifting through information and deriving lessons learned.
Group size	8–20
Estimated time	8–10 minutes
Props	Fables
Instructions	1. Ask participants to pair up.
	2. Distribute fables.
	3. Explain that fables and folk tales are short fictional narratives that illustrate a moral or a lesson. They are an indirect means of telling truths about life. Thus, they have a level of meaning beyond the surface story.
	4. Tell pairs they have five minutes to read two fables, and add a humorous moral to it.
	5. After five minutes, ask members to discuss possible morals to the story.
Variation:	Use fables without known morals, and ask the group to develop some.

Suggested Fables from Aesop

The Cock and the Jewel

A cock, looking to find food for himself and his hens, found a precious stone and exclaimed: "If your owner had found thee, and not I, he would have taken thee up, and have set thee in thy first estate; but I have found thee for no purpose. I would rather have one barleycorn than all the jewels in the world."

Moral: The ignorant despise what is precious, only because they cannot understand it.

The Crow and the Pitcher

A crow perishing with thirst saw a pitcher and hoping to find water, flew to it with delight. However, he discovered to his grief that it contained so little water that he could not possibly reach it. He tried everything he could think of to reach the water, but all his efforts were in vain. At last he collected as many stones as he could carry and dropped them one by one with his beak into the pitcher, until he brought the water within his reach and thus saved his life.

Moral: Necessity is the mother of invention.

The Ass and His Shadow

A traveler hired an ass to convey him to a distant place. The day being intensely hot, and the sun shining in full strength, the traveler stopped to rest, and sought shelter from the heat under the shadow of the ass. As this afforded protection only for one, and as the traveler and the owner of the ass both claimed it, a violent dispute arose between them as to which of them had the right to the shadow. The owner maintained that he had given the ass only, and not his shadow. The traveler asserted that he had, with the hire of the ass, hired his shadow also. The quarrel proceeded from words to blows, and while the men fought, the ass galloped off.

Moral: In quarreling about the unimportant we often lose the substance.

Title	New product offering
Purpose	To get members to see things differently and better understand the varying perspectives that members bring to the community.
Group size	8–24
Estimated time	30 minutes (will vary with number of subgroups)
Props	A common object, e.g., a feather duster, a stapler, or a yo-yo.
Instructions	1. Explain to the group that the object they see before them can be anything — anything other than what it actually is. Their job is to name the product, describe its uses, create a marketing strategy (including price), and present their new product offering to the community. 2. Organize participants into subgroups of three to five members. 3. Allow the subgroups to develop their ideas and practice their presentation (about 20 minutes). 4. Each subgroup introduces its new product offering to the group.
Tips	Lead the group in clapping after each performance.

Purpose of Systems Thinking

As a tool for collective inquiry and coordinated action, the purposes of systems thinking are:

- Foster team learning and collaboration.
- Tell compelling stories that describe how the system works.
- Discover the system structure behind problems.
- Describe our own mental models and those of others about why the system performs as it does.
- Test possible strategies against intended results and for unintended consequences.
- Identify higher-leverage interventions.

As a result, systems thinking enables us to:

- Understand how organizations and other complex systems really function.
- Change our own thinking to match the way such systems operate.
- Change our behavior so that we are working with these complex forces instead of against them to create what we want.
  - Develop greater appreciation for the impact of our strategies on others in the system.
  - Be aware of the impacts of time delays and the need to balance short- and long-term objectives and strategies.
  - Anticipate unintended consequences of well-intentioned strategies.

Steps in Systems Thinking

1. State the issue and tell the story: Begin your inquiry with the evidence. What are some of the facts that make you or others think that there is an issue?
2. Graph performance patterns over time: What are the trends?
3. Establish creative tension and draft a focusing question: When the trends are visible, we can state how this reality differs from our vision. A good focusing question describes the patterns in the context of what we want. For example: Why, despite our efforts to improve quality, do we continue to miss deadlines?
4. Identify structural explanations: What are key causes and consequences of the trends we observe? How do the consequences, particularly our own responses to the situation, become the cause of more problems?

5. Apply the going-deeper questions: What are the deeper structures that keep this set of causes and consequences in place? Is this system successfully accomplishing a purpose other than the stated one? Are beliefs and values causing the situation to persist?

6. Plan an intervention: Based on our understanding of the structure, what is our hypothesis about how to change it? What general approaches are needed? What specific actions?

7. Assess the results: Because our intervention is based on a theory of the situation, the results of our attempts to improve things provide new data, allowing us to continue through the steps again, if necessary.

Systems thinking usually adds value when situations are:

■   Problematic
■   Long-standing
■   Resistant to change interventions

Systems thinking is often helpful as a planning resource. In particular, a systems view can help you plan for growth, anticipate limits to growth, predict and avoid actions that can undermine partnerships, and avoid shooting yourself in the foot (by producing a worse situation than you already have).

In general, systems thinking rarely helps us find the single right answer; other problem-solving tools are more efficient in cases where there truly is an answer. Systems thinking provides the most value when it illuminates the possible choices embedded in complex, divergent problems, and their likely consequences. The final choice is ours.

Do use systems thinking to:

■   Identify or clarify a problem.
■   Increase creative discussion.
■   Promote inquiry and challenge pre-conceived ideas.
■   Bring out the validity of multiple perspectives.
■   Make assumptions explicit.
■   Sift out major issues and factors.
■   Find the systemic causes of stubborn problems.
■   Test the viability of previously proposed solutions.
■   Explore short- and long-term impacts of alternative or newly proposed solutions or actions.

Do not use systems thinking to:

- Impress people or win an argument.
- Validate prior views.
- Hide uncertainties.
- Blame individuals.

Systems Thinking versus Traditional Approaches

Traditional Thinking	Systems Thinking
The connection between problems and their causes is obvious and easy to trace.	The relationship between problems and their causes is indirect and not obvious.
Others (either within or outside our organization) are to blame for our problems, and must be the ones to change.	We unwittingly create our own problems and have significant control or influence in solving them by changing our behavior.
A policy designed to achieve short-term success will also ensure long-term success.	Most quick fixes either make no long-term difference or actually make matters worse in the long run.
To optimize the whole, we must optimize the parts.	Focus on policies that optimize the whole rather than each of the parts.
Aggressively tackle many independent initiatives simultaneously.	Target and orchestrate a few key changes over time.

L.4   BUILDING THE KNOWLEDGE BASE

Purpose	Provide a framework for building your community's knowledge base.
Expected outcomes	Establish knowledge inventory and folder structure
	A process for capturing documents for content management systems
	A framework to continually improve business processes leveraging lessons learned, and reusing best practices
	Identified target efficiencies in mission-related measures such as cycle time, customer service, and total ownership cost

Roles/ responsibilities	A CoP's knowledge base requires several roles for business process owners to successfully implement. These roles include the following: ■ Community sponsor ■ Community leader ■ Community members ■ Facilitator ■ Logistics coordinator These roles are mentioned and discussed in detail in Section L.2.
Products	Requirements traceability matrix (RTM); matrix of groupware functions that the community will focus on for its first release of the knowledge base. List of identified community media (documents, presentations, spreadsheets, etc.) that includes specific documents. List of folders used for organizing community media. Graphical model and supporting narrative of as-is media flow between the community and stakeholder organizations. List of community members and the folders that they have been assigned to for life-cycle development. Groupware electronic repository that features all of the functions listed in the RTM, all identified media, and a completed folder structure. Media will have been migrated to the groupware application under the given folder structure. List of asset rules that ensure all groupware transactions are done in a manner consistent across the community. Graphical model and supporting narrative of to-be media flow between the community and stakeholder organizations. Includes list of business performance measures and expected efficiencies (e.g., cycle time = 8 weeks; goal = 4 week reduction).
Key tasks	*Requirements:* Map identified collaborative tool functions to business requirements to simplify deployment, narrow training scope, and ensure more efficient use of the groupware. *Inventory:* Define knowledge assets in a business process context and identify whether created by the community or borrowed from other business owners.

	Taxonomy: Develop a business-context classification structure for organizing inventory. It should provide an intuitive navigation scheme for members and other interested communities. *Flow model:* Model as-is business processes based on the flow of inventory assets to and from customers. Focus on how assets are created and disseminated. *Migrate:* Provide necessary technical support to migrate inventory assets that exist in legacy repositories. Inventory should be organized, classified as relevant, and mapped to a classification owner. Owners are typically subject matter experts from within the community. *Map:* Identify owners of the inventory folders and designate life-cycle responsibility at a folders-structure level. *Asset rules:* Establish business rules for the use of the groupware to maintain consistency while performing business transactions. Designate which groupware functionality will be used to process specific transactions. *Transformation:* Identify, in priority order, high-value, low-risk business processes that provide the group with the highest value in terms of customer service, cycle time reduction, and total ownership cost. Members should focus on measures that correlate to related business performance measures. *Training:* Secure computer-training facilities to allow hands-on training for members. Transformed business processes will be simulated in a training environment for user testing and acceptance. *Help desk:* Enable a functional help desk specifically for community members.
Key task 1: Requirements	This task is aimed at narrowing the functional scope of the selected groupware application to only those functions that enable the achieving of mission-related measures (e.g., reduction in cycle time).
Narrow the functional scope of your groupware application	Given a groupware application, conduct a functional analysis of the application. At minimum, the analysis should include the following: ■ Function name ■ Description ■ Release

	List all of the functions that the groupware application is capable of performing (e.g., add a new document). This list should not include any extended or custom functionality. Focus on the base functionality of the groupware.
	Once a list has been prepared, convene the community members to review the list. Leaders should aim at obtaining consensus over which functions meet the general requirements of the community's needs within the first release of the knowledge base. Enter "1" for release if the community requires the function in the first release. Enter "2" or "3," respectively, if the community feels as though the particular function can be postponed to a later release.
Base your assessment on past experience and lessons learned	The community is expected to base its function decisions on lessons learned and past experiences. *Work product:* RTM — Excel spreadsheet containing the following elements: REQ ID, REQUIREMENT (or function name), DESCRIPTION, RELEASE (version of the implementation that will contain the corresponding function), NEW or EXISTING, FULL/PARTIAL, COMMENTS, and DOCUMENTS.
Key task 2: Inventory	Inventory offers community members the opportunity for identifying all media associated with established business processes.
Take an inventory of all community media	With the help of a facilitator or community leader, convene a session of community members, and conduct a brainstorming session on media that are either inputs to or outputs of the community's business processes.
Conduct both group and individual inventory	Once the list has been developed, assign each member the responsibility of reviewing the baseline list and adding media not captured during the community session. Compile the baseline list along with the individual input from community members. This will become the baseline inventory for the community. *Work products:* Inventory list — Excel spreadsheet containing the following elements: ASSET ID#, NAME, DESCRIPTION, BEST PRACTICE, and RECORDS MANAGEMENT METADATA.
Key task 3: Taxonomy	The objective of taxonomy building is to provide an intuitive structure for users who are interested in obtaining information from or contributing to a community's practice.

Build group and individual lists	Convene the community to brainstorm a list of categories based on the prepared inventory list. The objective of the brainstorming session is to develop as complete a list as possible. Disregard the length of the list. The actual list can be finalized during a separate community session.
Consolidate lists and assign inventory items to categories **Tip: Limit consolidated list to about nine categories.** **Limit subcategories to three levels.**	Once the group has developed a list, distribute the list to group members, and have them conduct a personal assessment of the list. Community members add, consolidate, or recommend deletions to the list. Community leaders will consolidate the group and individual lists into a single group list. Once completed, begin assigning inventory items to their respective categories. *Work product:* Taxonomy List–Excel spreadsheet consisting of the following elements: FOLDER ID #, CATEGORY, LEVEL, OWNERS, STATUS, DESCRIPTION, and REVISION NOTES.
Key task 4: Flow model	The purpose of flow modeling is to graphically illustrate how inventory items are transferred between organizations as business transactions are conducted. The model will present a view that allows for easy identification of as-is business processes.
Easy way to identify business processes	To begin, model the organizations involved in the inventory exchange as depicted in Figure L.3. **Figure L.3 Sample flow model.**

Layout stakeholder organizations	Using the baseline inventory list, illustrate how each item travels between community and organization. In some cases, an inventory item may traverse several paths between organization and community until the business process cycle is completed (Figure L.4).
Illustrate the inventory path between community and stakeholder	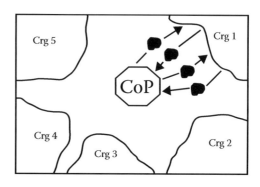
	Figure L.4 Sample flow model w/path example.
Model all core processes and associated inventory	The as-is flow model is complete when each of the inventory items has been illustrated on the model. Once the graphical model has been completed, the leader will write a narrative that describes the path of community inventory items. The general community member should write the narrative in terms that are easily comprehensible. Within the narrative, incorporate details that are not readily apparent within the model. *Work product:* As-is model and narrative of the business process and the knowledge assets transacted during the identified processes. Illustration of community, stakeholders, or customers, and the direction of flow of assets between services and customer.
Key task 5: Map *Community members share the responsibility of maintaining its workspace*	Mapping provides a means for the community to maintain its data. Community members will be designated as the point of contact for a particular category of data within the knowledge base. As with any community, all members must participate in the maintenance and upkeep of its locale. Similarly, the groupware community will also share the responsibility of maintaining its community.

Assign primary and alternate members to folders	Mapping is a relatively quick and informal process. Convene a meeting of community members. Using the established taxonomy list, have community members volunteer for folders that fall within their area of responsibility. Record these assignments in the ASSIGNED OWNER column of the taxonomy list. Additionally, have members volunteer for folders as an alternate point of contact. Therefore, each folder will have two community members who are familiar with the folder structure, content, and access privileges granted to the folder. *Work product:* See Taxonomy List — Excel spreadsheet of ASSET CLASSIFICATIONS and ASSIGNED OWNER.
Key task 6: Migration	Migration of data is important to demonstrating the capabilities of the groupware application. It also provides a means of validating what has been accomplished in terms of data organizations. Finally, it provides a context for discussing how inventory and taxonomy contribute to the community's business processes. Migration begins with validation of both inventory and taxonomy lists. This ensures that what has been gathered thus far accurately reflects the needs of the community. Convene the community, and conduct a quick review of both lists. Pay particular attention to those inventory items that (1) are not associated to a business process and (2) are not products of the community. Items that are not associated to a business process may be considered for removal. Items that are not a product of the community may exist as parts of an adjacent community. If so, eliminate redundancy by cutting out borrowed items. Once the lists have been validated, begin populating the project workspace according to the taxonomy. Data can be populated manually or in batches. Tools are available for large-scale conversions. *Work product:* Tool user accounts for all core group members and operational prototype of current release of the collaborative workspace.

Key task 7: Asset rules	Asset rules provide members with groupware guidelines for moving data in and out of the knowledge base. It also designates which groupware function will be used to support specific transactions in a business process.
	An example of an asset rule is using a compound document instead of a folder to collect and present periodic volume releases of a newsletter. In this case, two different groupware functions could be used to achieve similar results. Establishing asset rules provides a consistent means for interacting with the knowledge base.
	Sets of asset rules exist for each business process supported. Regardless of the size, rules must be put in place to avoid difference in practitioner usage. Asset rules will most commonly be identified with a business process. However, in some cases, specific documents may have an asset rule associated with it specifically.
	Begin with listing the different processes or documents that will require an asset rule. Remember, all transactions conducted within the groupware application will require a set of asset rules that provide guidance to the community members.
	For example, a particular community maintains a community calendar within its groupware application. The calendar is a Microsoft Word file. To provide guidance to the community on the use of this document, the following asset rules have been created:
	▪ Calendar only maintained by assigned owner ▪ Community members who need to add a date to the calendar will use the groupware's document Check-in/check-out function ▪ The community will maintain three months of its calendar — one month of past events and two months of future events
	All community members will create a change notification on the community calendar, thus allowing them to receive e-mail notification upon calendar update.
	Again, a set of asset rules should be developed for each process or document involved in a community business transaction. Asset rules should be reviewed periodically to ensure applicability and effectiveness.
	Work product: Asset rules — Excel spreadsheet including BUSINESS RULE NUMBER, BUSINESS RULE, DESCRIPTION, REVISION, STATUS, and COMMENTS.

Key task 8: Transformation	Transformation is key to achieving value from the knowledge base. The use of the knowledge base process implies that communities will undergo a transformation in how they do business. If transformation is not achieved, the community has done nothing more than increase its burden and develop another data repository.
	To transform, begin by selecting high-value, low-risk flows of inventory identified in the flow model stage. The flow selection should be based on that which the community believes would bring the highest value at the lowest risk to the community's mission. List and prioritize the flows that will be transformed into the groupware application such that all future transactions relating to the selected process will be conducted via the groupware.
	Once processes have been listed and prioritized in terms of value and risk, prepare an assessment or "gap analysis" of the as-is process and the to-be process. The analysis should include the following:
	■ List of stakeholders who will be affected by the process change.
	■ Changes to the process in terms of steps required to complete the process — are there any changes to the process? If so, document the changes.
	■ Measures and metrics for assessing the value achieved by transforming the as-is process to the groupware application environment.
	■ Document asset rules associated with conducting the process in the to-be environment
	Work product: To-be model and narrative of the business processes transacted. Includes a gap analysis identifying changes to as-is model and documented asset rules.

Key task 9: Training	Training ensures that all community members possess the necessary skill to function within the collaborative work environment. Community leaders should not assume that its members understand and can operate within the knowledge base without training and support.
	Training in this context includes more than just application training. It includes context-based training that is rooted in business process. That is, members are trained in both the use of the groupware application and the business processes it supports. This way, training has relevance to the community member and has immediate application.
	Training can be accomplished within the community by identifying a training lead for the community. Typically, this person will possess an above-average aptitude for information technology and has a good grasp of the business processes.
	The trainer will use the RTM developed earlier in the process to design a course for community members. The RTM provides the basis for the training. That is, it lists what groupware topics the trainer will cover. It is up to the trainer to select the business context of the functional topics. The trainer should develop a group of use cases or scenarios that illustrate to community members how the groupware will be utilized within the community's business environment. An example of a use case is:

	■ Update group calendar
	  – Log in to groupware
	  – Check-out calendar
	  – Add new calendar entry
	  – Check-in calendar

	There is no replacement for hands-on training. Where possible, utilize a training center to deliver training to community members.
	Training should be designed to be brief and specifically geared towards business processes. Long training sessions, greater than 1.5 hours, have proved to be ineffective. If training seems to be long, scale back on the coverage areas. Keep it manageable, applicable, short, and enjoyable for your community members.
Tools	Sample RTM Sample inventory template Sample taxonomy and mapping template Sample asset rule template

Sample Requirements Traceability Matrix

Req ID	Requirement	Description	Release	(N)ew/ (E)xisting	(F)ull/ (P)artial	Source	Comments	Documents
1.0	**Security**							
1.1	Log in	Used to verify that a user is authorized; also helps keep track of who added, modified, viewed, and otherwise accessed content	1					
1.2	Change password	Allow users to change secure encrypted password	1					
1.3	Log out	To prevent others from gaining unauthorized access, users are encouraged to log out when finished	1					
2.0	**Site Segments**							
2.1	Enterprise workspace	Central repository of your organization's knowledge; stores documents and other information that is meant to be generally available to all users	1					

Sample Requirements Traceability Matrix (continued)

Req ID	Requirement	Description	Release	(N)ew/ (E)xisting	(F)ull/ (P)artial	Source	Comments	Documents
2.2	Project or workgroup workspace	Team collaborative environment for projects to share and exchange specific project-related information	1					
2.3	Personal workspace	Allow users to create a customized view of their own personal data, project data, and enterprise data. Allow persons to share their workspace with other designated users.	2					
3.0	**Navigation**							
3.1	Standard navigational controls on workspaces	Provide a consistent means of navigating site and quick links to specific site content	1					
3.2	Provide consistent access to context-sensitive help	Make a help link available in every view	1					

Sample Taxonomy and Mapping Template

Folder ID #	Category	Level	Owner(s)- Mapping	Status	Description	Revision Notes

Sample Asset Rule Template

BR#	Business Rule	Description	Revision	Status	Comments
1.0	Update	Classification owners who have been designated as first point of contact have final approval authority over all content posted to the assigned area.	1.0	A	
2.0	Event expiration	Dated assets such as event or training schedule items will be scheduled for expiration one day after the item date.	1.0	A	
3.0	Periodicity	Update periodicity for an asset will be determined by the first and second points of contact assigned to the classification area.	1.0	A	
		If an asset requires updating, first point of contact will perform the update or reset the asset periodicity.			
4.0	Gatekeeper	Gatekeeper will have access to all classification areas. Access includes the ability to update, delete, restrict access, and renew assets, update periodicities.	1.0	A	

L.5 SUSTAINING COMMUNITIES

Purpose	Congratulations — your community has met and begun to form. The community is working together to develop and share best practices. How do you keep the community moving in a forward direction? How do you keep members coming back for more?
	This section is designed to help community leadership assess progress, recognize the natural evolution of community interactions, recognize and reward both individual and community contributions, and continuously foster innovation and growth.
Expected outcomes	Process adjustments
	Continuous infusion of new knowledge
Key tasks	Assess community progress.
	Understand community evolution.
	Recognize community contribution.
	Spark new knowledge creation and sharing.
Key task 1: Assess community progress	Once your community is up and running, community leadership should periodically check progress. In Section L.2, a CoP early progress checklist was introduced as a tool. In this section, that tool has been expanded to assess ongoing community effectiveness. This expanded tool, "CoP Regular Progress Checklist," is provided at the end of this section.
	As the community evolves, so may the strategic objectives of its members' organizations. A community should ask itself, "Have we satisfied our highest-priority knowledge needs? Do remaining needs still reflect strategic objectives? Have our knowledge needs changed?"
	Community members should be polled periodically to gain insights on how they believe the community is performing. In other words, is it serving its members, the organization, and the enterprise?
	One relatively simple method to gather member feedback is to facilitate occasional lessons learned discussions with the group. A template to capture this information was provided in Section L.2. A second way would be to collect written responses using a survey instrument. A generic community member satisfaction survey is provided as a tool at the end of this section. The survey should be tailored to your community's purpose and success criteria.

Key task 2: **Understand** *community evolution*	Similar to the stages of group development — forming, norming, storming, and performing — communities will also undergo evolutionary stages. As CoPs evolve, they go through stages of development characterized by different levels of interaction among members and different kinds of activities.
Key task 3: **Recognize** *community contribution*	When you reward people for certain behaviors, e.g., sharing knowledge, they will want to do more of it. Therefore, developing meaningful rewards is essential to sustaining community goals and achieving a KCO.
If you use it, say so	Meaningful recognition can come from peers as well as leadership. Community members should be encouraged to acknowledge individual and organizational contributions on a personal level. If knowledge culled from the knowledge base is useful to an individual's work, that individual should reach out to the contributor and personally acknowledge the contribution. It does not have to be formal — a simple phone call or e-mail expressing appreciation could suffice.
Peer nomination for rewards can be especially valued	People, if properly motivated and encouraged, will freely contribute if they know they are truly adding value to the enterprise. Peer nomination for rewards can be especially valued. An example might be a team of individuals contributing lessons learned on a particular assignment to the knowledge base. A second team utilizes these lessons on a similar assignment, resulting in improved decision-making capability and improved results. They nominate the first team for some kind of reward and recognition based on these results.
Blow your own horn	The community leader and core group should continuously promote and publicize individual and community contributions to organizational goals. Contributors could be recognized in newsletters, Web sites, staff meetings, luncheons, etc. Consider hosting or participating in knowledge fairs to show off your success.
Employees, personal acknowledgments from senior leadership	Another mechanism for community leadership to recognize contributors is to inform senior leadership of success stories. The information should be accompanied with a request for a personal note of appreciation from senior leadership to individuals or communities commending their work and acknowledging their contribution to the bottom line.

	Incorporate knowledge management expectations into formal performance evaluations and incentive compensation systems. For example, Ernst & Young evaluates its consultants along several dimensions, one of which is their contribution to and utilization of the knowledge asset of the firm. At Bain, a consulting firm, the partners are evaluated each year on a variety of dimensions, including how much direct help they have given colleagues. The degree of high-quality, person-to-person dialogue a partner has had with others can account for as much as one-quarter of his or her annual compensation.
Not invented here but I did it anyway!	Create a new award that promotes desired behaviors. For example, Texas Instruments created the NIHBIDIA Award — Not Invented Here But I Did It Anyway. Starting in 1996, TI's annual best practices celebration and sharing day (where all the best practice teams staff booths to publicize and answer questions about their practices) culminates in an award ceremony for those organizations that have most successfully shared best practices and knowledge — and produced great results. The organizations involved (and sometimes there are more than two involved) receive an award from the senior executives at TI for collaborating on the exchange of best practices. This is a highly prestigious award in TI, because it reinforces both the process and the results. Rewards and recognition may be healthy and useful in the early stages of building enthusiasm for transfer. However, in the long run and for a sustainable effort, employees have to find the work itself rewarding.
Key task 4: Spark new knowledge creation and sharing	Members should be continuously polled to identify new areas of interest or challenge. As needs evolve, the core group should seek interesting ways to bring knowledge to the community. Be creative — reach outside the organization for relevant seminars, training opportunities, tours and site visits to relevant industry and government operations, and guest speakers.
If only we knew what we know	Consider sponsoring cross-community forums to gain additional insights. Understanding the purpose and inventory of knowledge assets owned by other communities could essentially expand your community's knowledge base.

Look outside for innovations	In most professional disciplines, there is a plethora of relevant publications, Web sites, associations, etc. Who has time to read all of the available information? Perhaps your community would be interested in assigning members to scan specific information sources on a routine basis and cull interesting knowledge nuggets for the benefit of the entire community. If available, do not forget to use the corporate KM infomediary who can scan across knowledge bases to identify potentially relevant information.
Do not just stockpile new knowledge in a database	To counter the "if I build it, they will come" mentality, consider other vehicles to push knowledge gains throughout the enterprise. As best practices are identified, have them written up by professional writers, and have them embedded in all kinds of places — in training programs, possibly in policies and procedures — in as many different dimensions of the organization as possible.
Get to work and start talking	Try to create informal settings for member interactions. For example, coordinate bring-your-own-lunch (BYOL) sessions. Simply put, a BYOL means you get together over lunch, typically in a meeting room. Because everyone has to eat anyway, it takes little time away from busy schedules, members can come and go as they please, and prospective members can visit and check out the group, etc.
	The emphasis is open dialogue — informal, agenda-less weekly meetings with no pressure to come to resolution. Attendees can get input on any topic. The only structure is the time and place.
	Your community may decide to adopt this easy approach to informal networking and knowledge sharing. If so, have the community select a regular BYOL day and time, e.g., every other Wednesday at noon. To foster the process, the core group or the community leader should find a room that can always be used for BYOL day. Until the forum becomes habit, the leader should personally invite members and prospective members to drop in on a regular basis.
Tools	■ CoP regular progress checklist ■ Community member satisfaction survey

COMMUNITY OF PRACTICE

Regular Progress Checklist

1. Has the community revisited its purpose — is the purpose still compelling to leadership, active and prospective members, and their functional managers? Is the common purpose aligned with the command/enterprise strategy?
2. Is the community in agreement on the top priority that knowledge needs to tackle?
3. Has the community assessed its performance against its success criteria?
4. Are the functional sponsor and senior leadership kept abreast of community progress and issues?
5. Are core group members and the community leader strong content experts, enthusiastic, and able to sustain the community?
6. Do members' functional managers agree that time away from the job is valuable?
7. Do we have the right content experts to provide perspective and meaning in our membership?
8. Is there a shared space and context for dialogue, advice, and work?
9. Do we have enough members to keep the community alive?
10. How are the attendance trends?
11. Are collaborative tools, e.g., discussion threads or a Web site, in place? Are members set to use them?
12. What are usage trends for collaborative work tools?
13. Are needed resources, e.g., meeting rooms, VTC, participation in conferences, travel dollars, conference fees, etc., available?
14. Has a process been established for creating, organizing, publishing, storing, and sharing knowledge? Are common templates in place? Is there a process for distributing explicit knowledge and alerting others that it is available?
15. Can bottom-line improvements (cycle time, customer service, and TOC reduction) be demonstrated?

Community Member Satisfaction Survey		
Community Name:		
	Yes	No
Is there a common purpose that galvanizes community members to contribute to the knowledge base?		
Are you likely to recommend the community to your professional colleagues?		

Does your manager recognize and value your involvement in the community?		
Are community activities part of your job?		
Is there an acknowledged member base?		
Does the community share a mutual understanding of its identity?		
Does the community sustain a common methodology, process, and language?		
Does the community scan external sources for new ideas and innovations?		
Is the community free of the "not invented here" syndrome?		

	Rating				
	5	4	3	2	1
Technology is leveraged to support collaboration.					
The community serves as a reliable source for workable solutions or best practices.					
Needed information is quickly accessed and easy to apply.					
Community members enjoy open channels of communication.					
Community participation contributes to your individual success.					
Members enjoy continuous learning.					
Resources and effort are invested in developing a supporting infrastructure for the community.					
The community quickly mobilizes for ad hoc discussions.					

Ranking: 5 = exceeds expectations, 1 = does not meet expectations

- What do you like best about the community?
- What do you like least about the community?
- How would you improve the community?

NOTE

This appendix was adapted from the NAVSEA Community of Practice Practitioner's Guide. May 2001. Retrieved from http://knowledge.usaid.gov/documents/cop_practicioners_guide.pdf.

Appendix M

REQUIREMENTS ANALYSIS MATRIX

No.	Major Functional Requirement Area/Functional Requirements
1	**Content Management**
1.1	*Submit Raw Data and Upload Documents*
1.1.1	Submit text-based content through HTML forms.
1.1.2	Upload file types including: .doc, .pdf, .xls, .ppt, .gif, and .jpg to the content management system.
1.1.3	Categorize content based on site taxonomy as defined in Requirements Section 6 below.
1.1.4	Associate content with other "knowledge objects" on the site, including content, discussions, events, and people.
1.1.5	E-mail notification is sent to user after submitting content.
1.2	*Search and Retrieve Content and Documents*
1.2.1	Content searching integration into site search as defined in Requirements Section 6 below.
1.2.2	Retrieve content from search to view onscreen.
1.2.3	Print content and "Save as…" where appropriate.
1.2.4	"Save content" to a "personalized my content" area where the user can return later and easily access it.
1.2.5	Forward content to a friend by "Enter friend's e-mail address."

1.3	*Archive/Rank Content*
1.3.1	Archive content based on time horizon specified by administration and user search parameters to shorten searches.
1.3.2	Rank content on a scale of 1 to 10 based on its usefulness.
1.3.3	Search content based on ranking data.
1.3.4	Serve content to users based on ranking data.
1.4	*Manage Content Workflow*
1.4.1	Administrator can determine whether or not content must follow an approval process.
1.4.2	Administrator can determine whether there are 1 or 2 layers in the approval process.
1.4.3	If 1 level, administrator can update, approve, or reject content.
1.4.4	If 1 level, if content is rejected, it is routed back to original submitter for updating.
1.4.5	If 2-level approval process, administrator can determine who the first-level approver is before administrator approval.
1.4.6	If 2-level approval process, first level approver can update, approve, or reject content.
1.4.7	If 2-level approval process, if content is rejected at either step, it is routed back to original submitter for updating.
1.4.8	After content is approved by administrator, it is immediately available on the site.
1.4.9	Notification e-mails are sent to the original submitter when the status of the submitted content changes.
1.4.10	Administrator can "flag" content as important for users, adding it to the top of content lists and searches.
2	**Collaboration**
2.1	*Discussion Boards*
2.1.1	Create new discussion threads.
2.1.2	Create new messages.
2.1.3	Reply to messages.

2.1.4	Message author information is available to users.
2.1.5	Elect to post anonymous messages.
2.1.6	Administrator can delete messages.
2.1.7	Administrator can limit user rights to "read only" or "active participant."
2.1.8	Elect to have "discussion board" pushed to his or her e-mail box.
2.1.9	Discussion board acts like a listserve.
2.2	**Instant Messaging and Chat**
2.2.1	View a list of all users who are currently online/view directory.
2.2.2	Select user to initiate an IM session.
2.2.3	Initiate an IM meeting.
2.2.4	Conduct an IM session conversation.
2.2.5	Export conversation/meeting text records.
2.2.6	Administrator can create "open" chat rooms with specified topics on the site.
2.2.7	Administrator can determine who has access to IM and chat functionality.
2.2.8	Administrator can moderate or designate a moderator for selected chat events.
2.2.9	Archive chat content.
2.3	**E-mail Push**
2.3.1	New content is pushed to users.
2.3.2	New content is pushed to users based on user preferences.
2.3.3	E-mail push is available in text or HTML.
2.3.4	Other content such as events and people/expertise are pushed via e-mail.
2.4	**Web Conferencing/White Boarding**
2.4.1	Schedule a Web conference.
2.4.2	Integrate live video, video files, and PowerPoint files into video conferencing.
2.4.3	Draw and diagram using white-board functionality.

2.4.4	Invite users to join the conference.
2.4.5	Transfer (send/receive) files of various formats (file sharing).
2.4.6	Share programs.
2.4.7	Share active screen (e.g., other users can view the screen of any of the participants) and remote desktop sharing.
3	**Expertise Management**
3.1	***Expert Directory Linked to User Profiles***
3.1.1	Administrators can create the data fields to be completed by users for profiles.
3.1.2	Enter personal information when creating a user profile that can be accessed through a skills inventory.
3.1.3	Update user profiles.
3.1.4	Automatically reminded to update profile on a regular basis via e-mail notification.
3.1.5	Administrator can set frequency for e-mail reminders.
3.2	***Searchable Expert Directory***
3.2.1	Searchable by last name and first name.
3.2.2	Searchable by key criteria defined by the administrator.
3.2.3	Advanced search available to search by every field in the directory.
3.2.4	Retrieve search results and view onscreen.
3.2.5	Search and view contact information — integrated with user profile.
3.2.6	"Save person" to a "personalized my content" area where the user can return later and easily access it.
3.3	***Resource-Matching Capabilities***
3.3.1	Search interface catered toward matching; including adding resource availability to the expert directory.
3.3.2	Post description of need for an expert.
3.3.3	Search descriptions of needs for an expert.
3.3.4	Respond as an expert to a need.

3.3.5	E-mail push of expert needs; user can sign up to receive e-mail notification when another user requests skill.
4	**Personalization**
4.1	*User Can Create "myCoP" Page*
4.1.1	Create "myCoP" page accessible via a username and password.
4.1.2	Elect to include certain functions on the "myCoP" page, for example, content updates, experts, discussion boards, etc.
4.1.3	Elect to include certain topics from the taxonomy on the "myCoP" page: for example, include any HIV/AIDS–Africa item.
4.1.4	Access to "myCoP" page templates based on groupings within the CoP.
4.1.5	Administrators can customize the "myCoP" templates.
4.1.6	Administrators can specify functions that must appear on every "myCoP" page.
4.1.7	Administrators can specify certain topics from the taxonomy that must appear on every "myCoP" page.
4.1.8	Clustering of content and modules based on user profile, preferences, and actions on the site.
4.2	*User Profile Management*
4.2.1	Create user profile.
4.2.2	Update user profile.
4.2.3	Administrator can update user profiles.
4.2.4	Administrator can create user groups with customized rights.
4.2.5	Administrator can assign users to specified user groups.
5	**Events, Scheduling, and Tasks Management**
5.1	*Events Calendar (Submit and Read)*
5.1.1	Submit events through HTML forms.
5.1.2	Categorize events based on site taxonomy as defined in Requirements Section 6 below.
5.1.3	Associate events with other "knowledge objects" on the site including content, discussion threads, and people.

5.1.4	E-mail notification is sent to user after submitting event.
5.1.5	Event searching integration into site search as defined in Requirements Section 6 below.
5.1.6	Retrieve event from search to view onscreen.
5.1.7	Print event and "Save as..." where appropriate.
5.1.8	"Save event" to a "Personalized my content" area where the user can return later and easily access it.
5.1.9	Forward event to a friend by "Enter friend's e-mail address."
5.1.10	View events in an interactive calendar.
5.1.11	Administrator can elect whether to force events through workflow (see content workflow options).
5.2	***E-mail Reminders and Integration***
5.2.1	E-mail reminders sent when general events are scheduled.
5.2.2	Decide whether to receive these updates.
5.2.3	E-mail reminders sent for events in "Personalized content list."
5.2.4	E-mail reminders sent for personal tasks about to be due.
5.2.5	Send broadcast e-mail about tasks on an *ad hoc* basis.
5.3	***Task Management***
5.3.1	Enter personal tasks.
5.3.2	Assign tasks to user.
5.3.3	Track task completion.
5.3.4	View task completion reports for assigned users.
5.3.5	Tasks integrated with interactive calendar.
5.3.6	Associate tasks with site taxonomy.
5.3.7	Associate tasks with knowledge objects.
6	**Global Search, Taxonomy, and Data Management**
6.1	***Global Site Search of all Modules and Content***
6.1.1	Search based on content types.
6.1.2	Search based on modules.

6.1.3	Search based on module-specific parameters.
6.1.4	Search based on global taxonomy parameters.
6.2	**Simple and Advanced Search Capabilities**
6.2.1	Search based on simple-text-based search.
6.2.2	Search based on advanced search, allowing user to set values for all available fields.
6.2.3	Search based on natural language queries.
6.3	**Customizable Taxonomy/Metadata Attributes**
6.3.1	Administrator can set and manage global taxonomy.
6.3.2	Administrator can set and manage taxonomy for each module/content type.
6.4	**Data Mining and Warehousing**
6.4.1	Administrator can perform detailed ad hoc reporting and analysis.
6.4.2	Administrator can export data into another format.
6.4.3	Administrator can access back-end database and link to third-party tools (such as Crystal Reports).
6.4.4	Advanced reporting module available.
6.5	**Linguistic/Semantic Analysis**
6.5.1	Simple linguistic/semantic analysis managed by administrator.
6.5.2	Integrated with taxonomy/thesaurus.
7	**Technology Integration and Flexibility**
7.1	**Integration with Microsoft Outlook**
7.1.1	E-mail integration with Microsoft Outlook.
7.1.2	Calendar integration with Microsoft Outlook.
7.1.3	Task integration with Microsoft Outlook.
7.2	**Distance Learning (Offline from Internet and Network)**
7.2.1	Access while connected to Internet, but not to network.

7.2.2	Access and work with data without any Internet/network connection.
7.2.3	Download significant content portions.
7.2.4	Upload content.
7.3	**Technology Is 508 Compliant/Accessible**
7.3.1	Web-based technology is certified as 508 compliant.
7.3.2	Passes IBM Homepage Reader test as proxy for accessible technology.
7.3.3	Passes simple tests such as the use of "alt" tags for all images, table layout, and style orientation (css) method.
7.4	**Technology Is Easy to Use**
7.4.1	Pages are easy to understand and use.
7.4.2	Font is legible.
7.4.3	Do not need extensive training to learn how to use the tool.
7.5	**Customizable to CoP Brand**
7.5.1	Administrator can customize page colors to match CoP brand.
7.5.2	Administrator can upload a logo that represents the CoP.
7.5.3	Administrator can customize the header of all pages.
7.5.4	Administrator can customize the footer of all pages.
7.5.5	Administrator can customize the style sheet.
7.5.6	Administrator can choose from provided templates.
A	**Training**
A.1	**Robust Online Help**
A.1.1	Help section is preexisting on the site.
A.1.2	Help section is robust and matches offline documentation (meaning there is no need to access offline materials).
A.1.3	Administrator can update Help section.
A.1.4	Simple FAQ list is available in the Help section out of the box.

A.1.5	Administrator can create a custom FAQ based on CoP needs.
A.1.6	Online help content is downloadable in .doc or .pdf format.
A.2	**Robust Offline Help/Documentation**
A.2.1	Offline user documentation is preexisting and available.
A.2.2	Available in a one-page quick reference guide.
A.3	**Training/brown bag workshops available out of the box**
A.3.1	Vendor-provided content for training/brown bag workshops is available.
A.3.2	Vendor-provided training workshops for site administrators.
A.3.3	Vendor-provided training workshops for users (note that the system should be usable without extensive training).
B	**Implementation Costs and Scalability**
B.1	**Software Costs/Technical Environment**
B.1.1	Compatible platforms.
B.1.2	Cost of main "server" licenses for the software.
B.1.3	Cost of initial "seat" licenses for users within a single instance.
B.1.4	Cost for additional "instances."
B.1.5	Cost of seats for additional "instances."
B.1.6	Equation for determining license seats (price breaks for number of seats, etc.).
B.1.7	Discounting opportunities.
B.1.8	Data conversion costs with this package.
B.1.9	Owns current licenses?
B.2	**Hardware Costs**
B.2.1	Hardware environment specifications.
B.2.2	Estimated cost to purchase hardware.
B.2.3	Hardware can be supported on existing infrastructure?

B.3	*Scalability (to More Users within a CoP and to More CoPs)*
B.3.1	Software is easily scalable to additional users within a CoP.
B.3.2	Software is easily scalable to maintaining multiple CoPs with separate configuration.
B.3.3	Software has defined "load" requirements provided by the vendor.
B.3.4	Performance does not degrade based on target number of users.
B.4	**Vendor Stability**
B.4.1	Vendor provides similar qualifications.
B.4.2	Vendor has a stable history (x years).
B.4.3	Vendor is in good financial health.
B.4.4	Vendor has provided similar software to other U.S. federal government agencies.
B.4.5	Vendor has provided similar software to other non-U.S. federal government clients.
B.5	**Agency Enterprise Architecture Fit**
B.5.1	Software is part of existing agency property.
B.5.2	Has existing relationship with the vendor.
B.5.3	If not part of current architecture, software provides a unique fit and is compatible.
B.6	**Security**
B.6.1	Software can be reasonably accessible from behind the firewall.
B.6.2	Leverages existing architecture security standards (network log-ons, etc.).
B.6.3	Software meets all agency security requirements.
B.7	**Ongoing Maintenance**
B.7.1	Vendor provides warranty/maintenance support for x years.
B.7.2	Vendor maintains online knowledge bases for support issues.
B.7.3	Maintenance is estimated to be less than 40 hours/year.
B.7.4	Maintenance can be conducted in-house.

INDEX

D

Daemons, 12
Data
    access, 97, 120, 341
    administration, 107–109, 122
    backup, 113, 121–122, 147–148
    business intelligence (BI) and, 100–101
    capture, initial, 338
    cleansing, 103
    corporate, 122
    and databases, 95–96, 100, 109–110
    defined, 122
    development life cycles, 123
    elements, 123
    entry by sales forces, 161
    extraction, transformation, load (ETL)
        tools, 100, 103
    geographic, 94–95
    image, 94
    input and update, 114
    integrity, 113
    marts, 96, 100, 117
    meta-, 101, 124, 329–330, 457
    migration, 437
    mining, 168–169, 176–179, 184, 457
    model, 123
    multimedia, 95
    objects, 95
    quality, 156
    recovery, 113, 121–122
    replication, 97–98
    sampling, 178–179
    security, 114, 117–118, 204, 294, 460
    sharing, 108, 113, 118–119, 123, 126, 298
    source systems, 99
    sponsors, 104–106
    staging area, 99–100
    standards, 113, 127
    stewards, 106–107, 123, 127
    storage structures, 101–103
    stores, operational, 97
    submission of raw, 451
    text and numeric, 94
    tracking, 339
    visualization, 179–181
    warehouses, 96–97, 99–101, 117, 156
Data management
    change management and impact analysis
        in, 113
    components of, 94–99
    connectivity and, 113

data and mapping standards, 113
    data sharing and, 113
    data warehousing and, 99–101
    defined, 123
    guidelines, 115–122
    identification and enforcement standards,
        112
    input and update, 114
    master, 157
    metadata and, 114
    practices, good, 104–114
    privacy policies and, 117–118
    quality control, data integrity, and
        backup or recovery, 113
    responsibilities, 111–114
    roles, 104–111, 126
    security, 114
    terminology, 122–128
    training and, 114
Data Management and Data Warehouse
    Domain Technical Architecture,
    115
Data Management Association, 93
Database management systems (DBMSs),
    204
Databases, 95–96, 100, 122, 329
    administration, 109–110
    client use cases, 370
    design, physical, 125
    integrated, 124
    intelligent, 176–177
    logical design of, 120
    staff use cases, 372–373
Davenport, T. H., 79, 80, 82, 248
Debriefings, lessons learned, 34–38, 397
    forms, 233–235
Decision makers, types of, 3–4
Decision support
    for different types of decision makers,
        3–4
    filtering and, 4–5
    transforming information into
        knowledge, 5–6
Decision trees, 6–7
Deep Blue, 10
Defect density, 205
Demographic changes, 68
Denning, Stephen, 248
Design
    organizational, 322–324
    of space, 327–328

through on-the-job training (OJT), 38–39
storytelling, 40–42, 248–250, 402–403,
416–417
training and, 42
Transformation of information into
knowledge, 5–6, 439
Tree of Knowledge, The, 333
Trends in business intelligence (BI), 155–157
Truth maintenance, 9–10

U

Unexpected occurrences, 68
Unique identifiers, 128
United States Forest Service, 104
United States Nuclear Regulatory Agency,
138–139
Universal Studios Hollywood (USH),
163–164
University of Southern California Cancer
Registry, 177
Unpredictable risks, 227
Update, data, 114
Up-to-date knowledge, 189
U.S. Department of Defense, 58
U.S. Department of the Navy, 237
U.S. Post Office, 47
Usability
information dissemination and, 300
intranet, 129–130
web-based records, 145
Use cases
administration, 373–375
client scenarios, 369–372
staff, 372–373
Users
access, 341
principal, 125
profile management, 455

V

Validation of quotes, 414–415
Varela, Francisco, 333
Versioning, 345
Video, 95
Virtual teams, 322–323
Visibility, web site, 146
Visualization, data, 179–181

Vivisimo, 140–142
Voice data, 95
Von Krogh, George, 332

W

Wal-Mart, 168, 184
Warehouses, data, 96–97, 99–101, 117, 156
Web conferencing/white boarding, 453–454
Web harvesters, 148
Web sites. *See also* Internet, the
administrative updates, 374
global searches, 456–457
hyperlinks, 148
managing content of, 271–272
records management risks associated
with, 145–146
taxonomies, 456–457
tracking changes to content pages of,
147–148
use cases
administration, 373–375
client, 369–372
staff, 372–373
visibility, 146
Web-enabled online analytical processing
(WOLAP), 102
Weblogs, 135–136, 152
Wikipedia, 69, 81, 133–135
Wilson, H. J., 80, 82
Wilson, T. B., 89
Wisdom and knowledge, 13–15
Wishful thinking, 71
Work breakdown structure (WBS), 207–219
Working Knowledge, 248
World Bank, 248, 417
World Poker Tour, 69
Wriston, Walter, 5
5Ws and H technique, 70
Wurman, Richard Saul, 2

X

Xerox Corporation, 30

Y

Yahoo!, 136